Johnson, Nixon, and the Doves

Melvin Small

Johnson, Nixon, and the Doves

RUTGERS

Rutgers University Press

New Brunswick and London

Library of Congress Cataloging-in-Publication Data

Small, Melvin.
  Johnson, Nixon, and the Doves.

  Bibliography: p.
  Includes index.
  1. Vietnamese Conflict, 1961–1975—United States.
2. Vietnamese Conflict, 1961–1975—Protest movements—
United States. 3. Vietnamese Conflict, 1961–1975—Public
opinion. 4. Public opinion—United States.
5. United States—Foreign relations—1963–1969.
6. United States—Foreign relations—1969-1974.
I. Title.
DS558.S57 1988   959.704'33'73   87-20783
ISBN 0-8135-1287-5
ISBN 0-8135-1288-3 (pbk.)

British Cataloguing-in-Publication Information Available

For Sarajane, Michael, and Mark, and
the millions of other men, women, and
young people who exercised their
democratic rights to protest American
intervention in Southeast Asia

Contents

List of Figures

List of Tables

Preface

"One thing you learn, when you try to reconstruct an event from eyewitness accounts, is that each version is just someone's story, and that all stories mix truth and lies."*

—*MARIO VARGAS LLOSA*

I began thinking about a study of the impact of dissent on Vietnam-era decision makers when I was a minor actor in the drama, a foot soldier and petition signer for antiwar causes. As a young historian whose major focus was the relationship between opinion and policy, I was curious then about the effectiveness of the activities into which I had been drawn, often by physicists or philosophers who did not have the foggiest notion of how foreign policy was constructed in our nation. Was anyone in the White House listening to the chants of the thousands with whom I gathered at Golden Gate Park in November 1969? Did the ten dollars I paid to add my name to *New York Times* advertisements serve a useful purpose?

Although I thought often of those questions through the late 1960s and the 1970s, it was not until December 1979 that I decided to explore them in a scholarly study. The spark was again my role as participant-observer. After President Jimmy Carter reinstituted draft registration in response to the Soviet invasion of Afghanistan, student activists at my university invited me to a forum on the crisis. As usual at such events, most people in the audience were critical of the president's initiatives. They cheered when several veterans of the anti–Vietnam War movement proclaimed, "We did it before, we'll do it again!"

When it came my turn to speak, I remarked that much as I would like to have believed that the antiwar movement "stopped them," we did not know if that was the case. Little more than anecdotal evidence on both sides of the issue had been produced to assist scholars trying to answer that question.

---

*Mario Vargas Llosa, *The Real Life of Alexjandro Mayta*, translated by Alfred Mac Adam (New York: Farrar, Straus & Giroux, 1986), 118.

Perhaps we will never be able to answer such a question. Nevertheless, I decided to take a stab at it—to evaluate the impact of the demonstrators, petition signers, and editorial and letter writers on the policymaking process during the Vietnam War. The question was interesting to me for both personal and professional reasons.

After wrapping up other projects, I began working on this book in 1982. From 1983 through to 1985, I spent considerable time crisscrossing the country to interview key officials in the Johnson and Nixon administrations. The interviewing was the most challenging and fascinating research activity in which I had been engaged as a scholar.[1] Many of those people who generously gave of their time and their memories were the same people against whom I demonstrated. For the most part, I believe that I was able to separate my feelings about those individuals from my scholarly evaluations of their reminiscences. Indeed, I found myself liking almost everyone to whom I talked, a discovery that was, in many ways, as important for me as the material I turned up on my major research questions.

One theme ran through those many interviews. The major actors in the Vietnam tragedy in the United States were only human. To expect them to have acted any more rationally or intelligently than any of us is to misunderstand the nature of representative government. This is especially important to consider as scholars impose rational decision-making models on essentially normal and thus only sometimes rational human beings. I hope that I have been able to capture this important factor, a factor that plays havoc with any attempt to flesh out the motives behind policymaking and, especially, reactions in Washington to criticism of any sort. To distinguish between my interviews and other more traditional materials, I have adopted a stylistic convention to assist the reader. Recollections from interviews are reported in the present tense, those from books and manuscripts in the past tense.

The Lyndon Baines Johnson Foundation supported my visit to the Johnson Library with a generous grant. The staff of the library, especially David Humphrey, was very helpful. Most of the expenses incurred while interviewing were supported by an American Council of Learned Societies Grant. In addition, Wayne State University awarded me a sabbatical in 1983–84, during which time

I conducted many of my interviews and began making preliminary attempts at organizing and writing up my material. The university's Office of Research and Graduate Programs also provided me with support to make an eleventh-hour trip to the Nixon Presidential Materials Project in Alexandria, Virginia, where, in late June 1987, Joan Howard skillfully guided me through the newly opened files. The staffs of Wayne's library, the Michigan State University Archives, and the Richard B. Russell Memorial Library in Athens, Georgia, all offered valuable assistance. I am also indebted to William Bundy for permitting me to use his unpublished and uncompleted draft history of Vietnam-era policymaking.

Portions of this book were presented in lectures at Wayne State, Arhus (Denmark) University, Lund (Sweden) University, Boston College, and the State University of New York at Brockport. The faculty and students at those institutions provided much useful criticism. Among those who have read all or part of the manuscript and to whom I am most grateful are Otto Feinstein, Lloyd Gardner, George Herring, Chris Johnson, Lynn Parsons, and Athan Theoharis. Charles DeBenedetti's contribution to my work is incalculable. He and I began working on parallel studies around the same time; he concentrated on events outside the White House fence, I on the Oval Office. I profited immeasureably from our brainstorming, note sharing, and from his reading of several of my chapters. Unfortunately, he died in January 1987, before he could complete his own manuscript. His brilliant draft, now being edited by Charles Chatfield, will become the definitive book on the antiwar movement.

Virginia Corbin of Wayne State's History Department worked through innumerable versions of this book with her usual good spirit and keen editorial eye. Nancy Montgomery of Wayne's Word Processing Center was similarly helpful, efficient, and wise.

As she has throughout our marriage, my wife, Sara, offered unlimited encouragement, inspiration, and especially love. Of all my projects, this meant the most to her, a former McCarthy precinct delegate and indefatigable activist for peace and justice at home and abroad.

Royal Oak, Michigan
July 1987

List of Abbreviations

ADA	Americans for Democratic Action
AFV	American Friends of Vietnam
AID	Agency for International Development
ARVN	Army of the Republic of Vietnam
CAB	Minutes and Documents of the Cabinet Meetings of President Johnson
COSVN	Central Office for South Vietnam
DD	*Declassified Documents*
DSB	*Department of State Bulletin*
JCS	Joint Chiefs of Staff
LBJL	Lyndon Baines Johnson Library
MACV	Military Assistance Command, Vietnam
MFP	Memoranda for the President
MFRP	Memoranda from the President
MSU	Michigan State University
ND19CO312	National Defense 19 Country 312 (South Vietnam)
NP	Nixon Presidential Materials Project
NSA	National Security Agency
NSC	National Security Council
NSCDEP	National Security Council, History of the Deployment of Major U.S. Forces to Vietnam, July 1965
NSCVN	National Security Council Files, Vietnam
NVA	North Vietnam People's Army
PDS	Presidential Document Series
PH	President's Handwriting
POF	President's Office Files
PP	*The Pentagon Papers* (Senator Gravel edition)
PPF	President's Personal Files
WHCF	White House Central Files

Chapter One

Introduction: How Opinion Comes to the Oval Office

"Who gives a shit about William Sloane Coffin."
—JACK VALENTI*

I

n its extent and intensity, the antiwar movement in the United States from 1965 through 1971 was the most significant movement of its kind in the nation's history.[1] Its ultimate impact on policy, however, still remains a matter of conjecture, despite the publication of hundreds of books and thousands of articles on the United States and the Vietnam War. Indeed, aside from an article on the impact of the movement on the Senate, no one has studied how the decision makers were affected by the activities of the protesters and their leaders.[2]

One explanation for this gap in the extensive scholarship on the war is the difficulty of evaluating the impact of any social movement or even discrete event on decision makers. In his pathbreaking monograph published in 1961, James N. Rosenau listed factors that must be examined to determine how public opinion and foreign policy interact in the United States.[3] Because of the complexity of this problem, he identified three strata of the public, sixteen kinds of opinion makers, and ten channels of communication that could become the components of a formal model. We have not moved very far beyond Rosenau's "pre-theory" over the past several decades, despite the considerable scholarly attention paid to his problem.

Even decision makers are befuddled by this issue. Writing about

*Interview with Jack Valenti, Washington, D.C., February 10, 1984.

the White House in 1965 and 1966, presidential aide Bill Moyers described executive "frustrations of trying to divine public opinion toward foreign policy." On the other side of the fence, Senator George McGovern asked Assistant Secretary of State Charles Frankel in 1967 whether his antiwar speeches, as well as those of other prominent critics, had any impact on the executive branch.[4] If insiders like Moyers and McGovern encountered difficulties understanding the opinion-policy nexus, what hope is there for the historian?

Complicating matters is the recency of the Vietnam War era. Although a good deal of material is available in Lyndon Johnson's presidential library in Austin, Texas, much in the foreign area remains classified. As for Nixon, aside from his "Special File" partially opened in May 1987, few written documents or tapes dealing directly with national security affairs have been released to the public. It is true that most of the main actors, including both presidents, have written memoirs; these are no substitute for the paper trail left within the modern executive bureaucracy.

George Reedy, one of Johnson's press secretaries, is even suspicious of the value of that paper trail. In the first place, he emphasizes the complex nature of the mind of Lyndon Johnson, so complex that he doubts whether the president himself knew why he was behaving the way he did. Moreover, the memos available in the Johnson Library offer little indication of their impact on the president, since he rarely responded to them. According to Reedy, one could only be certain that a comment was noted when it appeared in a sentence or two in one of the president's speeches or press conferences.[5] Of course, Johnson was careful to initial much of what he read.[6]

Scholars of the Nixon administration will have an easier time of it. His aides generally stamped memos that he read "Seen by the President." In addition, Nixon made marginal notes on many of the documents that crossed his desk. Those interesting marginalia illuminate much more about his activities and thought processes than any comparable material in the Johnson Library.

Whatever the archives may ultimately reveal, there is an advantage in studying something as recent as the United States during the 1960s and that is the availability of sources for interviews. In fact, the major difficulty interviewing people in the 1980s is not only that some key figures have died, but that the memories of the living have already begun to fade. Thus, the more specific questions—did X say such and such at the July 21, 1965, meeting? —cannot always be answered through the interview process. Recognizing this problem, the presidential archives rush to complete oral histories within a few years after the end of an administration.

The recency of the subject to be analyzed is only part of the problem. Suppose, for example, the subject was the isolationists' impact on Franklin Roosevelt in 1940 rather than the antiwar movement's impact on Richard Nixon in 1970? Most likely, historians and political scientists would still maintain that the assessment of impact or influence, though important, is ultimately impossible, even with the mountains of documentation available for 1940.

One reason for this pessimism relates to the reluctance of decision makers to explain their foreign policies in terms of public pressures, unless they are looking for scapegoats. Whether one examines the documentation behind decisions to go to war, to increase troop levels, or to begin or stop bombing, the emphasis publicly is on strategic concerns and the president's concept of national security. Clark Clifford, for one, who was called in by President Johnson to reassess the Vietnam policy in early 1968, claims that he rarely factored opinion into his deliberations—he was concerned with military questions.[7]

Similarly, the reports of national security advisers McGeorge Bundy and Walt W. Rostow during the Vietnam War rarely included discussions of public opinion. Rostow wrote infrequently about opinion when discussing options in Vietnam because it was not within his charge of analyzing international security affairs. On the other hand, both McGeorge Bundy and Dean Rusk emphasize the importance of opinion to them. Bundy remembers many long conversations with President Johnson about opinion. Rusk explains that foreign-policy makers are like airline pilots, checking a variety of factors before takeoff, with opinion always important.[8] Yet a careful analysis of their formal memoranda and policy papers suggests that opinion was a negligible factor in most cases.

In their public statements, members of the executive branch, including the president, often talk about support as shown in opinion polls and how their adversaries should know that the American people stand behind their president. In private, to admit discussing or even to discuss the impact of public opinion on a foreign policy would be to abnegate their sworn responsibility to maintain national security, insulated from the vagaries of uninformed and emotional currents of opinion. It seems indecorous for presidents to raise the issue of the public, and thus politics and elections, when it comes to considering life-and-death questions in which only they and their aides allegedly have the information and expertise to make an informed judgment. They would agree with Edmund Burke, who told constituents, "I know you chose me, in my place, along with others, to be a pillar of state, and not a weathercock on the top of the edifice, exalted for my levity and versatility and of no use but to indicate the shiftings of every fashionable gale."[9]

Such noble sentiments may be related to the fact that in the United States, at least, elections have rarely been determined by foreign-policy issues.[10] Whether one considers the so-called League of Nations election of 1920 or the "mad bomber" election of 1964, foreign-policy issues in presidential elections have been only marginally important. The 1968 contest is an excellent example for the period in question. Although the Vietnam War was obviously a dominant public issue that fall, most voters were unable to exercise either hawkish or dovish options when they came to choose between Nixon and Humphrey.[11]

Of course, the public might always be there in the minds of the decision makers as the ultimate determiner of the boundaries within which they must operate. Since they have internalized the conception of what the public will bear, there is no need to discuss it. For example, when occasionally toying with the idea of a tactical nuclear threat to North Vietnam, the inner decision-making circle never needed to mention the probable public shock at such a demarche.

This argument weakens when we look at the historical record. The parameters for action allegedly established by the public can be shifted over time through the impact of events, as well as through "educational" campaigns led by the president. In 1943, the thought of stationing American troops permanently in postwar Europe seemed preposterous. The boys would have to come home posthaste at war's end. With the onset of the cold war, and only three years after Roosevelt had conveyed to Stalin the strongly isolationist preferences of his constituents, the American public accepted this unprecedented policy.

Presidents have occasionally explained a major policy in terms of public pressure. Most famous may have been William McKinley's decision to retain the Philippines, a decision he attributed to divine guidance and strong popular sentiment he discovered on a speaking tour. As with other tributes to the power of the people, historians have been skeptical about this justification as they point to the strategic and economic considerations that went into Mc-Kinley's decision to make the United States an imperial power.

More generally, the identification of motives for any individual act is a tricky business. Officials, as well as ordinary people, are not always able to explain with confidence why they behaved in a certain manner. This problem is compounded by leaders who often try to justify their programs in memoirs written many years after the events. The slippery nature of the evidence for motivation available on paper strengthens the argument for the efficacy of working in this area even before all the documents have been released.

There are mitigating factors that make the search for the impact of opinion on the decision makers somewhat easier in the cases of Johnson and Nixon. Above all, the number of participants in the making of foreign policy was quite small. Both men, especially on international issues, relied on only a few advisers who met in intimate settings where, alas, few notes were taken, although Nixon's tape recorders were rolling constantly.

By 1966, Johnson had come virtually to ignore the National Security Council, which, ironically, had been established, in part, because the cabinet was too unwieldy a body for foreign-policy deliberations. Instead, the president relied on the Tuesday Lunch group, which usually included the secretaries of state and defense, the director of the CIA, the chair of the joint chiefs, the president's assistant for national security affairs, and the press secretary. Despite its semi-institutionalized status, the Tuesday Lunch was more informal than it seemed; few notes or minutes were taken.[12]

A comparable, even less formal, arrangement obtained under the Nixon administration, with the president, his national security adviser, and sometimes the chief of the White House staff discussing major policy initiatives in the intimacy of the Oval Office. Most likely, under Nixon, there were even fewer meetings on foreign-policy matters in which the president was directly involved than under Johnson. Presidential counselor Bryce Harlow paints a picture of a president spending inordinate amounts of time by himself, away from the White House in the Executive Office Building, where, alone, surrounded by briefing papers, he contemplated the hard decisions. Nixon speechwriter and adviser Ray Price reports similarly that the president preferred memos to meetings with individuals.[13]

One reason for this centralization had to do with the greater efficiency of small groups. No less important, however, was the fact that both presidents, like many before and after them, were obsessed with the leaks that poured out of the larger cabinet and National Security Council sessions. William Bundy, former assistant secretary of state for Far Eastern affairs, feels that once a government group becomes larger than thirty, it is impossible to keep its secrets in Washington. Dean Rusk was delighted with the Tuesday Lunch arrangement because the handful of participants could debate openly without fear of finding their often frank statements in the media the next day.[14]

Undoubtedly, the more people involved in the decision making, the more likely the leaks, especially from members of the competing foreign-policy bureaucracies trying to protect their turfs and reputations. In both administrations, the presidents were troubled by officials in the departments of State and Defense, as well as by the National Security Council staff, who criticized one another to the Washington press corps.[15]

The fewer the chief advisers of the president and the more narrow the decision-making settings, the easier the task for the scholar. Although the bureaucracies continued to churn out long memoranda at all levels that were dutifully shuffled up a few levels, and the deputy and assistant secretaries held frequent coordinating meetings, much of this activity had little bearing on what went on inside Johnson's and Nixon's tight little groups. Of course, the secretaries of state and defense read some of these materials and they ultimately influenced the president. Nonetheless, the historian of this era should be wary of attributing too much importance to the mountains of paper emanating from those vast bureaucracies. One is reminded of the World War II historiographical problem when revisionist historians, looking for evidence of American anticommunist policies, found scores of such memos from assistant secretaries and desk people in the State Department. In reality, Franklin Roosevelt paid little attention to their analyses and chose to rely on his own intuition, ambassadors, and private advisers.

The decision-making groups under Johnson were small and insular. Senior staffers complained they rarely knew what was going on, even though charged with producing background reports that assumed full knowledge of American policy.[16] During the Nixon years, a scandal erupted when it was discovered that a military aide to national security adviser Henry Kissinger was leaking documents to the joint chiefs because even they did not know what was going on in American foreign policy.[17]

Clearly, it is difficult to determine how Presidents Johnson and Nixon were affected by opinion on their Vietnam policies. One should not begin a study of this issue with the formal, social-scientific models of opinion formation and submission that have been developed by academics. Public opinion is what government officials thought it was, whether or not their notions conformed to the neat flow charts created by the scholars. That is, even though presidents seemingly do not "understand" how public opinion works in American society, if they label some expression of opinion as an important reflection of *public* opinion, then in terms of impact on American policy, it is. And that is all that should matter to the scholar.

On occasion, presidents' impressions may indeed reflect the state of the sociological art, whether they know it or not. Johnson, for one, worried about intellectual dissent, even when the opinion polls were favorable to him. However, he most likely never thought about why the intellectuals were important; he just knew they were.[18]

Most politicians believe they can sense public opinion, with or without data provided by pollsters. There is evidence that people do become leaders in small groups in part because they are best able to understand what members of that group desire.[19] Harry S.

Truman, for example, prided himself on his ability to sense public opinion irrespective of what the media and polls reflected. In 1948, at least, he was right.[20]

George Christian, another of Johnson's press secretaries, was convinced that an advertisement in the *New York Times* featuring five thousand college professors opposed to administration policies was an important reflection of opinion. Although an academic public opinion analyst might be able to develop a convincing rationale for downplaying the significance of the published protest, Christian just "knew" the ad in question had to be taken into account when examining opinion in the United States.[21]

An even more astounding indication of this rejection of conventional academic wisdom is Dean Rusk's contention that the elite media and intelligentsia do not necessarily have a strong influence on foreign-policy issues with the rest of the population. According to this very experienced American statesman, when his "country cousins" in Georgia turned against the Vietnam War in the spring of 1968, they made up their minds virtually independent of currents of opinion emanating from the East Coast literary and journalistic establishment. With such an analysis, Dean Rusk denies the scholarly two-step-flow-of-information theory.[22]

In terms of the real world, then, academic experts who write about public opinion and foreign policy are, for the most part, out of touch with the real world. Or to put it another way, presidents and their advisers deal with public opinion in an idiosyncratic, unsystematic fashion that makes a mockery of the models that pervade the scholarly literature.

Both Bryce Harlow and Jack Valenti emphasize that their respective bosses were ultimately human beings who were quite capable of behaving irrationally and unpragmatically.[23] One lone picketer in Lafayette Park might arouse Nixon to a frenzy, and Johnson's day could be ruined because of a phrase in a report from an Associated Press correspondent.

Whether or not decision makers correctly assessed public opinion, it was important to them. How important and how the opinion ultimately affected the policymaking process is, of course, a difficult question. One way of getting at the answer is to examine the drift of opinion and, especially, the key activities of the antiwar movement, and then to determine how leaders perceived those activities and events. After those perceptions have been analyzed, one can move on to the even more difficult question of how they may have affected policy.[24]

First, one must determine how opinion arrives in the Oval Office. The most obvious and "scientific" source for opinion is the public opinion poll.[25] The most important polls were those that asked the same questions at periodical intervals: Are you satisfied with the president's handling of foreign relations? Was it a mistake to become involved in Vietnam? Johnson, as almost everyone knew, literally carried supportive polls in his pockets.[26] Nixon and his advisers were very keen observers and manipulators of the polls.[27]

There are polls and there are polls. One White House aide feels that the most important ones are those that are featured in newspapers or on television because they create opinion in their own right.[28] If the CBS/*New York Times* poll announced that 50 percent of those polled were opposed to further escalation, another 10 percent of the population might join with the majority that has sanctioned, for them, a critical attitude toward the war. Thus, a week after the poll had been published, the 50 percent might have become 60 percent because of the poll itself. Consequently, H. R. Haldeman, who looked at the Gallup Poll primarily as an influencer of opinion, commissioned his own polls to gauge actual public opinion.[29] At the same time, published polls during the Vietnam period had an effect on Hanoi as well.

In most cases, polls are too insensitive and crude an instrument for the president to employ to gauge reactions to foreign-policy initiatives. For one thing, they are often outdated by the time they reach the decision maker's desk.[30] Any poll on Soviet-American relations taken during the week before the 1983 Korean airliner incident would have been worthless the minute the news of the tragedy hit the airwaves.

In addition, Americans tend to support presidents' foreign policies more reflexively than their domestic policies.[31] This virtual knee-jerk support may be a product of deference relating to the public's alleged lack of knowledge in this complex and usually remote area.[32] Moreover, presidents can improve their approval rating merely by doing something in the foreign-policy sphere, the most famous case being the rise in John F. Kennedy's popularity after he publicly accepted the blame for the Bay of Pigs fiasco.[33]

Another potentially quantifiable and scientific source for general opinion is mail, telephone calls, and telegrams sent to the White House and executive departments.[34] This can be something of a two-way street with calls and telegrams artificially generated by party officials to demonstrate to the rest of the nation that people support the president's policy.[35] Generally, however, the correspondence and communication to the White House is spontaneous. Depending on the administration and the issue, departments keep records of this expression of opinion, which are forwarded to the president.[36]

Looking at the mail flow over a weekend period in early April 1965, National Security Council aide Chester Cooper counted 580 letters against and only 96 for the Vietnam policy. A worried Cooper noted that the letters did not look like they were part of an organized campaign and were "judicious and reasoned."[37] That 700 letters over a weekend in a population of 200 million could have an impact on the White House might seem surprising, but they apparently do.[38] It may be that a certain number of letters expressing a certain distribution of opinion becomes the norm and that when the number fluctuates or the opinion becomes skewed, the mail is considered potentially reflective of attitudes in the nation at large.

Skepticism about the meaning of White House mail should have been reinforced by the fact that people tend to write more frequently to their political friends than to their political enemies.[39] We also know that during the Vietnam period, letter writers tended toward the hawkish side of the argument, whereas demonstrators were more likely to be dovish.[40] Other scientific analyses of the meaning of the mail were available to White House operatives. However, when the president asks about the mail count or even asks to see a letter or two, the mail becomes an important indicator of opinion to him, an indicator that may have an effect on a policy decision.[41]

When we leave the polls and the mail (and, of course, election returns), the presidents' sources for public opinion become more unquantifiable and unsystematic. They are no less important, however, and in the case of the decision makers' acquaintances, friends, and family, they may be all important. The intimates to whom a president and his staff talk regularly, over the breakfast, conference, or cocktail table, both offer their own ideas about public opinion and reflect elite opinion. One can imagine, for example, Richard Nixon asking his daughter Julie what her classmates at Smith would think of such and such a policy, as well as what she thought of it.

It is true that both presidents seemed to surround themselves with sycophantic types. Or perhaps their forceful personalities and oversensitivity to criticism created sycophants out of previously strong-willed individuals. In any event, the presidents' intimates often found themselves in the position of telling them what they thought they wanted to hear. All the same, those intimates themselves were affected by family and friends, especially on the Vietnam War issue. Most important, the intimates were central to the opinion-presenting process, explaining to the president what was going on "out there." William Bundy remembers the way wives of officials often were confronted by harsh criticism on Vietnam policy from friends because those friends found it easier to open up to spouses. George Reedy recalls the role of his own wife, as well as the wives of other high officials, who fell off the Vietnam bandwagon early and told their husbands so in no uncertain terms. Bryce Harlow remembers an informal discussion with a group of his son's high school friends, none of whom was prepared to accept a draft call. The mother of Nixon's secretary of defense, Melvin Laird, as well as Laird's son, children of Gerald Ford, John Ehrlichman, Spiro Agnew, and Robert McNamara, among others, brought to their important relatives a feeling for the antiwar sentiment in the country.[42]

The same goes for social contacts in Washington and New York.[43] From 1966 on, more and more of the friends of the decision makers became critical of Vietnam policies and, until they became too strident, were able to relay that criticism indirectly to the Oval Office. George Christian feels that when influential figures like Dean Acheson and Matthew Ridgway privately and informally began to express displeasure with the way things were going in Southeast Asia, the president took notice.[44] In a study of the weapons industry during the period, one scholar discovered that friends and family were very important in affecting scientists' attitudes toward government policy, ultimately figuring prominently in their decision to leave war-related research.[45]

Congress is still another source of public opinion for the president.[46] White House staffers often interpret opinions from the Hill as surrogates for public opinion. Undoubtedly, publicly expressed opinion from prominent congressional leaders can affect opinion, as was probably the case with the Senate Foreign Relations Committee's televised hearings in February 1966.[47]

In general, however, congressional opinion is more a reflector than a shaper of public opinion, as legislators are loath to move out in advance of their constituents on an important issue. Bryce Harlow, for one, sees Congress as a "superb mirror" of public opinion.[48] Complicating matters is the suggestion that legislators and their constituents are least congruent on their opinions on foreign policy issues.[49]

A final source of opinion for the president is the media through which elite, congressional, and public opinion is reported and influenced. Bernard C. Cohen claims that the media play four roles—presenters of opinion, critics of government, policy advocates, and even policymakers.[50] It is the first of the four interrelated roles, presenters of opinion, that is of importance here.[51]

As has been said often, the media may not be able to tell people what to think, but they can tell them what to think about.[52] To some degree, the White House determines the news budgets of the electronic and print media through its own action, well-timed news releases, and even intimidation. President Johnson's staged media event, the Honolulu Conference of 1966, shifted attention away from the Senate Foreign Relations Committee hearings on Vietnam held during the same period.[53] Later, threats from Spiro Agnew produced a virtual blackout of television coverage for the massive Mobilization protest of November 15, 1969.[54]

Still, the media are not always manipulable. The *New York Times'* publication of Harrison Salisbury's account of the bombing of Hanoi in December 1966 and the same paper's publication of *The Pentagon Papers* in 1971 are good examples of journalistic independence.

Some media may be more influential than others as sources of public opinion on foreign issues. Perhaps because electronic media are supposed to be objective, editorial opinions expressed in newspapers tend to be those most noticed by the White House.[55] Although both electronic and print media affect and reflect opinion, electronic media are viewed by decision makers primarily as opinion influencers, print media as opinion reflectors.[56]

The *New York Times* and the *Washington Post* play a central role in the political life of the capital.[57] For people in the other media, the bureaucracy, and especially Congress, those two papers, which are required morning reading for conscientious officials, present not only opinions but also information unavailable to those not at the center of power.[58] For those making the decisions, the two papers represent a daily scorecard. They desire the approval of the "validators" of the *Times* and the *Post*.[59] Lyndon Johnson wanted Walter Lippmann to say nice things about his Vietnam policy, because of his ego as well as because of the fact that everyone else who counted read his column.[60] Richard Nixon, who did not expect much from the newspapers, nevertheless was distressed when they did not give him more credit for the way he was extricating the United States from Vietnam.[61]

Presidents often confuse the opinions they see in the *Times* and *Post* with public opinion. From time to time, their aides try to place a Reston or Lippmann column in perspective, to point out that the polls and 95 percent of the newspapers are supportive, but they usually fail to convince the president to ignore the criticism.[62] In part, Johnson and Nixon became "Washington types" who placed inordinate emphasis on the two major elite dailies, just like everyone else who is anyone in the capital.[63]

It is also true, as Senator J. William Fulbright reports, that since 90 percent of Congress does not know anything about foreign policy, the *Times* and the *Post* do reflect opinion if only because their opinions become opinion on the Hill. In Washington, then, the *Times* and the *Post* have an influence far greater than their national circulations might indicate because opinions presented in their pages have a disproportionate impact on leaders who read them each day.[64]

And this is not the entire story. Washington journalists interact daily with Washington officials. Not all of their influence comes from specific ideas presented in their columns. George Reedy talks of news people engaging in a "continuing dialogue" with policymakers. Thus, a few words at dinner concerning bombing in Vietnam from the publisher of the *Washington Post* to an assistant secretary of state were likely to have been reported to the president within a day or two and might have had as much impact as a published editorial or even a memorandum from a national security adviser.[65]

Presidents and their advisers find out about the media not just from the papers themselves but from prepared press summaries. Although most departments maintain their own clipping bureau, many rely on the *Current News*, an extensive daily summary of the media that is produced in several editions. Harry Zubkoff, chief of the News Clipping and Analysis Service at the Pentagon since 1970, has long been reputed to edit Washington's most thorough and authoritative review of the nation's press. To discover what decision makers are reading, one should look not only at the *Times* and the *Post* but also *Current News*.[66] The Nixon administration's clipping and pasting operation was, however, one of H. R. Haldeman's proudest accomplishments. He thought that it transcended any such Washington operation to that time.[67]

Presidents Johnson and Nixon received opinion from the polls, correspondence, friends and acquaintances, Congress, and the media. Each day they were exposed to a plethora of formal reports and informal observations concerning polls, mail flows, print and electronic journalism, congressional activities, and comments from intimates, all of which constituted the flow of perceived public opinion into the Oval Office. In a conventional sense, only the polls and the mail flow are sources of *public* opinion. Yet, as has been noted, presidents tend to see public opinion reflected in the other sources as well.

In both presidencies, no systematic attempt was made to coordinate the flow of public opinion, nor were any specific aides responsible for its monitoring.[68] It is unlikely that Jack Valenti or H. R. Haldeman, upon telling the president what the *Times* had to say that morning, also informed him that it was not public opinion but only opinion expressed publicly in a newspaper. On any day, the president and his advisers might be impressed by a poll result, or a comment by a television anchorperson, or a phone call from

Clark Clifford or Thomas Dewey, or an idea from a Georgetown professor in an undersecretary's carpool, or a letter selected at random from the mail sack, or any combination of the above. What was noted and taken seriously as meaningful public opinion depended on the mood in the Oval Office and the sort of opinion for which the president was looking.[69] Sometimes a "scientifically" sound datum became important; most of the time the public opinion that counted would not impress an academic analyst.

Presented schematically in Figure 1, in its simplest form, is the flow of public opinion on foreign policy to the president.[70] Yet the real world is not as simple and uncluttered as depicted in the figure, with the five main sources *directly* conveying public opinions to the White House.

Figure 2, a decidedly cluttered diagram, more accurately represents the ways alleged public opinion comes to the president. In the first place, the presidents do not passively receive spontaneously developed public opinion. They play a part in molding that opinion through their public and private statements to the media,

FIGURE 1.
THE PRESIDENT'S SOURCES FOR PUBLIC OPINION ON FOREIGN POLICY

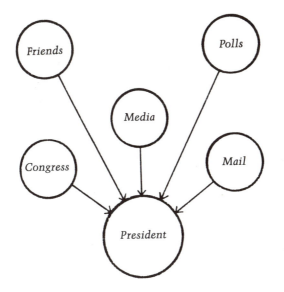

FIGURE 2.
INFLUENCES ON AND REFLECTIONS OF PUBLIC OPINION ON FOREIGN
POLICY

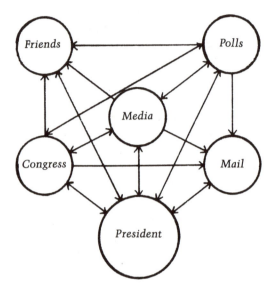

to friends, and to Congress, as well as in their role as national
agenda setter. After all, there was little expressed opinion on the
decision to bomb North Vietnam until that bombing started.

Moreover, almost all of the sources for opinion influence one
another. Thus, congressional opinion influences the opinions of
presidential family and friends, the media, the mail flow, and the
polls, while it is influenced by the media and the polls. Presidential
family and friends are influenced by opinions picked up in the
polls, the media, and Congress. The media influence the other four
sources and are influenced by Congress and the polls. Public
opinions in the polls influence the opinions of the other sources
and are influenced by the media and Congress.

During times of public debate, such as the Vietnam period, a
sixth source for opinion may emerge as depicted in Figure 3.[71] The
opinions expressed by the antiwar movement influenced opinions
reflected by all of the other sources and were influenced, in turn,
by the media and Congress. To place the ideas represented in
Figures 2 and 3 in another perspective, public opinions directly
presented by one of the six sources may appear to the president

filtered through almost any of the other sources. Thus, the president might learn about congressional reflections of public opinion from the media, from the antiwar movement, from friends and family, or from the *New York Times.*

Figures 2 and 3 suggest the chaotic nature of the way putatively *public* opinion on foreign policy is perceived by presidents in the modern era. That some of the things they consider to be public opinion are not is irrelevant. Complicating matters further is the fact, as we have seen, that presidents and their advisers rarely devote attention in public to the impact of their foreign policies on public opinion and vice versa.

Being able to identify sources of opinion in the Oval Office is only the first step in understanding how opinion influences policy. Both Johnson and Nixon were extremely sensitive men who were concerned about their image and the image of their policies and who easily took umbrage at criticism. They presided over large staffs who catered to their obsessions with the polls, the media, and other reflections of public opinion. In the documentary and archival records for both presidents are found thousands of items

FIGURE 3.
INFLUENCES ON AND REFLECTIONS OF PUBLIC OPINION ON FOREIGN
POLICY DURING THE VIETNAM WAR

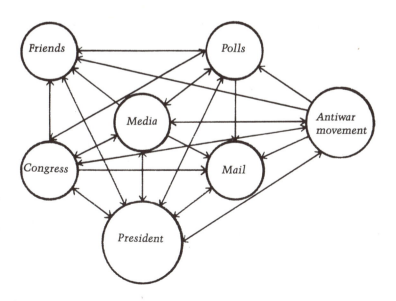

that suggest avid presidential interest in and response to opinion on the Vietnam War.

One Swedish scholar who discovered scores of references to Swedish antiwar activity in the Johnson Archives concludes that the administration did pay attention to his nation's critique.[72] Yet this scholar, as well as anyone interested in only one variable in foreign-policy making, has no way of knowing how much time and how much attention was paid to opinion during the waking hours of the president's day. There is simply no way to deal with this issue.

Johnson, who was more distressed with criticism than Nixon, in part because the latter was more used to being criticized, held a levée each morning devoted to the media and Congress. His aides gathered around his bed and received orders to respond to criticism in the *New York Times*, the *Washington Post*, and the *Congressional Record*, as well as all the television news programs that the president watched the night before, simultaneously. Sometimes he himself called publishers and network presidents to complain vociferously about their coverage. Nixon resorted to another and more indirect technique to lash back at his critics in the press. Early in his administration, he established an informal network of letterwriters who would complain to newspapers and television stations about "unfair" treatment of his policies.[73]

Experienced aides did not follow through on some of the more extreme requests for retribution against the opinion makers because they knew that sometimes Johnson and Nixon were merely reacting in anger.[74] Some of these brief, passionate outbursts were primarily of therapeutic significance. John Roche tells of Lyndon Johnson becoming exercised about a leak that he read in a Drew Pearson column concerning a top secret mission to Vietnam headed by Chester Ronning. Johnson wanted to find and destroy the leaker. Somewhat sheepishly, Roche explained that Johnson himself had given the leak to Pearson twenty-four hours earlier in order to demonstrate his constant search for peace.[75] Similarly, when one listens to Nixon's frequent threats on the infamous tapes, one must understand that most of them were soon forgotten by the president and his aides.

Clearly, the question of how much attention was paid to opinion and how seriously to take presidential hostility to critics can only be answered impressionistically. Interviews here do help, but they too have their shortcomings. Many government officials pride themselves on their thick skins, or at least believe that they are supposed to have thick skins. Thus, they report that although one or another of their colleagues may have been exercised about a march or a newspaper column, they coolly went on about their business. For example, although many contemporary observers described a state of siege in the White House during the March on the Pentagon in October 1967 and in the aftermath of the Kent State killings in May 1970, most of those queried were proud to report that they were not shaken by those tumultuous events.

Jack Valenti, however, does tell a revealing story about himself. From time to time, whenever Johnson became apoplectic about criticism in the media, Valenti tried to convince the president that almost all Americans loved him. "Who gives a shit about William Sloane Coffin," he would say. One morning, the president read from his bed a column full of nasty words presumably about himself. When he finished, Valenti, as usual, clucked his tongue and counseled patience and calm. The cagy Johnson then revealed that the column was about Valenti, at which point the presidential aide became apoplectic himself, threatening all sorts of dire retribution for the perpetrator of the attack.[76]

It is difficult to determine the way that perceived public opinion arrives in the Oval Office and how the decision makers evaluate the relative significance of expressions of support for or hostility to their policies. It is even more difficult to establish a link between those perceptions, responses, and decisions taken at some proximate later date. The problems multiply when one tries to relate antiwar activities to opinion to policy.

Scholars have discovered a general congruence between opinion and policy in the United States in recent years.[77] One sophisticated study even suggests that opinion changes more often than not precede policy changes.[78] The empirical research in this area, however, is macrosocial-scientific and deals with correlational, not causal relationships.

As for hard evidence of a link between dissent and opinion, it is likely that dissent did have some impact on congressional opinion.[79] Yet one scholar who crudely correlates demonstrations with national approval ratings for the president discovered no such impact. Indeed, he suggests that all of the marching, protesting, and petitioning had no effect on general opinion.[80] Here, he would be joined by almost all of the key decision makers in any administration who refuse to admit that they were affected by the rabble in the streets.

The historian interested in how discrete decisions were made during the Vietnam era cannot employ a rigorously empirical, social-scientific methodology. Like generations of humanistically oriented researchers, he or she must read most of the available documents and interview most of the participants willing to talk to scholars, and then come to some informed judgment concerning how opinion and dissent may have affected policy. Here one returns to the decision maker's perceptions of and reactions to public opinion, and one's impressionistic "measurement" of the attention given to opinion and the intensity of that attention. Unsatisfactory as this "method" may be, it is the only valid way to discover how the antiwar movement affected policy.

Although no one has studied the relationships between opinion, dissent, and policy in any rigorous manner, scores of scholars have offered their ideas on the subject. Few of them doubt that public opinion in general did play an important role in Vietnam decision making. According to Leslie Gelb, public opinion was "the essential domino," especially in the decision to deescalate.[81] Gelb does not, however, label the antiwar movement the essential domino.[82]

In fact, some contend that the antiwar movement had little or no impact on policy and, if anything, had an impact contrary to that hoped for by its leaders.[83] Proponents of this view maintain that most Americans perceived the movement as violent, hippie-led, and ultimately unpatriotic. Thus, the Johnson and Nixon administrations could wave the flag and uphold American values, confident that the majority of Americans were more upset about the unkempt, rowdy radicals than they were about the progress of the war.

Others even contend that the movement prolonged the war because citizens who were worried about administration policies in Vietnam did not want to associate themselves with the vocal protesters.[84] They reasoned that if *those* were the sort of people who were opposing the war, then they should be on the other side of the barricades.[85] According to this interpretation, many more Americans would have registered their dissent earlier had not dissent been linked to the well-publicized mass demonstrations.

The movement has also been judged counterproductive because of its negative psychological impact on Johnson and Nixon. The two strong presidents who disliked the protesters intensely might have been unwilling to adopt more conciliatory diplomatic postures because they did not want to appear to be truckling to the "nervous nellies," as Johnson called some of their leadership, or "bums," as Nixon labeled some students.

Finally, as Johnson and Nixon often claimed, the movement might have prolonged the war because it strengthened Hanoi's allegedly erroneous belief that it could win on American streets what it could not win in Vietnamese jungles. According to this line, Ho Chi Minh and his cadres would have been more forthcoming at Paris, and even earlier, had they not counted so heavily on their movement allies.

Despite considerable support for the notion that the antiwar movement had little or even a negative impact on policy, most observers think it contributed to the pressures that produced the American withdrawal from Vietnam. Although few go as far as Irwin Unger in saying "it forced the United States out of Vietnam," most analysts give it high marks for its effectiveness.[86] The existence of a strong antiwar movement by 1967, they argue, helped to compel Johnson to deescalate in the spring of 1968 and made it impossible for Nixon to reescalate. Through meetings, publications, and mass demonstrations, antiwar activists presented credible information to the public about the failures of American policies in Vietnam. Thus, the continuous decline of support for the war among the general population was, in part, a result of the well-organized campaigns that countered the line from Washington.

Another possible interpretation of the positive impact of the movement revolves around the unsettling environment created by the constant marches and demonstrations. The many disturbances and disruptions in daily life might have made politicians and citizens alike want to end the war so that they could return to a normal society where hippies and other ne'er-do-wells did not threaten domestic tranquillity.[87]

Some might argue that it is wise to distinguish between the two administrations when evaluating the impact of the movement. On the surface, it appears that it had its greatest impact with Johnson. The decision to wind down the war was taken in March 1968, and thereafter, presumably, the movement and public opinion declined in importance. In addition, most antiwar activists were Democrats from Johnson's constituency. Finally, Nixon ended the draft, a major issue for the armies of antiwar students and young people.

Not everyone agrees with such an analysis. One Vietnamese diplomat insists that he and his colleagues feel the antiwar movement was most successful with Nixon because it restrained his policy, which called for victory on the battlefield.[88] And it is clear that the Congress, perhaps in delayed response to antiwar activities, was its most hostile to escalation during the years after Johnson left office.

In the pages to follow, how antiwar activities were perceived by the decision makers will be examined. "Antiwar activities" is a rather broad term. It must be, since the concern here is with all important opposition to the war.[89] Obviously, "important" opposition activities had to have been visible enough to engage the attention of the decision makers and the public. From the start, with the teach-ins in the spring of 1965, the mass antiwar movement centered around the colleges, with professors and student activists playing leading organizing roles.[90] At first glance, one might dismiss college students as constituting a relatively insignificant pressure group. Yet by 1968, they numbered almost seven million, three times the number of American farmers and nine times the number of railroad workers.[91] This number had almost doubled since 1950, with more than one-half of all white youths of college age in college by the time the movement reached its peak.[92] Although most students were not activists and supported relatively conventional politics and life-styles, the elite colleges that produced the next generation of the "best and the brightest" were disproportionately dovish.[93]

The centrality of college students to the movement is best illustrated by the timing of the mass demonstrations. Almost all of them during the period, except for the Chicago Democratic Convention activities, took place in the spring or the fall. During the summer, the campuses, the easiest place to organize young people, were generally deserted.

The teach-in movement was the first, rather genteel, major antiwar activity. Although it faded when the students went home during the summer of 1965, it was soon replaced by other modes of protest that grew in intensity and scope through 1971.[94] These included marches and demonstrations in New York, Washington, San Francisco, and other major cities; the collecting and sometimes publishing of petitions signed by businesspeople, professors, doctors, writers, social workers, and other professionals; scores of meetings between peace leaders and administration officials; and individual and collective acts of civil disobedience, such as the burning of draft cards, fasting, and even self-immolation.[95] It also included increased media criticism, as well as the growth of the antiwar minority on Capitol Hill and in the Democratic party.

All of these activities captured the attention of the White House. At times, some were more important than others, and not all attracted the interest of all decision makers and their advisers. How they perceived those activities from 1965 through 1971 and how those perceptions may have contributed to the making of foreign policy during the Vietnam War is the subject of the discussion that follows.

Chapter Two

The Americanization of the War and the Rise of Dissent: November 1964–July 1965

"Distasteful as it is, elements in the intellectual community and other segments of the United States opinion do not believe in our South Vietnam policy."

—GEORGE BALL*

The United States first became directly involved in Vietnam in 1950 when President Harry Truman started to underwrite the costs of France's war against the Viet Minh. Presidents Dwight Eisenhower and John Kennedy increased America's political, economic, and military commitments steadily through the fifties and early sixties. Their activities in Southeast Asia were supported by that part of the American population that knew about them.

One reason for the support was the general bipartisan cold war consensus on strategy that lay behind any consideration of foreign policy during the period. In addition, given the many other crises around the world, ranging from the Korean War, Suez, Castro's revolution, and even the Laos problem of 1959–62, America's involvement in Vietnam was an obscure sideshow. Despite a growing economic cost when Lyndon Johnson assumed the presidency in November 1963, the attempt at nation building did not

*Ball to Lyndon Johnson, April 21, 1965, box 17, National Security Council Files, Vietnam, Lyndon Baines Johnson Library.

yet include significant participation in South Vietnam's *military* conflict with the insurgents of the National Liberation Front.

The military situation in the field and the political situation in Saigon, already deteriorating when Johnson took office, became even more problematic through 1964. To save South Vietnam from a communist takeover, the United States embarked on a policy that altered the conflict from one between Asians, assisted by fewer than twenty thousand American "advisers," to one in which the United States assumed the major combat role in the air and on the land.

The Americanization of the war in Vietnam and its extension to the North produced significant opposition during the first seven months of 1965. The decisions made in February to begin bombing North Vietnam and in July to assume the dominant combat role in South Vietnam, were opposed by some on the campuses, in the media, and the general population. After several silent generations, the campuses particularly came alive with new activism and even new battle tactics. An iconoclastic New Left emerged to cooperate with the Old Left on the war. Defectors within the Democratic party, as well as within the traditionally Democratic intellectual and journalistic community, joined in a cacophony of protest. The cold war consensus was beginning to fall apart.

During the period when those escalatory decisions were made, foreign-policy critics were perceived by the Johnson administration to be irritating but essentially manageable. The president still enjoyed overwhelming support for his foreign and domestic programs in the polls, the media, and on Capitol Hill. Nevertheless, most of his advisers agreed that if the war dragged on too long, the dissenters might become an important domestic political problem, one that could encourage the North Vietnamese and the Viet Cong to think that they could win in the streets of the United States what they could not win in the jungles and rice paddies of South Vietnam. Consequently, Johnson launched a modest offensive against his critics in an attempt to shore up domestic support for his programs. When, in July, he decided to begin the process that would ultimately send more than 550,000 American soldiers to Vietnam by 1968, he was confident that the dissidents had been contained.

TABLE 1.
MAJOR VIETNAM WAR–RELATED EVENTS OF 1965

Antiwar Activities	Percent Poll Respondents who Think War Was Mistake	Percent Poll Respondents for Withdraw
March 24: Teach-ins begin		
		April: 17%
April 17: Washington demonstration		
		May: 13%
May 15: Nationwide teach-in		
		June: 12%
June 8: New York demonstration		
June 14: White House Arts Festival		
June 15: Fulbright speech		
	August: 24%	
Oct. 15–16: Nationwide demonstrations		
Nov. 20: Berkeley demonstration		
Nov. 27: Washington demonstration		

Administration Activities	Troop Levels	Battle Deaths (6-month totals)
	Jan. 1: 23,300	
Feb. 7: Bombing of North Vietnam		
Feb. 27: White Paper on North Vietnamese aggression		
March 8: Marines land in South Vietnam		
April 7: LBJ Johns Hopkins speech		
April 23: Rusk attacks teach-ins		
May 12–17: Bombing pause		
May: Truth squads to colleges		
June 21: McGeorge Bundy debates Hans Morgenthau	June 30: 59,900	216
July 28: Draft calls increase by 50,000		
Dec. 24–Jan. 31: Bombing pause		
	Dec. 31: 184,300	1,153

Although most Americans were unaware of it, the war in South Vietnam was not going well in the fall of 1964. Despite the presence of more than twenty thousand American advisers and increasing levels of technical and financial aid, the anticommunist forces were not holding their own against the National Liberation Front. Moreover, the American-backed coup that overthrew President Ngo Dinh Diem the previous year had not produced the stable and efficient Saigon government for which Washington had hoped. The situation was so critical that Johnson and his advisers had begun giving serious consideration to a variety of escalatory proposals, including the bombing of North Vietnam. Almost all were convinced that the United States had to increase substantially its commitment in order to save South Vietnam.

As they contemplated their options in November, December, and January, they knew that they had little to fear from the American public. With the near unanimous vote in Congress for the Gulf of Tonkin Resolution in August and the smashing triumph at the polls in November, Lyndon Johnson's foreign policy had been approved in dramatic fashion by most citizens. In fact, the public perception of the president as a wise and restrained protector of national security, as compared to the hawkish Barry Goldwater, contributed significantly to his winning margin.[1]

This widespread popular and congressional support reflected the view that with Johnson as president, America's commitment in South Vietnam would remain limited. As Johnson himself said on August 29, the war "ought to be fought by the boys of Asia to help protect their own land. And for that reason" he had "not chosen to enlarge the war."[2]

Naturally, any major deviation from this approach to the war could produce an erosion in popular support. A few prominent senators and intellectuals had already begun criticizing American involvement in Vietnam during the summer of 1964. This still gentle criticism may have laid the groundwork for the mass antiwar movement that was to appear in the spring of 1965.[3] Nevertheless, it appeared in the fall of 1964 that with skillful presidential handling of the public relations aspects of the proposed escalation, the support of most Americans could be counted on for the year or two needed to bring the communists to the bargaining table.[4]

The position papers prepared in the State and Defense departments and the National Security Council during the period reflect this confidence in public support. At least, they rarely included considerations of the possible impact of the bombing on domestic opinion.[5] Conceivably, as William Bundy suggests, those who prepared such papers thought their job was to make military assessments; the president alone would make the political assessments, if any were necessary. The former assistant secretary of state cannot remember a time when the polls or public opinion were *explicitly* discussed in his circle from November through March 1965. Naturally, he and his colleagues knew what the polls revealed, as well as what prominent journalists were writing, but they did not spend much time talking about such things.[6]

On the other hand, according to Dean Rusk and Cyrus Vance, among others, the printed record does not tell the entire story of policymaking in meetings during the winter of 1964–65.[7] Early on, Under Secretary of State George Ball raised the issue of the Korean experience and predicted that the public would become increasingly restive as the war went on.[8] For his part, McGeorge Bundy clearly remembers several discussions with the president concerning the opinion variable on the eve of the bombing. Opinion, for example, was a consideration that crept into the conversations in a December 1, 1964, meeting, with Johnson worrying about "how to keep the problem from looking worse than it is."[9]

Somewhat removed from the inner circle, Vice President Humphrey was worried as well. According to James Thomson of the NSC staff, who had been "on loan" to Humphrey during the presidential campaign, the vice president did not think we would ever begin bombing, in part, because of adverse public reaction.[10]

The public may not have been a larger factor in the planning because of the belief that the bombing program would work and that the war would be over before it could become a political issue. The program was conceived as a short-term inducement to make the North Vietnamese reasonable. No one thought it would last almost four years.[11] Undoubtedly, had Johnson known that bombing would become a permanent part of American policy in Vietnam, he might have given more thought to its impact on the public and its potential for galvanizing dissent.

As for the existing critics of the war, not yet constituted as a "movement," many had been deflected by the election campaign against the apparently Strangelovean Goldwater.[12] The low-level antiwar activity that appeared in 1964, especially during the Gulf of Tonkin crisis in August, could be contained easily once the bombing began. To some like John Roche, its feeble but shrill protests came from the usual left-wing pacifist and sectarian groups who could always be counted on to oppose militant anticommunism.[13] Interestingly, when summing up the early results of the bombing campaign, Secretary of Defense Robert S. McNamara referred on July 30, 1965, to the "*new* school of liberals and peace groups" (emphasis mine) that had been spawned by the bombing.[14] This statement can be interpreted as obliquely indicating the virtual nonexistence of such groups before the bombing began.

Although the public was not an *immediate* worry, the trick was to escalate without appearing to escalate, or as President Johnson explained it to McGeorge Bundy, the bombing would be "not a change in policy but in what policy requires."[15] It was not just the public that concerned him. Worried about the reactions of the Russians and Chinese to a major escalation, Johnson had to make it less dramatic by concealing its import. Indeed, Johnson spent so much time personally overseeing target selection because of his continuing concern that a stray bomb might hit a Russian ship or installation.[16]

Another reason for approaching the bombing without much fanfare had to do with the hoped-for North Vietnamese response. Advocating a low profile, McGeorge Bundy did not want to "make it hard for Hanoi to shift its ground."[17]

At home, Johnson was concerned about Capitol Hill. If Congress believed that the bombing marked the beginning of an enlarged commitment in Southeast Asia, it might think twice about the emerging Great Society programs. The "if guns, no butter" argument would surely please conservative and hawkish budget balancers in Congress.

The attempt to escalate stealthily had a broader, long-term policy significance. Robert McNamara allegedly said that Vietnam was a test. Since limited wars were the wars of the future, Washington had to learn how to "go to war without arousing the public ire."[18] In a similar vein, a military analyst feels that the policy of fighting in Vietnam with draft deferments and without mobilizations and a declaration of war represented an attempt by Johnson not to "arouse the passions of the American people."[19] This unwillingness to arouse public ire relates to the fear of domestic criticism but also to the dangers inherent in the impatience of a public angry about fighting a war with its nuclear arm tied behind its back. Were the public not carefully managed the administration might be pressured into doing something that could lead to major-power confrontation.

Much of what came to be known as the "credibility gap" originated in the decision to obscure the degree of the Americanization of the war. At first, Johnson apparently got away with it in view of the initial reaction to the bombings and, especially, the almost total public indifference to the assumption by marines of a limited protective combat role around the Danang base on March 8.[20] But as early as May 23, the term "credibility gap" appeared in a newspaper.[21] Later, the developing belief that there was a credibility gap played a role in the growth of antiwar sentiment in the United States.

Of all the military activities of the United States in Southeast Asia, the initiation of the bombing of North Vietnam was the most dramatic—and the most useful to foreign policy critics. To be sure, as the ground war escalated and the American body count increased, more and more Americans began to feel uneasy, especially after 1967. Yet the well-publicized bombing of North Vietnam, a relatively small peasant nation that was not bombing the United States or even the South, hurt more in the long run in the battle for public opinion than it helped in the battle to control Vietnam. As William Bundy admits, the bombing "caused a maximum of fuss here and did minimum damage on the other side."[22]

The Johnson administration underestimated the extent and intensity of the opposition to the bombing. Perhaps the military had convinced the president and his aides that they could bomb surgically and destroy only legitimate military targets. Undoubtedly, the decision makers looked at bombing as just another tool of war, a tool that they thought had been used with great success and little public outcry during their war, World War II. Of course, World War II was fought with press censorship and without television.

For whatever reasons, this miscalculation was to cost the administration dearly. The bombing of the North catalyzed the antiwar movement and that elusive factor, world public opinion. It clearly stole the moral issue from an administration that hoped that its tales of Viet Cong atrocities and assassinations would win the propaganda battle. Bombing spawned the antiwar movement and sustained it, especially as the range of permissible targets expanded each time North Vietnamese leader Ho Chi Minh refused to bow to American demands.

Although most around Johnson agreed with the general strategy concerning the public and the escalation, some felt that the president should go to the people with a more complete explanation of the bombing policy lest it create political problems. McGeorge Bundy, assisted by his brother and George Ball, prepared material for such a speech, but the president insisted on his low-profile approach.[23] He was satisfied with a public statement demonstrating the link between his policy and that of his predecessors, emphasizing particularly President Eisenhower's 1955 commitment to President Diem. The bombing was presented as the logical extension of what had been American policy, Republican and Democratic for over a decade. McGeorge Bundy thinks that the statement did not represent a satisfactory justification for the bombing, which, to many, had to appear as a major escalation.[24]

Toward the end of February, as it became apparent to Americans and other observers that the bombing would continue indefinitely, the administration released a White Paper entitled "Aggression from the North." This jerry-built document convinced few who read it that the United States had to bomb because of North Vietnam's control of the Viet Cong. William Bundy, who had a hand in the work, considers it "a bust that got us into deep trouble." Bundy did approve of the idea of a White Paper but regretted that security considerations did not allow him to present all that he knew about North Vietnam's military and economic activities in the South. That is, to prove the case, he and his colleagues would have had to reveal evidence they had gathered through means not yet discovered by the enemy.[25]

Many of the factual underpinnings of the White Paper were demolished by I. F. Stone in his newsletter in such a brilliant fashion that the article was reprinted in the *New York Times* on March 8 by the antiwar Committee for a Negotiated Settlement.

The attempts by the State Department to refute Stone's critique were not very successful.[26]

Lyndon Johnson has been severely criticized by colleagues and historians for failing to level with the American public in February 1965, when he made the war in Vietnam an American war. One former official has argued that Johnson's obscuring of the nature of the war in 1965 through 1966 made it all the more difficult for him to convince his constituents that Vietnam was a major national security interest that demanded increasingly greater human and physical resources.[27]

Could Johnson have blunted the antiwar movement's later attacks by being more forthcoming about his view of the seriousness of the nation's plight in February 1965? Certainly such a position, perhaps presented in the speech prepared by McGeorge Bundy that was never given, would have weakened the credibility gap argument later on. But it would have opened up a debate on Vietnam policy in Congress and the public that would have presented an image to the enemy of a weakened home front. And a more forthright explanation of what the government was planning would also have been of assistance to that enemy. The antiwar movement would have emerged in any event, centering first around the issue of the bombing, and then around the growing cost of the war in terms of lives. Thus, one can understand why Johnson chose to keep a low profile, given the relatively few payoffs inherent in pursuing the other route. This explanation does not, of course, condone conducting an undeclared war in secret in a democracy.

Protests against the bombing mounted slowly. In the wake of the raids of February 7, the White House received about fifteen hundred telegrams, a medium-to-heavy outpouring according to McGeorge Bundy. More important, the telegrams were running twelve to one against the bombing, not yet announced as a permanent part of American policy. Bundy, who had earlier evinced concern about possible public responses to the escalation, told the president, "We have an education problem that bears close watching and more work."[28] Yet the telegrams did not reveal the entire story. Bundy aide Gordon Chase pointed out several days later that whereas telegrams were then running fourteen to one against the administration, the Gallup Poll showed 67 percent of the population supportive of the president's policy. "It goes to show something about telegrams to the White House," noted Chase.[29]

Picket lines slowly began to appear in Washington along with letters to the editor in the newspapers. On February 10, Dagmar Wilson led three hundred protesters from the Women's International League for Peace and Freedom and Women Strike for Peace to the capital. Later that week, the *New York Times* published a letter signed by faculty from twenty-five New England colleges calling for negotiations. During the same period, several people were arrested at a protest at the United Nations. More significantly, the Students for a Democratic Society (SDS) renewed its call for a mass demonstration in Washington on April 17.[30]

Much of this early activity involved groups like SDS, the Committee for a Sane Nuclear Policy (SANE), the War Resisters League, and a variety of left-sectarian and pacifist bodies that had been concerned about American involvement in Southeast Asia since 1962. Although several coalition antiwar groups were formed in the months and years to come, none ever dominated the disparate and diffuse movement.

Capitol Hill was another place where the bombing was of concern. On February 17, Senators Frank Church and George McGovern spoke out against the continuation of the bombing. This sort of criticism from members of his own party troubled the president more than the scattered public protests. Church's speech especially irked Johnson, who was quoted as telling the Idaho senator, "Okay, Frank, next time you need a dam in Idaho, ask Walter Lippmann for one."[31] Johnson probably did not use Lippmann's name, but the story made the rounds in Washington and was widely believed.[32] Among other senators who expressed their concern about the bombing to McGeorge Bundy were Wayne Morse and Ernest Gruening, the two opponents of the Gulf of Tonkin Resolution in the Senate, and Eugene McCarthy, Gaylord Nelson, and Stephen Young.[33]

On February 24, U Thant made known his own distress over Johnson's failure to explain to the American public the possibilities for a peaceful resolution of the conflict. The secretary general of the United Nations was implicitly critical of Washington when he responded to questions concerning a story about his diplomatic activities that had appeared in the *Chicago-Sun Times* on February 19.[34]

Although the debate over the bombing heated up in the months to come, at this point, the dissenters and the administration behaved genteelly toward one another. For example, both Dr. Benjamin Spock's protesting letter to the president and the president's response were couched in polite terms.[35] The president would rarely answer such mail in the future.

Most administration officials initially greeted these flurries of dissent with equanimity. Typical was the treatment of opinion in Assistant Secretary of Defense John McNaughton's memo of March 24, "Proposed Course of Action." The opinion variable in this very long memo appears under "Important Miscellany," where McNaughton mentions the need for an "information program [to] preserve US public support."[36] The appearance of opinion and dissent in such memos almost as an afterthought will be characteristic throughout the spring. Of course, like McNaughton, many officials felt that opinion or the domestic political variable was not their primary concern.

Characteristic also of administration responses during the first five weeks after the bombing began was its almost total disinterest in the first American self-immolation. On March 16, 1965, Alice Herz, a member of Women Strike for Peace and a refugee from Nazism, set herself afire on a Detroit street. The eighty-two-year-old woman died of her burns ten days later, the first of at least eight such American suicides during the war. According to her daughter, government agents showed no interest in Alice Herz's action, even though she left a statement equating the bombing of North Vietnam with the Reichstag Fire and the White Paper on "Aggression from the North" to the Nazi coverup of that fire. The media showed relatively little interest as well in what should have been a sensational act of protest. Interestingly, Herz's daughter feels that although her mother's action little affected the government or public opinion, it did "energize other peace activists."[37] One might conclude this about most of the early antiwar protests.

Not all in the White House were indifferent to the varied activities of the domestic critics. From his position on the NSC staff, James Thomson offered "One Dove's Lament" to McGeorge

Bundy, in which he worried about the growing polarization of opinion over the bombing issue. Thomson felt that the moderately dovish *New York Times* and some senators "have been speaking truth" on the issue.[38]

Another Bundy aide, Kevin Delaney, reported even before the teach-ins appeared on major campuses that most students were opposed to the new policy in Vietnam. Delaney, who felt that "we cannot afford to have campus attitudes . . . overwhelmingly one-sided," called for the dispatch of administration supporters like Robert Kennedy, Hubert Humphrey, and George McGhee to the colleges in order to turn things around there.[39]

Then came the teach-ins. They began at the University of Michigan on March 24–25 and spread to other campuses, including Wisconsin on April 1, New York University on April 19, Rutgers and Oregon on April 23, Washington and nationwide on May 15, with Berkeley on May 21–22. More than any other event up to that point, these protests at some of America's finest universities captured public attention. The media, according to Dean Rusk, overemphasized them and thus helped to popularize this mode of dissent.[40] For the movement in general, the teach-ins linked many American students to leftist intellectuals on campuses and elsewhere.[41] Within the government, a few quiet doves saw teach-ins as an important development that might serve as a "brake" on further escalation in Vietnam.[42]

Although several hundred colleges experienced teach-ins, most campuses were untouched by the short-lived phenomenon. Further, it all but disappeared as a vehicle for protest activity when the students went home for the summer. Above all, the vast majority of Americans were unaffected by the teach-ins and did not alter their views about Johnson's Vietnam policies. Nevertheless, from all indications, the teach-ins did concern the administration and contributed to the president's decision to present a major Vietnam address at Johns Hopkins University on April 7.

To understand Johnson's response to the teach-ins and later campus protest activity, one must examine his relationship to the universities. The president was proud of being a college graduate, albeit from the rustic and obscure San Marcos (Texas) State Teachers College. Much of what he thought about college professors and the life of the mind was a product of that limited exposure to the academy.

Most likely, Johnson never quite understood what professors did for a living or why many students went to college. One enrolled in colleges like San Marcos in the depression years to get a job or learn a trade. It is not surprising that during informal interviews with Professors Walter Prescott Webb and Eric A. Goldman, two distinguished historians, Johnson tried to recruit them to write political speeches.[43]

Compounding the problem was his unpleasant experiences with eastern intellectuals and academics during the fifties and early sixties. John F. Kennedy, with his Harvard connections, was a darling of that establishment, an establishment that Johnson rightly felt disdained the Texan. In early 1966, his suspicions were reinforced when several of them, including Arthur Schlesinger, Jr., began holding regular strategy sessions with Robert Kennedy in the Beekman Tower Hotel in New York.[44] This especially galled the president, since he felt that he had done more for education, intellectuals, and the arts than any president up to his time.

He had both envy and contempt for academics. Stories abound about how Johnson introduced visitors to his advisers—a dean from Yale, a professor from Princeton, a department head from Harvard—and then pointed out that they took orders from a graduate of a prosaic Texas teachers college. He was proud of his stable of academics from the best eastern colleges and even prouder of his command over them.[45] He once bragged about Walt Rostow, "I'm getting Walt Rostow as my intellectual. He's not your intellectual. He's not Bundy's intellectual. He's not Galbraith's intellectual. He's not Schlesinger's intellectual. He's going to be my Goddam intellectual and I'm going to have him by the short hairs."[46]

Jack Valenti suggests that one of the reasons Johnson hired him was because he was a Texan with a Harvard M.B.A. Valenti felt that the president "placed almost Olympian store by what he called educated people."[47] Similarly, George Reedy sees Johnson as envying those from Harvard and Yale as a member of the "jacquerie" envied the nobility. Indeed, Reedy thinks the president would have given almost anything to have gone to an Ivy League school and to have been a member of that cool, confident, well-connected group of leaders of the eastern establishment.[48]

It was not just Johnson. Many of his aides had close connections to academia or wished they did. People like Bill Moyers, Jack Valenti, Harry McPherson, and George Christian, as well as the Bundy brothers, wanted to be respected by intellectuals and elite college students. The self-proclaimed "anti-intellectual intellectual" John Roche, who was brought into the administration in 1966 as "a bridge to the liberal establishment and the academic world," remembers how hard Christian and McPherson worked (they "drove me nuts") to bring Johnson and the intellectuals together.[49] Most of the attempts at communication failed, to the chagrin of Johnson's staff. The University of Chicago–trained George Reedy, something of an intellectual himself, feels that many of the president's aides worried too much about the universities and only exacerbated the situation by trying to get the eggheads to communicate with the obviously uncomfortable Johnson.[50]

Like them or not, Johnson did think that the people who worked and studied at the Harvards and Yales were important. Impressed with the prestige universities, he may have exaggerated the significance of the teach-ins in conversations with his staff. Reedy suggests that most everything that happened around Johnson was exaggerated. He had "a gift for exaggeration." The former press secretary outlines the following scenario. Johnson began fretting out loud about the teach-ins, his aides responded by joining in his fretting, and thus magnified one another's concern through a sort of feedback process. On this issue, and others dealing with public opinion, Reedy portrays Johnson's staff as overemphasizing criticism because of the thin-skinned president's initial exaggerated sensitivity. In addition, many staff members, according to Reedy, were so politically inexperienced that they "couldn't get elected sheriff in Wise County, Texas."[51]

It was easy to see how young National Security Council and presidential aides became upset about protests on the campuses. Many who came from that milieu overemphasized their significance in the nation at large. On the other hand, such an explanation for the possible overreaction of the White House to the teach-ins is weakened by the fact that Johnson was a brilliant politician who should have known better than to be so bothered by scattered protest meetings on a handful of elite campuses.

Harry McPherson takes a different position in explaining why the president seemed to be so interested in the teach-ins. According to his former speechwriter and intimate adviser, Johnson "wanted to satisfy every legitimate group" and became distraught when any such group expressed opposition to a policy.[52] Curiously, perhaps, for a realistic politician, Johnson "wanted to be loved by" the entire nation—thus he was bothered by the teach-ins when they appeared on campuses in response to his escalation in Vietnam.[53]

Finally, teach-ins were a new and headline-attracting development in the history of American universities and protest movements. One can sympathize with those in the White House attempting to understand the significance of the unusual campus craze that appeared from nowhere in the spring of 1965.

Troublesome by the end of March, the teach-ins did not become a media sensation until the end of April. The first ones, however, indicated a general rise in the level of dissent, a rise that led the president to deliver his address at Johns Hopkins University on April 7. He had been disappointed when a March 25 statement that he was "ready to go anywhere at any time, and meet with anyone whenever there is a promise of progress toward an honorable peace," did not immediately silence the critics.[54] Something more was needed that would demonstrate formally his commitment to a speedy end to the war.

For several weeks, McGeorge Bundy and Bill Moyers, among others, had been trying to convince the president to tell the nation and the world about his noble goals in Southeast Asia.[55] Barbara Ward Jackson, a British Third World expert with whom an admiring Johnson had recently conferred, also contributed to the idea of a Hopkins speech. During their lengthy meeting, the two talked about a massive development program for all of Vietnam.[56] Thus it was at Johns Hopkins University that Johnson presented his Mekong River Delta Plan, to be headed by Eugene Black of the World Bank, a development plan that would aid all Vietnamese, North and South, once the fighting stopped.[57] In the hours before the speech, realizing that this carrot would not satisfy Hanoi or the antiwar critics, the president also committed himself to "unconditional discussions" with the enemy to bring about a peaceful resolution of the conflict.[58]

The Johns Hopkins speech was the first major example of the impact of antiwar and other dissenting activities on the making of foreign policy during the Vietnam War. George Reedy remembers the Hopkins speech as "a response to the teach-ins," whereas George Ball has "no doubt" it was directly related to the growing antiwar activities in the country.[59] William Bundy talks about the speech being given "to stabilize public opinion." It was not just the campuses that were bothering the president. On April 2, Canadian Prime Minister Lester Pearson had made critical remarks about American policy at Temple University. In addition, U Thant and some European leaders had been less than supportive of the United States during the previous week.[60]

Liberals in the Democratic party were becoming restive as well. McGeorge Bundy had suggested that one way of keeping them in line was to include material in the speech on John F. Kennedy's commitment to help our allies in South Vietnam. Such a statement would be "designed to give us protection and encouragement with some of the 'liberals' who are falsely telling each other that your policy is different from his."[61]

Among the most restive liberals were the Americans for Democratic Action (ADA), always suspicious of Johnson's progressive credentials. Some of their leaders met with him on April 2 and were even shown parts of the emerging Hopkins speech. The ADA briefing, at which Johnson was urged to rely more on the United Nations, led to a significant backlash. Although Johnson was polite to the liberals, he privately scoffed at their unrealistic suggestions and told a National Security Council group that met in the same room during the next hour about the foolish ADA recommendations. When word leaked out to ADA leaders about the derision to which they had been subjected, many became even angrier about the president's conduct of the war and his untrustworthiness.[62]

The ADA leaders were not the only ones to be treated to a preview of the Hopkins speech. Walter Lippmann was also accorded that honor.[63] Lippmann was more important to Johnson than the ADA. His widely syndicated columns meant a great deal to the president, who felt that they had tremendous influence throughout the nation. Although some thought that Lippmann, "more than any other man, determined Washington's critical taste buds," it is likely that his influence had peaked and that Johnson was incorrect if he thought that through Lippmann he reached the nation's intellectual and political elites.[64] People in Washington still read him, especially in Congress, and respected his opinions; intellectuals in other areas of the country may have begun to tire of his pontifications.[65]

To Johnson, Lippmann was an ambassador without portfolio. When Lippmann went abroad, he received entré to the chambers of world leaders. Thus, following his European trip in the fall of 1964, Lippmann was invited to the White House to brief the president on what Europe was saying about him and his policies.[66] Not all were happy with the state of affairs. Dean Rusk describes how, after taking office as secretary of state in 1961, Lippmann, as well as Arthur Krock of the *Times*, told him to feel free to drop by *their* offices any time.[67] Such was the price of trying to appear in a favorable light in Lippmann's column.

Lippmann was unhappy with the bombing policy. In March, Johnson tried to keep the columnist in line by having McGeorge Bundy meet frequently with him or talk to him over the phone and listen to his long-winded advice. The idea was to keep Lippmann on board by letting him think that his policy preferences were receiving serious consideration at the highest levels of the government. On the eve of a meeting between Johnson and the columnist, Bundy wrote to Johnson, "Like the rest of us, Walter is always flattered when he is asked for his own opinion." As the national security adviser commented, "A part of our purpose, after all, is to plug his guns."[68] Thus it was on April 6, with Lippmann beginning to fall off the wagon, Johnson revealed to him selected sections of the Hopkins speech.

This gesture turned out to be only a holding action. By the end of April, the columnist finally realized that the bombing was not a limited policy, and more important, that he had been had. He never returned to the White House.[69] McGeorge Bundy acknowledges that his period of trying to flatter the journalist and, to some degree, to obscure the drift of American policy cost him Lippmann's friendship.[70]

The Hopkins speech did the trick for a few weeks, in any event. The day before the speech, Chester Cooper worried about the White House weekend mail that ran 580 to 96 against the Vietnam policy. After the speech, the mail flowed in at a four-to-one ratio in favor of the administration.[71] Moreover, SANE approved of the president's apparent willingness to negotiate, as did the Fellowship of Reconciliation.[72]

Not everyone was satisfied with the speech, especially when it did not produce immediate results and the bombing continued. The protests continued, including teach-ins, picketing, even at the Johnson Ranch in Texas, open letters, and paid newspaper advertisements. More important, the Hopkins speech did not dampen enthusiasm for the long-planned April 17 Washington demonstration organized by SDS. Three days before the protest, the largest antiwar demonstration up to that point, McGeorge Bundy alerted the president to the left-wing student protest coming up that weekend. He advised that "a strong peaceloving statement tomorrow or Friday might help cool them off ahead of time."[73] Such a statement was never made, and would not have "cooled them off" in any event.

Between fifteen and thirty thousand demonstrators turned up in Washington for the demonstration, picketed the White House, and heard I. F. Stone and Senator Gruening, among others, assail American policy in Vietnam. Writing in 1966, Jack Newfield felt that the April 17 protest was a milestone in American politics, the day that the Silent Generation found its voice.[74] Activist Abbie Hoffman similarly remembers it as the beginning of the antiwar movement.[75]

Although the demonstration received wide media coverage, in part because it was the first of its genre, critics contend that, as in future protests, the radical element, especially the SDS, was given the widest play. According to sociologist and former SDS leader Todd Gitlin, the influential *New York Times'* coverage "depreciated, marginalized, trivialized, and polarized" the movement.[76] On the other hand, comrade-in-arms Tom Hayden doubted that the movement would have developed without media coverage, irrespective of their biases. Of course, by concentrating on the most sensational activities, the media tended to promote nationally the most radical leaders.[77]

One of the more curious aspects of the period involved the way the media tended to underplay the numbers involved, stress the violence and radical aspects, and thus convey a negative image of the protesters. The administration, however, generally tended to ignore or underestimate the significance of this skewed media coverage.

Complicating matters for Johnson was the invasion of the Dominican Republic that took place at the end of April. Although most Americans accepted Johnson's contention that he had to send in the marines to stop communists from taking over the country, the antiwar protesters found another reason to oppose their nation's foreign policies. It is interesting to note that Senator Fulbright's break with Johnson began over the Dominican Republic incident and not the Vietnam War.[78]

The month of April, with the Hopkins speech, the Washington demonstration, and the Dominican Republic invasion, marked a turning point in administration attitudes toward opinion and dissent. Although not worried about public support in general, Johnson and his advisers did begin to pay attention to the strong public dissent on Southeast Asian policy among a sizable minority of critics from the Left, the campuses, the media, and the Democratic party.

Within the administration, the most prominent dove, George Ball, told the president on April 21, "Distasteful as it is, elements in the intellectual community and other segments of the United States opinion do not believe in our South Vietnam policy. In fact, to many Americans, our position appears far more ambiguous —and hence far more dubious—than in the Korean War."[79]

Nevertheless, dissent over Vietnam was still only a minor if growing problem for the president. Early in May, Johnson was able to obtain an additional $700 million from Congress for the military in Vietnam without a fight. The votes in the House and Senate were 408 to 7 and 88 to 3, respectively. Congress was easier to handle at this stage than critics on campus and in the media, and, indeed, never during the Johnson administration did it fail to approve such legislation.

Congressional support notwithstanding, the administration found it necessary to mount an offensive against the foreign policy critics that went beyond the presentation of a peace program in the Hopkins speech. Dean Rusk, in particular, was the point man in the counterrattack. The discreet and loyal secretary, who commanded the president's respect, shared Johnson's views about the relationship between Vietnam and World War II. To the present, Rusk compares the antiwar movement of the sixties to European pacifism of the thirties. He had been at Oxford and on the continent in 1933 and continually harkened back to that experience when he and the unpopular interventionists had been correct and the isolationists had been dead wrong.[80] Rusk was personally angry at the new pacifists who had failed to learn the lessons of World War II.[81] In a speech to the American Society of International Law on April 23, 1965, he lashed out: "Once again we hear expressed the views which cost men of my generation a terrible price in World War Two. We are told that Southeast Asia is far away. . . . I sometimes wonder at the gullibility of educated men and their stubborn disregard of plain facts by men who are supposed to be helping our young to learn—especially to learn how to think."[82]

Rusk's periodic attacks on the demonstrators and critics in the media, many of whom came from the so-called eastern establishment, may also have reflected his animosity toward those insiders. When asked about the fabled Georgetown set and its parties, he responded that he was not invited to many of them. Johnson was not a favorite on that circuit either. Told that black militants were setting fires near the fashionable enclave, Johnson chortled, "Georgetown, I've waited thirty-five years for this day."[83] Rusk from Georgia, McNamara from California and Michigan, and Johnson from Texas were all outsiders in Washington and on the East Coast.

Other responses were more oblique than Rusk's slashing frontal attack. During this period, Jack Valenti received Johnson's approval for a "counter-offensive on campuses," in part because every antiwar demonstration "is priceless gold for the Viet Cong."[84] The first such counteroffensive was launched in May when a four-person Interdepartmental Speaking Team was dispatched to Drake University and the Universities of Iowa, Indiana, Illinois, and Wisconsin (Madison and Milwaukee) to respond to antiwar critics. Composed of Thomas F. Conlon from State, Earle Young from

AID, and Lt. Col. Rolfe Hilman and Lt. Col. Thomas Waitt from the Army, the committee expressed shock at the lack of knowledge among students about Vietnam. Further, Conlon reported that many of the faculty opponents of administration policy were from disciplines that had little to do with international relations.[85]

The truth squad encountered raucous heckling that earned it sympathetic headlines. In fact, the encounter in Madison probably turned out more hecklers than listeners. Following the squad's appearance on that politically active campus, six thousand students signed a progovernment petition.[86] In general, however, the truth squad approach was too adversarial in nature and, to some degree, counterproductive if free discussion was the goal. In addition, the speakers sent out were too junior to attract the attention of many students. After this initial foray into the Midwest, the program was dropped and replaced by more informal and ad hoc visits to campuses by higher-level government speakers.

Another offensive taken in the spring of 1965, proposed by Valenti, involved the sending of male college students to Vietnam that summer to work as civilian aides. A carefully selected group was exposed to the American aid program in the countryside and returned to present firsthand accounts of the peaceful intentions of their government to students on their campuses and elsewhere.[87]

Still another approach that continued through the war was to assist "friends" with speechwriting. The national commander of the American Legion, for example, through the good offices of FBI Assistant Director Cartha DeLoach, saw Johnson in June and received "specific suggestions" for his upcoming patriotic addresses.[88]

A more structured, nationwide counteroffensive was recommended by Chester Cooper, the NSC aide most responsible for opinion and dissent. Cooper called for the establishment of a project involving proadministration experts not officially tied to the White House, who would be available for speeches, seminars, and meetings. Cooper thought of such figures as Henry Cabot Lodge and Professor Wesley Fishel of Michigan State. The problem was money. Without directly helping out, the administration had to find a way to raise funds to support the propaganda effort. The major existing organization that could spearhead the effort was the

American Friends of Vietnam, but the AFV needed at least $25,000 to launch the operation.[89]

Although concerned about antiwar activity on the campuses and in intellectual circles in the spring of 1965, administration political strategists were confident that if properly directed, the vast majority of campuses would rally around the flag. Johnson's advisers saw nothing wrong in directing the directors under the table. After all, noted John Roche about a later public relations effort, the president is entitled to freedom of speech.[90]

It was easy to justify the back-stairs mobilization of support. Most in the White House thought their noisy critics came from small, well-organized left-wing groups that opposed any type of anticommunist program. They were not representative of the vast, but unfortunately unorganized, majority. As McGeorge Bundy reported, the real opinion on campuses was "not reflected in the efforts of a few pressure groups."[91] Beliefs such as these were reinforced by allegations from FBI director J. Edgar Hoover about the many communists involved in organizing positions during the April Washington demonstration.[92] Johnson himself told his cabinet on June 18, "I will see a line from Peking, Hanoi, and Moscow or [sic] about a month ahead of the time I see it here."[93] Thus it was that the administration turned to the American Friends of Vietnam for its primary "unofficial" cheerleading activities without qualms of conscience about the propriety of such a relationship.

Founded in 1955, the AFV had languished in the early sixties. It became energized when the war expanded in 1964. Led by Wesley Fishel, a Michigan State professor, and his executive director, Gilbert Jonas, the group's national committee included such luminaries as Emanuel Celler, Max Lerner, Roger Hilsman, Gale McGee, Claiborne Pell, Robert Shaplen, Angier Biddle Duke, and Leo Cherne. With a nudge from the White House, New York financier Sidney Weinberg began raising the $25,000 that Fishel said he needed to launch a speaker's bureau and a newsletter.[94] An initial AFV success was a June 1 Michigan State rally, which was, as Jack Valenti put it, "our counterforce to the anti–United States groups on American campuses."[95] Chester Cooper also expressed pleasure at the response to the rally at which Hubert Humphrey and Carl Rowan presented major addresses. But this would be only the start. He felt that proadministration forces must be rallied to raise money so that the AFV could publish a newsletter to rival *Viet Report,* which "the more rabid of the Teach-in set are launching." Although the students were going home for vacation that month, "the problem will still be with us in the fall."[96]

The AFV enjoyed its greatest successes during the year following the East Lansing rally. It did finally produce the supportive newsletter *Vietnam Perspective* in the fall. Further, during 1965, it sent out over a hundred speakers to many venues, especially college campuses. The AFV archives are crammed with copies of letters to the editor and columns that were printed and reprinted in scores of prominent newspapers and magazines. In addition, in the fall of 1965, the AFV arranged for a well-publicized American speaking tour for five South Vietnamese college students loyal to the Saigon regime. And when, in August 1965, Representative William Fitts Ryan held two days of hearings in New York City on the war, the AFV helped to arrange for progovernment speakers and even paid some of their travel costs.[97]

Although the White House cooperated with the AFV, it did try to keep the organization at arm's length for appearances' sake. The organization, for its part, kept Don Ropa of the White House and William Jorden of the State Department informed of its activities.[98] Occasionally, as was seen in the spring of 1965, and through that year, the White House helped raise money by inducing officials to lend their names to the cause. Thus, in an attempt to line up Ambassador Kenneth Young to serve on his board, Gilbert Jonas wrote that Henry Cabot Lodge was the honorary chair and that Lodge was "working directly from the White House."[99]

On the other hand, the White House apparently did not pull out all of the stops for the AFV. The organization was in constant difficulty trying to make ends meet and almost was unable to raise the rather modest $58,000 it needed to operate in 1965.[100] Surprisingly, this very active and visible organization spent only $71,000 in the 1965–66 fiscal year.[101]

The exposé of Fishel and Michigan State's undercover involvement with the Saigon regime that broke in *Ramparts* magazine on April 14, 1966, was a crushing blow for the AFV. By the end of

1966, it received refusals to serve on its honorary national committee from such stalwart anticommunists as George Meany, Douglas Dillon, Dean Acheson, and James B. Conant.[102]

The administration's support for the AFV undoubtedly helped Fishel sponsor programs and, especially, develop documentary materials that countered arguments of antiwar organizations. Pleased with progress in this area, Chester Cooper noted, "While we have been careful to keep our hand fairly hidden, we have in part, spent a lot of time on it and have been able to find them some money."[103] Yet the president could have done more in terms of financial assistance. The arm's length, short though it may have been, at which the AFV was kept from the White House reflected a degree of sensitivity to such operations, sensitivity not felt as strongly by the Nixon administration.

The activities of the AFV and other progovernment organizations and speakers, taken with the continued strong defense of American policies from administration spokespersons, helped to contain erosion in public support. Obviously, such activities were more important in keeping the troops in line than in converting those who had already turned against the policies. As the protests mounted in May and June 1965, the White House needed all the help it could get.

The antiwar movement, and domestic critics in general, played a role in the decision to announce a bombing pause from May 12 to 17.[104] Most likely, the administration did not expect diplomatic results from this first pause. Preparations were made hurriedly and, more important, indications suggested that Hanoi was not interested in talking to Johnson on his terms at that juncture.[105] James Thomson evaluates the pause as 50 percent directed to the domestic audience and 50 percent to the diplomatic arena. For his part, Chester Cooper thought that it was directed also to dovish officials inside the government.[106] Complicating matters was the continuing Dominican crisis. As is often the case, it is difficult for any government to handle two crises at once.[107] The pause had to take a back seat to the Caribbean in terms of the time allocated to it by the key players in the Oval Office. Given the long odds against any movement from Hanoi, the Dominican crisis, and the overall lack of preparation, it is clear that the pause was primarily a theatrical response to domestic and international opposition to U.S. bombing policy.

The decision to halt the bombing for five days was not taken easily. Maxwell Taylor, for one, feared that the likely failure of negotiations could lead to disappointment and a call for withdrawal. Taking a dim view of the pause because he did not think Washington had anything to offer Hanoi, George Ball reports that Johnson was worried that a failure could lead to hawkish demands from the Right for more bombing, demands that could spell trouble with China and the USSR. Finally, many in the administration believed that communists only understood strength. Consequently, premature pleas for negotiations might be taken as a sign of weakness.[108]

The debate within the Oval Office over the length of the pause reveals again the impact of domestic critics on high-level decision making. McNamara thought that the pause should be maintained for a few days longer than originally planned in order to respond to the *New York Times'* announced length preference. Johnson retorted, "We will never satisfy the *Times*"; moreover, he said that "the public wanted to continue the bombing," and he had decided to pause "because of the Fulbrights and the Mansfields."[109]

Jack Valenti plays down the role of the *Times* in such decision making. For him, the length of the pause was "a subjective call," and since it would make little difference whether the bombing stopped for five or seven days, why not consider throwing "a bone to the Doberman pinscher snarling at you" and "keep him quiet for a while"?[110]

As expected, the pause was too brief and hastily thrown together to elicit a response from Hanoi. It did not satisfy the *Times*, the Fulbrights, and the antiwar movement. However, its primary targets, uncommitted elites susceptible to the dovish line and restive European allies, were most likely placated for a while by this example of the peaceful intentions of the Johnson administration.

Antiwar activists carried on through the pause with their own programs. The scattered teach-ins had become more of a problem for Johnson when their organizers joined in a loose coalition, the Inter-University Committee for a Public Hearing on Vietnam. The committee began planning a nationwide teach-in to be conducted on television and radio, the centerpiece of which would be a debate between a prominent member of the administration and a dovish academic. After prolonged negotiations and several false starts, the committee obtained McGeorge Bundy's agreement to debate Professor George McT. Kahin of Cornell University in Washington, D.C., on May 15.

Bundy apparently accepted the invitation without checking with the president. Johnson was not at all pleased with his national security adviser's television date because he believed, as do most politicians, that one should not give one's opponents free publicity.[111] Johnson was correct, at least insofar as the networks only became interested in covering the event when Bundy agreed to appear.[112]

Bundy thought he should participate in the teach-in, in part, because he wanted to present the administration's position, in which he believed, in a free and open forum. Similarly, his brother, who went to Berkeley for a teach-in that same month, believed that college students and faculty were important because of their roles as ultimate opinion shapers in the nation as a whole. The assistant secretary continued to visit colleges until the fall of 1967, when at Stanford he realized that civilized dialogue was no longer possible.[113]

The Dominican Republic crisis presented Johnson with the excuse he needed to relieve Bundy of his May 15 commitment. On the eve of the debate, the president dispatched his adviser to the Caribbean to deal with a so-called diplomatic problem. Bundy now thinks his presence in Ciudad Trujillo was not needed and that Johnson sent him away to demonstrate displeasure with his television appearance.[114] The fifteen-and-a-half-hour teach-in was held despite Bundy's absence, with Berkeley political scientist Robert Scalapino, among others, standing in for the national security adviser. Connected through phone lines, perhaps as many as a hundred thousand people at over a hundred colleges listened to all or part of the day-long activities.[115]

Not entirely satisfied with their event, teach-in organizers still wanted to confront the administration head-on. For his part, McGeorge Bundy felt bound to honor his initial commitment, even though he knew that to do so would incur the president's displeasure. Bundy was pleased, however, with the new format for the debate that was painstakingly negotiated.[116] Trusted television journalist Eric Sevareid agreed to serve as moderator and Hans Morgenthau to be Bundy's major debating opponent on June 21.

Although antiwar partisans claimed that Bundy did not do well in the debate, he more than held his own.[117] Moreover, in a devastating ad hominem attack, he concluded his presentation with selections from Morgenthau's writings, writings that demonstrated how wrong the political scientist had been in the past. Some of the behind-the-scenes fireworks in the debate may have related to the role Bundy allegedly played in opposing Morgenthau's appointment to the Harvard faculty some years earlier.[118]

Looking back, nineteen years later, Bundy does not remember "winning" the debate. Moreover, the president never talked to him about it, something he would have done had he been pleased with his performance. More important, Bundy thinks that the teach-in was a "contributing factor" to the decline in his influence with the president and his ultimate departure from the White House in 1966. Johnson resented the independent streak he displayed in accepting the second teach-in offer, especially after he sent him to the Dominican Republic to avoid the first one.[119] It is also true that by becoming more of an advocate in public, Bundy might have hurt his image as an open-minded presidential adviser.[120]

Thus, the antiwar movement, through the national teach-in, contributed to the resignation of McGeorge Bundy in early 1966 and his replacement by the hawkish Walt Rostow. Of course, this would have occurred in any event as Bundy's support for the war began to waver in the months after the teach-in. Whatever the outcome, the well-publicized debate between Morgenthau and Bundy, a debate that afforded equal time for the antiwar position, made dissent more respectable.[121] Johnson's original knee-jerk opposition to sharing a platform with the doves was clearly justified.

During the same period, another major antiwar outburst was ignited by the seemingly innocuous White House Festival of the Arts. This day-long salute to the arts, planned primarily by Eric Goldman, the Princeton historian who was a part-time intellectual-in-residence at the White House, would demonstrate Johnson's commitment to the fine arts and would "particularly please the ladies."[122] Goldman worked with Jack Valenti and Bess Abell, Lady Bird Johnson's secretary, to pull together the apolitical event. The president was not involved in the planning, although Mrs. Johnson did take an interest in it.[123]

The failure of the May 12–17 pause and the consequent renewal of the bombing helped to turn an intellectual's lawn party into an embarrassing confrontation between major American artists and Johnson. The flap began on June 2 when poet Robert Lowell publicly refused to come to the festival because of the president's Vietnam policy.[124] His announcement, which was carried on the front page of the *New York Times*, was followed by a telegram of support from other dissident artists and writers, including Robert Silvers and Stanley Kunitz.

Johnson was furious as he railed about the "fools" who had transformed his cultural event into a conflict over foreign policy. According to Jack Valenti, who was taken by surprise by the contretemps, "None of us realized the depth of feeling about Vietnam and also the tawdry lengths that some people would go in impoliteness and incivility. It just never occurred to us that that would be the case." "Uneasy and anxious" about what was going to transpire on June 14, the president even contemplated canceling the entire affair.[125] He decided finally to limit his own attendance to a few moments and, more important, to orchestrate a media blackout of the festival.[126] Although he was able to keep the television networks from devoting much time to it, he failed with the print media. *New York Times* coverage of the June 14 event, again front-page news, concentrated on the antiwar issue, even though it turned out to be a minor part of the actual affair.[127]

The chief dissenting activity revolved around John Hersey's reading of an excerpt from *Hiroshima*. Mrs. Johnson, who tried unsuccessfully to get him to read from some other work, sat grimly through his performance and did not join in the applause for the author.[128] Critic Dwight Macdonald circulated an anti-Johnson petition to fellow participants. He did not reach many sympathetic ears, however, and according to Valenti "made an unmitigated ass of himself." The presidential adviser took pleasure when actor Charlton Heston "ate his ass out" as he told him what he could do with his petition.[129]

The entire affair reinforced Johnson's feelings about intellectuals and the Kennedy connection. He told Goldman, "I don't think I will ever get credit for anything I do in foreign policy because I didn't go to Harvard." He also decided to request that the FBI do a full security and political background check on all White House guests in the future.[130]

Although not a strong supporter of the president's Vietnam policy, Goldman was "appalled" by the tone of some of the letters and phone calls he received from colleagues in the academic and intellectual world. He thought the antiwar activities of many of them were affected by an "arrogance and smugness" that led them to see Johnson as a "baboon."[131]

The Festival of the Arts highlighted the breech between the president and segments of the intellectual community, especially in the New York area. As with the meeting with the ADA on the eve of the Hopkins speech, this event made communication between the two groups even more difficult. It might also have led Johnson to deemphasize their subsequent antiwar activities, since he realized there was little he could do to turn them around.

As the president scanned newspaper coverage of his Festival of the Arts on June 15, another prominent intellectual leader began to desert the ship. Senator J. William Fulbright, the head of the Senate Foreign Relations Committee and long-time Johnson supporter and friend, delivered a speech critical of administration foreign policy on that same day. At this point, Fulbright was most distressed about the Dominican Republic invasion and occupation. He completed his break with Johnson over this issue with an even harsher critique on September 15.[132]

Johnson was particularly angry with Fulbright over the speech and, in effect, removed him from the White House's intimate guest list after this point.[133] The Arkansas senator had moved full circle in less than a year from the loyal steward of the Gulf of Tonkin Resolution to the turncoat inspiring others to speak out against the president. To be sure, the hawkish Senate and House Armed Services committees were more powerful than the Senate Foreign Relations Committee, which Johnson could personally ignore in most instances. Yet with Fulbright's slide toward the doves, along with Wayne Morse, Joseph Clark, Albert Gore, Frank Church, and even George Aiken, John Sherman Cooper, and Johnson's trusted Senate friend Mike Mansfield, the Senate Foreign Relations Committee was becoming an irritating center of opposition.[134] Through 1967, however, the committee had far more influence on the national debate than it did on Johnson's policies directly.[135]

These embarrassing events held one compensation for the president. They took place, after all, in the middle of June and that meant that most of the campuses were emptying and that other potential activists were beginning to scatter to vacation spots around the nation. The last gasp of the mass spring activities was probably a Madison Square Garden rally on June 8 sponsored by SANE. Although seventeen thousand people turned out to hear Wayne Morse, Norman Thomas, and Hans Morgenthau, among others, administration observers could theorize that it was not difficult to fill the Garden in New York City.

Newspaper advertising and picketing continued through June, but by then they may have become so routine that they could be discounted.[136] Civility still marked the encounters with, for example, on June 16, Robert McNamara listening politely in his Pentagon to a group of antiwar protesters led by labor leader Sidney Lens.[137] The polls were overwhelmingly supportive of the president, the peace forces "thin and scattered."[138] More important, when Johnson met with his informal advisory group of "Wise Men" (Robert Lovett, John McCloy, Arthur Dean, Dean Acheson, and Omar Bradley, among others) on July 8, he was assured that the eastern establishment was solidly behind the administration.[139] No defection had appeared in those ranks yet. This was good news to an administration planning the second major escalation of 1965 —the decision to assume the dominant ground combat role in Vietnam. The announcement of the adoption of "combat support" activities by American soldiers on June 9 and the first "search-and-destroy mission" on June 28, both of which produced little public reaction, were only the tip of the iceberg in terms of the new American commitment.

As in the late fall of 1964, it was clear that things were still not going well in the war. Bombing alone apparently was not enough. The North had not been cowed by that policy. Infiltration of supplies and men had increased, not decreased, since February.

Further, South Vietnam had not proven able to combat the growing communist forces any more successfully than it had since the insurrection began. Thus it was in late June and through the first three weeks of July that the administration began considering new military initiatives. This time, although it did not figure prominently, public opinion was considered more seriously by the decision makers, a tribute, perhaps, to the activities of dissenters and journalistic critics.

At the least, Johnson and his key advisers recognized that the growing antiwar movement had some impact abroad. Vice President Humphrey, commenting on heckling he had been subjected to in San Diego, noted, "This is one of the reasons we are having trouble overseas." At a cabinet meeting on June 18, Dean Rusk reported that Hanoi's analysis of American problems involved three variables—military progress, domestic opinion, and international opinion. At that same meeting, the president commented on another, and one of his favorite, aspects of that issue. Discussing Vietnam, his "principal problem," he asserted that domestic critics were following the lead of North Vietnam and other communist states "then there will come out of the capitals—and some other places—a new line."[140]

Johnson saw well-organized communist dissenters, taking their lead from Hanoi, stirring up the home front, as part of the North Vietnamese battle against the United States. He was a good friend of J. Edgar Hoover, who also believed such an interpretation, and the president and his FBI director continued to feed each other's prejudices.[141] Whether dissenting activities were spontaneous or not, they did complicate decision making in the summer of 1965.

As June came to an end, McGeorge Bundy offered his views to the president on how United States involvement in Vietnam compared to the situation confronting the French government in 1954. Unlike the situation eleven years earlier, the American public had *"considerable concern"* but *"general support."* Articulate critics of the policy, found in academic and church groups, were "usually a minority within their own groups," but "have stimulated extensive worry and inquiry in the nation as a whole. With the end of the academic year, this protest movement has temporarily subsided." On the other hand, Bundy was confident that most of the public and most of the media were behind the president. All it would take to keep them in line would be assertive presidential leadership during the coming months.[142]

If anything, fear of the Right or "bombniks" was probably more in the minds of the decision makers that June than fear of peaceniks.[143] In arguing against the proposed escalation, George Ball pointed out that it could lead to public pressures for even tougher measures, pressures that could result in problems with the Chinese and the Russians.[144] Richard Russell, the senator Johnson most admired and the head of the Armed Services Committee, was never pleased about being in Vietnam but continually counseled: if we are there, let's get on with the job with massive force, and then get out.[145] McNamara also worried about pressure from the Right for an unrestrained bombing policy.[146]

William Bundy now admits that he and his colleagues probably overestimated the power and impatience of the Right.[147] The Right never became as much of a problem as predicted. The fear nevertheless, was a real one at the time.

As it contemplated escalation, the administration made an unusual attempt to improve its image when it invited Columbia University professor Henry Graff to the White House for the first of a series of interviews with the main foreign-policy decision makers. A diplomatic historian, Graff was a friend of Hayes Redmon of the White House staff. Graff now feels that Johnson approved the June interviews to demonstrate how "skillful" his team was in foreign affairs and not as a direct response to antiwar criticism.[148]

Well aware that he "could be used" for public relations purposes, Graff felt that he had an "amazing opportunity." He would have the rare chance as a scholar to interview contemporary decision makers as they constructed American foreign policy. Moreover, since the series would be published in the influential *New York Times* Sunday magazine section, Graff knew he would be making an important contribution to America's knowledge of the way the Johnson administration operated.[149]

His first article, generally favorable to the administration, did produce a minor controversy. Graff quoted McGeorge Bundy as referring to the United States as the "engine" of the world and the rest of the nations the "caboose." The *Times* ran an editorial on that phrase, chiding Bundy for his seeming arrogance. Given advance warning of the editorial, Bundy frantically tried to persuade Graff to retract the quote and the *Times* to drop the editorial.[150] Bundy claims that his concern was caused not by what the statement might mean in the Vietnam debate, but because he was the president's chief adviser and the *New York Times* was considered an official newspaper of record by many around the world.[151]

Graff had been in the White House at a critical juncture. During the first weeks in June, major position papers were drawn up in State, Defense, and the National Security Council, and numerous departmental and interdepartmental meetings were held on the proposed escalation, preparatory to the final high-level meetings of July 21 and 22. Throughout, opinion was still a secondary variable in the printed materials. Most of the dialogue involved military tactics and strategy, hardware and software, and the usual contingency plans. The best books on the subject of the July escalation rarely allude to public opinion.[152] As one examines how dissent and opinion may have affected the decision to increase dramatically U.S. troop levels, the analytical focus centers on only one part of the problem, and a relatively small one at that.

Undoubtedly, the Johnson administration was leaning toward ordering an increase in both troop levels and combat activities as it moved closer to the July 21–22 decision point. Whether or not Johnson had made up his mind irrevocably ahead of time is another matter. George Ball, Bill Moyers, Harry McPherson, and Jack Valenti, for example, are among those who feel that Johnson's mind was still somewhat open until July 22. According to McPherson, he was searching for conclusive arguments against escalation, but did not find them, even from Ball, whom Johnson felt was arguing primarily from a narrow, Eurocentric point of view.[153]

On the other hand, in a July 1 memo concerning four proposals from presidential advisers, McGeorge Bundy advised the president to listen "hard to George Ball and then reject his proposal." Bundy's brother is not certain when the decision was made, but he feels it probably occurred before the July 21–22 meetings.[154] By that time no longer a Johnson insider, George Reedy nevertheless considers those allegedly epochal meetings a charade. According to the press secretary, Johnson "could script a meeting like nobody else I ever heard of," and people like George Ball never understood that. It was typical of the president to exaggerate the significance of the meeting, then have Ball's dissent leaked to the press so that people on the outside would think he had listened to all sides before making his important decision.[155] The complex Johnson, however, was not entirely happy with the leak that depicted Ball as the administration dove; he preferred to have him considered a "devil's advocate" for the dissenting position.[156]

Was the July 21–22 meeting a charade? The decision was certainly in the cards before Johnson gathered his key people around him at the end of July. Yet Jack Valenti paints a picture of a man "troubled by this war," hoping against hope that he could find some *practical* dovish advice; or at least, hoping to find more widespread disenchantment with the escalatory policy. If, for example, Rusk, Cyrus Vance, Mike Mansfield, or Treasury Secretary Henry Fowler had added some or all of their voices to Ball's, the president might have reconsidered. Even though Johnson, according to Valenti, was impressed with Ball's arguments and carefully read his memos, Ball "had no allies in the White House." Ball himself agrees with Valenti—the outcome might have been different had a few others joined him in July.[157]

It was difficult, if not impossible, to be a dissenter in the Johnson White House.[158] George Ball got away with it because he was recognized as house dove at worst, devil's advocate at best. Jack Valenti does not remember anyone, including Reedy, raising their voices in dissent inside the White House that summer, except for Ball. Similarly, Dean Rusk recalls somewhat bitterly that some of those in the cabinet who later became outspoken critics never complained while in government. He remembers sitting next to some of those turncoats who never gave an inkling of their hostility to the Vietnam policy while they were in government, even though they later claimed they had always been internal doves.[159]

The decision to escalate was made irrespective of the fact that it could lead to some erosion in popular support for the president. As with the earlier bombing decision, the potential erosion was thought to be not serious enough to jeopardize the overall policy in Vietnam.

Since late 1964, George Ball had been telling Johnson, and anyone who would listen to him, that the American public would not stand for a long, inconclusive war. At the July 21–22 meetings he emphasized that point, employing charts that reflected the decline in popular support for the Korean War effort over time.[160] Not a dove, ad hoc adviser Clark Clifford, who attended the July 22 meeting, also predicted difficult domestic problems should the war drag on.[161] The military was more confident about opinion. Marine Corps Commandant General Wallace Greene, Jr., reported that the public would accept as many as five hundred thousand American soldiers committed for as many as five years.[162]

As with Nixon some years later, Johnson's options were limited in terms of domestic politics. He could only withdraw or refuse to escalate if he obtained an honorable peace—a peace with some sort of victory. And that was not possible in July 1965. He felt that he could not afford to be the president who lost Vietnam.[163] The absence of widespread opposition to his Dominican invasion also may have encouraged him.[164]

Adopting what could be called a "dawk policy," Johnson thought that with pressures from the Right and the Left, he might find himself in good shape in the center with the extremists canceling one another out.[165] More specifically, he told William Bundy that he had the support of the public for an escalation on the ground at that point at around a 65-to-35 ratio.[166] As a good politician, he knew that things would not get any better as the war dragged on. At this point, however, he worried less about the antiwar movement's opposition than general public irritability about the potential costs of an interminable and inconclusive military commitment.

One desirable option, rejected because of public opinion and domestic politics, was the calling up of the reserves.[167] This would be an issue that haunted Johnson throughout the war, for it made good strategic sense to call up the reserves to contribute to American forces in Vietnam and elsewhere that were being stretched thin by the new combat commitment. In addition, a reserve call-up would serve as a psychological ploy to awaken the United States to the seriousness of the Vietnam War.[168]

The reserves were, in part, a refuge for middle-class young people or, at least, a relatively pleasant way for such people to fulfill their military obligations. From a political perspective, Johnson could have safely called up reserves had that call-up been combined with a strong resolution of support from Congress. However, William Bundy felt that although the Senate harbored only a dozen doves, they would force a noisy debate that would be harmful. It was clear also to Bundy that Congress would not welcome such a demarche.[169]

The public had not been formally told about the February bombing decision. This time Johnson announced, in a July 28 television address, the outlines of the July 21–22 decision, but refrained from making too much of it.[170] This low-key approach had its opponents. As usual, McGeorge Bundy worried about the public response to the escalation and wondered about how to sell the policy over the long haul. He thought, "The country is in the mood to accept grim news," although "no single speech will be sufficient to reassure the American people."[171]

There was always the problem of creating too much public attention on the issue, by, for example, publishing supportive advertisements. John McCloy advised Bundy that such an approach could lead to a self-defeating battle of the advertisements.[172] On the other hand, political consultant Horace Busby advised Johnson that he should organize a speaking campaign featuring popular cabinet secretaries to sell the new policy to the nation. Similarly, meeting Mike Mansfield's concern about public support, McNamara called for the formation of a task force to explain the war to the American people to "try to keep up the momentum built up during the public discussions last spring and early this summer."[173] This was not done in any formal sense, although the administration did offer behind-the-scenes assistance to a nationwide support group headed by diplomat Arthur Dean that would emerge in the fall.[174]

As with the decision not to go very public in February, domestic political considerations may again have been preeminent.[175] How could one produce the Great Society while fighting a larger war in Vietnam? Even Franklin Roosevelt called off the New Deal when war was on the horizon. This low-key approach to publicizing the increasing American involvement in full-scale war would cost Johnson dearly in the months to come. It would only work if the war ended quickly. And that was not to be.

Chapter Three

The Opposition Gathers: July 1965–November 1966

"This thing is assuming dangerous proportions . . . and giving our enemies the wrong idea of the will of this country to fight."
—LYNDON B. JOHNSON*

Between the late summer of 1965 and the fall of 1966, the American military effort in Vietnam accelerated in conformity with the twin decisions to escalate taken during the first half of 1965. The number of air sorties over the North increased from 25,000 in 1965 to 79,000 in 1966; the bomb-tonnage figures from 63,000 to 136,000. More important, the list of permissible targets expanded incrementally, with, for example, in the summer of 1966, the petroleum storage facilities in and around Hanoi and Haiphong approved as fair game for American airmen.

The raids inflicted very heavy damage on North Vietnam's military and civilian infrastructures. Yet despite an occasional peace rumor amid the scores of failed diplomatic initiatives from the Johnson administration, the communists were unwilling to talk on the terms laid out by Washington. Moreover, irrespective of the bombing, the infiltration of materiel and men through the Ho Chi Minh trail network increased during 1966. Finally, the bombing was becoming costly in terms of American planes lost and contributing to the erosion of domestic and international support for the overall war effort.

On the ground in South Vietnam, the attrition tactic of "search and destroy" called for the engagement of larger numbers of GI's in combat. While the enemy was being ground down, at least in

*Lady Bird Johnson, *A White House Diary* (New York: Holt, Rinehart, 1970), 360.

terms of weekly body counts provided by the Military Assistance Command, Vietnam (MACV), so too were Americans and South Vietnamese. The more than five thousand Americans killed in battle in 1966 troubled many young people and their parents, among others, in the United States.

Most, however, were still willing to give the president time to win the war. If the boys would not be home by Christmas of 1966, they surely would be home by the following Christmas. The president and his respected advisers continued to exude confidence in public about the wisdom of their policies.

The antiwar movement grew slowly during this period, as did the number of critics in Congress and the media. The administration met their thrusts with a variety of parries, in most cases successfully. Teach-ins faded as a tactic for protesters who instead concentrated on organizing large-scale demonstrations, the most notable of which took place in October and November 1965 and March 1966. The numbers that turned out were not especially impressive—in hindsight 1966 proved to be a breathing spell for activists between the exciting and newsworthy start-up period of early 1965 and the dramatic series of confrontations of 1967.

At the same time, the administration paid attention to antiwar activities. For one thing, the omnipresent hecklers and placard carriers who hounded Johnson and his colleagues whenever they stepped out of the White House were personally irritating and physically debilitating. Moreover, with Senator Fulbright's televised hearings in February 1966, Capitol Hill became a focal point for antiwar criticism. The president's huge majorities on Capitol Hill held, but a few outspoken dovish senators maintained a barrage of criticism, much of which was picked up by the media.

As the war dragged on through 1966, administration officials began to worry more and more, publicly and privately, about the impact of dissenting activities on Hanoi. Most thought they could contain politically the allegedly left-wing and misguided college students and the handful of rogue senators and journalists, but they feared that the communists would get the wrong idea from their well-publicized statements and demonstrations. More and more, public opinion and, consequently, antiwar critics became a crucial factor for Johnson as he fashioned his military and diplomatic strategies.

With much of the potential opposition dispersed for summer vacation, Johnson's decision to escalate in late July 1965 did not spark widespread adverse reaction. The teach-in held at Harvard on July 15 was characteristic of the antiwar movement's logistical problems. Despite the participation of media personality and author Norman Mailer, only two thousand summer school students showed up for the event. Similarly, although the administration was worried about the potential for mass civil disobedience in Washington from August 6 through 9, only a few thousand attended the centerpiece of the Assembly of Unrepresented People's demonstration, a joint appearance by folk singer Joan Baez and venerable pacifist leader A. J. Muste.[1]

Nonetheless, the Washington conclave did result in the establishment of the National Coordinating Committee to End the War in Vietnam. Based in Madison, Wisconsin, the Coordinating Committee, the most important such group of the early years of the movement, began to plan nationwide protests for October. August also witnessed the Watts uprising in Los Angeles, the first of the major black urban riots that convulsed the nation from 1965 through 1968. Those unprecedented disturbances contributed to the general sense of national disorder that plagued the last two years of the Johnson presidency.

Along with most other observers, the president did not view August's protest and riot as a necessary augury of things to come. In the late summer of 1965, he confidently took the advice proffered during the July meetings to begin selling his Vietnam policy aggressively. During this period, the administration produced an elaborate pamphlet entitled "Why Vietnam?" that was sent out by the thousands to newspapers, legislators, business leaders, and almost anyone who had a query about the reasons for American involvement in Southeast Asia.[2]

The White House welcomed a Freedom House advertisement in the *New York Times* in late July that supported the administration's quest for peace. A pleased McGeorge Bundy told Johnson, "Any knowledgeable academic men would know that this list of supporters is a whole lot more distinguished and knowledgeable than any list of critics yet published." An equally pleased president instructed aide Marvin Watson to send copies of the Freedom House release to members of Congress.[3]

Johnson felt confident enough on August 4 to speak before

thousands of students working in Washington for the summer. His address, which began with "My fellow revolutionaries," was greeted enthusiastically. Of course, the speech did contain a gaffe when it was discovered the Robert Lowell quote that he mischievously read to the students was really a misquote of Matthew Arnold.[4]

The administration kept up the offensive on several other fronts. Senator Thomas Dodd of Connecticut was assisted with material and ideas for a Senate speech to meet Senator Fulbright's criticisms. McGeorge Bundy talks of giving "some help" to Dodd. Such activity, according to the national security adviser, was only a "normal kind of staffwork."[5] The nineteen American college students who had spent the summer in Vietnam working with AID came back with positive public statements about what they had seen. In addition, White House aides worked closely with Young Democratic leadership to keep that restive organization in line.[6]

The most successful action was the launching of the Committee for an Effective and Durable Peace in Asia. Headed by veteran diplomat Arthur Dean, the committee took out advertisements in fourteen newspapers on September 8. Among the influential people who signed the proclamation of support were Dean Acheson, Robert Murphy, Douglas Dillon, David Packard, Whitney North Seymour, Walter Annenberg, John McCloy, Roswell Gilpatrick, and David Rockefeller.[7] This impressive bipartisan list, which reflected the high level of approval for the president in establishment circles, overshadowed any comparable list put together by the doves.

The media was, nevertheless, a concern for the Johnson administration. Characteristic was Johnson's remark at an August 5 meeting: "We are getting bad things from the press." A Defense Department aide responded that only a minority of the correspondents in Vietnam were unfair and that protests should be made to the editors to present "a balanced picture in their news efforts."[8]

That night, Johnson's "bad things" became worse when CBS television offered one of the first sensational documentaries on the war. Narrated by Morley Safer, the film revealed, after denials from officials that such things could happen, an American marine setting fire to a peasant hutch with his handy Zippo.[9] An irate

Johnson called CBS president Frank Stanton the next morning and began his conversation, "Frank, are you trying to fuck me? Frank, this is your president and yesterday your boys shat on the American flag." Johnson also ordered a security check on the Canadian-born Safer.[10]

The networks responded to administration bullying, as well as to what they perceived as public interest in the war, with several specials. CBS offered a four-part "Vietnam Perspective" later that month; NBC offered a "Vietnam Weekly Review"; and ABC countered with "Scope." All network programs did poorly in the ratings.[11] Most of the material they presented was favorable to Johnson, although scattered critical comments were heard. Despite the positive treatment afforded administration policy by the broadcasters, the presence of reasonable critics, even in minor roles, further legitimized dissent and may have first exposed many inactive citizens to dovish opinion.[12]

The administration's concern about its image soon led to the pulling together of all relevant public relations operations into a Public Affairs Policy Committee for Vietnam in August 1965. This committee, later the Vietnam Information Group (VIG), met regularly throughout Johnson's tenure in office.

Behind Johnson's irritation with the media and his increasingly thin skin was the realization that antiwar activities could affect international perceptions of American policy. In late September, Harry McPherson informed him of a disquieting incident involving Averell Harriman and a Viet Cong representative. The sometime roving ambassador was accosted in Warsaw by the diplomat, who proudly brandished columns by Walter Lippmann and other critics. Not entirely sold on American policy, Harriman nevertheless muted his criticism because he felt that it might hurt the chances for peace. McPherson regretted that "other public figures did not share his actions."[13]

With the return of the students to the universities in the fall and the noticeable rise in American combat deaths, organized antiwar activities picked up in intensity. General Maxwell Taylor was one of the first to confront the new, sometimes uncivil, activism. Unruly young people in San Francisco, one of the hotbeds of antiwar protest, picketed his hotel and called him a war criminal. A few broke in and even began banging on the door of the manager's office, where a nervous Taylor had taken refuge. For the general, this was a frightening example of the public relations problem with which Johnson had not successfully dealt.[14]

This was only the beginning of the first tumultuous autumn of major antiwar activities. In Washington, the administration girded itself for the so-called International Days of Protest scheduled for October 15 and 16, as well as a SANE-led demonstration on November 27.[15] With an eye to the media, McGeorge Bundy urged Johnson to launch a radio and television campaign to counter the protesters. Only he had the prestige to obtain the positive media coverage needed to deflect attention from their activities.[16]

Johnson was not just worried about the impact of the demonstrations on domestic and international opinion. He was genuinely concerned about both White House security and the misleading impressions created by the image of a government under siege. In addition, he personally did not like having to observe protesters in Lafayette Park almost around the clock. Lady Bird Johnson, who shared her husband's distress, counted 166 separate White House picketings in 1965 alone.[17]

Early on, J. Edgar Hoover recommended a ban on picketing within the vicinity of the White House. Such a ban, however, would have necessitated congressional action, something that was most unlikely from a Democratic majority.[18] Instead, Johnson (and Nixon) combated the picketers through a variety of legal and illegal harassments, including limiting their numbers in certain venues and demanding letter-perfect permits for every activity. It was a constant battle in which Johnson could never claim total victory. The unkempt picketers, foul-mouthed chanters, and placard carriers, in large and small groups and as individuals, maintained a presence around the White House that irritated all within its confines.

Johnson was not without weapons to deal with protesters in the District and in the nation at large. He could have taken the low road (as his successor would later do), appealing to a silent majority, waving the flag, and, especially, impugning the loyalty of antiwar critics. But this would have been unseemly for a Democrat in 1965, especially one trying to earn his liberal spurs. Moreover, it would have torn the party apart even more than the war issue itself.

In general, the president adopted the public line that although he recognized the right to dissent, the dissenters were encouraging the enemy and ultimately prolonging the war. Bill Moyers advised Johnson to stress the fact that the demonstrators represented a small minority. For his part, Eric Goldman warned the president about "liberal McCarthyism" and urged him to acknowledge the patriotism of his opponents.[19]

A bit ruefully perhaps, the more pragmatic Joseph Califano also reports that Johnson rejected a move to the Right and a campaign of superpatriotism. Califano felt that Johnson and his advisers may have "misjudged the eventual power of the left in American society, particularly its influence on the formulation of American public opinion."[20]

Johnson's relatively high-minded approach to demonstrators is even more surprising given his apparent conviction that many of those who opposed his Vietnam policies were influenced by Russian and native communists. Trusted friend J. Edgar Hoover did little to disabuse the president of his suspicions. Why, Johnson asked, was Soviet ambassador Anatoly Dobrynin's car seen frequently in front of opinion maker James Reston's house? He had heard that certain senators were being fed the Soviet line as well.[21]

Whether Johnson really believed that the antiwar movement was another communist conspiracy is difficult to determine. One must remember that once the president picked up an issue, his sycophantic aides tended to repeat and reinforce his prejudices in an almost endless feedback procedure.[22] If Johnson believed that there were communists in demonstrations, his advisers would find some for him, and then he might believe even more firmly that communists were in control.

Blaming the movement on communists does make sense in terms of Johnson's own self-image. He was proud that "he had done more for education than anyone else" and felt he was something of a hero to college-age youth and liberal activists. Thus, the demonstrations had to be "contrived and artificial," not representative of the vast majority of young people.[23]

Compounding his problems in understanding or in perceiving the issue accurately were the "young people" with whom he came into daily contact, the junior White House and NSC staffers. Well mannered, neatly groomed, and properly deferential, these were the youth of America, although most had already moved out of their twenties.[24] In addition, he and Mrs. Johnson spent an inordinate amount of time with White House Fellows, young interns whose company he apparently enjoyed.[25] If they were the real representatives of the Ivy League, then those noisy, hairy, unkempt people he saw on television or out his window in Lafayette Park were obviously counterfeits.

Yet something held him back from adopting a red-baiting strategy. One wonders if beneath all of that opportunistic, pragmatic, amoral facade, Johnson really meant what he said about the right to dissent in a free society. That he rejected the route Richard Nixon ultimately took, despite the fact that he was offended more than his successor by the taunts of the demonstrators, may reflect his democratic inclinations. In addition, he was a genuinely intelligent man who received "conflicting reports" on communists in the movement. While Hoover, Mayor Richard Daley of Chicago, and others stressed conspiracy, Johnson was informed by some of his aides that the movement was "authentic."[26]

A final reason Johnson may have refrained from red baiting was the assistance he received from the media. According to the *New York Times*, the nationwide mass antiwar demonstrations of October 15–16 were successful, with as many as a hundred thousand people turning out in over ninety cities.[27] About ten thousand attended the protest organized by the Vietnam Day Committee in Berkeley and thousands of others appeared at demonstrations organized by the National Coordinating Committee to End the War in New York, Chicago, Philadelphia, Madison, Columbus, and Ann Arbor. Although the SDS was not the only organizer of the events, the radical organization received much of the media attention, especially for the scattered acts of civil disobedience.[28] The media's portrayal of the October demonstrations as SDS-dominated helped the administration. George Ball, for example, although pleased by the demonstrations, was upset about their apparently radical tone.[29]

In a front-page story during the following week, the *Times* shifted more attention away from the large demonstrations by describing the success of a variety of proadministration support groups around the nation. McGeorge Bundy told the *Times* that the protests were unrepresentative of the strong backing for the president on campuses, an assertion supported by an AP poll of college administrators taken the week after the demonstrations. Perennial cheerleader though he was, Hubert Humphrey may have been correct when he informed Johnson of a "rising tide of support . . . among the college students."[30]

Despite the evidence that most Americans and even most American students supported the president, the White House did take seriously the demonstration planned for Washington on November 27.[31] In part, this nervousness may have reflected the relative novelty of these affairs in the fall of 1965. It is also true that administration officials *and* march organizers from SANE were worried about possible radical violence in the streets of the capital. SANE head Sanford Gottlieb met several times with Chester Cooper to consider ways to keep the protests reasonable and civil. Cooper was successful in convincing Gottlieb to send a letter to Ho Chi Minh calling upon the Vietnamese leader to make an effort for peace as well.[32]

Between twenty and forty thousand demonstrators showed up in Washington on November 27 for a peaceful protest, marked, according to the *New York Times*, by its middle-class, adult character.[33] March leaders Norman Cousins, Homer Jack, Benjamin Spock, Coretta Scott King, and Sanford Gottlieb met with a variety of officials, including Humphrey, who lectured them on the need to be evenhanded and also the need to keep radicals from their ranks.[34] SANE was joined in leading the demonstration by two new groups, the Catholic Peace Fellowship and the larger and ecumenical Clergy and Laymen Concerned about Vietnam. The relatively moderate nature of the organizing coalition and the protest itself was undermined somewhat when the *New York Times* reported that the antiwar critics received public congratulations from the Viet Cong.[35]

The appearance of Coretta Scott King at the rally reflected the slow but inexorable movement of civil rights leaders into the antiwar van. The fusing of the two powerful movements increased pressures on Johnson in the months to come.

As the marchers were pounding the pavement in Washington, *Look* magazine hit the newsstands with a story concerning Adlai Stevenson's "troubled last days." A good friend of his, respected news analyst Eric Sevareid, revealed that U Thant initiated a peace probe under United Nations auspices in late 1964, about which Stevenson was optimistic, only to have the Americans shoot it down. When Johnson heard about the *Look* story, he claimed to have no knowledge of Thant's proposal and even asked Moyers for more information.[36]

As in the spring, the administration met these sallies from antiwar critics with offensives on the domestic and the international fronts. On November 28, the day after the Washington rally, Freedom House issued a statement signed by 104 notables, including Dean Acheson, Richard Nixon, Lucius Clay, James B. Conant, Douglas Dillon, Max Lerner, Sidney Hook, and John Dos Passos, that called for a mobilization of the heretofore mostly silent supporters of the president. During the following week, Wesley Fishel of the American Friends of Vietnam produced a statement from 190 professors from Harvard, Yale, and other New England institutions, as well as two former heads of the ADA, supporting the administration. Fishel claimed that academics opposed to the Vietnam policy were rarely experts in relevant fields, whereas more than half of his cadre were from the social sciences.[37]

Not sanguine about the success of such committees, Chester Cooper urged the president in December to go to the people directly to separate "the confused or worried liberals from the hard-core left-cum kooks." Although antiwar liberal intellectuals were few in number, Cooper worried that "they were giving prestige and respectability . . . to the organized protesters of the left."[38]

Johnson did not go to the people directly to sell his policy, but certainly appealed to them with his thirty-seven-day bombing pause, which began on Christmas morning of 1965. The pause, and the subsequent diplomatic whirlwind of missions and missives, was the most celebrated peace probe of the Johnson administration. Unlike the May pause, this one was apparently serious, although the president was not optimistic about its chances for success.

The main problem with such pauses and the administration's other peace initiatives in 1966 and 1967 was the basic incompatibility between American and North Vietnamese bargaining positions. The North Vietnamese said that they would not sit down

with the Americans until they stopped their bombing unconditionally. The Americans would not stop the bombing until they
received concessions from Hanoi. And there matters stood.

That bombing was not yet doing the trick, as demonstrated by
Hanoi's intransigence, as well as by the NLF and NVA's relative
success on the ground in the South. Further escalations in terms of
the territory and targets to be bombed had been recommended by
the military to increase pressure on Hanoi and to cut supply lines.
The proposed escalations would look better at home and certainly
defuse criticism if they were preceded by an apparently genuine
attempt to bring Hanoi to the peace table.

Whether or not American officials were sanguine about the
peace prospects of the pause, coming as it did after the fall
demonstrations, it could appear to be a response to antiwar critics.
If it was, it was an indirect one with the emphasis on demonstrating to all American citizens that their government was responsible
and peace seeking.[39] At one point during this period, Maxwell
Taylor remarked that the pause was "good . . . if only to show
government sincerity." Dean Rusk struck a comparable note in his
explanatory memo to Ambassador Lodge in Saigon. He saw the
main benefit of the pause not in producing negotiations, but in
driving a rift between the communist powers and in gaining
support for American policies at home.[40]

Robert McNamara may have been the prime mover behind the
pause.[41] When he recommended the gesture to Johnson at the
Texas ranch, he argued that it would improve international opinion
of the United States, not pose a military problem (a commentary
on the ineffectiveness of the bombing), and just might produce
diplomatic negotiations.[42] McNamara did not stress the domestic
front in his presentation. He knew that Johnson did not want to
appear to take such a dramatic international initiative because of
domestic critics. The joint chiefs were not as excited about the
pause. They worried about "the ability of the political-decision
makers in Washington to resist the pressures from the 'peace
movement.'"[43]

They would not have been happy had they been invited to the
important December 17 and 18 meetings in the White House at
which the decision for the pause was taken. There, the public, and
tangentially the dissenters, figured prominently in the discussions.

On December 17, Johnson met with Rusk, McNamara, McGeorge Bundy, George Ball, and Jack Valenti and on the eighteenth with the same cast of characters and Clark Clifford, William Bundy, Deputy Under Secretary of State U. Alexis Johnson, and Supreme Court Justice Abe Fortas. On the seventeenth, Johnson revealed his willingness to "gamble" on the pause, although he was not very optimistic about its chance for success either diplomatically or politically. "You have no idea about how much I've talked to the Fulbrights and the Lippmanns. They're not coming aboard," he complained. He then read aloud a part of a Norman Cousins editorial and noted that the government had to look peaceful because, "the weakest link in our armor is public opinion." Naturally, as was the case at most of these decision points, Johnson expressed concern about the hawks and the joint chiefs. George Ball felt that if the pause failed, the Right might demand more, the Right that was "the Great Beast to be feared."[44]

On the following day, Dean Rusk picked up the president's theme. He wondered about the ability of the American people to stand firm. They were "isolationists at heart." As in the earlier meeting, when the domestic front was discussed, the emphasis was on general American opinion, not the antiwar movement and the need to throw it a bone.[45] On the other hand, the two were related implicitly; the need to appeal to general opinion was generated, in part, by the appearance of foreign policy criticism in journalistic and public forums.

Public opinion and antiwar critics also were important variables in the decision concerning the length of the pause. Too long a pause without diplomatic progress would disturb the military, nervous about the negative strategic implications of a bombing cessation. Too short a pause, on the other hand, would disappoint the doves and maybe even the general public. As Johnson noted, considering the fallout when the pause would have to end, "People will be upset and AP and UPI will provoke them."[46]

Assessing the first week of the pause, a week full of furious diplomatic activity without tangible results, McGeorge Bundy remarked that at least the *New York Times* was pleased with the gesture. At the same meeting, McNamara gloomily predicted the loss of some "respectable political leaders," when and if the bombing began again.[47] Several days after he made this comment, in a sort of self-fulfilling prophecy, the defense secretary, who met informally with Kennedy people Arthur Schlesinger, Jr., John Kenneth Galbraith, Richard Goodwin, and Carl Kaysen, heard warnings about the reaction to the resumption of the bombing.[48] McNamara met often with Kennedy people and may have had a foot in both camps in general, and on the escalation issue in particular. Concerned about the ultimate Kennedy challenge and Vietnam policy as a lightning rod for disaffected liberals, Johnson was not pleased when he discovered that McNamara had been consorting privately with the "enemy."[49]

As the pause moved into its fifth and last week, worry about the impact of renewed bombing increased in administration circles. Jack Valenti reflected Johnson's views when he predicted what would happen once Washington announced that the pause had failed to produce the hoped-for diplomatic breakthrough. "The minute we resume . . . the doves, the Lynd-liners, and the *Times* will shriek," Valenti remarked. No matter what concessions they were given, they will ask for more—"like lava pouring over a volcano, the flow is resistless." Among the Lynd-liners, Valenti included Senators Claiborne Pell, McGovern, and Fulbright, as well as Walter Lippmann.[50]

On the other hand, the Right would howl as well. At a bipartisan White House meeting on January 25, Johnson informed a mostly friendly congressional delegation of the decision to resume the bombing. Senator Richard Russell, the influential head of the Senate Armed Services committee and a man Johnson, according to George Ball, "revered," advised his old friend to "go all the way. . . . This is an unpopular war but the people want us to win." Senate Minority Leader Everett Dirksen chimed in with comparable hawkish advice.[51]

Two days later, McNamara advised the president that since everyone expected the resumption of bombing sooner or later, he had best get on with it. The longer the delay after the obvious failure of diplomacy, the noisier the public debate and the more dramatic the polarization of opinion. Worried about the Senate, Johnson considered obtaining a resolution of support for the bombing resumption.[52] He knew he could get one, but not without a divisive and potentially damaging public debate. Richard Helms later told Bill Moyers that if twenty senators publicly voted against the president on Vietnam, Hanoi would be encouraged, and the United States might soon resemble France in 1954.[53] Above all, Johnson wanted to look tough to Hanoi and his critics. "I don't want to back out—and look like I'm reacting to the Fulbrights." He had to resume bombing even though that act "will lose a good part of the Senate." Johnson was being told by advisers like Admiral Sharp that the United States could not let up on the bombing because Hanoi might think that "international and domestic pressures . . . were having an effect."[54]

On January 28, at a large meeting devoted to the termination of the pause, Clark Clifford worried about how the administration could show Hanoi that it had the support of the American public. He feared that the communists were misperceiving the political situation in the United States. "They hear Senators and protests and they are convinced we are losing the support of the people." Maxwell Taylor then repeated what he had said on previous occasions about doing a better selling job with the public.[55] Of course, adopting that approach would mean making Vietnam a major political issue. Johnson still wanted to avoid going to the public or the Senate for support in fear of the debate that would be provoked on the way toward obtaining that manifestation. Moreover, it was still less than a year since the bombing began and only six months since American ground escalation; the war could still be a short one, especially if one believed the more optimistic evaluations of the joint chiefs. Thus, why make too much of the growing division in the United States if the war would be over by next Christmas?

On January 29, at the last of a series of meetings before the pause was to end two days later, Johnson called for a continuance of the peace offensive, primarily for show, even after the bombing began again and was expanded, "because I certify that the Fulbrights and Morses will be under the table and the hard liners will take over—unless we take initiatives." And then, as if to say I told you so, Johnson reminded his aides that he had been against both pauses, because, among other things, they "created a situation of doubt" as to what the country's true policy was.[56]

Johnson did not approve another full-scale bombing pause until October 1968. The failure of the thirty-seven-day pause was important in the development of his attitudes toward the doves.

According to Chester Cooper, Johnson considered the acceptance of the pause "his worst mistake" and that he had been "led down the garden path by doves among his advisers." William Bundy reports that Johnson was "disillusioned" about the efficacy of diplomacy after the pause.[57] Reluctant to go through with the pause, Johnson felt he had been pressured by domestic and international opinion. He had gone the last mile to appease the doves with his frenetic global diplomacy, his relentless search for signals, and in the resultant presumed military advantage gained by Hanoi during the pause. And still the North Vietnamese were unresponsive. The failure of the pause made it easier for the majority of the population to accept renewed escalation. It is interesting to note that in 1966 the mass antiwar movement never reached the proportions it reached in the fall and early winter of 1965.

As expected, the bombing resumption produced a flurry of public protests. SANE held a vigil at the United Nations, thirty Stanford professors refused to teach, and about a thousand demonstrators sat down in Times Square.[58] It was the winter, of course, not a good time for mass protests, and the public, including antiwar activists, had been expecting the bombing resumption. Thus, the immediate political fallout in the streets and the media was not especially significant.

The expected fallout in the Senate was another matter. Senator Fulbright was anguished about his inability to influence America's Vietnam policy. In January, he came up with the idea of transforming routine hearings on supplementary aid for South Vietnam in his Senate Foreign Relations Committee into an extensive, public review of all of American activities in the war. He later called his hearings "an experiment in public education." Doubtful he could have much of an immediate impact on policy, Fulbright hoped that he might affect developments over the long haul by influencing some senators, and maybe their constituents.[59] Because of his outspoken criticism, Fulbright had made the Foreign Relations Committee a place to which the president rarely turned either for advice or support. The powerful committees in Congress were Armed Services and Appropriations, where the proceedings were dominated by Johnson loyalists, even hawks.[60]

Yet Fulbright was not completely alone in the Senate. On January

TABLE 2.
MAJOR VIETNAM WAR–RELATED EVENTS OF 1966

Antiwar Activities	Percent Poll Respondents who Think War Was Mistake	Percent Poll Respondent for Withdra
		Feb.: 19%
Feb. 8: Fulbright committee hearings begin on television		
	March: 25%	
March 25–27: Nationwide demonstrations		
May 15: Washington demonstration May: Antidraft activities, Madison, WI		
Summer: Campaigns for congressional doves		
	Sept.: 35%	
	Nov.: 31%	
		Nov.: 10%
Nov. 7: McNamara assaulted at Harvard		
Dec. 25: Harrison Salisbury's accounts of Hanoi bombing in *New York Times*		

Administration Activities	Troop Levels	Battle Deaths (6-month totals)
il 12: B-52s over North Vietnam		
e 29: Hanoi oil dumps raided	June 30: 267,500	2,511
c. 23–March 1: Partial bombing pause		
c. 24–26: Complete bombing pause		
	Dec. 31: 385,300	2,497

27, fifteen Senate doves, led by Vance Hartke, sent a letter to the president urging him to continue the bombing pause. It is interesting that Fulbright's celebrated hearings, which "infuriated" Johnson, began on January 28, the day he decided to resume bombing on January 31.[61]

The initial hearings were not televised because the networks were not certain how to deal with the unusual proceedings. Secretary of State Dean Rusk was the chief witness that first day. Accounts of his forceful presentation received three and five minutes, respectively, on the CBS and NBC evening newscasts. Journalists covering the opening day saw in the clash between the administration and critical senators the stuff from which gripping real-life drama was made. When the hearings resumed in February, the networks were there with live coverage.[62]

On February 10, however, CBS suspended its coverage and ran its normal daytime fare, including reruns of the "I Love Lucy" show. Respected news director Fred W. Friendly's resignation over this incident fueled speculation that Johnson's friend Frank Stanton, the president of CBS, had something to do with the change in programing. Friendly himself did not think the White House was behind the decision to replace scholar-diplomat George Kennan with Lucille Ball.[63] In any event, NBC did cover that day's testimony, which included a sophisticated, genteel critique of American policy in Vietnam.

Johnson was angered by the hearings, especially when they were shown live.[64] Part of this anger related to his growing disenchantment with Fulbright. Although the former master of the Senate "admired" antiwar critic Wayne Morse because he had been consistent and had also supported the Dominican Republic intervention, he was upset with Fulbright's flipflop.[65] Fulbright claims that the president did everything possible to ruin his hearings, including sending potential witnesses out of the country and simply refusing to allow others to testify.[66] His most dramatic attempt to push the hearings from the front pages was his calling of the Honolulu Conference. Jack Valenti thinks that Johnson arranged the hastily planned conference on Vietnam to shift attention from Fulbright to himself, or at least, Valenti says, he "wouldn't put it past him." William Bundy refers to the conference as a "preemptive act by Lyndon Johnson."[67] If the Honolulu

Conference, with its attendant policy statements and publicity, was indeed fabricated *only* to divert attention from the Senate hearings, then once again antiwar criticism had influenced important policy. Although the conference was soon forgotten, Johnson's unnecessary meeting with Vietnamese President Nguyen Cao Ky at Honolulu could have inadvertently affected American policy.

Johnson himself did pay careful attention to the hearings. After he saw Dean Rusk on the first day, he congratulated him for his spirited defense of the administration and even asked for a copy of the briefing books that looked so impressive on television when Rusk referred to them.[68]

Most of the witnesses who appeared before the committee defended administration policy. The two chief critics, Kennan and General James Gavin, called for tactical changes without condemning the original intervention. The main problem for the administration was the pointed interrogation by dovish senators, especially Morse, Church, Clark, and Case. Several witnesses worried about the impact the hearings might have on Hanoi, revealing, as they did, senatorial opposition to Johnson's policy. Senator Case defended his committee's probing, pointing out that Americans needed to be educated about Vietnam; the administration could not expect support from the public for a policy that it did not understand.[69]

Reactions to the hearings were mixed. Of 1,207 letters sent to the State Department, 1,028 were counted as approving of Rusk's presentation.[70] Wayne Morse received an umbrella in the mail, the Neville Chamberlain symbol of appeasement. Senator Albert Gore, not one of the harshest critics, reported that his office was flooded with mail and phone calls supporting the idea of the hearings. Pleased with the estimated television audience of 22 million, Gore told an anecdote about a journalist's wife who was so transfixed by the educational experience that she told her husband when he arrived home one evening, "You have an unclean house but a highly informed wife."[71]

In the short run, however, the hearings had little impact on the polls or the president's general level of support.[72] As for Congress, according to George Christian, Johnson retained the support of a majority of the senators and representatives right through to the day he left the presidency, although it became increasingly difficult to work with them. Jack Valenti thought his boss "probably survived them [the hearings] in good shape" and that the White House had anticipated the worst. George Ball agrees. To a dove like himself, the hearings were "disappointingly docile."[73]

Johnson thought the hearings muddled. Moreover, he accused his detractors of not knowing very much about the communists. At this point, he was confident that his defenders had the best of the argument on television. General Maxwell Taylor, for example, reported much positive mail applauding the manner in which he responded to senatorial grilling.[74] Nevertheless, it may not have been coincidental that, in April, the White House hired Robert Kintner, former head of NBC, to coordinate public relations activities.[75] And for Johnson, the memory of the hearings lingered on through the spring. In May, he joked bitterly at a public meeting, "You can say one thing about those hearings, but I don't think this is the place to say it." On another public occasion, he made sarcastic remarks to Fulbright's face about the arrogance of power.[76]

It is difficult to evaluate the significance of the hearings for the antiwar movement and American foreign policy. They probably had some cumulative long-term effect since, for the first time, aside from the June 1965 teach-in, reasoned dissent obtained a platform on national network television and seemed respectable. Those who found fault with administration policy on television, people like Kennan, Gavin, Church, and Fulbright, were noted reference figures who added luster to the antiwar movement. Critiques by professional military experts like General Gavin were especially impressive to a national audience that respected its generals.[77] At the same time, Kennan, in particular, went to great lengths to distance himself from the students and their teach-ins.[78]

Another measure of the hearings' importance was Fulbright's increasing celebrity. During the first four months of 1966, he received 736 invitations to deliver speeches. In Chicago, on March 14, delegates to the National Conference on Higher Education greeted the senator with a standing ovation.[79]

The networks, however, did not broadcast hearings again until 1968.[80] Moreover, after a spate of specials and even weekly programs on Vietnam in the fall of 1965, such shows virtually disappeared during 1966. The absence of Vietnam from prime time during that year reflected more a lack of interest from the public than pressure or displeasure from the White House.

The resumed expanded bombing program and the hearings spurred a new round of protests in February. On February 13 the *New York Times* featured a full-page advertisement with the names of mostly eastern academics who opposed the resumption of bombing. The day before the ad appeared, in a sort of point-counterpoint, Dean Rusk addressed ten thousand enthusiastic supporters at an Atlanta rally. Senators Richard Russell and Herman Talmadge also spoke and a representative of the South Vietnamese government was presented with a petition bearing the names of two hundred thousand Americans who approved of their government's policies in Southeast Asia.[81]

As comforting as such petitions were, in addition to the constant overwhelming support in the polls, the administration was again becoming worried about antiwar criticism. To be sure, that criticism came from only a small minority, but that minority was growing, especially in terms of dissenting journalists and politicians. Although mail counts to government agencies are not the most sensitive and reliable indicators of opinion, the vast majority of letters to the Defense Department in January supported administration peace initiatives but opposed escalation. During this same period, Mrs. Johnson quoted her husband as saying on February 13, "This thing [antiwar movement] is assuming dangerous proportions, dividing the country and giving our enemies the wrong idea of the will of this country to fight." A week later, she lamented that Vietnam "is about two thirds of what we talk about these days."[82]

Mrs. Johnson was not the only one who listened to the president's harangues about domestic opposition to his war policies. Meeting with congressmen on February 24, Johnson claimed that he could not "understand why Americans who dissent can't do their dissenting in private. Once we are committed to a program of action, there never has been public dissent. You have to go back to the Civil War. . . . Men can't understand why prominent men in the United States continue to criticize our policy." At the same time, Averell Harriman chided the *New York Times* and Walter

Lippmann for contributing to a perception among allies that the United States lacked will.[83]

To such elite criticism were added the voices of those who joined the International Days of Protest from March 25 through March 27. Organized by A. J. Muste, the Fifth Avenue Peace Parade Committee took the lead in planning the protest and remained on the scene to organize future New York actions. The largest demonstration of the three-day period was held in New York with smaller ones in San Francisco and Chicago, as well as cities in other countries. Prior to the protests, White House aides worried how the crowds and media coverage of them might affect the nation's image.[84] Other demonstrations that spring included the Fifth Avenue Vietnam Peace Parade on April 16 and a SANE and Women Strike for Peace rally at the White House on May 15. More ominous in a political sense, perhaps, were the clashes over Vietnam at the United Auto Workers' convention in May and protests on elite campuses in early June against honorary degree recipients from the administration.[85] Finally, the well-publicized announcement on June 30 by three soldiers, the Fort Hood Three, of their refusal to go to Vietnam opened a new and troubling dissenting front in the armed forces. All of this activity suggested that Jack Valenti's May 1 comment to Johnson that the "Vietnam debate is about over," and all he needed to do was "rally the sound 60% of the country to sweat out the next stage with confidence," was wishful thinking.[86]

Fueling these activities was the growing size of the American military commitment and casualties in the war. With almost three hundred thousand troops in the field and more aggressive tactics in the bloody war of attrition, the Vietnam engagement began to threaten the future of more and more young people and their parents.

On June 5, the *New York Times* ran the largest antiwar advertisement to date. At a cost of $20,800, the Ad Hoc University Committee for a Statement on Vietnam and the Committee of the Professions published the names of over sixty-four hundred academics and professionals who opposed administration policy in three pages in the Sunday "News of the Week in Review" section.[87]

The purchase of newspaper advertisements in prestigious publications by political and humanitarian groups is a common activity in American society.[88] Most who become involved in such campaigns cannot be certain how the administration being petitioned is affected by them. They simply accept as an act of faith that the time and expense involved in advertising campaigns is a worthwhile contribution to their various causes. Their faith may be merited.

We do know that White House staffers clipped and filed most of the advertisements from the major newspapers. Further, someone read them and underlined the names of prominent scholars or public figures. Certainly, in the most general sense, the incessant bombardment of advertisements served as a constant reminder to readers of the *New York Times*, especially, of the unrelenting opposition "out there." In Washington, almost everyone who was anyone read the Sunday *Times*. In addition, the more such advertisements appeared with the names of prominent mainstream figures, the more other citizens might think that dissent was legitimate. Finally, the ads, with their return coupons soliciting money, financed antiwar organizations and produced enlarged network lists.

George Reedy claims that although he paid little attention to the advertisements, many people around Johnson did, particularly those with little or no political experience, like the young, well-educated National Security Council staffers. The former press secretary thinks that Johnson too was impressed with some of the ads because, in part, he "assumed a potency to words" and "wanted to track down and squelch words derogatory" to him. One of Reedy's successors, George Christian, reports that the major ads were "duly noted" and represented "another chink in the defenses." He thought as he read them in 1967 and 1968 that they affected opinion, especially when signers were Nobel Prize winners or college presidents. That is, if it appeared that the "smart" people were opposing intervention, then others might conclude that dissent was not unpatriotic. Among those who also remember scanning the ads are Douglass Cater and George Ball. Ball was pleased with anything that offered hope of stopping the war.[89]

Others in the White House were more cavalier about the ad campaign. College professor Walt Rostow was not impressed by college professors in the *New York Times*; he was confident that the administration knew what it was doing in Asia. Unlike the political economist heading the National Security Council, those well-meaning academic signers were not experts in foreign policy. Similarly, McGeorge Bundy does not remember paying much attention to the ads when they first appeared in 1965 and 1966. He categorized many of the signers as the sort who would oppose any anticommunist activity from their government. To Bundy, all the ads combined did not match, within government circles, the significance of George Ball's dissent.[90]

One might expect that as the ads increased in frequency through 1966, 1967, and 1968, as with demonstrations, they would have become more commonplace, a part of everyday life that could be ignored by administration and public alike. Although such an approach makes sense, the administration did monitor the longer advertisements right through to 1968, evaluating the importance of the sorts of people who were jumping aboard the antiwar bandwagon.

Harry McPherson was worried about the sorts of people he met on a New England vacation in the summer of 1966. These were conservative, well-educated, internationalist types, whose support was "vital." Yet he found very little support for the "extremely unpopular war." What's more, according to McGeorge Bundy, those who opposed the bombing policy were much more passionate in their convictions than those who favored it.[91]

Professors, professionals, and other members of the opinion-making elites who opposed the war did not just sign advertisements. Joseph Califano, for example, was nervous about the possible impact of the decision by a group of University of Chicago professors to foil the draft by refusing to provide the Selective Service with students' transcripts.[92]

Throughout the war, the influential internationalist and liberal National Council of Churches lent its pulpits and publications to antiwar activities. When Harry McPherson heard in early October that the council was preparing to make a strong statement against the administration, he asked Bill Moyers whether he knew "someone in State who can get to them." The proposed council statement would make "front-page news" and would leave the administration with the support only of the fundamentalists.[93]

The spring 1966 activities, the petition drives, and the development of new permanent organizations troubled the president. In
public and private he and his aides began to worry more and more
about how the antiwar movement was affecting domestic and
international opinion, and especially, how the movement was
evaluated in Hanoi. Was it possible that they were so unyielding
diplomatically because of the movement in America, he wondered?
In one of his strongest public attacks, Johnson railed against the
"nervous nellies" in a Chicago address in May. Most likely, he was
concerned about senatorial and journalistic dissent when he used
the famous phrase. A few weeks later, Bill Moyers sent him a
twelve-page memo on how to improve his deteriorating relationship with the media.[94] Labeling them nervous nellies was not the
best way to go about that fence-mending operation.

Problems with the media over Vietnam were a subject for
discussion at several cabinet meetings that summer. At one meeting on July 26, Johnson told his colleagues, "Don't believe our
newspapers and Republican critics—the country is for our Vietnam policy."[95] The president wanted to convince people inside and
outside the administration that the government was not moved by
the dissent and that, moreover, the dissent did not reflect most
citizens' views of the Vietnam policy. According to Arthur Goldberg in a London speech, "The differences in our national debate
are concerned with how these objectives are to be achieved, not
with the objectives themselves." Several weeks later Dean Rusk
told a Denver audience that Hanoi was "mistaken" if it hoped that
dissent here would bring victory in Southeast Asia. The president
himself told an Omaha audience, "I hear my friends say 'I'm
troubled, I am confused, I am frustrated,' and all of us understand
these people. Sometimes I almost develop a stomach ulcer listening to them."[96]

Johnson's growing exasperation was evidenced by the flap he
created when he asked the commander of Jewish War Veterans, *in
public*, why so many Jewish leaders were against his war effort.[97]
Whether or not Johnson was correct in his evaluation, he displayed
poor judgment to air such criticism. Arthur Goldberg had to be
called in to put out the fire. Meeting with forty Jewish leaders who
were disturbed by the implications of Johnson's remarks, Goldberg
assured them that the president did not mean to sound anti-

Semitic, nor did he threaten American support for the state of Israel.[98]

Although friendly and neutral international opinion was never as important to Johnson as domestic opinion, he did worry about the way his policies in Southeast Asia were perceived abroad. In the spring of 1966, negative international reaction was one variable affecting the decision to limit bombing escalation. Similarly, Dean Rusk was concerned in June that too dramatic an increase in American military activities might sabotage the attempt by Canadian diplomat Chester Ronning to open up lines of communication with Hanoi.[99]

Walt Rostow had an eye on international opinion when he advised Johnson on strategies to follow during his Asian trip in the fall. Since October was a proclaimed month of prayer and peace for Catholics around the world, Rostow felt that it was "politically important in the United States and throughout the world" to stress peaceful themes in the meetings in Asia and Australia and New Zealand.[100]

It was Hanoi, however, that drew special attention from everyone in the administration. How the North Vietnamese evaluated the strength of dissent in the streets and in Congress was thought to be a crucial element in their political and military calculations. Thus, on that fall trip, on October 21, Johnson repeated his by then familiar theme as he warned in Melbourne not only Australians but Vietnamese, Russians, and Chinese: "but so far as my country is concerned, don't be misled, as the Kaiser was or as Hitler was, by a few irrelevant speeches. . . . So don't misjudge our speeches in the Senate."[101]

Some who were concerned about the freedom to dissent in the United States thought that the president was exaggerating this theme in order to contain critics in Congress and elsewhere. He may have been waving the flag and attacking the patriotism of those who were allegedly giving aid and comfort to the enemy in wartime in order to improve his political fortunes in the United States, not his military fortunes in Vietnam.

The issue of the impact of dissent on Hanoi raises two difficult questions. First, was the Johnson administration serious in its admonitions to the antiwar movement to mute its protests lest the communists underestimate the strength of America's commitment to the war in Vietnam? And second, naturally, how did the North Vietnamese evaluate that growing dissent? Did it encourage them to maintain a stiffer diplomatic and military posture?

In general, those few in the administration who were dovish did not think that Hanoi counted very much on American dissenters when it contemplated its strategies. George Ball and James Thomson, for example, doubt whether Hanoi was affected by the movement's activities in 1965 and 1966. Thomson remembers advising McGeorge Bundy in December 1964, as they pondered the bombing option, that the North Vietnamese would fight on because of "national, cultural, and geographical realities," irrespective of American actions. Thomson recalls Bundy suggesting that he might be correct. Both Ball and Thomson left the administration before the movement matured. Moreover, Thomson is certain that Johnson and many of his advisers did believe what they were saying when they expressed concern that Hanoi would get the wrong message from the spirited American public debate over Vietnam policies. According to Thomson, if you keep on saying things long enough, you come to believe them in a sort of "self-deception," whether or not you truly believed those things at the outset.[102]

John Roche thought that Ho and his advisers were interested in American opinion and isolationist trends, in general, not in the intellectuals and the students in the streets.[103] Of course, if American opinion and the polls were being affected by the movement, then Ho had to be interested in its activities.

Another former academic, Walt Rostow, struck a variation of the Roche theme. According to Rostow, Ho saw himself involved in a "war of public opinion against American public opinion." He knew that Americans did not like long and indecisive wars and "systematically took this into account" in his policy planning. Further, he thought that the Vietnamese were very sophisticated on this issue and would not exaggerate the limited significance of a protest march or a petition in the *New York Times*.[104]

Dean Rusk, Cyrus Vance, and Maxwell Taylor were among those who directly link the movement to Hanoi's calculations. Somewhat bitterly, Rusk reports that the movement had its "principal impact on Hanoi." The North Vietnamese had "no real incentive to negotiate" and played games with the American public by inviting dovish peace missions to North Vietnam that would return to the United States "eight months pregnant with peace." Vance, one of the Paris negotiators in 1968, is convinced that the activities of the antiwar movement were indeed a factor in Hanoi's calculations. For his part, Maxwell Taylor suggested that one of the major North Vietnamese defenses against American bombing was their propaganda campaign "abetted by American doves."[105]

Such observations from inside the administration must be evaluated carefully. Defense Department aide Phil Goulding claims that he and his colleagues never really knew what the North Vietnamese were thinking.[106] Nevertheless, if the administration did believe that the peace movement was assisting North Vietnam and that Ho did indeed include it among the factors in his decision making, then, in fact, the movement affected the strategies of those in Washington who were trying to interpret Hanoi's policies.

The problem of divining North Vietnamese policies and perceptions during the Vietnam War is difficult even today. Hanoiology is an even finer art than Kremlinology. Opinions from experts in this arcane field are mixed, although most agree that antiwar activities helped the North Vietnamese. Stanley Karnow reports that though General Giap paid tribute to the antiwar movement in America, the major battlefield was Vietnam. Denis Warner sees the movement playing a more significant role in Giap's strategies, with evidence that even on the district level, National Liberation Front and NVA cadres monitored demonstrations and sent funds to assist their American supporters.[107]

In a carefully prepared interview, Bui Xuan Ninh, a counselor at the Vietnamese legation in New York in 1983, offered what was most likely the official line on the movement. The diplomat contends that Americans were uninformed and apathetic about their "aggression" in Asia until leading American "social scientists" like Benjamin Spock, Stanford professor Linus Pauling, and Martin Luther King began to speak out against their government. Through the "application of their specialized knowledge," they awakened the American people and became one of the most "decisive elements" in Hanoi's struggle. Bui also calls attention to the importance of Harrison Salisbury's December 1966 stories from Hanoi as an important milestone along the way toward general American disenchantment with the war. The counselor deems the opinion makers to be more important than the student demonstrators. Hanoi knew this and thus invited many of them to North Vietnam to observe American "aggression" and return with reports to the American people that aided the communist war effort. Bui applauds the "courageous acts" of the American visitors who came out of a "sense of humanity and justice." In addition, he sees a link between the American movement and the development of favorable international opinion led by people like Olof Palme of Sweden. Nevertheless, Bui does think that the American antiwar movement came "a little late" to halt the destructiveness of the war.[108]

No doubt the antiwar movement in the United States assisted the North Vietnamese. Although not responsible for maintaining their resolve, as Johnson suggested, it did encourage them. Thomas Powers may have been on the mark when he suggested that Hanoi felt the failure of American arms in Vietnam would create the opposition to the war, not the other way around.[109] That is, the antiwar movement, which became an important factor late in the game, did not lead directly to America's defeat. The failing military policies helped create the mass antiwar movement, which then had some impact on Hanoi and its analysis of the correlation of forces in the world.

Antiwar protests were also beginning to have an intensely personal effect on those officials and their families against whom the protests were being directed. Of special concern was the possibility that Luci Johnson's wedding on the White House lawn in August 1966 might be ruined by obstreperous protesters.[110] With careful advance containment preparations and not very many protesters in the near vicinity, Luci's wedding ultimately took place amid the proper pomp and ceremony, but not without a few sleepless nights for the proud first family.

Wherever they traveled, Johnson and his family began to be subjected to rowdy picketers and often profane verbal abuse, the likes of which had not been experienced by any other American president. In September, for example, Mrs. Johnson had to face unruly protesters in New York, outside the Metropolitan Opera, and in San Francisco, outside the San Francisco Opera. Lady Bird's diary entries for 1966 more and more included comments on whether or not pickets were present. Antiwar placards, chants, and jeers were even in evidence in New Zealand and Australia. George Christian remembers particularly being distressed by the number of picketers and vocal critics in crowds in Australia, rowdy crowds "vividly" recalled by Christian's aide, Tom Johnson.[111]

At times, in the summer and fall of 1966, Johnson and his entourage had to feel beleaguered. It was during that period that he allegedly asked, after rejecting an option to bomb Hanoi and Haiphong, "How long will it take five hundred thousand angry Americans to climb the White House wall out there and lynch their President?"[112]

Robert McNamara may have been the individual in the administration most distressed by the antiwar opposition in 1966. He had been mildly skeptical about the efficacy of the bombing from the start although, as a loyal member of the administration, he helped to plan it. The protests that the bombing produced in the United States and the apparent lack of results in North Vietnam reinforced his skepticism by the middle of 1966. Even after Paul Warnke revealed in his hiring interview of August of 1966 that he was a dove who opposed the bombing policy, McNamara brought him into the Defense Department.[113] The secretary was especially upset about protests on the major university campuses against "his" bombing.[114] Despite the image that he projected as the cool, brilliant, unemotional crisis manager, McNamara was a surprisingly sensitive man, with an "overly human heart."[115]

On November 7, at Harvard University, his car was surrounded and rocked by a group of radical students and for a moment he was in great physical danger—the secretary of defense in a life-threatening situation at Harvard, America's most prestigious university. McNamara was greatly shaken by the attack, "a searing experience."[116] One might have expected that he would have rationalized the incident; after all, only several hundred students protested, only a handful behaved violently, some of the leaders were not real students, the dean of Harvard apologized the next day, and two days later, over three thousand Harvard students sent him a letter of apology.[117] Nonetheless, this direct encounter with the passions his bombing had aroused, even considering all of the possible rationalizations, apparently made a deep impression on McNamara.

Despite McNamara's harrowing experience, antiwar activities in the fall of 1966 were less of a problem for the administration than those in the fall of 1965. To be sure, the president and his aides confronted the by then usual meetings, demonstrations, marches, and petitions, but none compared in drama with the events of the previous fall. In part, this relative breathing spell was related to the tactics of some peace movement leaders who had decided to devote their energies to defeating hawks and electing doves in the congressional elections. They failed. Hawkish senator Paul Douglas did lose in Illinois, dovish senator Mark Hatfield (a Republican) won in Oregon, and over 40 percent in a Dearborn, Michigan, referendum expressed antiwar sentiments. Nevertheless, if the returns meant anything, the vast majority of Americans still supported the president and his perceived middle-of-the-road policy between hawks and doves. It is probable that antiwar Democrats may have hurt their cause more than they helped it by splitting their party in some districts and allowing Republicans to win.[118] At bottom, however, foreign policy may, as usual, have taken a back seat to more parochial concerns in the election.[119] Over the next two years, Democratic insurgents concentrated their attention on gaining control of their party in order to affect the race for the presidency. There, at least, they hoped that foreign policy issues might become the primary factor for many Democratic voters.

A Freedom House advertisement that appeared in the *New York Times* on November 29 reflected the broad support for Johnson's leadership on the war among national leaders in the fall of 1966. Attacking irresponsible critics, the ad was signed by former president Eisenhower[120] and 137 other luminaries, including Jacob Javits, Robert Murphy, James A. Farley, and James B. Conant.

Nevertheless, more and more troops were being sent to Vietnam, more and more casualties were being recorded, the bombing was intensifying around populated areas in North Vietnam—and no end was in sight as 1966 came to a close. It was only a matter of time before dissenters in the media and in the streets would intensify the pressure on the administration.

Chapter Four

Coming Apart: December 1966—January 1968

". . . this dissent has [not] contributed much to any victories we have had. . . . Please count to 10 before you say something that hurts instead of helps."
—*LYNDON B. JOHNSON**

Nineteen sixty-seven was the worst year of Johnson's presidency and one of the most turbulent years in all of American history. The war in Southeast Asia and the war at home in the streets and on the campuses dominated the headlines and the attention of the White House. To make matters worse, 1967 witnessed more urban riots, the most deadly of which took place in Detroit and Newark. It was also the year of the hippies, Haight-Ashbury, drugs, and a wholesale assault on conventional morality and middle-class values. All of these singular happenings were magnified by the media, which careened wildly from one sensation to the next.

There was nothing sensational to report from the field in Vietnam, however. No doubt, the Americans and South Vietnamese were doing better in 1967 than in 1966. The problem was that the slow pace of that progress made unlikely any chance for a speedy termination of the war. All the while, the human and fiscal costs were mounting. By summer, draft calls were averaging thirty thousand a month and American combat deaths had reached thirteen thousand. On the domestic front, the president was compelled to request a surtax in August to finance the increasingly more expensive engagement.

Department of State Bulletin 57 (December 11, 1967):777,779.

The limited bombing policy that outraged so many at home and abroad was not working. Secretary of Defense McNamara was prepared to give it up. Others in the military and Congress preferred escalation to bomb the North Vietnamese back into the Stone Age until or unless they were willing to talk peace on reasonable terms.

President Johnson wanted to end quickly and honorably the war that was crippling his presidency and paralyzing the nation. Although preferring not to escalate, he refused to cut and run and thus was stuck with a middle-of-the-road policy that satisfied few. He could not understand why Ho Chi Minh would not sit down and talk to him, considering the heavy price that the communists were paying to maintain their war effort. A frustrated Johnson expanded the range of permissible targets in the north again and gave his military some but not all of the additional troops they requested. He also tried to sweeten his offers to the North Vietnamese in October by softening American terms for a cessation of the bombing. But he would not stop the bombing unconditionally, the communists sine qua non for negotiations.

The war was becoming more and more unpopular at home. By the middle of 1967, close to a majority of Americans began telling pollsters that the original involvement in Vietnam had been a mistake. More ominously for Johnson's political prospects in 1968, little more than a quarter of the population approved of his handling of the war.

To be sure, many of those fed up with the way the war was going were hawks who wanted to remove the shackles from the generals. Nevertheless, Johnson's critics among the doves were more troubling to him. In the first place, they were far more vocal and visible than the hawks, appearing at large, well-organized demonstrations and, in smaller numbers, wherever he, his aides, and their families appeared in public. Even more disconcerting were the continuing defections from the media, the Democratic party, and the intellectual community. What had been a slow trickle in 1966 became a flood by the fall of 1967. By then, important newspapers and magazines such as the *New York Times*, the *Wall Street Journal*, the *Washington Post*, *Time-Life*, and the *Saturday Evening Post* all had begun calling for an end to the war. The most dramatic antiwar

TABLE 3.
MAJOR VIETNAM WAR-RELATED EVENTS OF 1967

Antiwar Activities	Percent Poll Respondents who Think War Was Mistake	Percent Pol Responden for Withdr
	Feb.: 32%	
		Feb.: 6%
April 15: New York and San Francisco demonstrations	May: 37%	
May: Vietnam Summer activities begin		May: 6%
	July: 41%	
	Oct.: 46%	
Oct. 16: Oakland Draft Resistance week		
Oct. 21–22: Pentagon march		Nov.: 10
Nov. 30: McCarthy enters primaries		
Dec. 4–8: New York draft protests	Dec.: 45%	

Administration Activities	Troop Levels	Battle Deaths (6-month totals)
. 8: LBJ letter to Ho Chi Minh		
. 8–12: Bombing pause		
. 24: Firing over DMZ		
rch 18: Request for 200,000 more troops		
:il 6: Second LBJ letter to Ho		
y 11–June 4: Partial bombing pause		
y 23–24: Complete bombing pause		
	June 30: 448,800	4,899
e 11–Aug. 1: Partial bombing pause		
t. 29: New LBJ peace proposal		
:. 24–25: Complete bombing pause		
:. 31–Jan. 2: Complete bombing pause	Dec. 31: 485,600	4,478

event of the year was the March on the Pentagon in October, the turning point for the Johnson administration emotionally and politically.

With public support for Johnson's conduct of the war fading rapidly and the opposition becoming bolder and more audacious, the president fought back by unleashing his intelligence agencies and, especially, by overselling the modest gains that his military commanders claimed to be making. This overselling of the war's progress played a major role in creating the domestic crisis produced by the Tet Offensive in early 1968. Although the marchers were unable to levitate the besieged Pentagon, their activities, as well as the activities of their supporters and antiwar critics around the country, ultimately contributed to the redirection of American policy in Vietnam in 1968—and the destruction of the presidency of Lyndon Johnson.

The distinguished *New York Times* journalist Harrison Salisbury visited Hanoi from December 23, 1966, to January 7. His unprecedented reports from an enemy capital in wartime provided a dramatic shot in the arm to an antiwar movement, which had been treading water since the Fulbright hearings almost a year earlier.

Critics had denounced the bombing policy, which, they claimed, caused massive civilian loss of life. Now, writing in America's most prestigious newspaper, Salisbury apparently confirmed their charges with accounts of destruction to dwellings, schools, and hospitals in the North Vietnamese capital. Administration claims that it employed only "smart bombs" and "surgical strikes" were damaged amid the stories and pictures of rubble and ruin in Hanoi.

Salisbury considered his reportage to be an effective antiwar action.[1] Paul Warnke remembers the trip causing "quite an impact," especially on McNamara. Warnke also points out that Salisbury's accounts were reinforced by journalists Harry Ashmore and William Baggs, who visited Hanoi during the same period.[2] Assistant Secretary of Defense Phil Goulding, who referred to a "traumatic" reaction in the White House, regretted that the president did not immediately explain how it was possible for a few accidents to happen, given Hanoi's topography, antiaircraft fire, and the way civilian structures abutted military facilities. Goulding felt the administration "bungled" the issue and created "a national disaster."[3]

William Bundy thinks that the reaction to the Salisbury stories in the United States might have finally convinced Hanoi that dissent could affect White House strategies; the North Vietnamese were "heartened" by the controversy Salisbury's series spawned. His evaluation of the stories as a turning point is reinforced by journalists David Kraslow and Stuart Loory, who reported that Hanoi, reeling under American escalation in 1966, might have been ready for more serious peace talks had it not been for the blow that the White House took from the *Times* feature.[4]

The president responded briefly in public to Salisbury's charges on December 31. The next day, Dean Rusk told a "Face the Nation" television audience that Hanoi was relying on dissent here to undermine the American war effort. He urged protesters to demand concessions from Hanoi as well as from Washington.[5]

Salisbury himself became a popular speaker at antiwar gatherings over the weeks following his series in the *Times*. In general, he found support for his perspective as he traveled around the country.[6] Needless to say, he was excoriated in private by the White House. Upon seeing him, one official allegedly said, "Here comes the man from the *Hanoi Times*." Rusk met with the journalist to lecture him on the damage he had done to his country. Following the cool conversation, the secretary called the influential *Times* columnist C. L. Sulzberger to express his displeasure. Some months later, after the Pulitzer Prize advisory board overruled its selection committee's recommendation of Salisbury for an award, few doubted that the administration played a behind-the-scenes role.[7]

Hanoi stepped up its propaganda attacks against the bombing in the wake of the Salisbury exposé. We will talk peace, they maintained, as soon as the bombing of our women and children stops. The administration met that argument with a demand for specific military concessions before it would ground the planes.

The week between Christmas and New Year's was not a good one for the administration. Liberal political organizer Allard Lowenstein masterminded a campaign that produced an open letter to Johnson from over one hundred college student-body presidents and editors. In a civil and well-reasoned presentation, the young leaders questioned the basis of American policy in Vietnam. The letter made front-page news in the *New York Times*.[8]

Always nervous about elite dissent on the campuses, Harry McPherson urged Johnson to reason with the students, to offer them a low-key response, since they were not "wild men of the new left."[9] Johnson left it to Rusk to offer the initial response, a long, historical analysis of American policies and goals in Southeast Asia. At the end of January, the secretary met with forty-four student leaders to explain further his position. Johnson himself did not meet with them.[10]

In addition to the exchange with the student presidents and editors, the White House received other protests from academia. Another long series of advertisements was published in the *Times*, with 462 Yale faculty calling for an end to the bombing on January 15 and 239 Cornell professors offering a comparable petition on January 30. On January 26, fifty Rhodes scholars publicly queried the Johnson policies. All of this activity in January was topped off by a day of fasting on February 1 that may have involved as many as one million people nationwide.[11]

As had been the case in the past, the flurry of bad public relations beginning with the Salisbury story and including leaks about botched peace proposals, as well as the protests from the universities, contributed to pressures on Johnson to produce yet another peace gesture. On February 2, he wrote directly to Ho about negotiations. Delivered to North Vietnamese representatives in Paris on February 8, Johnson's letter announced that he was "prepared to order a cessation of the bombing . . . as soon as I am assured that infiltration into South Vietnam . . . has stopped." Hanoi was given three days to respond during a truce period from February 10 to 13. The president knew that Ho's position on an unconditional cessation of the bombing was a firm one. On February 15, the North Vietnamese leader rejected the proposal.[12] Further, Ho violated what the president thought was diplomatic etiquette by going public with his rejection. Did Johnson make the gesture for the record to mollify, perhaps not the peace movement, but those who were being affected by the antibombing propaganda campaign? The suddenness with which he reacted and the likelihood that Ho would not find his gesture acceptable suggest as much.

The Salisbury sensation did not have as lasting an impact as Johnson's break with Robert Kennedy over Vietnam policy. Reports of their acrimonious meeting on February 6 became public in *Time* magazine in March. For the president, the defection of the Kennedys and their supporters, whom he had not trusted for years, augured ill for him and the party in 1968. According to Kennedy partisan Arthur Schlesinger, Jr., Johnson was paranoid about the threat from Robert Kennedy. Perhaps he had good reason to be paranoid. Kennedy people had been meeting on and off with Democratic leaders throughout 1966, testing the waters for a Dump Johnson movement. John Roche is proud to report that he got Pierre Salinger tipsy on a transcontinental flight that year and then wormed out of the former press secretary details of the secret strategy sessions, which he duly revealed to Johnson.[13]

Until the revelation of the February meeting, Robert Kennedy had been a mild critic of Vietnam policy in public. At that meeting, after listening to his suggestions for moving negotiations along, Johnson allegedly lectured Kennedy, "If you keep talking like this, you won't have a political future in this country within six months. In six months all you doves will be destroyed. The blood of American boys will be on your hands."[14] Several weeks after the meeting, Kennedy publicly called for an unconditional bombing halt. His differences with the administration on this issue encouraged Kennedy supporters, middle-class opponents of the war, liberal Democrats, and perhaps the North Vietnamese, who had an added inducement to fight it out at least until November 1968.[15]

As if Johnson did not have enough political problems, the nation's most respected civil rights leader, Dr. Martin Luther King, Jr., who had heretofore been only a guarded critic of America's Vietnam policy, broke with Johnson in speeches in March and April. His celebrated dovish statements fused elements of the civil rights and antiwar movements.

On March 23, King made front-page headlines when he spoke out strongly against Johnson's policies in Vietnam. Two days later, he led five thousand protesters in Chicago in a demonstration. On April 4, he became co-chair of Clergy and Laymen Concerned about Vietnam. Later that month, along with Democratic activist Joseph Rauh, King organized a new antiwar group and campaign, Negotiation Now!, and then associated himself with the student-run Vietnam Summer at Cambridge.[16]

The highlight of those April activities was his appearance at a massive New York rally on April 15, part of the Spring Mobilization demonstrations, along with black activists Harry Belafonte, Floyd McKissick, and Stokely Carmichael. The civil rights movement had become linked to the antiwar movement. The *New York Times* reported a crowd of a hundred thousand, whereas organizers claimed at least four times that. A crowd of fifty thousand in San Francisco's Kezar Stadium heard Coretta Scott King and Julian Bond attack American policy on that same day. It was at these rallies that the first pro-Ho signs appeared en masse.[17]

Johnson was very distressed about King's dramatic entry into the leadership ranks of the antiwar movement, especially given what he perceived to be his administration's ultraprogressive record on civil rights.[18] Pro-Johnson black leaders had cautioned King about challenging the president on Vietnam, hinting at political and financial retribution if he went too far. One bit of political retribution involved an anti-King offensive launched by George Christian, who leaked information about the civil rights leader's "communist" aides to conservative black columnist, Carl Rowan. The president read the FBI reports about the April 15 demonstration and took note of the rumors of a King-Spock ticket in 1968. Although black aide Clifford Alexander assured him of mainstream black support, Johnson had to be uneasy about the charismatic King's activities in April.[19]

Alexander's comforting reports were matched by those from other official cheerleaders who told the president what he wanted to hear: the critics were in the minority and the people, overall, supported their president. The ever-optimistic Hubert Humphrey, reporting in mid-April on a moderate Norman Cousins article in the *New York Times*, noted: "Some of our effort that we are making to get the more sensible members of the peace groups to take a look at the position of Hanoi is beginning to pay off." William Bundy chimed in with his May 9 report that the " 'dove reaction' to the April program of increased bombing has not been too serious." That this may have been merely the case of the messenger being unwilling to bring the bad news to the king can be seen in Bundy's retrospective oral history when he recalled a troubling increase in protests during this period.[20]

Another indication of the growth of the antiwar movement in the spring of 1967 can be seen in an intensified public relations campaign to counter naysayers and nervous nellies. On April 20, Harry McPherson suggested that the White House unofficially support a committee that planned to send encouraging telegrams to soldiers in Vietnam. McPherson thought that the administration might be able to obtain the aid of former presidents Truman and Eisenhower in the venture. Similarly, the White House assisted the organizers of the "Support our Boys in Vietnam" parade in New York on May 13. That assistance for organizer Charles Wiley involved liaison with congressional and labor leaders. According to the *New York Times*, the parade drew seventy thousand flag-waving supporters of "our boys." In addition, the day before, the *Times* ran an effective ad associated with the parade that juxtaposed pictures of dead American servicemen with scruffy-looking demonstrators.[21]

The telegram-writing scheme evolved into the most important White House support group of the war, the National Committee for Peace with Freedom in Vietnam, headed by former Senator Paul Douglas. John Roche was the main figure in the White House working with committee organizers, along with the interdepartmental coordinating body, the Vietnam Information Group (VIG). The committee originally used the term "the Silent Center" to attract inactive moderates. It was later stolen, according to Roche, by Nixon for his more successful appeal to "the Silent Majority."[22]

The campaign's centerpiece was to be the honorary co-chairmanship of Truman and Eisenhower. Although both presidents supported Johnson, getting them to work together was not easy, especially when it came to the feisty Truman. Truman was not very fond of Douglas and also feared that Eisenhower would get most of the attendant publicity. Ultimately, Roche, working with McPherson and long-time Johnson political adviser James Rowe, played important behind-the-scenes roles in organizing the committee.[23] Roche, who says he just "got the ball rolling," sees nothing wrong with his activities. The president, he feels, was entitled to the same sort of freedom that his critics enjoyed, and thus administration activities in support of his allies were consonant with the operation of a free give-and-take in a democratic society. Of course, he did not boast about such activities at the time; he assured the president, "I will leave no tracks" to the White House in his work with Douglas.[24]

Roche was pleased when the committee, chaired by Truman and Eisenhower, was formally introduced on October 16 with a news release and, then, with an impressive advertisement in the *New York Times* on October 26. The head of the USIA, Leonard Marks, felt that the formation of the committee served as a signal to Hanoi and Peking that Americans really did stand behind their president. For his part, Rowe gloated to Johnson, "You will be interested to know that at least two Harvard professors will be on the Committee."[25]

One prominent supporter of American involvement in Vietnam, Richard Nixon, did not lend his name to the committee. He had been advised by an aide to steer clear of the organization because it did not reflect American public sentiment.[26] The events of the next few months, at home and in Vietnam, suggest that the prescient aide was correct in his advice to candidate Nixon.

Along with the support groups came a constant verbal barrage from the administration warning Hanoi that Americans, by and large, approved of administration policies in Vietnam. Appearing on "Meet the Press" immediately following the New York antiwar demonstration in April, Dean Rusk downplayed the size of the crowds and once again expressed concern "that the authorities in Hanoi may misunderstand this sort of thing and that the net effect will be to prolong the war and not to shorten it." He also called attention to communist support for such demonstrations, a theme that appeared more frequently in 1967. For example, in another television appearance the next month, he talked about "highly organized demonstrations of minorities here and there in the country." Highly organized could be a euphemism for communist. To this day, Rusk is convinced that the movement was responsible for lengthening the war, and also that subversive forces were influential in its ranks.[27] During the summer, John Gronouski, ambassador to Poland, offered a variation on this theme when he referred in a Madison, Wisconsin, speech to intellectuals in the

United States: "There seems to be just one position —prefabricated, offered inviolate, and all too often followed by rote."[28]

The extent of communist or subversive influence in the antiwar movement is a complicated issue. The FBI, and to some degree the CIA, suspected that antiwar leaders accepted money and guidance from unfriendly governments. Nevertheless, it was the White House, in most cases, that pressed the intelligence agencies to discover the links between the movement and subversive elements and foreign governments. Obviously, proof of those links would help undermine the growing middle-class support for antiwar activities. In addition, it is likely that even without that political motivation, Johnson did believe in the conspiracy explanation for dissent. After all, how else to explain the often excellent organization and leadership of presumably ad hoc, grass-roots campaigns?

Small, left-wing groups such as the Socialist Workers Party (SWP) and the Socialist Labor Party (SLP) did play disproportionately important roles in planning many of the largest demonstrations. They enjoyed the advantage of being among the few experienced cadres in amorphous, impermanent antiwar coalitions. But the SLP, SWP, and other groups were not foreign directed.[29]

J. Edgar Hoover believed that the movement was unpatriotic and subversive in the most general sense, and his obsession with the hippies, yippies, and reds fed into Johnson's developing obsession.[30] As usual, Hoover operated independently of his titular chiefs, Attorneys General Kennedy and Clark. The key liaison between Hoover and Johnson was Cartha DeLoach, who did not have to go through Justice to obtain access to the Oval Office.[31] The FBI director and his agents worked diligently to provide Johnson with what he wanted to hear.[32]

This was not exactly a new development. At Franklin Roosevelt's request, the FBI searched for Nazi influences in the isolationist America First Committee in 1941. To Roosevelt's chagrin, the Bureau was unable to find much of substance that the president could use.[33] Johnson would be similarly disappointed.

In April 1965, just as the antiwar movement was getting off the ground, Hoover met with Johnson at the White House to discuss organized domestic opposition to his policies in Vietnam. The director reported that the president had "no doubt" that communists were behind the antiwar movement. Hoover agreed, pointing to the early organizing role played by SDS. When he issued one of his first formal reports on the movement several weeks later, he repeated what Johnson wanted to hear—communists were indeed involved in the demonstrations.[34]

In May, the FBI was requested to prepare a full-scale report on SDS, a request that was followed by, among other things, name checks on dovish telegram and letter writers, reports on SANE, journalists Joseph Kraft and Peter Arnett, and even the monitoring of the February 1966 Fulbright hearings to see how closely senators' lines matched those of the Communist party.[35] The FBI eagerly complied with White House requests, as for example on June 4, 1965, when agents ran name checks on selected critical artists and intellectuals, including Hannah Arendt.[36]

The administration was most concerned with intelligence gathering, not the disruption of New Left and antiwar activities. The latter sort of "dirty tricks," as they came to be called in the Nixon administration, originated in the Bureau, although operatives knew that the Johnson White House was not adverse to some of them.[37]

The Rockefeller Commission Report on intelligence, however, does conclude that the CIA's "Operation Chaos," which included dirty tricks, was developed, in part, because of "continuing and insistent requests" from the White House.[38] Even before the establishment of Operation Chaos in August 1967, the CIA had begun to infiltrate dissident groups in the capital, allegedly because of concern about the protection of CIA and other government installations. In February 1967, for example, the CIA began to observe regularly and to infiltrate Women Strike for Peace, the Washington Peace Center, SANE, and CORE, and then, later, the National Mobilization Committee, the War Resisters League, and the Washington Mobilization for Peace. The Secret Service was similarly concerned, as evidenced by its agents' attendance at a meeting of only seventy people in May 1967 called by the Washington Ad Hoc Vietnam Draft Hearings Committee.[39]

The intelligence agencies, especially the FBI, did more than just observe and infiltrate. The overall goal of the FBI was to make it difficult for antiwar critics to receive a public hearing. Thus, agents sent phony letters to editors of major publications defaming the movement and movement leaders. It is interesting to note that the FBI assumed that a planted letter to the editor in *Life* in the fall of 1968 might have some impact on public opinion. FBI officials also leaked information to friendly journalists on the alleged subversive backgrounds of antiwar leaders, even to the extreme of revealing the communist background of the wife of a professor who was involved in Eugene McCarthy's campaign to unseat Lyndon Johnson.[40]

The Internal Revenue Service operated its own Special Service Staff (SSS), which was charged with investigating political organizations and activities. For example, the SSS was asked by the CIA to examine *Ramparts* magazine's tax situation, a request precipitated by the publication's exposé of the CIA's ties to the National Student Association.[41]

Ramsey Clark, whose Justice Department generally did not work closely with the FBI in domestic intelligence, established his own intelligence agency, the Interdivision Information Unit (IDIU), which was primarily involved in coordinating riot control efforts in the government. In general, Clark was protective of the civil liberties of dissenting groups, as reflected in his repeated refusals to authorize wiretaps of the National Mobilization Office in the spring of 1968 in conjunction with security for the upcoming Democratic convention.[42]

The energies expended by the intelligence agencies in monitoring dissenters and their organizations suggest again the growing importance of the antiwar movement. The attempts to disrupt and harass, generally not at the *direct* behest of the White House, reveal the fear that Johnson and his advisers had of the power of the movement.

On the other hand, if the president and his aides could convince themselves that the antiwar movement was subversive, they might be able to dismiss it as unrepresentative of American opinion. Robert Kintner prodded the attorney general to investigate the movement because the demonstrations were so "well planned" and involved "in many cases the same people." Or similarly, when Fred Panzer, another White House operative, told the president about the similarity of tactics described in the publication *New Left Notes* with those actually used in demonstrations against

Arthur Goldberg at Harvard and Hubert Humphrey clear across the country at Stanford, the notion of a small conspiracy was reinforced.[43]

At bottom, it is difficult to determine the motives behind the exhaustive search for common tactics, leadership, and foreign and left-wing influences in the antiwar movement. It may have reflected a serious belief on the part of Johnson and his colleagues that the movement was something that could be ignored because dissenters were either dupes or subversives. Just as plausibly, it may have reflected an attempt to defame and smear a potent political enemy. The truth probably involves a combination of both motives.

Other evidence in the spring and summer suggests that the administration did consider public opinion, irrespective of alleged subversive activities of antiwar critics, to be more and more the key variable in Vietnam strategies in Washington and especially Hanoi. Alain Enthoven, of the Defense Department's Systems Analysis Office, reported in late April that Ho was waiting patiently for dissent at home and anti-American international opinion to drive the United States out of Vietnam. In addition, he warned, increasing the troop levels would arouse even more adverse opinion among Americans. Consequently, Enthoven advised McNamara on May 1 that the United States had to build a strong South Vietnam before domestic pressures pushed American forces out of Southeast Asia. Unfortunately, Hanoi was well aware of the problem and the American race against the clock.[44]

More significant in terms of the source was Assistant Secretary of Defense John McNaughton's analysis later that month that underscored the growing unpopularity of the war, especially among the youth, the underprivileged, the intelligentsia, and women. Even more ominous for him was the absence of dissenting opinion within the White House as those who disagreed with the president quietly left government service. "Mac Bundy, George Ball, Bill Moyers are gone. Who's next?" Like Enthoven, McNaughton feared that massive call-ups would result in more dramatic protests from the doves, including more militant draft resistance. That development could be followed by reaction from the Right and demands for escalation. McNaughton saw in this scenario dangers of intervention from the Soviet Union and China. The joint chiefs, however, who did not buy McNaughton's line, tended to downplay domestic problems at this juncture.[45]

Other advisers agreed with McNaughton. John Roche, although not impressed by the movement, told the president on March 27 that Ho was counting on public opinion, especially America's traditional isolationism. Walt Rostow confided to Richard Whalen during the same period that the war in Vietnam, since 1966, had been about American politics, with Hanoi's military losses balanced by Johnson's decline in public opinion. The president himself some months later acknowledged that Ho believes "our will is weakening."[46]

McNaughton's question "Who's next?" referring to officials falling off the Vietnam policy bandwagon, might have best been applied to his boss, Secretary of Defense McNamara. Never an enthusiastic supporter of the bombing policy, especially considering the fact that it apparently was not working, McNamara had been moving away from official policy for more than a year. He had been shattered by his Harvard experience, distressed by the defection of the Kennedys, and moved by Jonathan Schell's *New Yorker* piece of July 15, 1967, on the village of Ben Suc.[47]

The end for McNamara may have been reached in August, when he testified on the effectiveness of the bombing program before Senator John Stennis's Armed Services Committee. Opposing escalation, McNamara testified as a moderate or even a dove who thought the political costs of increasing the bombing outweighed its dubious strategic value. He refers to his appearance on August 25, 1967, before an executive session of the committee as "quite an ordeal."[48] His clash with the more hawkish members of the committee weakened his position in the government, especially considering the power and influence of Senators Stennis and Russell. It also revealed that the president still had much to fear from the Right, even though dovish senators and their supporters received more media attention.

One exception was the more obscure hearings of the Senate Foreign Relations Committee held during the same month and virtually ignored by the media. Senator Fulbright's National Commitments Resolution, a resolution that would have restricted the president's ability to send troops into combat, received its first hearing during August. Johnson ally and friend Richard Russell supported the idea in general on the floor of the Senate. Although invited to testify, Dean Rusk refused and sent Deputy Secretary of State Katzenbach in his stead. From the Fulbright hearings of early 1966 until January 1968, Rusk ducked all invitations to appear on Capitol Hill.[49]

The activity in the Senate in August reflected a national concern with the way the war was going, as more and more critics on the Right and the Left reported to their respective constituencies that the United States was not winning the war. Johnson spent a good deal of time with media representatives that summer trying to explain how well American military strategies were working in Vietnam. At one luncheon meeting with his chief aides at which he outlined his personal campaign to enlighten journalists about American battlefield successes, "the President said he cites these reports, some of which are so optimistic that he believes Komer must be writing them. But . . . we have no songs, no parades, no bond drives, etc., and . . . we can't win the war otherwise." And it was not just the doves who were pressuring him. Republican hawk Senator Everett Dirksen told Johnson that he was worried about his mail "saying someone in Washington is putting the reins on the military commanders."[50]

Two weeks later, at another luncheon session, Rusk talked about his correcting *New York Times* columnist Tom Wicker's reportage on Vietnam and revealed that the editors of *Time-Life* were considering an editorial shift away from support for the American military effort in Vietnam. The president made arrangements to give them and other editors and publishers access to top American military commanders so that they could appreciate the extent of the progress in Vietnam.[51]

The campaign to accentuate the positive in reports of military success is central to an understanding of the shock experienced by Americans when the first news and film footage of the 1968 Tet Offensive reached the media. As opposition to administration policy grew from 1966 through 1967, the military in Vietnam was under pressure to demonstrate that the increasingly costly effort was paying dividends.

This pressure on the military not only to win in Southeast Asia but also in Congress and the media led to the order-of-battle controversy that reached its denouement in the celebrated Westmoreland versus CBS lawsuit of 1984–85. The testimony in that suit sheds light on the impact of the antiwar movement, or at least the importance of dissenting opinion in the United States during the last two years of the Johnson presidency.

In the fall of 1966, CIA analysts began to question the Pentagon's estimates of total enemy strength.[52] Over the next year, the battle of the estimates raged with CIA operatives in the field and in Washington challenging General Westmoreland's lower figures by a factor of as much as 50 percent. Who was correct is not important here. The rationale often given for accepting the lower estimates, however, is, since it illustrates the serious concern felt by MACV and Washington about public opinion.

The affidavits filed by the defense for CBS to meet the libel charges of General Westmoreland against the 1982 CBS Report titled "The Uncounted Enemy: A Vietnam Deception" reveal the military's felt need to present optimistic reports to Washington. For example, army colonel Elmer Martin states that "General Westmoreland was under tremendous political pressure to demonstrate progress in the war effort." Another officer, Donald Blascak, who monitored a call from Walt Rostow to George W. Allen of the CIA, remembers Rostow saying in 1967, "The president needs your help. He is depressed about progress being made in the Vietnam War and needs encouraging news." CIA analyst Ronald C. Smith felt that Johnson was having problems with "resolve at home" in 1967 and to have raised estimates of enemy forces "would have been a source of extreme embarrassment to the Johnson administration." Finally, Colonel John Barrie Williams directly alludes to the movement: "as the antiwar movement grew there was growing need to demonstrate success."[53]

Westmoreland agrees that "public opinion did play quite a major role in the course of that war," although he denies that it ever affected his order-of-battle figures. Several of his closest aides disagree with his disclaimer. General Joseph McChristian remembers when he advised Westmoreland to send new and higher estimates, in May 1967, the general responded, "If I send this cable to Washington, it will create a political bombshell." Another aide,

Captain Kelly Robinson, recalls Westmoreland wondering out loud over and over how the public and press, especially the *New York Times*, would react to an upward change in the estimates.[54]

McNamara denies categorically that he or his staff were under instructions to accept the more positive estimates from the field. More important, he claims that he knew full well about the order-of-battle controversy and treated it as an apolitical dispute between two well-meaning rival intelligence agencies.[55] Even if this was the case, one variable in the army's ultimate decision to stick to its original estimates was the difficulty in explaining the change, and the apparent lack of progress, to the American people.

If the military was compelled to place the most optimistic interpretation on operations because of the fear that the public, influenced to some degree by the antiwar movement, would not support an apparently endless war, then the movement did play a most important role in Vietnam policies in 1967. The false light at the end of the tunnel perceived by the military and described to Johnson and his aides made it all the more difficult for them to explain how it was that a reeling Viet Cong was able to penetrate into the Saigon embassy compound in early February 1968.

Pressures on the military from domestic critics increased in October, when the single most impressive peace demonstration to date, the March on the Pentagon, took place. According to Ramsey Clark, it was "the moment that the fever broke in the whole antiwar movement." He did not mean that it represented a major turning point for policymakers, although, as we shall see, it might have, but that it was a catalytic event for the rest of the nation. The March on the Pentagon, from Clark's perspective, "energized antiwar forces and spelled the beginning of the end for American involvement in the war" in Southeast Asia.[56]

The march came after an eventful late spring and summer during which protesters and riots dominated much of the news. On the antiwar front, May saw the formation of the Business Executives Move for Peace and Bertrand Russell's anti-administration War Crimes Trial in Stockholm. The following month, heavyweight boxing champion Muhammad Ali was sentenced to jail for his celebrated draft resistance. That summer, Captain Howard Levy's trial began. Levy was an army doctor who refused to train men destined for Vietnam. On the political front, dissident Democrats met in Chicago at the National Conference for New Politics in September. Even more troubling to the administration were the riots in the ghettos of Newark and Detroit. The Detroit uprising was an especially shocking event in a summer full of such events. The final shocking event of 1967 would be the March on the Pentagon.

March organizers expected that their October demonstration would be a large one. Given the prior success of the Spring Mobilization in New York, they talked of bringing hundreds of thousands, perhaps even one million, demonstrators to Washington.[57] As they made their preparations, they were carefully monitored by the FBI and other intelligence agencies.[58]

Serious White House "defense" planning began at a September 20 meeting attended by Clark, McNamara, Katzenbach, and Interior Secretary Stuart Udall, among others. The attorney general reported that New York march organizers were trying to rent 1,000 buses for their event, but would most likely end up with only 150. In addition, although organizers predicted a crowd in excess of 200,000, the FBI estimated that only 40 to 50,000 would eventually show up in Washington. Some present at the September 20 meeting suggested that the president make arrangements to be out of town that weekend in order to limit the potential for violence around the White House.[59]

Johnson's September 29 speech in San Antonio, Texas, outlining the American negotiating position, was presented in part with an eye to opinion and the upcoming demonstration. The San Antonio formula, America's basic negotiating position through the next few months, offered a cessation of the bombing without a demand for *formal* concessions from North Vietnam. In exchange for this unilateral concession, Johnson assumed that productive discussions would commence quickly and that the communists would not engage in any buildups during the cessation period. Tucked in the generally conciliatory message was another warning to Hanoi not to "mistake dissent for disloyalty" and that they should "not think that protests will produce surrender." Johnson was pleased with the initial public response to his speech, which produced 105 favorable telegrams to the White House to only 47 unfavorable ones.[60] It is again interesting to see how few telegrams, in a nation of millions of potential correspondents, could attract the attention of the president and his aides as reflecting some sort of meaningful public opinion.

Johnson did realize that the San Antonio speech would not stop the marchers from invading Washington. He evinced concern about their potential impact, as demonstrated in his October 3 memo: "I want some kind of report from him [Clark] or Mr. [Warren] Christopher, his Deputy, on the progress and what they are doing on the demonstration, together with new FBI information. Have in my office before 8:00 P.M." The next day, at a cabinet meeting, Clark presented what he and the FBI knew up to that date and then outlined government strategy to contain the political damage. Estimates of the size of the demonstration ranged as high as a hundred thousand, although attempts were being made to "create other diversionary events on the day and night of March."

Johnson then asked: "Who are the sponsoring groups? Pacifists? Communists?"

CLARK: "They are a combination of both. There is a heavy representation of extreme left wing groups with long lines of Communist affiliations. . . . They are doing all they can to encourage the March."

JOHNSON: "Is this a secret?"

CLARK: "No."

RUSK: "Wouldn't it help to leak that?"

JOHN GARDNER: "The people have got to know that . . . they must know that!"

(Strong vocal agreement from the Cabinet.)

CLARK: "The fact of Communist involvement and encouragement has been given to some columnists."

JOHNSON: "Let's see some more."

McNamara then reported that he had over twenty-five thousand troops available to protect the capital. Clearly, with that show of force, the government would be ready for all eventualities. The only eventuality not planned for, perhaps on purpose, was bathrooms. When Dean Rusk discovered that Clark was doing little to aid in "port-a-john" procurement, he feared for the State Department's facilities: "that means that they'll all be on top of us . . . we're the closest to them."

An exasperated Johnson closed the discussion with: "It is time that the Administration stopped setting back and taking it from the Vietnam critics." Rusk chimed in, claiming that some critics were "practicing a gross fraud on the American people."[61]

Rusk struck back on October 12 at a news conference with one of his favorite lines of attack, the antiwar intellectuals don't know anything about international relations. He lambasted those "who know about enzymes" but are uninformed about Southeast Asia. Johnson stressed the same theme when writing to thank Harvard historian Oscar Handlin for his support, remarking that "much of the academic opposition to the war in Vietnam has struck me as irrational rather than rational, as anti-intellectual rather than intellectual."[62]

The leaks to the press defaming the alleged communist leadership of the march may have created new pressures from people like Congressman Carl Albert and Senator John Stennis for Johnson to crack down on the subversives. Similarly, Selective Service director Lewis Hershey demanded that the Justice Department bring charges against draft impeders Dr. Benjamin Spock and the Reverend William Sloane Coffin.[63]

With a week to go before the march, an anxious Johnson was assured by Joseph Califano, his liaison with the Defense Department, that all was in readiness for the twenty-five to fifty thousand expected. The White House and the Pentagon were well defended. Further, the material that had been leaked to the media about the number of communists in the demonstration "should discourage many less extreme antiwar sympathizers from attending."[64]

As for the rumored mass draft card burning, Johnson prepared to prosecute to the fullest extent of the law to squelch this potentially dangerous development. He ordered Clark to "inform me promptly" about the burnings, and, on copies to Hoover and Hershey, Johnson noted, "I want you to be personally responsible for keeping me informed on this."[65]

Thus, the administration dug in for a long and dramatic weekend of protests, some uncivil disobedience, and numerous arrests. As usual, estimates of the size of the crowd on October 21 varied, with the organizers claiming well in excess of a hundred thousand participants and the administration fewer than fifty thousand.[66] There was no disagreement about the major events of the demonstration, with the first, peaceful series of speeches and musical presentations taking place at the Lincoln Memorial. Then many of the participants marched to the Pentagon, where some tried to levitate the building while others challenged the soldiers guarding the command center of the American military establishment. For most Americans, the events that weekend were probably symbolized by television images of dirty-mouthed hippies taunting the brave, clean-cut American soldiers who confronted the unruly demonstrators. Given the relatively small size of the demonstration and the unpleasant image of hippies versus soldiers, the March on the Pentagon should have been made into a propaganda victory for the Johnson administration. It was not.

James Reston's lead story on page one of the *Times* was characteristic of much of the coverage. Titled "Everyone Is a Loser," his account dwelt on the violence and ugly incidents at the Pentagon. Editorially, the *Times* did note that there were two demonstrations, with the largest at the Lincoln Memorial very peaceful. *Time* was also impressed with the Lincoln Memorial gathering, but referred in a headline of its cover story to "Nudism and Napalm" and lavished attention on a loutish, drunken Norman Mailer. Further, the newsweekly's staff estimated a crowd of only thirty-five thousand at the Pentagon. *Newsweek* also made fun of the violent hippies and Norman Mailer. Even the liberal *Nation*, in its favorable account, tended to emphasize the Pentagon activities in "Bastille Day on the Potomac." Robert Sherrill, the author of the *Nation* piece, did, however, take the media to task for their unbalanced coverage.[67]

The networks' approach to the march assisted the administration. With CBS in the lead, they decided not to devote large amounts of time to the Washington events; as was becoming common, only the most sensational activities were stressed.[68] It is possible that the wilder the activities, the more civic leaders worried about the alienation of youth. At least, that is how movement leader Tom Hayden interprets such media coverage and its impact.[69]

To be sure, most of the organizers of the demonstration tried then to disassociate themselves from the Pentagon activities and claimed that the Lincoln Memorial gathering was the significant and representative affair of the weekend.[70] According to one White House adviser in a memo titled "Keeping the Doves on the Hook," the doves had been successful in getting that point across to David Brinkley on his October 23 NBC television newscast.[71] But even if Brinkley was convinced, the vast majority of Americans had to be shocked by the Pentagon protests, which dominated most accounts of the Washington demonstration.

Reaction within the administration varied. Johnson and his aides were well prepared for almost anything that weekend. They certainly paid careful attention to both the activities of the demonstrators and how the media framed them. When it was over, one official suggested that they went overboard in security protection for the White House. Demonstration control cost the government in excess of $1.4 million.[72]

On Sunday, October 22, after having attended church, the Johnsons and daughter Lynda drove around the Lincoln Memorial because the president was "interested in what a hippie looked like." One wonders if he knew the difference between hippies and more politically involved demonstrators or whether he confused them on purpose, as many movement critics did. In any event, Mrs. Johnson was shocked by the litter around the memorial, a clear affront to her campaign to beautify America.[73]

The president was also informed that the local demonstration was paralleled by protests in London, Paris, and Berlin, among other world capitals. According to the head of the USIA, they produced the "worst riots in memory."[74] Reports such as these reinforced Johnson's notion that internationally organized subversives were at the roots of the American antiwar movement.

Looking back at the major demonstration of the period, many key officials either do not remember it well or consider it only one of many such demonstrations.[75] Nevertheless, those hazy recollections must be evaluated because the administration's response at the time was to deny that the Washington gathering even captured much of its attention. To estimate the march's impact on resolve, morale, and policy, one must sift through the retrospective comments with care to discern a pattern.

When interviewed in 1984, Senator Fulbright could recall nothing at all about the March on the Pentagon. Although especially interested in such things, Harry McPherson remembers it only vaguely as just another big demonstration similar to the ones following the Columbia University riot and the death of Martin

Luther King in 1968. For him, the entire period from the spring of 1967 through the spring of 1968 was just one long period of disturbances, "a dog's breakfast"; a revolutionary era with the Pentagon, Tet, Ché Guevera, the Chicago Convention, urban riots, and Paris all blending into one turbulent time.[76]

Clark Clifford, who walked over to the White House from his office on Connecticut Avenue three or four times during the week of the Pentagon march, does not remember it having much impact on the president. The more gentle, moving, candlelight-type marches stick out in his memory. The bigger disorderly demonstrations were too extreme, not representative of the American people. Dean Rusk, who does remember it, claims that the Pentagon march was "not all that cataclysmic," although it was "troublesome." He does admit to being "annoyed" by some activities, especially the dumping of excrement on American soldiers. Walt Rostow recalls spending the afternoon of the march engaged in business as usual as he, the president, and Indian diplomat B. K. Nehru discussed agricultural projects. They had little time that day to devote to reports on the demonstrations.[77]

This vagueness about the march and the downplaying of its impact is difficult to comprehend given one noted participant's celebrated memoir. Norman Mailer describes an electric, excited Washington on the eve of the demonstration. The streets were full of people late at night. "The air was violent, yet full of amusement, out of focus."[78]

Other key officials remember the march most clearly and attest to its power. The dovish Paul Warnke was "pleased" by the weekend's events in the main. The "remarkably good-humored" protest was a "healthy thing," well handled at the Pentagon by McNamara. There were no "mass incarcerations," nor did he remember much violence—the flowers in the gun barrels of the soldiers impressed him, as did the crowd of fifty thousand. He himself walked around the besieged Pentagon and did not feel at all threatened. As for the president, Warnke is certain that it affected him, especially when one realizes that Johnson, who "liked to be loved," was very sensitive to any criticism.[79]

Inside the Pentagon, Daniel Z. Henkin, the head of public relations for Defense, along with Warren Christopher from the Justice Department, were monitoring events. Henkin remembers trying to show the world that the Pentagon could not be closed down, even to the point of holding a most unusual Saturday morning meeting of the joint chiefs to demonstrate that the government was functioning. It was not, of course. Ultimately, Henkin felt that a few hundred rowdies at the Pentagon gave the administration a public relations "victory," something that saddened him, since he had compassion for the peaceful protesters. As for the crowds themselves, he was not impressed. It is easy, he maintains, to turn out fifty thousand or so demonstrators in Washington almost any weekend.[80]

The crowds may not have been impressive, but their unusual behavior was. McNamara, who carefully followed developments and who feared having to shoot at the demonstrators, told a reporter, "Christ, yes I was scared. . . . It was terrifying . . . a mess." Most distressing was the way civil disobedients forced their way into the Pentagon—the Pentagon could be taken with Ghandi-like tactics. Abbie Hoffman still revels in the impact worldwide of the besieging and breeching of the Pentagon.[81]

John Roche remembers it as "one hell of a demonstration." As a veteran organizer, he admired the way the young people put the entire thing together. Although Roche does not think the march ultimately affected policy, Johnson, who wanted all young people to love him, was "outraged." Ramsey Clark saw the affair as representing a "benevolent infection" of the population. And rather than being distressed, the former head of the Justice Department is now amused that demonstrators were able to penetrate the heavily guarded Pentagon.[82]

Former press secretary George Christian was very impressed with the march and, more important, sees it as a major turning point for the Johnson administration. Christian's recollections ring true. Despite all the advance planning, he and his colleagues were surprised by the size of the demonstration, although he admits that he "was always surprised by the magnitude of such events." He recalls a tense White House, the feeling of siege. At the least, remembers Christian's aide Tom Johnson, the march was "troubling" to the president, who monitored television news all weekend and was impressed with the number of people participating. In the weeks that followed, according to Christian, White House staffers began to look around for new jobs after 1968. For many, the March on the Pentagon marked the beginning of the end for the Johnson administration.[83]

One of those who soon found a new job was Robert S. McNamara. His drift away from administration policy had become obvious to many by the time of his Stennis committee appearance in August. It may not have been coincidental that the drift became a break at lunch on October 30, a week after his plant, the Pentagon, had been besieged.

On that occasion, the defense secretary made his first strong statement of disapproval of Vietnam policy. Convinced that the bombing was not working, disheartened by the youthful protests, including the most recent one, and influenced by his friends in the Kennedy (or as Roche refers to it, the Jacobite) camp, McNamara followed up his critique with a formal resignation on November 1.[84] Johnson accepted the resignation, which may have been requested, and announced that McNamara would soon be moving on to the presidency of the World Bank. Although the president was distressed over having lost McNamara's support, he rewarded him with the World Bank post for being a loyal soldier up to that point. McNamara was to stay on at Defense as a lame duck through February 1968.

He earlier had assured Henry Graff that antiwar opposition did not influence national security policy.[85] Whatever the direct cause, his relative dovishness became apparent, according to one source, as early as November 1965. Former Secretary of the Army Cyrus Vance traces it to early 1966. Certainly by the spring of 1967 the Defense Department had developed a dovish reputation, with many of McNamara's civilian aides a matter of concern to military men like Admiral Sharp. McNamara is a very complicated man who talked little in public about his resignation. From most accounts, he was overworked, perhaps even "burned out" by the fall of 1967. To George Christian he looked "completely frazzled." John Roche feels that the compassionate president was nervous about the state of McNamara's health and may have even worried about having another Forrestal on his hands.[86]

Antiwar activities, beginning with the Harvard incident the previous fall, had taken a personal toll on the sensitive, even emotional McNamara. He was widely targeted as the architect of the bombing, as a cold, unfeeling man who was "murdering"

North Vietnamese women and children. McNamara knew well the role that he played as a villain in the hawkish aviary. One Johnson aide evinced concern about the impact the announcement of his resignation might have at Harvard and other elite universities. They might interpret it as their victory.[87]

In a related vein, Leslie Gelb remembers that the march produced new attacks from the Right against moderates in the Defense Department. The Pentagon analyst saw the use of the violent hippies line as a "powerful tactic" of Johnson's supporters in the wake of the march.[88]

McNamara's resignation was not the only apparent fallout from the tumultuous October demonstration. In the weeks that followed, senators became bolder in their attacks against the president. Among those who issued strong statements in opposition to the Johnson policy were Case, Morton, Cooper, and Kennedy. After Representative Morris Udall questioned the policy, his mail ran forty to one in his favor. At the same time, Johnson's approval rating for his conduct of the war fell to a low of 28 percent.[89] The poll result was most likely related to the success of the antiwar movement in the fall of 1967, as well as to the growing concern that dissent was splitting the nation apart, as reflected in that unprecedented Pentagon confrontation.

The *Saturday Evening Post,* a conservative bellwether, might have been reacting to this latter issue when its editors criticized Johnson's handling of the war in its November 18 issue. That same month, former presidential aide Bill Moyers told the president that he had declined an invitation from Richard Goodwin, Arthur Schlesinger, Jr., and John Kenneth Galbraith to head up a new antiwar organization.[90] Finally, on the last day of November, Senator Eugene McCarthy threw his hat into the ring. The Minnesota backbencher would challenge his party leader and president in the upcoming primaries, almost exclusively on the war issue.[91]

Things did not improve for the president in December. David Halberstam published an article in *Harper's* December issue that was so effective an aide complained to Rostow, "I wish we had people on our side who could write like he does." The desertion of influential intellectuals was a serious problem. So important was the Halberstam piece that the administration prepared an official response to his charges.[92]

Nor was the cause helped by the well-publicized Bermuda Conference. On December 12, a group of moderate influential Americans, including Harding Bancroft of the *New York Times,* General Matthew Ridgway, and diplomats Charles Yost and Ernest Gross, drew up an unsolicited dovish series of recommendations to bring the war to a close.[93]

The president met this new round of criticism in a variety of ways. Most important, he called the Wise Men together on November 1 to consider the state of the war in Vietnam and at home. The distinguished group of foreign-policy influentials still supported the president.[94] According to Clark Clifford, had a vote been taken, it would have been 11.5 for Johnson and only 0.5 (George Ball) against him. Of course, this was a short series of meetings, hastily called, with the most superficial of briefings for the advisers. Abe Fortas, for example, after hearing a glowing review of success in Vietnam from the CIA's George Carver, commented that "the nation is totally unaware of this side of Vietnam conflict."[95] The Wise Men later remembered these positive reports from military and intelligence analysts when they met again in March in the wake of the Tet Offensive, an offensive that was impossible according to the November briefings.

The one area that troubled the Wise Men was the erosion of support for administration policy. All agreed that new efforts had to be made to inform the public of the progress made and the importance of Southeast Asia to national security.[96] William Bundy remembers a suggestion that called for a government truth ombudsman who might address the issue of the credibility gap. The assistant secretary of state obtained Rusk's approval to bring Edward Thompson, the recently retired editor of *Life,* to Washington, to vet all public statements emanating from the government concerning Vietnam. Bundy was particularly upset about the over-optimistic reports from the White House, especially the "hype" from Rostow's NSC. Just as Thompson was preparing to assume his responsibilities, Tet occurred and the plan was jettisoned. The editor stayed on in Washington, however, and founded the journal of the Smithsonian Institution.[97]

The prominence of the opinion variable in the deliberations is evident in Rostow's briefing memo to Johnson. He reported that discussion during the preliminary, prepresidential meetings of the Wise Men centered around two issues, domestic support and the bombing program. He advised Johnson to ask the Wise Men five questions on the morning of November 2, with the fifth being how to rally support for his policies. Following Rostow's suggestions, Johnson himself told his prestigious advisers that "he is deeply concerned about the deterioration of public support and the lack of editorial support for our policies. . . . So the question is how do we unite the country?"[98]

McGeorge Bundy served as rapporteur for Johnson. At the meeting he advised, "Don't let the communications people in New York set the tone of the debate. Emphasize the 'light at the end of the tunnel' instead of the battles, death and danger." In his summation of what had been accomplished, forwarded to the president on November 10, he noted that all agreed they had problems explaining the administration position to "doves and moderates." Bundy thought that Zbigniew Brzezinski, Katzenbach, or his brother might be good spokespersons to make clear that the administration wanted to negotiate and that Hanoi did not. Above all, Bundy noted, the president somehow had to take the lead in "a contest that is more political in its character than any in our history except the Civil War." The former national security adviser felt that "public discontent with the war is now wide and deep. One of the few things that helps us right now is public distaste for the violent doves—but I think people are really getting fed up with the endlessness of the fighting."[99]

The Wise Men's recommendations had immediate effect, evidenced at a Tuesday Lunch meeting of November 4 when Johnson asked Rusk, Wheeler, Helms, and McNamara to put together a task force to produce a brief pamphlet to answer the public's questions about Vietnam. He then inquired as to when Ambassador Bunker and General Westmoreland were returning to the States for consultations and speeches. Bunker was due on November 9 and Westmoreland on November 15. Their trips to Washington were part of the new propaganda campaign that was spurred by the increasing levels of dissent. Further, Johnson had not lost his interest in the campuses; he complained that "Senators Hartke, Fulbright and McCarthy are going to all the colleges and stirring up problems and we are not answering them." Johnson added a footnote: "Princeton got a resolution just yesterday." On a related theme, he stated, "I'm not going to let the Communists take this government and they're doing it right now." He had "been protecting civil liberties since he was nine years old but I told the Attorney General that I am not going to let 200,000 of these people ruin everything for the 200 million Americans. I've got my belly full of seeing these people put on a Communist plane and shipped all over this country."[100]

Johnson thus prepared his campaign on several fronts. He and his chief aides were going to take on the dissenters with a new round of positive reports on progress coupled with warnings, once again, to Hanoi to ignore the protesters and to the protesters, if they were patriotic, to think before they spoke.[101] In addition, he directed the intelligence agencies to find that elusive foreign link between the dissenters and the communists.

The first front was by far the most important. Here, the president overreacted to the call for a propaganda campaign and ignored Bundy's concern about "hype." At a press conference on November 17, Johnson offered a civil libertarian approach to dissent during wartime, beginning in 1775, but, he pointed out, presidents had always been proven correct. Although he understood the dissenters' position, it disturbed him since "this dissent has [not] contributed much to any victories we have had. . . . Please count to 10 before you say something that hurts instead of helps." In December, on a television program, "A Conversation with the President," he suggested that if the public got in line, Hanoi would be convinced that it could not win the war in American streets.[102]

Aside from media appearances, Johnson went on a speaking tour of military bases in November, places where he knew he would receive a warm reception.[103] The other two big guns in the cheerleading campaign were the experts from the scene, Bunker and Westmoreland. McPherson had suggested the campaign even before the March on the Pentagon, having concluded that the nation should be receiving the same sort of positive reports the president was receiving from the men in charge of operations in Vietnam. Bunker himself wrote to Rostow after the March on the Pentagon of the "overriding need to demonstrate our progress in grinding down the enemy."[104]

The elderly and rather bland ambassador did not cut quite the attractive figure of the handsome and more youthful general who was the star of the campaign. Westmoreland offered press briefings on November 11, 17, and 22, and delivered major policy statements on "Meet the Press" on November 19 and at the National Press Club on November 21. Over and over he assured Americans, as he told a television interviewer on November 16, that he was "very, very encouraged" and that we were "making real progress."[105]

Paul Warnke is convinced that Westmoreland came home primarily to combat domestic dissent. At the least, if he did come home for other reasons, he certainly was used for that purpose while he was here. At the same time, Warnke believes that Westmoreland did not dissemble—he really believed in his progress reports and felt that the nation had no real understanding of how many American goals had been achieved. Although some in the intelligence community did not agree with his rosy outlook, there was a genuine divergence of opinion on this issue.[106]

Dean Rusk sees many of the statements by Westmoreland, Bunker, Johnson, and himself in November and December as paralleling the approach taken by Franklin Roosevelt and his aides during the dark days of World War II in 1942. Rather than look at the defeats in Asia, Roosevelt emphasized the successes in an attempt to keep up morale. Clark Clifford agrees—there was a need to calm the public and to assure Americans that things were on course in Vietnam.[107]

Walt Rostow does not recall the general public being his primary concern in the fall of 1967. Irritated with the media, he thought the new propaganda campaign was directed to the networks and newsweeklies, which were not presenting an accurate picture of the war to their audiences. On the other hand, Congress, according to John Roche, was the primary target. He and his colleagues worried about the constant complaining from the Hill about constituent pressures to end the interminable war. In charge of Defense public relations, Daniel Henkin agrees with Roche, but is quick to point out that Westmoreland's activities were orchestrated by the White House. The Pentagon had little to do with them. It is true that McNamara had to warn Westmoreland about speaking out too harshly against dissent.[108]

Whatever the direct target, the "people" did receive very optimistic reports, especially from Westmoreland, a general from the field they could trust. He clearly "built up expectations" of victory.[109] The propaganda campaign of November and December came home to haunt the administration after the shock of the Tet Offensive. Those expectations of the fast-approaching light at the end of the tunnel were dashed as films of the attack on Saigon and most other southern strongholds hit the airwaves. Americans only three months before had been assured that the enemy was on the ropes. If so, how could he have launched what appeared at first to have been such a devastating and massive attack?[110]

If it is correct to link the reaction to Tet to the propaganda campaign of the previous fall, then antiwar critics surely affected the policy changes adopted in March 1968. That is, if Johnson had to oversell progress in order to defend himself against the growing antiwar movement, and if that overselling helped to explain American reluctance to believe reports of new "successes" in the weeks after Tet, then the antiwar movement enjoyed a signal victory on March 31, 1968, when Johnson began the process of American withdrawal from Vietnam.[111]

While Johnson, Westmoreland, and Bunker were traveling around the country on their ill-fated public relations campaign, the CIA and FBI went to work in their most intensive effort to date to investigate the links between unfriendly foreign powers and the movement. What made the situation a matter of national security was the impact of draft resistance and draft card burnings on the military. From his side of the barricades, David Dellinger was pleased to note that some of the higher brass were nervous about the unwillingness of their men to carry out orders and even alleged defections from those guarding the Pentagon on October 21. As for the draft card burnings, Johnson maintained a bold front before a group of congressional leaders on October 31. Of the 256 people who burned their cards that Saturday, according to Johnson, "a substantial number were crazy people who had previous history in mental institutions." Moreover, some of that 256 burned only photostats, not the real documents. Despite this apparent lack of concern, he also told the legislators that he "did not want to be like a McCarthyite, but this country is in a little more danger than we think and someone has to uncover this information."[112]

On a related subject during the same period, Joseph Califano worried about the president's inability to move around the country and speak freely to his constituents because of the increasingly violent demonstrators. He wondered whether there might not be an organized plan to keep Johnson from speaking. Warren Christopher from Justice began to examine legal ways to stop those who were violating the president's freedom of speech. Further, as early as December 16, Ramsey Clark informed Johnson about radicals' plans to disrupt both parties' conventions the following summer.[113]

National security adviser Walt Rostow, always disturbed about foreign influences in the antiwar movement, wrote to Johnson the day after the march about David Dellinger's "direct ties to Hanoi." In December, he forwarded to Johnson a MACV intelligence report from a captured member of the Viet Cong leadership in Bin Thuan province. The official recounted a tale of attending a meeting in July at which it was reported that a Viet Cong intelligence organization had been created in the United States led by Vietnamese students, Soviet agents, and other communist diplomats. Its purpose was to assist doves and even to help a dove get elected in 1968.[114]

The MACV report was farfetched. Nevertheless, it was true, as Dean Rusk told his audience in Columbus, Indiana, on October 30, that a North Vietnamese official had referred to the Pentagon marchers as "comrades in arms."[115] It was in this context that the intelligence agencies mounted a renewed effort to penetrate movement organizations.

In the first of several reports on this issue, the CIA presented the president with "International Connections of the US Peace Movement" on November 15. A compendium of analyses from the CIA, the FBI, and NSA, the document concluded that there was little evidence of foreign financial support for the peace movement and no evidence of direct contact between movement leaders and foreign embassy personnel. Almost apologetically, because he knew of Johnson's interest in "proof" for his prejudices, CIA director Richard Helms claimed that evidence was fragmentary because of the difficulty of obtaining such information, if it did exist. Perhaps as a sop, he noted that many of the peace movement leaders did have close connections to communists. However, "They do not appear to be under Communist direction." And while it was true, according to Helms, that the American Communist party was benefiting from the movement, the party did not inspire or direct its leadership. There was some celebrated public contact between North Vietnamese and movement figures, but very little with any other unfriendly government.[116]

Johnson simply did not believe the CIA's initial conclusions.[117] Another report of December 21, 1967, failed to turn up any smoking guns. A third "Report of the Foreign Connections of Peace Groups," produced on February 29, 1968, offered a few "new twists" but nothing that could please Johnson. Back to the drawing boards went the CIA, with an apology from Helms for the vagueness of his reports and a suggestion that the FBI use "more advanced investigative techniques" to assist his research.[118]

It is unclear whether the FBI used more advanced techniques to aid in the preparation of the CIA's major report, "Restless Youth," in which radicals the world over were surveyed. Again, investigators had to conclude that communist parties were not involved either in leadership positions or as financial angels. In the United States, of the estimated 6.3 million college students, only 120,000 were activists, and when blacks and feminists were eliminated from that cadre, the number of hard-core college activists dropped to thirty to thirty-five thousand. In addition, the entire world was experiencing youthful protests, little of which was coordinated or organized across national boundaries. Helms's findings were affirmed in Johnson's last report on the subject, presented to him only three days before he left office. Ambassador George McGhee, who had been appointed head of an ad hoc Student Unrest Study Group, could find little domestic or international communist party involvement in the New Left in America.[119]

As Johnson left the White House on January 20, 1969, he remained unconvinced of the intelligence findings. It is interesting to note that Richard Nixon continued where Johnson left off, again dispatching operatives in the CIA and the FBI to find the communist conspiracy. He too was disappointed with the results.

Yet as 1967 came to a close, Johnson had every reason to feel like a target of some well-organized, well-financed, devilish conspiracy. How else to explain the unprecedented series of large demonstrations on campuses, coming at a time when the cities were aflame for other reasons? From September through December, there had been seventy-one significant antiwar protests on sixty-two campuses. This was an augury of the future, as the first six months of 1968 would see such activities on 101 campuses. Some solace could be found in the fact that this was still only a minority activity, unpopular with most Americans. In the summer of 1967, 40 percent of those polled did not feel that students had a right to protest against the war.[120]

Such poll results may have comforted Dean Rusk, who was the target of a noisy demonstration when he appeared in San Francisco on January 11. More distressing because of the source, 94 percent of students polled at Harvard that week opposed Johnson's handling of the war.[121]

Even Mrs. Johnson suffered from the impolite excesses of antiwar critics. She hosted a January 19 White House luncheon devoted to the issue of crime in the United States, at which one of her guests, entertainer Eartha Kitt, shocked the audience with her reportedly intemperate and extracurricular speech against the war. The president was upset about the incident; Mrs. Johnson referred to it as "a nightmare." This insult to the president's wife, however, brought the Johnsons sympathy. To many, Eartha Kitt appeared to be an ungrateful guest attacking the wrong person. The *Times* called the affair "a rude confrontation" and editorially empathized with Mrs. Johnson.[122]

The family came in for more sympathy when protesters were ejected from its Washington church, the National City Christian Church, on January 21. The president was not in attendance, making the indecorous behavior even more unseemly.

Such unruly and rude protests helped the president in the polls. If antiwar protesters were scruffy, radical hippies, then middle-class Americans opted to support the president, even though they had their doubts about the war. On the other hand, Johnson, his family, and his aides had become captives in the White House, unable to appear in public without drawing an unfriendly crowd. It is one thing to rationalize in one's home about the minority nature of the worst of the protesters. It is another to confront them daily, listening to their chants and taunts, expecting them and their outrageous acts at almost every turn in the road.

At the beginning of 1968, despite the irritating omnipresence and obstreperousness of the antiwar movement, Johnson still felt that he could weather the storm, supported by a plurality of Americans against the smaller groups of doves and hawks. Some of this support had been eroded and more important, major elite groups and influential figures in academia, the media, and Congress had fallen off the bandwagon. Yet the military seemed to be turning the corner; progress in pacification had apparently made great strides; the worst at home and abroad, if one listened to Westmoreland and Bunker, might indeed be over. Few, including Johnson, were prepared for the shock that awaited the world as the Vietnamese began to celebrate their Tet New Year's holiday at the end of January.

Chapter Five

The Beginning of the End:
January 1968–January 1969

"What seems not to be understood is that major elements of the national constituency—the business community, the press, the churches, the professional groups, college presidents, students, and most of the intellectual community—have turned against this war."

—*CLARK CLIFFORD*

With the previous fall's glowing accounts of progress in Vietnam still ringing in their ears, Americans from the White House to Main Street were shocked to learn about the communists' massive Tet Offensive on January 31, 1968. Although Hanoi ultimately failed in its main military objectives, it won the battle for American public opinion.

MACV contended that by March, American and South Vietnamese forces had their enemies on the run. Further, all it needed was one final troop call-up and the tide of battle would be turned. Such requests, backed by promises of victory, had been heard before. This time they were not heeded.

Most Americans did not view Tet as a victory for the United States. The offensive demonstrated that Johnson had been painting too bright a picture of progress in Vietnam; the war was apparently endless. Critics of administration policy on the campuses, on Capitol Hill, and in the media seemingly had been right after all.

For the first time, the state of public opinion was *the* crucial factor in decision making on the war. By the end of March, Johnson became convinced that the continuing commitment to South

*Townsend Hoopes, *The Limits of Intervention* (New York: David McKay, 1969), 219.

TABLE 4.
MAJOR VIETNAM WAR–RELATED EVENTS OF 1968

Antiwar Activities	Percent Poll Respondents who Think War Was Mistake	Percent Poll Respondents for Withdraw
	Feb.: 46%	
	March: 49%	
March 12: New Hampshire primary March 16: Kennedy enters primaries		
	April: 49%	
April 23: Columbia University siege April 26: 800 campus demonstrations April 27: New York demonstrations		
August 28: Chicago Convention riots		
	Oct.: 58%	
		Nov.: 19%

Administration Activities	Troop Levels	Battle Deaths (6-month totals)
ı. 3–March 31: Partial bombing pause		
ı. 31: Tet Offensive begins		
b. 28: Military requests 206,000 more troops		
arch 31: LBJ halts bombing beyond 21° and begins deescalation		
ıril 3: North Vietnam agrees to talks		
ıril 9: 541,400 troop ceiling announced		
ay 13: Paris peace talks begin	June 30: 534,700	9,592
:t. 31: Complete bombing pause		
	Dec. 31: 536,100	4,997

Vietnam was crippling the United States. The military's request for further escalation would produce even greater domestic turmoil, threatening the very fabric of American society. This had been one of the conclusions of his Wise Men, who had been summoned to the White House to consider American military and political options in the wake of Tet.

On March 31, 1968, Johnson announced that he was placing the United States on the road toward deescalation and that he was offering the communists generous terms to open peace talks. He also withdrew his candidacy for reelection. Antiwar critics interpreted those stunning decisions as a major victory in their struggle against the war.

Those Americans who wrote, marched, and picketed against the war no doubt contributed directly and indirectly to the president's decisions. In a personal sense, their demonstrations fatigued and disheartened him and his advisers. Further, although Tet was the catalyst, their arguments had affected the attitudes and opinions of the general public. Important here were major reference figures and newspapers and magazines who publicly doubted the wisdom of American policy in Southeast Asia.

Although formal peace talks opened in Paris on May 13, the war dragged on, as did the protests. The movement sought a presidential candidate who would extricate the United States from Vietnam as quickly as possible. Johnson worked behind the scenes to promote the candidacy of his vice president, Hubert Humphrey, someone who would continue his foreign and domestic policies. The Democratic Party Convention in Chicago in August spawned violent confrontations between young activists opposed to Humphrey and the Chicago police force.

In the meantime, as the war continued to take its bloody toll and the peace conferees debated procedure, the nation prepared to elect a new president. The antiwar movement inadvertently helped Richard Nixon win the election because of its lack of enthusiasm for, and sometimes opposition to, the potentially more dovish Humphrey. As Johnson's unhappy term of office came to an end, antiwar critics and Hanoi prepared to do battle with their new adversary.

On January 31, 1968, at the start of the Lunar New Year, or Tet holiday, the National Liberation Front and its North Vietnamese allies launched a massive offensive throughout South Vietnam. The American military had expected major attacks during the period, but nothing so extensive and on such a broad front. After all, given MACV's optimistic reports of the previous fall, the enemy should have been incapable of mounting such a complex nationwide campaign. Although he never publicly expressed his initial reaction to Tet, even President Johnson was "very surprised" by the offensive.[1]

The communists were surprised as well when their countrymen in the South, especially in Saigon, did not rise up to greet them as liberators. They too were captives of their propaganda. As guerrilla war expert Sir Robert Thompson noted, the North Vietnamese expected a "mass uprising in Saigon. What they got, of course, was a mass uprising in the United States."[2] As things turned out, the U.S. uprising may have been more important for their strategic goals than the one they had expected.

Most Americans were shattered by the first television accounts of the "invasion" of Saigon, highlighted by films of Viet Cong sappers inside the American embassy compound. During the first few days, three images stood out: the Associated Press story from the village of Ben Tre that quoted an American officer saying, "We had to destroy it in order to save it"; the *Life* magazine photograph of George Jacobson, gun in hand, peering out of the window of the besieged embassy; and above all, film of the assassination of a suspected Viet Cong infiltrator in cold blood by South Vietnamese General Nguyen Ngoc Loan on a Saigon street.[3]

Today it is clear that the North Vietnamese and Viet Cong did not win their Tet Offensive. That is, there was no mass uprising, the South Vietnamese army performed better than expected, and finally, and most important, the battering that the Viet Cong took destroyed their offensive capabilities for several years. The joint chiefs, the president, and his advisers all were convinced that the United States had turned the tide by the time the dust had settled after the second week of the battle. Despite heavy costs in casualties and disruption of the pacification program, the United States and South Vietnam won perhaps their biggest military victory of the war. Unfortunately for the administration, few Americans believed it.

Lyndon Johnson had claimed victory once too often. The gaping credibility gap was now perceived to be total as Americans asked themselves, Haven't we heard such claims before, and if things were going so well, as we were assured three months ago, how could the enemy have reached Saigon in the first place? As Major General Tran Do of North Vietnam admits, his nation's military objectives were not attained through the Tet Offensive. He now suggests that the offensive had political objectives as well. Whether or not Hanoi expected it, as Dean Rusk laments, they won "a brilliant political victory here in the United States."[4]

The Tet story was a media sensation. To some critics, like Peter Braestrup, the media exploited the early defeats and generally underplayed or scoffed at the administration's claims of victory. Moreover, according to Braestrup, those most affected by the events in Vietnam were journalists themselves and Washington officials exposed to their unbalanced reportage. To make matters worse, even after the communists' main thrusts were turned back throughout the country, television kept Tet alive with nightly coverage of the long siege of Khe Sanh that neatly "filled a journalistic need."[5] Whatever the truth in Braestrup's searing allegations, and there are those who have challenged his account,[6] Tet was the turning point in the battle for the hearts and minds of Americans.

On March 31, 1968, two months to the day after the launching of the communist offensive, Lyndon Johnson took to the airwaves to announce a new peace initiative, bombing limitations, that additional ground troops would not be sent to Vietnam, and that he would not run for president again. The background to Johnson's startling announcements and the role of opinion and dissent in the decision-making process are, as usual, both complex and ambiguous. Complicating matters is the fact that George Christian and Tom Johnson, at the president's request, drafted an "I shall not run" statement for the State of the Union address well before Tet.[7]

Townsend Hoopes, who acknowledges the difficulties in interpreting the causal factors behind the March 31 decision, is confident that although "it will take a lot of digging and a lot of time . . . who can doubt that in the end, after some distant spring thaw, historians will uncover the bones of actuality and piece them together in a sensible mosaic."[8] Perhaps that spring thaw has arrived, and the sensible mosaic can now be constructed.

During the weeks following Tet, Johnson's approval rating on the war, which had risen to 40 percent since the previous fall, plummeted to 26 percent.[9] Many of those expressing their displeasure were hawks not doves. As Harry McPherson points out, when Eugene McCarthy almost won the New Hampshire primary in March, he received many votes from people who wanted the United States to do more and not less in Southeast Asia. Walt Rostow not only now thinks that Johnson could have gotten away with dramatic escalation; he was one of the few to recommend such a course right up to March 31. We had the enemy on the run, he avows, even though the American population did not realize it. Escalation, however, such as invading North Vietnam, according to Harry McPherson and Clark Clifford, did raise the still troubling specter of Russian or Chinese intervention.[10]

Although Johnson did contemplate a continuation of the attrition strategy that called for the sending of over two hundred thousand more troops to Vietnam, escalatory moves that would have pleased the hawks were never a serious option. In the month before Tet, the North Koreans seized the *Pueblo* and there was a flurry of concern about a new Berlin crisis. The United States was simply stretched too thin to risk an expansion of the war in Southeast Asia. Further, Johnson was convinced that while many among the dissatisfied public wanted to win the war and get out, few of them, let alone the rest of the public, would have accepted the more brutal military measures that an all-out strategy demanded. Thus, the debate over American policy during February and March 1968 centered around modest escalation in the mode of previous escalations—or deescalation.

Johnson's own health was another background factor. For some, this was the most important factor.[11] General Earle Wheeler describes Johnson in early 1968 as exhausted, "worried about the dissent," and Mrs. Johnson as "worried about his health." Harry McPherson talks about a "sick and tired" Johnson, and Clark

Clifford remembers him as being "worn to a frazzle," with Mrs. Johnson urging him not to run again. Douglass Cater used Clifford's word *frazzled* as he described "tired men pushed beyond capacity," with Johnson going through an immense "personal crisis." Others see the entire Tuesday Lunch group in general as "embattled" and "besieged."[12] The parallel domestic crisis in the cities, the black urban rebellions, contributed to the debilitation of the administration as well.

Several of Johnson's aides remember vividly discussions with him about his health and how he feared becoming incapacitated in the White House, another Woodrow Wilson. In fact, Rusk claims that when informed of the president's decision not to run again while on the way to a meeting in New Zealand, he was not at all surprised. Clifford, on the other hand, a presidential intimate, was not prepared for the announcement.[13]

Whether or not the decision surprised many people in the inner circle, Johnson was a beleaguered man when he made it. Part of his condition had been caused by the antiwar movement that had made life so miserable for him, his family, and aides over the previous several years. If this is the case, then again, one can credit the movement with having an impact on the decision making in February and March 1968, if only by contributing to the deteriorating state of Johnson's mental and physical health.

In the wake of Tet, the administration began a major reevaluation of Vietnam policies, the likes of which had not been seen since July 1965. The process involved three stages. First, in late February, Johnson drafted Clark Clifford to head an internal study group or task force that included Rusk, Rostow, Wheeler, Warnke, Taylor, Treasury Secretary Fowler, and McNamara. On March 1, Clifford was sworn in as defense chief. His briefing papers were prepared by Gelb, Warnke, Enthoven, Morton Halperin, and John Steadman, most of whom were, by then, relative doves, with Enthoven, in particular, concerned about the home front.[14] No formal minutes were taken at most of the group's meetings, although briefing papers are extant in several files.[15]

The chief task confronting the study group was to recommend action on an old request from General Westmoreland for 206,000 more troops, a request withdrawn the previous spring. The request was not Westmoreland's idea, but emanated from the joint chiefs, who, in effect, asked Johnson to ask Westmoreland to make it. At this point, Johnson apparently approved of the need for the additional 206,000 troops.[16]

The second stage in the process was the convening of the Wise Men on March 25 for advice and analysis of the discussions, documents, and conclusions of the Clifford group. The final stage involved a series of meetings between Johnson and a handful of intimates as he contemplated the Wise Men's recommendations and prepared the March 31 address. Affecting all participants in these consultations were several crucial events in February and March that altered the domestic environment.

Most important may have been the March 12 New Hampshire primary election that Johnson won, but over an obscure senator and only by a 49-to-42-percent margin.[17] To the North Vietnamese, Tet was Dienbienphu and McCarthy was Pierre Mendes France, the man who pulled France out of Vietnam.[18] One product of Senator McCarthy's shocking symbolic "victory" was the March 16 decision by Robert Kennedy, a more formidable opponent, to enter the primaries.[19] In an election year, politicians, including Johnson, were coming to realize that the war was a losing issue for those committed to maintaining then current administration policy.

A flurry of war-related activities on Capitol Hill also affected political perceptions in Washington. Fulbright's Senate Foreign Relations Committee began holding hearings on February 20 on the Tonkin Gulf issue, the censored transcripts of which were released to the press on February 24. Then, on March 7, in a well-publicized Senate debate, Fulbright, Mansfield, and others issued general attacks on the Johnson war policy. Johnson's friend Richard Russell had to inform the president during this period that he was fast losing the Senate. Clark Clifford and Earle Wheeler received similar reports.[20]

The Foreign Relations Committee hearings on the foreign aid bill, which were televised in part on March 11 and 12, featured a defensive Dean Rusk being badgered by almost all committee members, even conservative Karl Mundt. The latter, who talked about the "bewilderment" of the American public, pointed out that those who were dissenting were not just street mobs.[21] For the first time in two years the networks decided to provide live coverage of such hearings.

Congressional attitudes, especially as expressed in the media, affected public opinion, which in turn affected the media's presentation of the Vietnam debate, which thus, in a feedback process, affected legislators. Several other major television events were part of the process that contributed to Johnson's loss of support. The defection of Walter Cronkite on February 27, 1968, was a blow to the president.[22] The nation's most distinguished and respected anchorperson had gone on his own investigative tour of Vietnam during the middle of February. He returned to the CBS network in a special documentary highlighted by a rare editorial in which he reported that the war was not going well, that the administration's policies were failing. Johnson watched a recording of the Cronkite editorial the next day. He was impressed with the potential impact on Middle America of Cronkite's pessimistic account. In addition, he reasoned that if Cronkite, a moderate and a patriot, was turning on his policies, then he must be losing millions of like-minded Americans as well.[23] Johnson, who had "enormous respect" for Cronkite, always had considered him "fair." Now this fair-minded opinion leader opposed him in what was a "turning point" of the period.[24]

Although not as important, only two days earlier the "Smothers Brothers" television show made antiwar headlines. The previous fall, CBS censored folk singer Pete Seeger's satirical, allegorical attack on the Vietnam policy, "Waste Deep in the Big Muddy," owing to its concern about Johnson's reaction. Now, on February 25, Walter Cronkite's network permitted Seeger's song to be aired all over the country.[25]

A final media spectacular was the printing, on March 10, by the *New York Times* of an exclusive story outlining "Westmoreland's" secret request for an additional 206,000 soldiers. After the pre-Tet propaganda campaign and after claims that Tet really was a victory, the military was asking for a huge increase in ground troops. The leak to the *New York Times* and its attendant negative publicity offered an early-warning indicator of the public's displeasure with the troop request.[26] The proposed escalation was a signal that there was no end in sight to the interminable war. Dean

Rusk feels that he lost Americans like his conservative and patriotic "Cherokee County cousins" in Georgia when he could no longer tell them when the war would be over.[27] The bombshell of the 206,000 troop request weakened Johnson's remaining support in journalistic, congressional, and ultimately public opinion.

It is difficult to determine with any degree of precision how Johnson was affected by the march of events from Tet to the evening of his speech, in part because he did not discuss his feelings much in public or private. Tet had to be a "brutal surprise" for the president, as it was for others in the White House, such as George Christian. Johnson never did go to the nation to explain it and its aftermath, although he was urged by Rostow to take "on the peace issue squarely" and to give "a war leader speech." Concerned about the impact of Tet on the public, the national security adviser felt that the president still could rally the nation behind him with a strong speech.[28]

Analyzing the vagaries of American opinion, Rostow told the president, "If the war goes well, the American people are with us. If the war goes badly, they are against us."[29] No doubt Rostow was correct. The problem for Johnson at this time, a week after the Tet Offensive began, was how to explain to the public that the Americans were winning when the television footage and news photos seemed to indicate the opposite. The credibility gap was too wide to be closed by such a speech.

Although the president did not speak out directly on the military situation in Vietnam in the first weeks after Tet, he and Rusk again cautioned American critics about their impact on Hanoi. On February 6, Johnson told participants at a congressional breakfast, "I wish Mike [Mansfield] would make a speech on Ho Chi Minh. Nothing is as dirty as to violate a truce during the holidays. But nobody says anything bad about Ho. They call me a murderer. But Ho has a great image." A few days earlier, Rusk presented the same message to a group of college editors: "One of the problems is that Hanoi watches this debate very closely. There is no doubt they are encouraged by dissent in this country, no doubt about it."[30]

Johnson and his military advisers—Westmoreland, Wheeler, and Taylor, among others—blamed the media, senators, and dissenters for making the American public believe that the communists had won the offensive. The head of the USIA noted how communists the world over were quoting American politicians on the bankruptcy of their own policy in Southeast Asia after Tet.[31]

In his memoirs, Johnson lists four factors that he took into consideration as he moved toward his March 31 decisions. He thought that another Tet was unlikely, that the South Vietnamese were becoming stronger, that the American economy was weakening, and that the public was discouraged about the Vietnam venture. On the latter, he commented that the "state of mind and morale on the domestic front" were important to him. He does not link the movement to the state of mind after Tet, and he told journalists at a news conference on February 12 only that their actions "saddened me, troubled me."[32]

Whether there was a link between dissenters and public opinion was an academic question in February 1968. By February 12, Rostow could assure Johnson that the United States had won the military battle; Ho had failed in his main objective. However, he "shook U.S. public opinion."[33]

As usual in such periods, the administration tried to counter the increasingly bad news emanating from Vietnam. The director of VISTA suggested that dispatching more veterans to college campuses might turn opinion around in that volatile milieu. A Johnson aide recommended taking action against the fifteen hundred federal employees who had signed an antiwar advertisement that was to appear in the *Washington Post* on April 1.[34]

A dramatic example of the administration's concern about dissent in high places revolves around a March 7 meeting of the presidents of MIT, Duke, Yale, Cornell, and Princeton. After discussing the war, the educators agreed to release a mild antiwar statement to the press. When the president of Cornell, James Perkins, informed Douglass Cater about the proposed demarche, the White House proceeded to squelch it. The president agreed that Rusk should meet with some of the presidents to convince them not to go public with their apparently damaging press release. After meeting with both Rusk and Clifford, presidents Howard Johnson of MIT and Douglas Knight of Duke agreed to hold their fire.[35]

The attention devoted to the college presidents' rather innocuous gesture by the secretaries of state and defense, who took time out from their own feverish activities in March to put out the brush fire, reflects a recognition that the establishment was deserting Johnson en masse. These college presidents from elite institutions, except for Kingman Brewster of Yale, had been silent on the war issue through the years. Walt Rostow talks of such activities as sadly, for him, reflecting "the end of the American establishment's consensus on foreign policy," a consensus that had existed since the 1940s.[36]

Clark Clifford had worried in March about the increasing alienation of the American business community. The defense secretary thought corporate leaders were troubled both by the effect of escalation on the economy *and* their own children.[37] One can link Clifford's observation to the college presidents' dissent. Prestige colleges are connected to boardrooms of Wall Street through their trustees. The presidents' defection could contribute to that of key members of the corporate community. In any event, the attention lavished on the college presidents reveals how seriously the Johnson administration took such opinion makers. On the other hand, Dean Rusk denies that what he did in March was anything special; he had always met frequently with college presidents, professors, students, and industrialists.[38] A skeptic might suggest that such public relations activities probably became less frequent during times of crisis.

Clark Clifford was a quintessential man of the establishment whose advice had been sought by presidents and business leaders for more than twenty years. Throughout his administration, Johnson had relied more and more on Clifford and Abe Fortas, two friends who generally supported his strategic programs and could not at all be considered dovish. In fact, from January 1966 on, both had opposed bombing pauses. According to Rusk, Clifford had been "one of the biggest hawks in town."[39]

Until he was called into service in February 1968, the widely respected Washington lawyer was a prominent ad hoc adviser who, with a moment's notice, could be at the White House, a short five-minute walk across Lafayette Park from his office at the foot of Connecticut Avenue. Because of his previous support for presidential policies, as well as his celebrated discretion, Clifford had the most influence of the presidential advisers during five weeks of agonizing reappraisal of Vietnam policies. George Reedy, especially, emphasizes Clifford's sensitive handling of the president, whom he allowed to come to his own conclusions at the eleventh hour. Paul Nitze thinks that as one of Clifford's chief advisers, he was influential in turning his boss around.[40]

When he agreed to head the study group, Clifford's mind was not made up. Had Johnson known that Clifford was going to lead a dovish conspiracy within the White House, he never would have called him into the government. He was angered by his friend's defection. Clifford maintains that his relationship with Johnson was never the same after he finally recommended the dovish option at the end of March.[41]

The defense secretary designate, along with Rusk, received a memo from Johnson on February 28 in which the president raised twelve questions for the task force to answer. Only the last question related directly to the opinion variable. Clifford remembers his group working primarily on strategic issues and that public opinion was not a significant part of his mandate. He set out to examine past policy and to determine what it would take to win the war in Vietnam. Obviously "conscious" of opinion throughout the weeks of study and discussion, he considered it only a background factor. One thing he did discover, now that he was on the inside, was that he and the Wise Men had been "misinformed" by the American military. He thus began, as George Christian puts it, "second guessing" the reports from the field.[42]

As an indication of the role that opinion played during the deliberations, hovering in the background but rarely forgotten, Clifford asked at a meeting the day before the task force began its work, "How do we avoid creating the feeling that we are pouring troops down a rathole?" Johnson talked in a similar vein in his memoirs: "How could such an increase be justified to the American people?"[43]

The briefing papers prepared for the March deliberations concentrated primarily on military and international political questions with the effectiveness of the bombing, the progress shown by the ARVN, and the other side's capabilities reappearing over and over. The historian interested in tracing the role of opinion and dissent in the March 31 decision must again rely on fragmentary written traces of allusions to the public and the general impressions of participants after the fact. As usual, most participants began from the premise that the president was the best judge of opinion and domestic politics. They were called in to analyze military reports and make recommendations on troop levels and other strategic initiatives.

At the start of the deliberations, around the beginning of March, some confident souls thought that if nothing worse than Tet occurred in the near future, the administration would regain some of its popular support. For example, William Bundy concluded early in the process that unless Hanoi suddenly accepted the San Antonio formula, "We believe that peace pressures will not rise to serious levels." At the same time, since the public and Congress had lost confidence in the administration, it had better show progress soon.[44] Naturally, when the military responded that it could show progress only with an additional 206,000 men, and then could not estimate how long it would take to achieve that progress, even with the massive escalation, Bundy's relatively confident assessment of opinion became shakier.

More and more, the prime consideration became the need for a quick victory. A staff paper prepared around March 1 adopted a line similar to Bundy's stressing that although the majority of the public would support increasing troop levels again, the win-or-get-out sentiment was growing. Some public affairs specialists thought popular support might be regained with yet another propaganda campaign, but most seemed to think it was too late for words alone to bolster morale. Another report prepared for Clifford and his colleagues predicted that although the doves alone could be contained, they would get somewhat stronger. The problem was that the administration had to contend with the hawks as well, who, with the doves, might create "a whipsaw effect" that would weaken the center and lead to a polarized, "prolonged and divisive debate."[45]

Others were even more distressed about the state of public opinion. Assistant Defense Secretary Phil Goulding was convinced that the only viable option in terms of American domestic politics was no further call-ups. Paul Warnke similarly worried about the problems that would be created by the need to dip into the reserves to replace the 206,000 soldiers who were to be sent to Vietnam.[46] Dipping into the reserves would affect many middle- to upper-middle-class families.

Aside from the issue of domestic support, Realpolitik could also be invoked in arguments for deescalation. Asia of 1968 was not the Asia of 1965. Indonesia had joined the West after the deposition of Sukarno and the Sino-Soviet split made any Chinese threat to intervene much less serious.[47]

As early as March 4, even before the leak in the *New York Times*, Clifford appears to have begun to move away from his long-held hawkish position.[48] It had taken him and most of his colleagues less than a week to become disillusioned with the generals, who could not produce a plan for a speedy victory.

As his advisers pondered their reports, Johnson's aides tried to console him. On March 15, Tom Johnson told him of a fall 1967 *Newsweek* poll that revealed that 71 percent of all college students had never joined a march or written a protest letter, 34 percent of those polled favored escalation, and only 17 percent wanted to stop the bombing. The poll was dated. The game had changed after Tet, despite Tom Johnson's attempt to find a silver lining.[49]

After three weeks of study, William Bundy altered his view of the domestic front. Public opposition to a long-term commitment in Southeast Asia, he acknowledged, had grown by the third week in March. This opposition was impressive because it was not attributable to the activities of such notable dissenters as presidential candidates Kennedy and McCarthy. Here Bundy echoed Rusk's view that the ordinary people had decided enough was enough, irrespective of what the movement and dovish leaders had been saying.[50] It is, nevertheless, impossible to disassociate the well-publicized critiques of Robert Kennedy, Walter Cronkite, or the *Wall Street Journal* from the development of antiwar sentiment in the nation as a whole. Decision makers, nevertheless, may find it comforting to say that they are bowing only to the public will and not to the noisy attacks of their political opponents, who clearly had some effect on that will.

One bit of advice that was eschewed was Harry McPherson's proposed genuflection to the American public with an insincere bombing pause that would be rejected by Hanoi. The "purpose of this exercise: to show the American people that we are willing to do every reasonable thing to bring about talks."[51]

Basing his conclusions primarily on the military situation and what it would take to win quickly in Vietnam, Clifford took the lead in his task force in opposing Westmoreland's request for the additional 206,000 troops. To bolster his position, he suggested that Johnson again summon his Wise Men to consider the task force's reports. At this point, the president did not know where Clifford stood. The discreet lawyer now claims that he saw himself engaged in a "conspiracy" during those last two weeks in March, a conspiracy to rally support among Johnson's advisers for a deescalation in Vietnam. Within the Oval Office his ally was presidential aide Harry McPherson, "our secret dove." Katzenbach in State, Fulbright in the Senate, and even Richard Russell were those whom Clifford called upon as he planned his strategy. As he wandered through the corridors of power looking for support for his plan to convince Johnson that the game was up in Vietnam, he found himself whispering to friends, "Is he one of us?"[52]

The Senior Advisory Group on Vietnam, the Wise Men, met in the White House on March 25 and 26. They included Dean Acheson, George Ball, McGeorge Bundy, Douglas Dillon, Cyrus Vance, Arthur Dean, John McCloy, Omar Bradley, Matthew Ridgway, Maxwell Taylor, Robert Murphy, Henry Cabot Lodge, Abe Fortas, and Arthur Goldberg. This glittering galaxy of American leaders was presented with briefing papers, met with military and civilian officials, discussed the issues among themselves, and finally met with the president. Compared to previous Wise Men sessions, the military briefings were detailed, frank, and not optimistic. The prospect of a war without end revealed in those papers and discussions shook their faith in administration policy. They simply did not believe that the nation could afford to prosecute the war indefinitely. Unlike the participants in the task force, the Wise Men emphasized the opinion variable in their deliberations.

It was clear to Johnson at his luncheon with them on March 26 that the Wise Men had executed an about-face since they last met in early November. The doves were now ascendant. The twin themes of the troubling divisions in American society and the general erosion of popular support for the war dominated the discussions. Again playing the role of rapporteur, McGeorge Bundy reports that opinion played "an absolutely critical role" in the meetings. Indeed, he thinks that his colleagues were less affected by the military scenarios sketched by Clifford than by the public opinion polls and, especially, their own sense of what was going on in the nation. A clear majority of those present were "in agreement with Dean Acheson that we could no longer do the job we set out to do in the time that American opinion would permit us."[53]

There was a minority position. Speaking for moderate hawks who included Murphy and Bradley, Maxwell Taylor was "dismayed. . . . Let us not concede the home front; let's do something about it." Taylor had urged similar action in November. In addition, the general and former ambassador to South Vietnam thought that the Wise Men were unduly affected by media biases, especially those expressed in the *New York Times* and the *Washington Post*.[54]

In any case, most of the Wise Men reacted to the opinion shifts produced by Tet. Only four months earlier, they had put their stamp of approval on administration policy. Now they were deeply concerned about popular support for that policy. Apparently, most felt powerless to shape or lead opinion at the time. According to any power elite theory, the Wise Men were representatives of an establishment that controlled what appeared in the media. How could opinion get out ahead of them?

One can fit this apparent paradox into a power elite analysis such as that which has been applied to the 1898 crisis when opinion leaders split on entry into the Spanish-American War and the establishment's consensus was temporarily shattered.[55] The uncertainty and conflict within the corporate community especially over the war issue in 1898 created a demand for something decisive to be done so that the nation could get on with its business. Undoubtedly, the United States confronted a comparably chaotic time in the weeks after Tet, when, according to Clifford, the establishment had fallen apart.[56]

In addition, even had the Wise Men been able to control the media, they could not control their own young people, members of the establishment of the future.[57] Something had to be done to bring the Yales, Harvards, and other elite institutions back into the fold in order to preserve the continuity and consensus in America's political, intellectual, and corporate leadership.

Other factors came into play as well for the Wise Men, and two, in particular, involved the opinion variable. The first was the growth of draft resistance and how it might accelerate with any attempt to continue the apparently failed military policies.[58] The other had to do with a reported rush of gold buying in the international financial community, an early sign of lack of confidence in the United States' military plans, a lack of confidence that had to be related, in part, to the general domestic climate.[59]

The Wise Men shocked Johnson. Many had swerved 180 degrees since Tet. Presented with their majority recommendation for deescalation, he considered his options during the last few days of March. After listening to the bad news from old friends and colleagues, Johnson still had not made up his mind and, if anything, was prepared to announce a modest escalation.[60] Characteristically, it seemed, the Wise Men had met only for show, to demonstrate that Johnson listened to all options before acting. Only this time, the meeting was not scripted, the Wise Men did not play the role they had played in July 1965 and November 1967. Clifford portrayed the Wise Men as the representatives and interpreters of the national "jury"—on Vietnam policy, the media, and the public. The verdict was in, and this time the Wise Men could not ignore it.[61] Johnson finally accepted the verdict at the eleventh hour, a turnabout that surprised even Clifford.[62]

Clifford's surprise was understandable given the draft of a speech that Johnson circulated to him, Rusk, McPherson, Rostow, and William Bundy on March 28, two days after the Wise Men had departed. It was a hard-line speech that ignored their dovish recommendations. Clifford determined that it could not be given. "What seems not to be understood," he complained, "is that major elements of the national constituency—the business community, the press, the churches, professional groups, college presidents, students, and most of the intellectual community—have turned against this war."[63]

Rusk and Rostow did not oppose Clifford's criticism of the

speech, although Rostow did agree with president. McPherson, with the defense secretary's blessing, set about to write a new speech that was "almost a complete reversal" of the original draft.[64] McPherson's draft, without Johnson's surprise announcement not to seek reelection, was ultimately accepted.

What happened to Johnson between March 28 and March 31 is difficult to determine. He reached his decision after consulting few people, save his wife and children. The most charitable explanation is that he decided to end the war and realized that he could not do it while running for president. The war had been his greatest failure. The loss of American life had caused him "great pain"; he was "frustrated by his inability to move toward peace." For the good of the nation, and perhaps to restore his place in history as a great president, he could sacrifice his gargantuan need for power.[65] Public opinion weighed heavily in his decision.

Herbert Schandler, who has written the best study on the subject, concludes that the impact of opinion on that decision can never be evaluated with certainty. Nevertheless, Leslie Gelb was correct when he termed it "the essential domino." As William Bundy noted, Johnson's speech "reflected a generalized response to what was happening in public opinion all around us during that month."[66]

The presidency for Johnson had been, in the words of historian-participant Henry Graff, "a great burden." Clark Clifford talks about his "rugged five years" on the Vietnam issue, citing Johnson and Lady Bird being spit upon in a hotel in their beloved Texas, while Douglass Cater refers to the war as a "killer" for Johnson.[67] The president finally realized that he "could not unite the country" on the Vietnam issue. The time had come for him to ease his own and the nation's trauma and to end the division in the country over the war that troubled him so.[68]

Johnson did not come easily to his decision. Clark Clifford, who knew him better than most of his advisers, points out that he was "not a timid man" and would not "have been scared off" in most situations; he "would have said to hell with them." Thus, when he finally decided to deescalate without the communist coonskin nailed to the wall, the new policy "did not sit well with him." In fact, Walt Rostow reports that not only did Johnson second-guess himself, but in the last year of his life he confided that military escalation after Tet might have been the wisest course. Johnson was influenced at that point by the relative success enjoyed by Nixon in *his* escalations.[69]

Second-guessing or not, Johnson never recognized the potential strength of his foreign-policy critics until it was too late. Part of his problem was that the public opinion polls and congressional votes both continually demonstrated that he always had a healthy majority supporting him from 1965 through most of 1967. The change in grass-roots public opinion that Dean Rusk began to sense during the second half of 1967 was not fully revealed in the objective measures of public opinion, including the Democratic primary campaigns, until after Tet.[70]

There is no doubt that the president felt he had lost the country on March 31 and that his party had fractured on the war issue. How the antiwar movement was linked to those developments and Johnson's state of mind can only be inferred from scattered bits of evidence and surmise. It was clear by the spring of 1968 that antiwar antics over the previous two years had contributed, at the least, "an extra dimension of strain."[71] The vilification, the picketing, and the obscene chants against the prisoner in the White House had all taken their toll. One can imagine him saying to himself as the red light on the television cameras shut off on March 31, at last my family and I will have some rest from this relentless attack directed against us. To be certain, he was not a quitter, but thinking that those scruffy, vile hippies would finally leave him alone must have given him some comfort.[72]

Even the most insensitive man would have been anguished by the treatment meted out to Johnson by the youthful dissenters.[73] No president in history had been pilloried in public so abusively. He tried to shrug it off, but few believed him. Bryce Harlow recalls a visit to the ranch in 1969 when the subject of antiwar students was broached. The former president made some charitable remarks to Harlow, but just as the discussion was about to be concluded, Lady Bird interjected, visibly angry and upset. She expressed in no uncertain terms to Harlow her "most intense resentments" of the movement.[74] Most likely, she was speaking for her more diplomatic husband as well.

Maxwell Taylor, for one, feels that Johnson and some of his colleagues may have exaggerated the power of the movement. The public was with Johnson most of the time. Nixon's successful appeal to the Silent Majority demonstrated one way of dealing with the noisy minority. Yet how does one deal with the human problems caused by the protesters? To avoid demonstrations, for example, travel plans had to be made on the spur of the moment. To press secretary George Christian, the situation was a "nightmare," always "feeling that you are going to be attacked the minute you get out of your castle." He remembers feeling "under siege" to the point that Johnson's visit to EXPO 67 in Montreal had to be announced with fifteen minutes lead time in order to foil demonstrators' plans. And he has not forgotten the raucous hecklers in places like Los Angeles, Honolulu, Australia, and even Texas.[75]

The usually calm Hubert Humphrey has written of his own anger with impolite students and how he was bothered by heckling, even if only a few protesters were involved. Indeed, the hecklers made him a less effective campaigner in the 1968 campaign. Abbie Hoffman on the outside and Tom Johnson on the inside cite Johnson's recognition of his own inability to campaign as a contributing factor to the decision not to run.[76]

The personal attacks on administration families were even harder to take. William Westmoreland found out only years later how upset his son had been to see his father burning in effigy at Harvard. Walt Rostow tells of pickets in front of his house on several occasions and even how his mother-in-law received a telephoned death threat meant for him.[77] The influence of family and friends on decision makers should not be understated. Even Johnson's views of the movement and his Vietnam policies must have been influenced, if only subconsciously, by the fact that his two sons-in-law were in the military in Vietnam. Both Charles Robb and Pat Nugent wrote extensive reports to him through their wives that often included heart-rending descriptions of killed and wounded.[78]

In the inner circle, McNamara's son Craig was opposed to administration policy and later, in 1970, emerged as a student activist in California. McNamara's wife felt the strain as well.[79]

Notable wives who became doves before their husbands included Lillian Reedy, Gertrude Califano, and Clayton McPherson. Some official spouses were so upset about the war that they had difficulty being civil in Johnson's presence.[80]

Whether or not they opposed the war, wives were often on the firing line in social gatherings. Opponents of the war, uncomfortable about broaching the subject to William Bundy, for example, subjected his wife to criticism at dinner parties. Bundy also remembers conversations with nieces and nephews strongly opposed to the war and an especially "anguished letter" from a relative. This dissent within the Bundy family troubled the assistant secretary more than crowds of anonymous students demonstrating at Yale, his alma mater.[81]

Johnson officials were not even safe on vacation. McNamara had trouble finding tennis partners on Martha's Vineyard. Further, someone put a sign on his glass house retreat: "People who live in glass houses shouldn't drop bombs."[82]

The largest target for such attacks was the president himself. No matter the support in the polls or media, criticism even from a small minority wounded him. He was surprisingly sensitive for a man who rarely received more than 60 percent of the vote in any election, for a man who had honed his political skills in the rough and tumble of Texas politics. Yet he wanted to be accepted or loved by everyone. He "regarded the political process entirely in terms of popularity."[83]

Johnson was convinced that as president, especially on foreign policy issues, he deserved the unswerving support of the entire nation. The guardian of national security, he was merely following the guidelines established by those very popular chief executives, Eisenhower and Kennedy. The latter's popularity especially rankled him since he viewed himself as a far more successful president than Kennedy and, naturally, knew all of the gossip about his predecessor's character flaws.

Like many of his advisers, Johnson was exasperated with the antiwar movement since he was convinced that it had prolonged the war. He knew that all wars provoked some dissent. The dissent on the Vietnam War, however, had "passed the bounds of reasonable debate and fair discussion." Americans were "defeating ourselves" in 1968. By the time of Tet, the biggest foreign policy problem was "the divisiveness and pessimism at home."[84]

Nevertheless, he claimed to sympathize with the young people who opposed him. He told a colleague after he left the presidency, "I don't blame them. They didn't want to be killed in a war, and that's easy to understand." He seemed almost melancholy as he recalled the "Hey, Hey LBJ" chants and of the "long gulf between them and me. I was doing what was right for them, but they didn't understand history and our commitments."[85] He heard those chants often in the living quarters of the White House, but they caused much more "pain" than anger.[86] These sentiments fit with those reported by other observers who maintain that Johnson bore no animosity toward the students and did not fear the New Left on campuses. He reserved his anger for the professors and others in the forefront of the movement who had led the students.[87]

According to Jack Valenti, Johnson found the antiwar protests "troubling." He was "stricken" by the fact that though his Great Society had given "young idealistic people what they wanted," they hated him. He could not understand how the current generation of young people could include both brave young marines and "hippies and draft-card burners."[88]

George Reedy, who felt that Johnson was out of touch with his critics among the student population, now thinks that he should have urged the president to meet with more of them. On the occasion of one genteel sit-in during the early stages of the war, Johnson expressed an interest in going down to the public area of the White House to chat with the protesters. Reedy and others in Johnson's entourage advised against the encounter, an action that the former press secretary now regrets.[89]

It is doubtful that meeting with protesters would have contributed much to Johnson's understanding of, or sympathy for, the arguments of antiwar students. Such meetings did not seem to affect Dean Rusk's views. He recalls one in particular when, minutes after a proper exchange of views with students and editors, a press release was on the street, obviously prepared in advance, that excoriated the administration. Rusk sympathized with those of a pacifist persuasion but not with the politicos of the New Left. Similarly, it is difficult to determine what was accomplished by McNamara's liberal open-door policy for protesters in the Pentagon.[90]

Occasionally, right through to the end of his administration, Johnson and his aides took solace in the fact that the antiwar movement was a factor on only a minority of campuses. Selective Service director Lewis Hershey experienced few problems in American universities except for the top fifty colleges, places like Yale and Columbia.[91] The problem was that, despite the numbers, it was precisely at those top fifty colleges that Johnson and his aides wanted support.[92] And perhaps they were correct, for the positions of President Kingman Brewster at Yale or the editor of the *Harvard Crimson* were more important than any number of presidents or editors at "normal" schools in the Midwest.

Johnson's relationship with elite dissenters was complex. He despised the eastern establishment, but also wanted to be respected by it. Criticism from that quarter might have made him more stubborn, unwilling to confess error and give his enemies something to crow about.[93] Further, he probably was not very confident about his Vietnam policy from the start and thus might have overcompensated for this lack of confidence by adopting an unyielding posture.[94] In addition, he clearly perceived himself as a moderate on that policy who should not have been branded a hawk and a baby killer.[95] As criticism mounted in 1966 and 1967, Johnson, Rusk, and a few other loyalists dug in, an ever-smaller group that reflected a siege mentality. According to psychologists, members of small groups like these turn to one another for reinforcement against outsiders.[96] The loyalists surrounding Johnson did not just pull their wagons around themselves to defend their position against the movement and other foreign-policy critics. They were also leery about the way their opponents influenced some of their own aides.

There were those in the administration at the fringes of the inner group who had become increasingly disenchanted with the way the war was going, especially after 1966. Many were personally affected by the movement and the rancor of the national debate. Their disaffection had some impact on Johnson, if only indirectly. When the internal arguments did arise out of Johnson's earshot, however, they were generally over tactics, not fundamental assumptions.[97] Among those he knew or suspected were distressed with the war were cabinet members Clark, Udall, and Wirtz, and McNaughton, Warnke, Katzenbach, Ball, Reedy, and Moyers. According to Clark, this is one of the reasons Johnson held so few cabinet meetings.[98]

Just as Johnson knew of the silent dissenters in the White House, they knew that he abhorred criticism.[99] Most likely, given his paranoia on the loyalty issue, he imagined there were even more critics in his entourage than there really were, since he knew that they knew that he demanded complete loyalty. This is a subtle issue, for aside from Ball and perhaps Moyers, who were considered house doves at times, few dissenting voices were heard in and around the Oval Office until March 25, 1968.

As Earle Wheeler commented on the lack of criticism at the Tuesday Lunch meetings on Vietnam policy, "You just don't go in there and piss in the President's soup." James Thomson explained why the Johnson White House (or perhaps any White House) was not the place for a free and open exchange on the Vietnam policy, especially after 1966, when things started going badly. Johnson simply would not accept criticism. Thomson himself tells how he often contemplated a "Walter Mitty" action in which he would call the press, burn his White House pass, and join the marchers outside the fence. But then he would lose all of his ability, modest though it may have been, to influence policy. After he left government and wrote a parody of a Rostow staff meeting in the May 1967 issue of the *Atlantic Monthly*, Rostow allegedly threatened him with professional punishment in a message relayed by his Harvard superiors. Johnson was similarly vindictive to such "traitors."[100]

Whether or not the suspected doves inside the administration had any direct impact on Johnson, he worried about them. Further, the attacks on administration officials by the antiwar critics produced a good deal of "wear and tear" on them. Because they were less used to politics than Johnson, they took the criticism in the media and among their intimates even more seriously than the sensitive president.[101]

Johnson's defenders reject the depiction of a little group of insular men, unwilling to listen to criticism. Rusk and Roche remember many lively exchanges with the president over Vietnam policy with, according to the former secretary, the leaking of dissent to the media the biggest problem.[102] It was that, not criticism in private, that the president could not abide.

As late as 1968, Johnson told Henry Graff that he was still listening to critics like Ambassador Edwin Reischauer, James Gavin, Robert Kennedy, George McGovern, even Eastern bloc ambassadors, most of whom he found to be simpletons.[103] He did, however, tend to put all critics, from hippies and yippies to the Fulbrights, in the same bag and then dismissed their suggestions.[104]

As Eric Goldman notes, Johnson listened to them, but he was the president charged with the defense of national security and they were not. Jack Valenti goes further and suggests that the president might even say to a Lippmann or a Fulbright, "OK, I agree, but what do I do specifically—I have to give an order." Short of pulling out of Vietnam, they offered few options that Johnson found politically practical. Valenti draws the distinction between the "troubled academicians and the fellow who has to make a decision." Rusk echoes his sentiments, referring to the gulf between the "world of opinion" and the "world of decision."[105]

Looking back at how the dissenters in the streets, the salons, and the media affected Johnson and his advisers in the early spring of 1968, we must take refuge in an ambiguous conclusion. All along, the administration had dealt with them in an inconsistent and indecisive manner. George Reedy may be correct when he sees Johnson being "baffled" by the critics, uncertain how to handle them, how to respond to their incessant and allegedly irresponsible demands. George Christian simply thinks that he and his colleagues, as well as the president, did not handle dissent well, although he is at a loss to explain what he would have done differently today. Undoubtedly, he is correct in maintaining that Johnson never had a "political plan" to deal with the troubling antiwar critics, short of FBI surveillance. As his colleague Harry McPherson has written, the rallying of the population behind the war was "a neglected task."[106]

Given the energies Johnson devoted to the rallying of the population right through to March 1968, it may not have been a neglected task, merely a task not well done. Perhaps even that criticism is unfair, since the administration was aware of the dangers inherent in arousing the population too much. Given that constraint, the creation of enthusiasm for a limited war that seemed endless by early 1968 was an enormous, maybe even impossible, task. As was suspected as early as the first escalatory moves in the late fall of 1965, a limited war, even without organized dissent, as was the case in Korea, is difficult to manage in a democracy with periodic elections. Ho Chi Minh certainly knew this as he waited eagerly for the 1968 presidential election.[107]

Two dissent-related military issues also had to weigh heavily with Clifford and his task force, the joint chiefs, the Wise Men, and Johnson in February and March 1968—the draft and the state of morale in the armed services. As the draft began to penetrate middle-class defenses that included educational deferments, the reserve option, and medical and theological exclusions, antiwar activities increased. It is too facile and certainly unfair to dedicated antiwar movement leaders and their foot soldiers to credit their success, especially after 1966, solely to young people's fear of the draft, but it undoubtedly played a role. More important, perhaps, middle-class parents became increasingly critical of the war as it threatened to take their own children.[108] There is a relationship between the decline of the antiwar movement and Nixon's winding down of the draft in 1972. Even antiwar partisans see the link between the increased appeal of the movement and the impact of the draft on young people.[109]

As early as 1966, a hundred student leaders warned Johnson about the unpopularity of the draft and the growth of resistance. In 1967, James Reston concluded that as many as 25 percent of all college students would resist a draft call. Those numbers of potential and real resisters grew in 1968. With the end of graduate school deferments in 1968, things became even worse.[110]

In addition, as General Westmoreland lamented, the antiwar movement was having an impact on ROTC on college campuses, decreasing the pool of eligible officer candidates. The numbers of those enrolled in such programs dropped from 212,400 in 1968 to 75,000 in 1973.[111]

Once in the army, the new recruits tended to be more radical, less passive, and generally poorer material for soldiering than earlier cohorts. In 1967, the coffeehouse movement near the bases, countercultural military newspapers, increases in desertions and AWOL's, even mutinies and assassinations (fraggings), began to capture public, as well as the Pentagon's, attention. General Westmoreland was particularly concerned about the part played by SDS and the National Mobilization Committee in organizing the subtly subversive coffeehouses.[112] Paul Warnke, however, does not remember morale in the army being a major factor in the spring 1968 deliberations, although there was considerable discussion of the reserve issue. Army morale in Vietnam became increasingly important in 1969 and 1970 as more and more troops began coming home.[113] Nevertheless, it was a troublesome issue in 1967, and 1968 as well. To the extent that it had become a matter of concern, it represented another victory for antiwar forces.

Whether we look at the media, Congress, the military, the Democratic party, or opinion in general, one cannot ignore the link between the antiwar movement and the growing opposition to the war in February and March 1968. Dissenting messages, presented over and over in many forums in 1966 and 1967, conditioned the public and the decision makers for the deescalatory arguments following Tet. Douglass Cater talks about a "mushrooming effect" in which people of "national standing" opposed to the war affected others.[114]

Cater's observations conform to theories of opinion analysts that see antiwar messages transmitted to the public through the *New York Times*, the *Washington Post*, Walter Cronkite, or a senator's statement eventually filtered down to the public in the so-called two-step-flow-of-information theory. Dean Rusk, who denies the validity of that approach, argues that when the American people determined that enough was enough in 1968, they made up their minds independent of the antiwar activities of the previous three years. Nevertheless, his own comments on March 22, 1968, belie his contention. At a White House meeting that day, he acknowledged that "there has been a dramatic shift in public opinion on the war, that a lot of people are really ready to surrender without knowing they are following a party line."[115] Implicitly, Rusk linked the shift in opinion to the movement.

Even if Rusk does not believe it, the public, and especially the activists, thought that the movement had been instrumental in forcing Johnson to present the concessions in his March 31 speech. Almost immediately following the completion of his speech, students poured out of dormitories all across the nation in spontaneous demonstrations, congratulating themselves and shouting "the hawk is dead."[116]

With the withdrawal of Johnson from the primary campaign, the agreement in early April by Hanoi to open peace talks, and the lack of new or dramatic military activity in Vietnam, the peace movement lost some of its energy. Johnson had curbed the bombing, refused to send more troops to Vietnam, and begun talking to the enemy in Paris. Nonetheless, and even considering the fact that the students soon left the campuses for summer vacation, some antiwar activity did pick up again in the late spring, most of it directed against the candidacy of Hubert Humphrey. Having apparently won a major victory on March 31, antiwar students and politicians did not want to see it snatched from them by Johnson surrogate Humphrey.

In addition, a new element appeared on the scene that made a media splash, the alliance of hippies and the New Left. Abbie Hoffman and Jerry Rubin's Youth International (Yippie) Party, considered "crazies" by political organizations in the movement, announced the formation of their party with a chaotic "invasion" of Grand Central Station in New York on March 23. Although the Yippies were not a serious party and never commanded much support from activist youth, they may have weakened the antiwar movement in the eyes of middle-class America by calling attention to the countercultural, almost revolutionary, tendencies of some of its adherents. Abbie Hoffman denies that charge, claiming that his group specifically and consciously targeted part of the youth "market," while others, consciously, targeted other groups in the grand antiwar coalition. Moreover, he insists that most of those who had earlier composed the crowds listening to the Spocks, Coffins, Kings, and other relatively middle-class antiwar leaders were indeed hippies and "freaks" who were there mostly for the music. Although they did not often see eye to eye, Tom Hayden agrees, in part, with Hoffman. Commenting on a later demonstration, he noted, "Without the musicians you couldn't get the youth base."[117]

Aside from the headlines grabbed by the Yippies, more tradition-al activism continued apace, with a nationwide protest on April 26 in which over two hundred thousand college and high school students cut classes to mark the occasion. The following day, as many as one hundred thousand people turned out for antiwar rallies in New York and San Francisco to hear such luminaries as Coretta Scott King and Mayor John Lindsay of New York. And as if Johnson had never made his speech, the ads continued in the newspapers, with five hundred student leaders signing a huge Clergy and Laymen Concerned advertisement in the April 28 issue of the *New York Times*.[118] At the same time, as Humphrey toured the nation in quest of the nomination, he was harassed and confronted by demonstrations and walkouts at such places as Kent State on May 2, Bucknell on May 4, New York on July 23, and at Los Angeles on July 28.

The demonstrations at the Chicago Democratic Convention in August that turned into bloody riots were viewed as another antiwar protest. Insofar as citizens generally supported the police over the "radicals," those activities hurt the antiwar movement.[119] More important from the point of view of the left wing of the Democratic party, the nomination of Humphrey, the perceived undemocratic nature of the convention, and the so-called police riot on the streets of Chicago helped to elect Richard Nixon in November. Not only were middle-class, moderate, and conserva-tive Americans horrified by the alleged excesses of the movement, but many on the Left were similarly outraged by the excesses of the police and the Democratic party and sat out the election or voted for a third party. In addition, even those who voted for Humphrey from the left wing of the Democratic party most likely did so unenthusiastically and withheld their labor from the campaign. The antiwar movement, then, had something to do with the creation of Vietnam policy in 1969 by contributing in several ways to the victory of Richard Nixon, whose programs were quite different from those planned by Hubert Humphrey.[120]

Though a lame duck, Johnson did not stop trying to defend himself against his critics through the remainder of his term. Two weeks after the speech of March 31, political aide Fred Panzer, who again raised the credibility gap issue and "the insidious media impact your antiwar critics were able to achieve," called for a new public relations campaign to rally support for the administration. In June, Johnson told Rusk and Clifford that they were not "communicating adequately" and suggested that they hold more press conferences, the texts of which they should send to him.[121]

His renewed public relations offensive, which was not as spirited as earlier offensives, had two main purposes. The first was to assist the candidacy of Humphrey. Even diplomatic strategy was tied in with that campaign. The Paris peace talks could not break off until his nomination and perhaps even election was assured. As Clifford noted late in May, "If we do anything to wreck Paris, Bobby [Kennedy] shoots up. . . . We need to keep the talks going through August 26."[122] Kennedy's drive for the nomination ended when he was assassinated on June 5 by Sirhan Sirhan.

The second purpose, and one that involved national security in a less political fashion, had to do with the continuing attempt to convince the North Vietnamese that the movement was not American opinion. Cyrus Vance, W. Averell Harriman's second in command at Paris, was acutely aware of Hanoi's interest in American antiwar activities in the summer of 1968. Similarly, presidential adviser Abe Fortas saw the North Vietnamese "testing to see if your [Johnson's] hands are tied by dove sentiment." On August 28, in public remarks at Paris, Harriman explicitly warned his opposite numbers to stop trying to influence opinion in the United States; they did not really understand how opinion and policy worked in a democracy. Dean Rusk echoed those sentiments on an October 6 "Issues and Answers" television program: "I think the North Vietnamese watch public discussion in this country very closely. They from time to time quote to us the most obscure statements made by someone in this country. They put great weight on the demonstrations and the signs of dissent in this country. But they are confused and misled about what the meaning of 50,000 demonstrators at the Pentagon really is."[123]

Whether or not the North Vietnamese understood the meaning of demonstrations, they did understand the American electoral system. When Richard Nixon was elected on November 5, they had a little more than two months to prepare for the alterations in the style and substance in American policy that the Republican leader would bring with him. The antiwar movement, part of the coalition of allegedly unpatriotic and violent Americans against which Nixon railed in his politics of resentment, also began preparing its strategies for the man who claimed to have a secret plan to end the war in Vietnam.

Chapter Six

Hanoi and the Movement Confront a New President: January 1969–December 1969

"North Vietnam cannot humiliate the United States. Only Americans can do that."
—*RICHARD M. NIXON**

Richard Nixon assumed the presidency with a ballyhooed secret plan to end the war. Although most doves were not optimistic about the prospects for a speedy American withdrawal from Vietnam under Nixon, they, and the public in general, were prepared to give him time to execute the plan. Further, a "new" Nixon had apparently replaced the old one, a development that temporarily neutralized his antagonists in the press and on Capitol Hill.

Nixon never had a plan to end the war, but he did have a general strategy—to increase the pressure on the communists, issue them a November 1, 1969, deadline to be conciliatory or else, and to keep all of this secret from the American public. Thus, the level of hostilities—and casualties—increased in the late winter and spring from the previous fall and Nixon ordered the covert bombing of Cambodia as a signal to North Vietnam that the rules of the game had changed. At the same time, he increased the pressure from the Justice Department and the intelligence bureaus against the more radical of the left-wing activists.

*Public Papers of the President, Richard Nixon, 1969 (Washington, D.C.: GPO, 1971), 909.

It did not take long for antiwar critics and organizations to take up where they had left off with Lyndon Johnson. When little progress had been made by the spring of 1969, they geared up for another campaign of petitioning and demonstrating. The center-pieces of 1969's activities were the Moratorium of October and the Mobilization of November. The former was the more threatening to the Nixon administration because it promised not only to involve middle-class, apolitical types in a civilized and gentle series of protests, but also because it was planned to become institutionalized as a monthly activity during which time support-ers refused to do business as usual—until the war was over.

Despite the increase in American and South Vietnamese mili-tary activity on the land and in the air during the first six months of 1969, the North Vietnamese did not respond to Nixon's ultimatum. Consequently, his aides began planning Operation Duck Hook, a series of possible major escalatory blows that would be administered to the recalcitrant communists after November 1.

The deadline came and went without Operation Duck Hook and without movement on Hanoi's part toward the American negotiat-ing position. One explanation for Nixon's failure to follow through with his strategy was the rejuvenation of the antiwar movement centered around the very successful Moratorium of October 15. Millions of Americans took part in some form of moratorium that day and millions of others sympathized with the protest. With the Mobilization only one month away, Nixon feared that the public, led by a confident antiwar movement, would demand a much quicker withdrawal from Vietnam than he had planned. Moreover, he was convinced, as Johnson had been, that such demonstrations bolstered Hanoi's morale.

In early November, Nixon appealed to the Silent Majority to back his self-proclaimed prudent policy of gradual Vietnami-zation, which would bring peace with honor and maintain American national security. His speech, as well as Vice Presi-dent Spiro Agnew's attack against the eastern media and tele-vision networks, struck the right chords. Nixon had temporarily won the battle for the American public. There was a silent ma-jority in the land that not only supported his policies in Vietnam but was angry at the media, the youth, liberals, and all of those who were apparently tearing down the flag. That majority,

TABLE 5.

MAJOR VIETNAM WAR–RELATED EVENTS OF 1969

Antiwar Activities	Percent Poll Respondents who Think War Was Mistake	Percent Poll Respondent for Withdra
	Feb.: 52%	
		March: 26
April 5: New York demonstration		
		June: 29%
	Sept.: 58%	
		Sept.: 36%
Oct. 15: Nationwide Moratorium		
		Nov.: 21%
Nov. 15: Washington Mobilization		

Administration Activities	Troop Levels	Battle Deaths (6-month totals)
e 8: Nixon announces withdrawal 5,000 troops	June 30: 538,700	8,340
t. 16: Nixon announces withdrawal 35,000 troops		
v. 3: Nixon Silent Majority speech		
v. 16: My Lai report 15: Nixon announces withdrawal 50,000 troops	Dec: 31: 475,200	3,874

although willing to accept gradual Vietnamization, was not in a hawkish mood, as Nixon discovered the following spring.

Most voters who went to the polls on November 5, 1968, found little to choose between Humphrey and Nixon on Vietnam policies.[1] Both candidates promised to bring the troops home from Southeast Asia and to continue the Paris peace talks. If anything, some might have reasoned that Nixon offered a brighter prospect for a speedy peace, since he had a secret plan. Without revealing its details, he told dovish Michigan Republican congressman Donald Riegle that the war would be over within six months of his assumption of office. With that deadline approaching, in May 1969, Henry Kissinger asked a group of Quakers to give *him* six months. If the war isn't over by then, "you can come back and tear down the White House."[2]

The secret plan to end the war did not exist. Senator Fulbright reports bitterly how he was "hoodwinked and misled" by Kissinger, who promised him an end to the war through the application of the "plan."[3] That plan was a campaign gimmick designed to close the gap on the war issue between the perceived hawk Nixon and the more moderate Humphrey. Instead of a specific plan, the Nixon administration fashioned a strategy that it hoped would bring the war to an end in 1969 on terms favorable to the United States and South Vietnam. Its outlines were still dim during the weeks after November 5.

As Nixon and his aides met in the Hotel Pierre in New York during the interregnum between the election and the January 20 inauguration, they confronted an unusually wide variety of domestic and international problems, not the least of which was Vietnam. Nixon had been elected not only to end the war but also to deal with the unprecedented wave of civil disturbances and the fragmentation of American society. The fact that he could learn from his predecessor's unsuccessful attempts to manage the dual crises was a considerable advantage. Nixon later wrote that the antiwar movement "frustrated Johnson . . . then it disillusioned and finally it destroyed him."[4] To understand his own relationship to the movement, it is important to examine how policy was made in the new administration, especially the way it dealt with public opinion and the media.

Although several task forces prepared extensive position papers on domestic and international problems, most of the high-level discussions at the Pierre involved the structure of and personnel in the new administration. John Ehrlichman, who was one of the president's two chief White House advisers (the other being H. R. Haldeman), does not remember any particular strategy sessions concerning the antiwar movement. He, John Mitchell, and William Rogers, among others, were, of course, briefed by Deputy Attorney General Warren Christopher about civil disturbances and radicalism and how the Justice Department and the FBI were dealing with them.[5] For his part, Haldeman recalls planning the implementation of the campaign's "Bring Us Together" theme. He and his colleagues thought it would be especially important for the new administration to maintain a dialogue with young people. That was one area in which the Nixon team felt Johnson had been weak.[6]

Early in the administration an attempt was made to coordinate the public relations aspect of Vietnam policies at home and abroad. Representatives from Defense, State, the CIA, NSC, and the JCS composed a Coordinating Group on Vietnam Policies, something akin to Johnson's VIG.[7] Nevertheless, as with the Johnson administration, no specific officer or structure was established to deal with the antiwar movement or critical opinion. As former Appointments Secretary Dwight Chapin jokes, there was no "Secretary of Dissent" in the Nixon administration.[8] As in the Johnson period, foreign policy aides generally "left political judgements to the president." Naturally, those who prepared position papers for the National Security Council, for example, took the public into consideration because their recommendations had to be realistic in terms of political acceptability. In addition, in order to evaluate the impact of a policy on Hanoi, diplomatic experts tried to assess Hanoi's view of the American public. Nevertheless, most advisers in most instances deferred to Nixon's celebrated political acumen when it came to the opinion variable.[9]

Quite different from Johnson in many ways, Nixon was every bit as fascinating a public and private figure. Former Eisenhower aide and long-time Washington insider Bryce Harlow was one of Nixon's chief congressional operatives. Harlow found his new boss to be "one of the most intelligent" men who had ever occupied the

Oval Office. A master politician, Nixon had an uncanny sensitivity for "visceral behavior down at the precinct level clear across America." Further, unlike Johnson, who often bogged down in details, Nixon knew how to distinguish trivia from the truly important. That was one of the reasons Nixon spent so much time alone in an office in the Executive Office Building across the street from the White House. There, surrounded by his omnipresent yellow pads, he was able "to keep the crap from consuming the president of the United States." Helping him from being consumed by that crap was H. R. Haldeman, "a remarkable administrator," according to Harlow.[10]

Haldeman was Nixon's "gatekeeper,"[11] with vast powers as the president's right-hand man not seen since Eisenhower's Sherman Adams. "Nearly everything went through Bob Haldeman's office," notes a speechwriter. Some in the Nixon kitchen cabinet were not pleased with this arrangement, which limited their access to the president. Nevertheless, on occasion, key assistants such as William Safire and Ray Price were able to see Nixon without first being ushered through the door by Haldeman.[12]

Despite some resentment over the concentration of power in the hands of one man, most of Haldeman's colleagues hailed his general fairness, especially the way he presented differing views to the president.[13] Haldeman himself takes great pride in the media summaries that he provided for Nixon, analyses of the print and electronic media that surpassed in comprehensiveness previous White House compilations. Nixon devoured Haldeman's summaries as well as analyses of both privately commissioned and published public opinion polls.[14]

Unlike Johnson, Nixon encouraged his aides to express their differences in briefing papers in the early policymaking stages. He was well aware of the ideological biases of his staff and, for example, discounted ultraconservative pleas from speechwriter Pat Buchanan and liberal laments from White House counselor Leonard Garment. To be sure, the political spectrum within the administration ranged within the confines of Republican philosophy. Yet Nixon did encourage his aides to speak their mind, especially during periods when policy was still being formulated.

He did not exactly allow them to *speak* their mind, since this very shy man preferred to read memos than listen to counselors in person. In part, he found this was a more efficient way for him to tap their ideas. He also did not like confronting unusual or dissenting ideas in person.[15] In addition, such a procedure made it easier for a memo writer to be bolder than he or she might be reporting at a conference table. Even the third-in-command in the White House, John Ehrlichman, recalls worrying about dissenting in a public forum at which Nixon presided. One never could be certain of one's latitude. One oral misstep could lead to being frozen out of the inner circle for weeks.[16]

Overall, although Nixon presided over fewer important formal policymaking sessions such as Johnson's Tuesday Lunches, he may have been exposed to as wide a variety of views and information as was his predecessor. Even when Nixon emerged from seclusion to discuss the proposals he had handwritten on yellow pads, aides were still able to offer gentle critiques. Once beyond that point, however, absolute loyalty was demanded, especially in formal meetings. If one could not get on board, he or she was supposed to resign swiftly and quietly.[17]

As for foreign-policy decision making in particular, the inner circle was very small, involving fewer people than the previous administration. Aside from domestic political issues with a bearing on foreign relations, such as the antiwar movement in some cases, foreign policies were devised by Nixon, Kissinger, and one or two others, with Alexander Haig and Brent Scowcroft playing some part in the last two years of Nixon's tenure.[18] John Ehrlichman expands this circle to include, on an ad hoc basis, Attorney General John Mitchell.[19]

The protective wagons were drawn even tighter around Nixon than around Johnson to defend the president against leaks to a press dominated by eastern media and bound to give him a rough time. Nixon perceived himself as "hated" by the media. Johnson had earlier thought that the media considered him a "boor." A boor, however, was better than an object of hatred. Expecting less, Nixon apparently worried less than Johnson about media criticism. In early 1970, he thought that 15 percent of the press was friendly to the administration, 20 percent fair, and 65 percent negative and unfair. That 65 percent could never be won over, he advised. Thus, among other ploys, he tried to call on the 15 percent of friendly journalists at his press conferences.[20]

To Ray Price, the media represented a "beast"; to White House colleague Jim Keogh, an "adversary." Keogh thinks the media treated Nixon much more harshly than they treated Johnson.[21] Perhaps Keogh is correct, but this is a relative matter. The historic hostile relationship between the western conservative Nixon and eastern liberal journalists may have made it easier for the president to deal with the expected attacks. For Democratic reformer Johnson, they may have been more difficult to accept, even if they were gentler. In addition, when he first took office, many old antagonists gave Nixon the benefit of the doubt, especially considering the developing image of a "new" Nixon. If anything, at the start of his administration Nixon's media treatment may have been better than expected. Only when the new Nixon began to fade into the old Nixon, at least in the eyes of the press, did the treatment become harsher.

Whether the critiques were harsh or muted, Nixon, not surprisingly, did not like them. Although he did not hold a Johnson-like levée, Nixon often railed against the press, dispatching aides to attack his antagonists. Enemies lists were dutifully drawn up and elaborate campaigns were directed against media and other critics of his policies. Nevertheless, as was the case with Johnson, aides learned to ignore Nixon's initial outbursts of anger and the resultant intemperate orders and to wait until the rational, politic Nixon replaced the thin-skinned recipient of criticism. For this reason, the famous "tapes" may be misleading, since his astute aides did not carry out many of his orders.

Through his years in office, depending on the issue, Nixon and his advisers varied in their reactions to the media. In general, they claim to have been frustrated by their inability to get out the truth. The problem, according to Ray Price, was not bad news but the "bad reporting of the news."[22]

Nixon's defenders consider his anger and even outbursts against the press and other critics as different from Johnson's. Most of the time, Nixon did not take criticism personally; he was angry because he knew that his unfair treatment in the press affected national security as well as his domestic program. Thus, the rational Nixon sometimes placed an embargo on contacts with the *New York Times'* James Reston not because he was angry at the influential columnist personally, but because he was angry at the damage Reston had done to his program. Nixon had no expectations of being loved or admired by a man like Reston. Or similarly, when he angrily embargoed the entire *Times* after it published *The Pentagon Papers*, he cited its irresponsibility and unpatriotic behavior for his draconian order.[23] This idealized view of the pragmatic decision maker is difficult to juxtapose with the image of a man constantly concerned with how his actions were being reported for the historical record.

The more moderate or even liberal the adviser, the more likely he or she was to be troubled personally by the bad press and to think that the not-so-conservative and pragmatic Nixon was as well. Adviser and friend Leonard Garment thought that *New York Times* criticism especially bothered Nixon. Like Johnson, Nixon "craved legitimacy" and was "resentful" when the most important American paper did not support him. He "tried not to let it get under his skin," but for a man who thought he was a "liberal" or at least a "centrist," such a lack of acceptance was irritating.[24]

John Ehrlichman claims he had no personal antagonism toward individual journalists and, for example, enjoyed good relations with the *Washington Post*'s Katherine Graham and Ben Bradlee. These good relations almost flourished during the honeymoon era in 1969, a time of tentative liberal support for some of Nixon's domestic programs. On the other hand, Ehrlichman was one of those in charge of trying to shift national interest from the ten or so major eastern papers to the five thousand in the rest of the nation. He and his aides tried to "flank the wire services and the eastern establishment" by developing regional media contacts and lavishing attention on them out of proportion to their previous experience.[25]

The media were not the only critics of government officials. Like their predecessors in the Johnson administration, Nixon aides were subject to pressures from family and friends who were opposed to a continuation of the war. Washington was full of such people in 1969.

As for the influential Georgetown set to which many Johnson Democrats had aspired entry, Nixon Republicans were "not as thirsty" for respect by that group of political and social tastemakers. Someone as highly placed as H. R. Haldeman did not even feel himself a "part of the social life" of the District.[26]

Irrespective of Haldeman's general indifference to Georgetown, like their predecessors in office, family members of administration loyalists often took the brunt of criticism from antiwar friends. Haldeman's daughter dated an antiwar leader at Stanford; a young NSC aide, Peter Rodman, recalls how his parents were occasionally assailed by liberal Boston intimates; and even Henry Kissinger's thirteen-year-old daughter was asked to sign an antibombing petition.[27]

John Ehrlichman's social life in Washington was not affected dramatically by the war, in part because he seemed always to be placed next to Mrs. Richard Helms at dinner parties. Although he knew that most of the National Symphony people with whom he socialized were against the war, he got along quite well with them. His children, one of whom was of draft age and at Stanford, were another story. For him and them it was a "rough time" full of "anguish." Two of his boys once discussed Vietnam with Henry Kissinger at San Clemente and Peter called his father during the Cambodian invasion to express his concern.[28]

Of all of Nixon's major advisers, Henry Kissinger, the most important Vietnam policymaker, was the most sensitive to criticism from the so-called eastern intellectual-journalistic establishment. The powerful national security adviser came from the center of that establishment, Harvard, and if not a Democrat most of his life, he was certainly a Rockefeller Republican in 1968.[29] Walt Rostow, his predecessor as national security adviser, was rejected by colleagues at MIT, his old home university and Harvard's neighbor along the Charles, when he wanted to return to his original post in 1969.[30] From the start, Kissinger worried about ending up like Rostow, persona non grata in Cambridge. On several occasions, especially during some difficult days in 1970, Kissinger joked nervously about not being taken back by Harvard or not having his leave extended, or even having to accept a post at someplace like Arizona State.[31]

Throughout his years in office, Kissinger courted successfully his friends in the press and in intellectual circles in the East, leaking information to them and suggesting that he was different from his neanderthal colleagues. He was quite "sensitive" to their criticism, but generally "skillful" at using them. And like Nixon, according to Kissinger's supporters, it was not just ego—the scholar-diplomat knew how the media could affect policy if not in Washington, certainly in Hanoi.[32]

His skill was shown as late as December 1972, when he was able to convince many of his intellectual and journalist friends that he had opposed the B-52 bombing of Hanoi. Most likely, he was a supporter of that tactic. At least H. R. Haldeman remembers him that way and expresses a hope that the "tapes" will soon be released so that the rest of the world could see how hawkish Kissinger really was.[33]

Kissinger carefully monitored and sometimes catered to antiwar critics in the eastern establishment and on eastern campuses. He recognized their importance in opinion formation and also in their contributions to the images of America developed by foreign allies and enemies. For Kissinger, who came from their midst though ultimately remaining an outsider as a German-Jewish emigre, the relationship may have been somewhat more personal than for Nixon, always an outsider and only recently a New Yorker. Nevertheless, both men, despite the tough talk, were nervous about the media, the intellectuals, and the college students who contributed so much to Johnson's downfall.

The ambiguity in the Nixon approach to the establishment was evidenced in the appointment of Daniel Patrick Moynihan to a prominent post as White House adviser. Earlier discussing staffing, Nixon ordered Haldeman, "None of them in the Cabinet, do you understand? None of those Harvard bastards!"[34] Yet one Harvard "bastard" made it to the kitchen cabinet: Harvard Professor Moynihan, a Democrat as well.

Moynihan sent his new boss an unsolicited memorandum on January 5, 1969, in which he predicted a one-term presidency unless the Vietnam War ended soon. The war could easily destroy him, as it had destroyed Johnson. Most important, counseled Moynihan, the scorned liberal Left in the United States did have power, more power than the insular Johnson ever understood. Few of his new Republican bedfellows shared his perception at the time. Moynihan now is certain that his warning was prescient.[35]

President Nixon did not have long to wait to confront antiwar demonstrators. They turned out for his inauguration, along with other left-wing and radical activists. The relatively small number of visible demonstrators organized by the National Mobilization Committee were not able to spoil the day that Richard Nixon finally made it to the top of American politics. He was fortunate that the antiwar movement was in one of those breath-catching modes, comparable to 1966, waiting to see how the secret plan to end the war would turn out. Leaders of the movement who suspected that Nixon did not have a viable plan realized that many potential foot soldiers were not ready to march on the Pentagon again until he was given a fair chance. After all, troops were being withdrawn, the bombing had stopped, and diplomats were talking in Paris.[36]

Moreover, the movement was in organizational disarray with factional disputes occupying as much energy as the larger dispute with Washington. The Nixon administration itself contributed to the disarray by beginning to strike at the more radical leadership of the movement. In March, a federal grand jury indicted David Dellinger, Tom Hayden, and six others for their activities at the Chicago convention. Nixon's vigorous prosecution of left-wing opponents, as well as black militants, accelerated the tendency on the part of some of them toward revolutionary violence. Such violence helped to shore up Nixon's support among the Right, the center, and even Democrats who were appalled by such actions as the Weathermen's "Days of Rage" in Chicago later in the year.

Although the organized antiwar movement in particular was relatively quiet during the early days of the Nixon presidency, the number of radical and violent protests increased dramatically in 1969. Several people were injured in a rash of bombings at such places as Pomona in February and San Francisco State in March with, according to the Scranton Commission (President's Commission on Campus Unrest), over eight thousand bombings or threats of bombings recorded between January 1, 1969, and April 15, 1970. During the 1968–69 academic year, over four thousand people were arrested on college campuses for political violence; the next year the number rose to seventy-two hundred.[37] Such spectacular violence, often unrelated to the war and mainstream antiwar activity, would be used by Nixon when he went on the offensive against the doves in October.[38]

The by now unspectacular and even "normal" picketing, leafleting, marching, and petitioning did continue during the first six months of the Nixon administration, albeit without any large-scale centerpieces. Despite their disappointment in not capturing the presidency, antiwar critics had to feel confident in their ultimate power, given their perceived role in the "defeat" of Lyndon Johnson.

Typical of the continuation of normal antiwar activities was the February meeting between leaders of the Clergy and Laymen Concerned group and Henry Kissinger in which the national security adviser outlined the administration's policies. Several weeks later, over thirteen hundred members of the Women Strike for Peace, a group Nixon privately labeled a "front," picketed the White House.[39] These were relatively obscure activities and, more important, were not treated as significant events by the media. For example, when critic Dwight Macdonald and actress Viveca Lindfors presented a petition at the White House signed by nine thousand people, the *New York Times* chose to cover the story with a brief item on page 5 of its April 13 edition. It would take larger and more dramatic antiwar actions to capture media attention, especially during the honeymoon period when Nixon's secret plan was allegedly being placed in motion.

In the current absence of the richness of documentary evidence available for the Johnson years, one is left chiefly with impressionistic clues as to the importance of petitions in newspapers during the Nixon years. Given their antieastern, antiestablishment biases, and the conviction that professors and intellectuals were not their natural allies anyway, Nixon people took such manifestations of criticism less seriously than Johnson people. Bryce Harlow, who had seen many petitions since he began working in Washington in 1938, was not impressed with "a bunch of names." Like George Reedy, however, he did lament the fact that some of the more inexperienced young people in the White House did pay attention to them. On at least one occasion, John Ehrlichman took note of an advertisement. On the eve of the October Moratorium, he tried to discover the sources of the funds that paid for an ad in the *New York Times* that had been signed by fifteen prominent antiwar critics. H. R. Haldeman, the master of the opinion analyses, on the other hand, claims that he never looked at them.[40]

As in the previous administration, antiwar petitions published in the *New York Times* and other newspapers influenced the attitudes of those who read them. The main difference may have been that there were fewer people left exposed to such manifestations of opposition who had not already made up their minds about the war and Richard Nixon. Nevertheless, sitting in the White House on a Sunday morning, leafing through the *New York Times*, Nixon aides had to be disheartened by the numbers of important educational and cultural leaders who continued to add their names to those petitions.

Similarly, although they expected them, mass demonstrations also had to dishearten those who had hoped that with deescalation on track, the protesters would stay off the streets and the Mall. The general pattern of one large spring and one large autumn demonstration held up through Nixon's first spring with a crowd estimated at between twenty-five to a hundred thousand gathering in New York on April 5 to protest his policies. It could not compare to previous spring marches, perhaps because Nixon had not yet disappointed those who were prepared to give him the benefit of the doubt.

Even campus leaders tried to reason with the new occupants of the White House. After a group of 253 college editors and politicians signed a declaration of conscience on the war and asked for a meeting with Nixon, their representatives were granted time with Kissinger and Ehrlichman on April 29. As had been the case with such sessions during the Johnson era, the youthful activists were not convinced by administration arguments.[41] Some of the leadership of this group helped to organize the October Moratorium.

As might have been expected, graduation and honorary degree time produced embarrassment for administration dignitaries. Over two-thirds of Brown graduates turned their backs when Henry Kissinger stepped forward to receive his degree at their commencement on June 2.[42] This was the last time Kissinger accepted such an honor. Ohio State University mustered 150 protesters at a ceremony at which Vice President Agnew was feted on June 7, and the next day 77 percent of the Yale graduating class signed a protest against administration policies in Vietnam.[43]

As in previous years, administration officials breathed a sigh of relief when the campuses cleared for summer vacation. Things could have been much worse. Nixon and his colleagues did not look forward to the fall. On June 30, the Vietnam Moratorium Committee issued its call for a nationwide moratorium on all work-related activities on October 15, and less than two weeks later the Student Mobilization Committee called for a student strike and a massive Washington demonstration on November 15. In addition, the White House heard of plans for a nationwide student strike in the fall, a strike that adviser Bud Wilkinson began trying to foil. He wrote to Kissinger in July about how "the White House should *not* be directly involved with the effort. It must appear to be a spontaneous reaction by students. There are a number of ways that might be done."[44]

Nixon had been in office more than five months. To many, the secret plan to end the war either did not exist or had failed. It was time for the movement to turn up the heat.

Contributing to national impatience with Nixon's policy may have been *Life* magazine's June 27 issue, an issue devoted to pictures and stories of the 242 American war dead the previous week. The unprecedented somber tribute from that influential publication reminded readers that despite America's commitment to deescalate, her boys were still dying in the jungles of Vietnam.[45] The *Life* issue was especially important, since the networks had decided informally after 1968 to spotlight the peace talks and other diplomatic issues and to deal only lightly with combat stories. The evening newscasts that now delivered their obligatory nightly report on Vietnam from Paris, not Saigon, may have lulled some viewers into thinking that the shooting had stopped.[46] Here, interestingly, the much-maligned media were apparently foiling Hanoi's attempt to concentrate its fire on American and not ARVN soldiers to arouse antiwar sentiment in the United States.[47]

Although the movement was relatively quiescent during the first half of 1969, Nixon faced increasing dovish activities in Congress, particularly the Senate. Vocal Senate doves influenced fellow senators, the public, and the media, and, in turn, were influenced by the media and the antiwar sentiments of their constituents.[48] One former NSC aide still cringes when he talks about how North Vietnamese negotiator Le Duc Tho quoted dovish senators to Kissinger. For his part, Nixon asked Kissinger to document the number of times communist negotiators referred to such dissent so that he could use those data in a fall speech.[49] Despite occasional bursts of activity by Fulbright, Church, and other legislators during the 1966–68 period, doves in Congress were probably underrepresented in numbers and influence compared to the amount of dovish sentiment in the country.[50] This situation changed in the Nixon years.

First, of course, Congress was Democratic and the president was Republican. During the early years of the war, complains H. R. Haldeman, Johnson "euchred" Congress. Now, some Democrats who earlier had been quiet doves could speak out without challenging the party leader, who held many of the purse strings for their favorite domestic programs.[51] Second, the doves gained in the elections of 1968 and 1970, with antiwar senators often replacing those more moderate on the war.[52] Finally, according to Haldeman, the Senate leadership was not as effective under Nixon as it was under Johnson in keeping the troops in line. For example, Haldeman expresses disappointment with Mike Mansfield's inability to calm antiwar Democrats, even though he was kept informed about the progress being made in Paris and in the later secret talks.[53]

Bryce Harlow, Nixon's point man in Congress, knew that his boss was walking into "a lion's mouth" on Capitol Hill. The first problem is that Congress often has little confidence in a new president's staff, many of whom "can't even find the men's room." To help build confidence and to quiet potential antiwar senators, Harlow held secret briefings in Georgetown, every six weeks, between Henry Kissinger and a "clot of dissident senators." Senators Fulbright, Mathias, Percy, Cooper, and Symington were among the regulars at the informal meetings. They convened at one another's homes, "sucked a little juice to get warmed up," and listened to the national security adviser explain how Nixon was getting the country out of Vietnam. According to Harlow, Kissinger "dominated them with his mind," and often, in intellectual exchanges, "humiliated" them. Not everyone remembers the secret meetings that way. Fulbright himself does not think that they were very important, nor did they help to keep much of a lid on dissent, especially after the first few months that Nixon was in office. Further, laments Fulbright, Kissinger belonged in the Senate chambers, testifying publicly, something that Nixon would not permit.[54]

However one explains it, the Senate, especially, became more and more of a problem for Nixon, even after the era of mass demonstrations ended. From June 1966 through July 1973, Congress took 113 votes on Vietnam War–related items. Ninety-four of those were taken during Nixon's presidency. Of the 86 in the Senate, 62 involved reducing appropriations or military options.[55]

More specifically, in January 1969, Senator Fulbright set up an ad hoc committee, the Symington Committee, to study security arrangements and commitments abroad. The committee, which held hearings primarily on Southeast Asia, also produced a resolution defining a "national commitment" in June. Then, in December, Congress approved for the first time a resolution to restrict American operations in Laos and Thailand. Another straw in the wind early in the Nixon term was a 350-to-40 vote on the military appropriations bill in the House in May, with the 40 opponents the highest number of presumed antiwar voters up to that date.[56] Capitol Hill posed many more problems for Nixon than for Johnson, especially as time began running out on his secret plan to end the war. Nixon revealed his extreme displeasure when he ordered Haldeman to say on the "Today" show in 1972 that some senators were "consciously aiding and abetting the enemy."[57]

Antiwar critics began to become more active by the spring of 1969 because the war was not winding down as fast as they expected, especially considering the administration's secret peace plan. When Nixon took office, over 540,000 American soldiers were still in Vietnam. American combat deaths for the first half of 1969 increased rather than decreased during the time in which the plan was supposedly being implemented. But that was part of the plan.

Nixon really did have a plan to end the war, although not in the six months he told Representative Riegle, nor was the plan as dovish as he implied. He hoped to end the war during the second half of 1969 through a covert threat to the North Vietnamese that he would unleash American power if they did not become more conciliatory at the bargaining table. The deadline was November 1. If progress had not been made by then, Hanoi would face unimaginable escalation. This secret strategy employed the reasonable Kissinger as the good cop and his chief, the anticommunist Nixon, as the bad cop. Kissinger let it be known that if the Vietnamese were unable to accept his generous terms, they would have to face the irrational hawk who had spent his life fighting bolshevism.[58] In the meantime, he sought to pacify the public with troop withdrawals and moderate-sounding offers to the North Vietnamese, as seen in his first televised speech on Vietnam on May 14.

In the summer of 1969, National Security Council aides began to work on Operation Duck Hook, a series of proposed escalations intended for use against the North Vietnamese should the November 1 deadline pass without any movement from them. Although the strategists considered a wide variety of options, including bombing the dikes, blockading Hanoi and Haiphong, and invading the North, Duck Hook never advanced beyond the planning stages.[59] The absence of a formal plan as the November 1 deadline came closer suggests that the elaborate secret strategy employed by Nixon and Kissinger may have been a bluff.

Bluff or not, in the period preceding the deadline, Nixon authorized a series of secret escalations meant to demonstrate his toughness. Early in his administration, American marines were sent into Laos on covert missions to counter new NVA incursions, and most important, Nixon ordered the secret bombing of Cambodia in March. The bombing, which became an issue during the Watergate investigations, was kept secret in part to keep the antiwar movement quiet, as well as to avert a crisis with Hanoi's allies and, especially,[60] to avoid embarrassing Cambodia's leader, neutralist Prince Norodom Sihanouk. Kissinger worried particularly about domestic reaction to the bombing, an escalation that few Americans would understand was calculated to bring the war to a speedy close.[61] The bombing was also a signal to Hanoi that Nixon could escalate without arousing the antiwar movement.[62]

Nixon and Kissinger claimed not to have been *personally* worried about the movement's reaction to the bombing. They could have weathered any storm antiwar activists might have created, they assert. However, they did worry about the impact of that storm of protest on Hanoi. Like their predecessors, they saw Hanoi using American doves in all of their political and military activities, especially the Paris peace talks.[63]

A new approach to Vietnam was only one of their foreign policy initiatives. Nixon and Kissinger had embarked on a grand series of linked strategies of détente, the cornerstone of which was America's strength of purpose. The Russians, Chinese, and other powers were watching to see if Nixon could establish mastery over his turbulent nation. Any truckling to the mobs in the streets could send the wrong message to Moscow and Beijing.

Nixon and his colleagues were confident that they could have bested the antiwar movement in a contest for public opinion. On the other hand, they reasoned, if the story of the bombing of Cambodia leaked out, the bombing of a neutral country not yet formally involved in the war, more than just doves would have been disturbed. Such a perceived escalation certainly would have aroused strong criticism in the media and in Congress.[64] Most Americans would have reacted negatively as well to any escalation of a war that was supposed to be winding down.[65] If this was the case, then the November 1 deadline looks all the more like a bluff. If the general public could not have been expected to accept the secret bombing, then how did Nixon propose to institute the much more devastating blows envisaged in Duck Hook?

Whether or not Nixon was bluffing, he and administration representatives talked frequently in public about the dangers posed by Hanoi's thinking that dissent might hamstring the new American policymakers. Taking up where Johnson and Rusk left off, Nixon and Rogers tried to educate the North Vietnamese about the American system and the relationship between noisy dissenters and the public.[66]

At a March 4 press conference, Nixon explicitly drew the link between Hanoi's military strategies and the state of American public opinion. At that time, he thought that he could maintain strong American support for his policies as long as he explained them carefully and completely.[67] This implicit critique of Johnson's old credibility gap sounds especially ironic, considering the fact that it was precisely at this time that Nixon was devising his secret bombing of Cambodia.

On several other occasions during the summer and fall of 1969, the president stressed the by then timeworn theme that if only the public would unite behind his programs, North Vietnam would be forced to negotiate in good faith.[68] Henry Cabot Lodge, the chief negotiator in Paris, chimed in when he remarked in May that Hanoi was still waiting for a sign that "American public opinion is going to collapse." With an eye on those negotiations, Secretary of State William Rogers echoed Rusk when he claimed that although he did not oppose criticism of the administration's Vietnam policy, such criticism was not constructive during a period of delicate negotiations.[69]

As the Nixon forces conducted their still low-key offensive against mainstream foreign policy critics, they never imagined that the October 15 Moratorium would be as successful as it turned out. To be sure, the president's California White House in San Clemente was picketed by over three thousand protesters on August 17, but the Pacific community was near Los Angeles, with its large, easily mobilized young population.

The Moratorium was a novel sort of protest. It was not held on the weekend, nor did it take place in only two or three cities. It was a nationwide protest in which predominately moderate and even apolitical types would join clean-cut college and high school students for dignified activities. Early indications of support for the Moratorium were seen in advertisements in the *New York Times* on September 21 and 28, the latter of which included endorsements from Republican Senators Charles Goodell and Mark Hatfield and Democratic Senators George McGovern and Eugene McCarthy. Further, Moratorium organizers began to plan a continuing series of monthly moratoria until the war in Vietnam was ended. There would be no "business as usual" while American soldiers remained in Vietnam, they promised.

The fall activism was a major problem for the administration. Ray Price saw it as "the most profound challenge of this century to the continued stability of the democratic system itself." Henry Kissinger, particularly, took it very seriously, along with antiwar resolutions introduced in Congress in September and October. He called up images of Weimar Germany in the twenties and how the mobs in the streets paved the way for Nazism.[70] The president and his aides were determined to demonstrate once and for all to the Vietnamese—and the Russians—that American foreign policy would not be influenced by the minority of demonstrators in the streets and on the campuses.

An informal offensive against the college protesters began as early as June, with Nixon addressing students at conservative campuses, General Beadle State and the Air Force Academy. As the Moratorium itself approached, the president dramatically announced on September 26 that he and the government would not be affected by the upcoming demonstrations.[71] When his statement produced widespread complaints that the president was not listening to the people, Ray Price helped him counter the protests. The speechwriter selected a letter from an antiwar student and made it public, along with a civil reply from Nixon, on October 13. Nixon explained that although all Americans had the right to protest, he himself did not think he could learn anything new from the Moratorium.[72]

Privately, he took actions to weaken the Moratorium's impact. He encouraged friendly senators and representatives to become more vocal in support of administration policy, tried to defeat a major antiwar resolution in the Senate precisely on October 15, and ordered leaks to the press about the allegedly radical nature of the Moratorium's leadership, especially the Socialist Workers and Communist parties. The retirement of the head of Selective Service, Lewis Hershey, on September 20, may also have been part of the Nixon campaign to dampen enthusiasm for the Moratorium among young people.[73]

A parallel offensive was launched on September 26 by Vice President Agnew, who took on the media for its biased coverage of antiwar protests. His main targets were the television networks, whom he hoped to bully into not devoting much time to the Moratorium and the November Mobilization.[74] In both cases, he was successful in affecting network decisions on the extent of live and filmed coverage of the demonstrations. The Moratorium did receive considerable attention, but nowhere as much as one might have expected given its middle-class coloration and unprecedented nature. Offering no live pick-ups during prime time, television news bureaus made late-night wrapup specials the highlights of their coverage.[75]

Irrespective of the extent of the advance coverage, the Moratorium was the single most important one-day demonstration of the entire war. During the week preceding the event, momentum had begun to build. On October 7, the Harvard faculty voted against American involvement in Vietnam by a 255-to-81 vote and supported the Moratorium by a whopping 391-to-16 tally. This election was the first of its kind in the over-300-year history of America's most prestigious university. On October 10, John Laird, Melvin Laird's son, announced that he planned to participate in the Moratorium. Later it was revealed that Kim Agnew, Spiro Agnew's fourteen-year-old daughter, also had wanted to join in. On October 11, five of the eight Ivy League college presidents issued a call for Nixon to speed plans for the withdrawal of American troops from Vietnam.[76] Despite the attempt of friends of the administration to blunt the Moratorium with a new patriotic campaign, the Tell It to Hanoi campaign,[77] on October 15, millions of Americans in hundreds of locales took off from work and school to join with people like Coretta Scott King and Averell Harriman[78] in New York, and luminaries in Washington, Boston, Detroit, and Miami, among other cities, who were distressed by the lack of progress toward peace in Vietnam. Ninety percent of all New York City high school students did not attend classes on that remarkable day. The administration itself documented over two hundred major demonstrations on October 15.[79]

The "effete corps of impudent snobs," as Vice President Agnew labeled them, attracted worldwide attention, including that of the leaders in Hanoi. It is possible that the North Vietnamese hurt the cause somewhat when Premier Pham Van Dong wrote a public letter to Moratorium leaders supporting their efforts. At least, the administration, that called it privately a "kiss of death" letter, tried to tar Moratorium participants with the charge of aiding and abetting the enemy, as demonstrated by the letter.[80] On October 16 in Paris, Henry Cabot Lodge again warned his opposite number, as had Harriman in 1968, not to judge American opinion on the basis of an altogether normal democratic demonstration by a minority of the population.[81]

As has been the case with previous demonstrations, Nixon aides have trouble recalling their reactions to the Moratorium. Clouding memories here is the fact that the Mobilization came only one month after the Moratorium. In general, the party line is: "We realists concerned with protecting national security were not affected in the least by the Moratorium."

The younger and more moderate members of the Nixon entourage were impressed by the numbers of people participating in the various Moratorium activities. One young NSC aide, Peter Rod-man, recalls how some of his friends from out of town used his place to "flop" while they attended the Moratorium. He himself observed the crowds, in part to look at the "cute girls." He remembers feeling "sad" as he watched the demonstrators because they could have an effect on the realistic foreign policies of the Nixon administration. Another young NSC staffer, Winston Lord, also had friends among the participants in the Washington Morato-rium. The success of the event "helped to drive [him] to a relatively dovish position" on Vietnam. The older Leonard Garment, per-haps the most liberal White House counselor after Moynihan, and former Nixon law partner, was impressed with the "awesome crowds" and recalls being somewhat "shaken up" by the Moratori-um. He met with some of the leaders and was distressed to see evidence of the breadth and depth of the antiwar opposition—the situation for Garment was "out of control." White House mail and telegrams also reflected support for the Moratorium.[82]

Such analyses are not common among the Nixon forces. Accord-ing to James Keogh, the Moratorium did "bother" and "worry" President Nixon. However, he and his colleagues were quite sincere when they said that such protests would not affect *their* policies. The problem was that they perceived the demonstrations as influencing the North Vietnamese—Rogers called them "their best ally"—and if they influenced Hanoi, then they had to affect Washington.[83]

The key, for Ray Price, was the "effect of the demonstrations on the media and the public" and how Hanoi interpreted that effect. Likening the Moratorium to a "big be-in," similar to Woodstock, he was not impressed with the crowds. It was easy to "mass bodies" for such events in 1969. Unfortunately for Nixon's White House, the media, the public, and Congress did not view the Moratorium in that manner. Especially distressing to John Ehrlichman was the way the media "hyped" such demonstrations, thus affecting Congress, the public, and ultimately Hanoi.[84]

H. R. Haldeman is convinced that the two fall 1969 demonstra-tions "prolonged the war three and one half years." The White House second-in-command is confident that Nixon could have obtained his peace with honor some time in the fall of 1969 had not the demonstrations, in effect, "eliminated the possibility of a negotiated settlement."[85] That is, Hanoi's resolve was stiffened by the movement in October 1969.

This cannot be the entire story of the impact of the Moratorium on policymaking and the secret November 1 deadline. That deadline came and went. Hanoi did not change its negotiating stance and Nixon did not escalate. The best Nixon came up with in the way of concessions was Hanoi's agreement to secret peace talks, which began in August. But there, the old diplomatic stalemate of the public talks continued. Was it possible that the November 1 deadline and the vague Operation Duck Hook was a colossal bluff and that Nixon knew all along that Congress and the public would never accept major reescalation?

According to this interpretation, when the Moratorium succeeded in engaging the participation of millions of Americans, after Hanoi refused to accept Nixon's terms, the bluff failed. The president may have suspected all along that it would be difficult, if not impossible, to carry out his threat in the face of pervasive public unwillingness to escalate.[86] It was true, as Haldeman points out, that Nixon knew that the vast majority of Americans supported his Vietnam policy, even after the Moratorium. Of course, that policy was based on negotiation, deescalation, and withdrawal. Certainly, Secretary of Defense Laird, among other key Nixon aides, feared that poll support would dwindle when and if the administration started to make good on his threat to escalate.[87]

It is possible, of course, that despite all of his tough words, the Moratorium's remarkable success convinced Nixon himself that he could not go through with the escalation. This argument suggests that Nixon had not been bluffing. Up through October, he simply underestimated the moral and political power of the movement and his other critics at home and abroad. Thus, he was compelled to jettison Duck Hook because of the reaction to the Moratorium not in Hanoi but in the Oval Office, Congress, the media, and the nation as a whole.[88]

If Nixon could have obtained his version of peace with honor by convincing Hanoi that he might escalate, even if he did not plan to, then one might agree with Haldeman that the Moratorium prolonged the war. On the other hand, if, as is more likely, Hanoi was not about to give up what it had fought for for more than thirty years, the Moratorium did contribute to Nixon's own decision. It may have convinced him not to deliver the series of savage blows envisioned in Duck Hook, blows that might have threatened world peace and domestic tranquillity without moving Hanoi any closer to surrender. In either case, this one massive demonstration played the decisive role during one of the major decision points of the Vietnam War.

A final contributing factor, unrelated to opinion, was the conclusion of NSC staffers that the Duck Hook escalations would not bring Hanoi to its knees.[89] The North Vietnamese had held out so long that only the most unthinkable actions, actions that risked destruction of the incipient détente policy, might have some impact on those dogged communists. Nevertheless, one would have expected some reprisal against North Vietnamese intransigence after November 1, even if only for symbolic value. Nixon might have lashed out with such a reprisal had the public and the rejuvenated movement not stood in his political way.

Nixon, angered and worried by the successful Moratorium, more than ever saw himself engaged in a contest "with the antiwar movement for the public mind in the United States and the private mind in Hanoi." He had lost the first round. It was not going to happen again. He would not "allow national policy to be dictated by street demonstrations."[90]

On October 21, six days after the Moratorium and three days after Henry Kissinger's Harvard visit, during which he discovered that almost everyone on campus opposed his policies, Nixon began to work on his famous November third Silent Majority speech. He thought that this was his most important speech, the turning point in the battle for public opinion. Peter Rodman remembers the White House abuzz with excitement over "the Speech" a full two weeks before it was delivered.[91]

Although Nixon had been participating in sporadic guerrilla warfare against the movement through November, the Silent Majority speech was his formal declaration of war against all radical and liberal activists. His short-run goal was to weaken the Washington Mobilization demonstration called for November

15.[92] Advance intelligence suggested it might be the largest one-city demonstration to date, with perhaps as many as five hundred thousand coming.[93]

The Silent Majority strategy involved an embrace of the patriotic, conservative, and neo-McCarthyite rhetoric that Johnson had eschewed, even though his own 1967 support group called itself the Silent Center.[94] Nixon and Kissinger knew the majority of Americans were angered by the 1960s' assault on their traditional value system. William Safire, who discussed the speech with his boss, suggests that in its "pluralistic ignorance" the majority did not even know it was a majority. It needed to be awakened. Kissinger emphasized that a leader must not follow the loudest critical voices when the unmobilized majority supported him. Even at his lowest point on the Vietnam issue in 1969, Nixon enjoyed a 44- to 26-percent approval rating in the Gallup Poll, although the momentum before the Speech may have been in the dovish direction. He announced that he decided "to go over the heads of the press to the people and do this by TV. . . . Ted Agnew has done well with this."[95]

Nixon wanted to show the world, once and for all, that he "was not going to be pushed around by the demonstrators and the rabble in the streets." His use of the term "rabble" reflects the visceral nature of Nixon's antagonism toward the protesters.[96] As he confided to an interviewer, "With college students I was so frustrated. It was hard for Julie. I couldn't even go to her graduation." At times, he concentrated his fire on the professors who led the students, "the sanctimonious frauds on campus . . . faculty leaders and professional agitators." But he also lashed out at the "pampered kids on campus who were out screaming . . . around the White House." Sometimes the screaming was so loud he could not sleep.[97] And why were they protesting? Quite simply, according to Nixon, because they wanted to avoid the military, "to keep from getting their asses shot off." He complained that even some well-to-do cabinet offspring were involved in the protests.[98]

Given this view of spoiled kids and a minority of left-wing agitators and professors egging them on, one can see how Nixon, like Johnson, convinced himself that communists were somehow involved, especially since the movement was helping Hanoi. This was still another reason to take off the gloves with the movement.

To be sure, not everyone in the White House was as combative as Nixon. Even as late as 1969, Patrick Moynihan thought civil dissenters should be listened to—it was still possible to reason with them. Kissinger, as well, reports his opposition to the frontal assault in 1969.[99] Interestingly, however, in his book *The White House Years*, he titled his key chapter on the movement "The Unpacifiable Doves" and argued that they would never be pleased with his initiatives, even though in secret negotiations he had gone beyond moderate dove positions.[100] Despite his close ties to dissenting professors and his wish to be acceptable along the Charles River, Kissinger too had written them off, albeit more quietly than Nixon.

According to the national security adviser, the Silent Majority speech that reached at least 50 million Americans "turned public opinion around completely." Nixon artfully defended his policies in the speech, holding out the prospect of peace with honor. Vietnamization would be the key that would allow American boys to come home and South Vietnam to defend itself. The problem, he told the nation, was that the protesters were irresponsible, recklessly impatient, and through their actions, unpatriotic. The "great silent majority" should rise up, he exhorted, and send a message to Hanoi. "North Vietnam cannot humiliate the United States. Only Americans can do that."[101]

Nixon expressed pleasure in the way the speech worried the Moratorium and Mobilization organizers, helped to frustrate their attempts to hold monthly protests, and even drove some to counterproductive violence.[102] White House strategists envisioned stressing the violent and radical in the movement to frighten peaceful protesters into staying home, especially on November 15.[103]

The Silent Majority speech dovetailed with the Agnew attack on the media, an attack that accelerated after the Moratorium. The vice president writes about becoming "enraged" by what he saw on television during the October 15 event, especially "a gang of scruffy-looking characters proudly carrying a Viet Cong flag down Pennsylvania Avenue."[104] Undoubtedly, like other White House operatives, Agnew was on a short leash when he assumed the offensive. Yet he was personally involved in his effective campaign as witnessed by his emotional response to the Moratorium. His most important speech came ten days after Nixon's. The networks were strongly advised to cover in detail that November 13 address in which he excoriated them.[105] Agnew lambasted the eastern networks and journalists, whom he deemed responsible for all that was wrong in American domestic and international interactions. This dressing down took place only one day after Seymour Hersh broke the My Lai massacre story, which, as it unfolded over the next two years, contributed to the growing distaste for the war.

The terrorizing worked. The Mobilization, which brought at least 250,000 people to Washington on November 15, received no live coverage and scant TV news coverage. Moreover, the limited coverage emphasized the violence, especially at the Justice Department. NBC reporter John Chancellor remembers the impact of Agnew's attack and how he began to think not just twice but three times about the way he covered the movement. Another example of the chilling effect of the vice president's speech were the problems encountered by Senators McGovern and Hatfield just *buying* network time for an antiwar presentation to answer Nixon.[106]

The Mobilization was not just another demonstration. From November 13 to 15, as a prelude to the main event, over forty thousand Americans paraded past the White House in a March of Death, calling out and then depositing in canisters at the Capitol the names of Americans killed in Vietnam. Veteran activist Sidney Lens thought it was one of the "most moving" demonstrations that he had ever seen. Most Americans, however, caught only glimpses of it on their newscasts. Further, the Nixon-Agnew stress on violent protesters may have made the demonstration on November 15 more radical than originally planned by convincing some middle-class antiwar people not to go to Washington.[107]

Some aspects of the Nixon offensive against the movement were covert, as he picked up where Johnson left off with the surveillance, and sometimes harassment, of movement leaders and leftist radicals in the United States and in leaking stories about subversives in the movement to the press. In many cases, where Johnson was aware of illegal activities, Nixon explicitly authorized them.[108] Even more than his predecessor, Nixon was convinced that antiwar leaders were working with national and international communist parties, and like Johnson, Nixon demanded evidence for his beliefs from the FBI and the CIA.[109] The infamous and aborted Huston Plan of 1970, Nixon's attempt to establish his own intelligence program, stemmed in part from his lack of satisfaction with the work of the FBI, CIA, and other intelligence agencies in uncovering the communist links to the movement. The CIA's Operation Chaos and the FBI's programs were not enough for the president and his advisers.[110]

Although Nixon was dissatisfied with the operation of the agencies in this area, he and his Justice Department enjoyed much warmer relations with the FBI than did the Democrats. This relationship paid off for him in many ways. For example, after October 15, Attorney General John Mitchell approved an FBI request to wiretap the Moratorium and other movement organizations. Similarly, in December, Hoover informed the White House that Clark Clifford was preparing a magazine article critical of the administration. His warning set Jeb Stuart Magruder and others to work to counter the possible deleterious effect of such an article. Finally, during that same month, Hoover sent out to the American embassies in London and Tokyo his proof that the majority of Americans did not support the Moratorium. He had heard that the North Vietnamese were spreading rumors to the opposite effect in both capitals.[111]

The Silent Majority speech, Agnew's temporarily successful intimidation of the media, and the stepped-up intelligence campaigns strengthened Nixon's hand as he considered his options in the late fall of 1969. The momentum toward the doves had slowed.[112] Yet, if Nixon was so successful in rallying support against his Vietnam critics, he should have escalated as planned, perhaps not on November 1, but in December or January. The Silent Majority speech and the offensives against the movement on several fronts did not give him a free hand, although they did buy him "a lot of time and a lot of room."[113] The population had rallied around his perceived moderate policy.[114] Most Americans, even congressional and media leaders, accepted Vietnamization, the continuation of peace talks, and, especially, the staged withdrawal of American troops.[115] The pressure on Nixon to withdraw precipitously eased after the fall of 1969. Nonetheless, both he and the North Vietnamese knew that the moderate policy supported by most citizens would lead ultimately to a total American withdrawal. Nixon had to devise a new strategy that would enable Vietnamization to produce a strong pro-Western political and military force in the South before the last American soldier departed. However, his Silent Majority was not prepared to follow him too far down the road toward an expansion of the war. Moreover, the movement now abominated by many in an increasingly polarized society, was not completely neutralized, as Nixon discovered in the spring of 1970.

Chapter Seven

The War and the Movement Wind Down: January 1970–April 1975

"Christ, they surrounded the White House, re-member? This time they will probably knock down the gates and I'll have a thousand incoherent hip-pies urinating on the Oval Office rug. That's just what they'd do."
—*RICHARD M. NIXON**

The antiwar movement reached its high-water mark in the fall of 1969. From that point on, except for a tumultuous period in the spring of 1970, it became increasingly fragmented and isolated. Nixon's Silent Majority strategy ultimately prevailed.

That strategy did not provide the president with a blank check to work his will on Hanoi. His support from the public rested on its belief in Vietnamization, a policy of gradual but steady withdrawal of American combat troops from Southeast Asia, and a continuation of the peace talks. Vietnamization posed several problems for Nixon. He had to discover a way to make the North Vietnamese more forthcoming at the bargaining table before the last American soldier left the battle theater. The public, however, was in no mood for reescalation. Further, the probability that the South Vietnam-ese would be able to hold their country together when the Ameri-cans departed was slight.

In May 1970, Nixon gambled that he could buy time for Vietnamization through an attack on Cambodian sanctuaries to

*Benjamin F. Schemmer, *The Raid* (London: Macdonald and Jane's, 1977), 164.

TABLE 6.
MAJOR VIETNAM WAR–RELATED EVENTS OF 1970

Antiwar Activities	Percent Poll Respondents who Think War Was Mistake	Percent Poll Respondents for Withdraw
	Jan.: 57%	
		Feb.: 35%
	March: 58%	
	April: 51%	
April 15: Nationwide demonstrations		
	May: 56%	
May 4: Kent State killings		
May 9–10: Washington demonstration		
May: Universities close all over U.S.		
		Sept.: 55%
		Nov.: 40%

Administration Activities	Troop Levels	Battle Deaths (6-month totals)
ril 20: Nixon announces withdrawal of 150,000 troops ril 30: Cambodian invasion		
	June 30: 414,900	2,876
	Dec. 31: 334,600	1,345

destroy communist command-and-supply infrastructures, while containing the protests that he knew his action would provoke. His gamble failed when the killing of four students at Kent State University made the expected protests much worse than anyone in Washington could have foreseen. The Nixon administration was besieged. The wave of demonstrations on hundreds of college campuses paralyzed America's higher-education system. Congress, with the Senate taking the lead, threatened to pass legislation that would severely limit the tactical prerogatives of the commander-in-chief of the American armed forces.

The reaction to the Cambodian invasion demonstrated to Nixon the dangers inherent in any attempt to increase the pressure on Hanoi by using American troops. He thus devised other strategies to obtain the peace with honor that he promised the nation.

He continued the pace of troop withdrawals while increasing the aid packages to the South Vietnamese. He further modified the American bargaining position at the secret talks that had been taking place since August 1969 between Henry Kissinger and Le Duc Tho. And finally, he unleashed his intelligence agencies in forays against the antiwar movement, critics in the media, and radicals that weakened an already fragile and, to some degree, burned-out group of dissenters.

When he sent ARVN and not American troops into Laos on an ill-fated invasion in February 1971, the protests were scattered and ineffective. Nevertheless, he had to confront one last major Washington demonstration, the late April–early May series of protests beginning with an encampment of the Vietnam Veterans Against the War and ending with mass arrests of the May Day demonstrators.

When the North Vietnamese launched a major offensive in the spring of the following year and Nixon responded with stepped-up bombing and the mining of the Haiphong harbor, he met little serious opposition. The boys were almost all home, the movement was in disarray, radicals and hippies were discredited, and the détente policy had sublimated the wrath of the Russians and Chinese.

The weakness of the Left in the United States was demonstrated by Nixon's smashing defeat of left-liberal Democratic candidate George McGovern for the presidency. His margin increased when

Henry Kissinger announced on the eve of the election that he had negotiated a peace agreement with the communists. When the agreement fell apart after the election, Nixon had to resort to the most savage bombing of the war during the Christmas period. The initial spirited protests to that bombing faded away when peace talks reopened.

This is not to say that the antiwar movement had failed. Its arguments had been accepted in general by the majority of the population, which agreed that the involvement in Vietnam had been a mistake, perhaps even an immoral mistake. When, in the period from 1973 to 1975, first Nixon and then Ford tried to increase support for the fast-failing Saigon regime, Congress, backed by the vast majority of the population, refused to reescalate. Almost all of America had joined the anti–Vietnam War movement.

As 1969 came to a close, the antiwar movement and Richard Nixon had reached a standoff. The president had contained the critics of his policy of slow withdrawal with his Silent Majority strategy of the fall.[1] The critics and their supporters in Congress and the media had flexed their muscles enough to convince Nixon that peace through escalation was not a viable option. He did not have a free hand to use the force he felt necessary to produce a swift diplomatic breakthrough. Vietnamization would have to do; Vietnamization imposed on Nixon as the only strategy acceptable to the American public.[2]

As long as the president continued the peace talks and the troop withdrawals, he could count on the support of most Americans. Only 21 percent of those polled in late November called for immediate withdrawal from Vietnam. Of course, as Nixon well knew, the North Vietnamese had little reason to accept American peace proposals, since someday, in the not-too-distant future, the last GI would leave Southeast Asia. Moreover, Hanoi was aware that those remaining GI's had their eyes on the withdrawal schedule as well. Why should they take chances in a war that their president had apparently written off as far as American combat participation was concerned?[3]

Nixon still maintained some hope that Vietnamization might work. The gradual American departure from the South was coupled with a massive buildup of ARVN forces and equipment, new land-reform programs, and increased air support. Whether nation building would finally work in South Vietnam before the last GI departed was problematic, however.

On December 15, Nixon announced his intention to withdraw an additional fifty thousand troops in early 1970. From 1970 on, MACV strongly opposed the withdrawal of so many troops at a time when the ARVN showed little disposition or capability to assume the American combat role. Knowing this, the North Vietnamese could not have taken Nixon seriously when he told them again that month that they were wrong in thinking that "division in the United States would eventually bring them victory."[4] Even the president's faith in that position would be shattered when he confronted the unprecedented nationwide protests against his invasion of Cambodia in the spring of 1970. Division in this country was one of the keys to a peace settlement favored by the North Vietnamese, as Nixon feared all along.

The president did enjoy a good late winter and early spring as far as organized antiwar activity was concerned. For example, the Moratorium Committee had prepared to do battle with him through peace action days to be held every month until the war ended. After the gigantic October and November demonstrations, however, the December activities fell flat. Even less impressive were the peace action days in January, February, and March 1970. It was proving difficult to rouse the faithful so frequently in the absence of an escalation, a break in the peace talks, or an end to the withdrawal program.

A Clergy and Laymen Concerned antiwar offensive also did not attract much attention. A call for a seventy-day partial fast from February 11 through April 27, or from Lent through Passover, to protest the slow pace of withdrawal from Vietnam, drew limited participation.

As had been the case since 1965, the weather had to warm up before the antiwar troops again pounded the pavement. On April 15, in demonstrations organized by the Moratorium, the Mobilization, and the Student Mobilization, ten thousand turned out in Boston and twenty-five thousand in New York City to denounce Nixon's policies. The crowds for the events were comparatively small, the speeches lacked fervor, and the radicals in attendance garnered most of the headlines. The *New York Times* highlighted the over $100,000 worth of damage produced by rampaging students at Harvard and Berkeley.[5]

The unimpressive April 15 demonstrations represented another victory for Nixon. Given the increase in incidents of violence on college campuses that spring and the widening split between moderates and radicals in the movement, he profited from the public perception that those in the streets were violent and uncivil. He had to be cheered when, on April 21, the Vietnam Moratorium Committee disbanded, recognizing its inability to produce large, effective, and peaceful demonstrations.

Only the day before, Nixon had contributed to the general sense of satisfaction with his policies when he announced a phased withdrawal of another 150,000 American troops. As he wrote in his memoirs, he took the action to "drop a bombshell on the gathering spring storm of antiwar protest," protests that would surely be provoked by the invasion of Cambodia in two weeks' time. He hoped that the news of the largest withdrawal to date would weaken those protests. Throughout this period, Nixon used the "controlled exits" from Vietnam in an "artful" manner, gaining the maximum political payoff from the inevitable withdrawals.[6]

He knew that Hanoi would interpret his troop withdrawal announcement as further confirmation that he was unable to take effective military action in Vietnam. He would thus demonstrate to the communists their misreading of American opinion with his bold escalation of April 30.

The motivations behind the Cambodian invasion were manifold. At bottom was the military dimension. If Nixon could destroy the North Vietnamese sanctuaries in Cambodia and maybe even capture the mysterious headquarters of the Central Office for South Vietnam (COSVN), he would buy more time for Vietnamization by weakening Hanoi's ability to launch new offensives. This was his prime consideration, although once having decided to show the world who was boss, he oversold the military value of the incursion.

In addition, he had been embarrassed when he did not call

Hanoi's bluff on the previous November 1. The Cambodian invasion was one way to pay them back for their unwillingness to meet American negotiating demands in 1969.[7] On a personal level, he was angered by the wave of campus violence and his inability to attend the spring graduations of his daughter Julie at Smith and his son-in-law David at Amherst.[8] The invasion could be a response to antiwar critics and radicals who thought they had weakened the president's ability to conduct the war and even travel freely in his own country.

He was also still bristling at the Senate because it had just rejected two Supreme Court nominations. He was alleged to have told his advisers that the Cambodian invasion was meant as a signal to senators that they too could no longer push him around.[9]

Finally, he felt that he would be criticized by the movement and critics in the media no matter what he did to end the war with his self-styled moderate approach, so he might as well order the escalations that military necessity required. As he remarked to aide Charles W. Colson, "We'll catch unshirted hell no matter what we do so we'd better get on with it."[10]

Nixon wanted to show the protesters, the Senate, the media, the North Vietnamese, and the Russians and Chinese that he was still the boss. He warned North Vietnam once again on April 20 that it was making a "fatal miscalculation" if it was counting on dissent to weaken the president of the United States.[11]

During the last week in April, as the president briefed members of his inner circle about the Cambodian invasion, he told them to expect some strong dissenting activity.[12] He did not think it would be too serious, in part because he was convinced that the young protesters were mainly interested in the draft and the body count, both of which he had reduced and would reduce still further.[13] Henry Kissinger briefed his own aides on April 24, emphasizing the likelihood of mass protests over the invasion. He himself had to confront angry dissent from some of them that resulted in the resignations of Anthony Lake, William Watts, and Roger Morris. The national security adviser referred to such dissent as character-istic of the "cowardice of the eastern establishment."[14]

Despite their warnings about the protests on the eve of the invasion, both Nixon and Kissinger were unprepared for the quantity and quality of the antiwar activities that their policy produced. Gerald Ford felt that neither had "foreseen . . . the furor that the incursion would provoke outside Congress."[15] Consistent with his managerial style, once he made up his mind on the invasion, he avoided those in his entourage whom he knew would be distressed by it. Rogers and Laird were brought on board only very late in the game.[16] Perhaps Nixon would have been better prepared had he listened to those he knew would oppose the invasion. When he heard that Nixon thought that his April 30 speech explaining the invasion would unite the nation, Rogers allegedly commented, "This will make the students puke."[17]

No single event of the antiwar period so inflamed the college campuses as the Cambodian invasion. Nixon's attempt to explain the escalation as a way to bring the war to a speedy end did not convince hundreds of thousands of young people, who protested in myriad ways on their campuses and in their communities. It was the spring, the traditional time for protests, with the weather making outdoor demonstrations feasible in almost all parts of the United States. In addition, the campuses had experienced increasing violence during the period preceding the invasion, a fact that contributed to the unprecedented burning and trashing of many buildings.[18]

Nixon contributed to his problems when he referred to "bums blowing up the campus" in the wake of the first reports of widespread protests. He quickly explained himself as referring only to the most extreme radicals and hangers-on, the nihilistic sort who were presumably responsible for the burning of almost a dozen studies at the Center for Advanced Study in the Behavioral Sciences on Stanford's campus a week earlier on April 24. Stanford had been experiencing a stormy series of antiwar protests just before the incursion. Although no one was injured in the fire at the independent study center, several scholars lost valuable research materials, with M. N. Srinivas, a distinguished Indian sociologist, hit the hardest.[19]

It is impossible to know what would have happened on the campuses after the first few days had not four students been killed by the National Guard at Kent State University on May 4. During the first hours after the invasion, but before May 4, Columbia University announced a one-day moratorium and the New Mobilization Committee to End the War called for a Washington demonstration for the weekend of May 9–10. Yet the outrage and anger might have been contained had it not been for Kent State.

Kent State was one of those universities that experienced more than the normal amount of protests in the several days after the president's speech. After a campus building was burned and the town of Kent itself experienced some damage, the governor of Ohio called out the National Guard. On May 4, poorly trained Guardsmen shot into a crowd and killed four students.

The Kent State killings "ignited a conflagration" on campuses around the nation.[20] Strikes, rallies, and other forms of protest began or were planned on most major campuses on May 5. By May 6, over eighty college administrations announced their intentions to close down from one day to the remainder of the school year. As a precaution against violence, Governor Ronald Reagan closed the University of California. On May 7, Kingman Brewster, the president of Yale, announced that he was going to bring 1,000 Yale students to Washington to lobby with alumni in Congress and the executive branch. Between May 4 and May 8, campuses experienced an average of 100 demonstrations a day, 350 campus strikes were called with varying degrees of success, 536 colleges shut down, and 73 colleges reported significant violence in their protests.[21] On the weekend of May 9–10, from 75 to 100,000 people gathered to protest in Washington. By May 12, over 150 colleges were on strike.

The problems Nixon faced from the movement after April 30 were compounded many times over by the Kent State tragedy. According to him, the days following the killings were "among the darkest" for his administration. Ultimately, over 450 colleges closed down for at least some of the period in May and the National Guard had to be called out at least twenty-four times. By June, a majority in a Gallup Poll thought that campus unrest was America's number-one problem.[22] As the situation whirled out of control, Nixon could easily conclude that the issue was not the Cambodian invasion, which most of the public, including the young people, would have swallowed; it was Kent State. For many around Nixon, Kent State was the key to the national crisis confronted by the administration during the first two weeks in May.[23]

Looking back on those turbulent days, many of the major actors in the administration, including Kissinger, remember Washington as "a besieged city." John Ehrlichman refers to "extraordinary measures taken to protect the White House," H. R. Haldeman remembers sleeping in the White House bomb shelter for several days, and even tough political operative Charles Colson felt as if he was in a Central American country, with the palace surrounded by the army protecting the government against a coup. Daniel Patrick Moynihan recalls a panicked press secretary Ron Ziegler announcing "We're at war" and is still grateful for Nixon's thoughtfulness when, without being asked, the president ordered Secret Service protection for his and Kissinger's homes in Cambridge. Moynihan also remembers thinking then that Nixon would most certainly be a one-term president after Cambodia. Among the distraught aide's written suggestions to the president was a call for the formation of a "national government" to unite the country.[24]

The White House's relative "isolation" from the nation contributed to its initial underestimation of the reaction to Kent State according to Herbert Klein. Taken by surprise, the government stopped most of its business in order to contain the protests. Even those with links to the liberal camp like Winston Lord, who was prepared for an "unpopular domestic reaction," were shocked by the events of May. It was a painful time for him because he had opposed the invasion, in good part because he feared that the domestic reaction would ultimately affect Hanoi's perception of American resolve. Another dovish aide, Leonard Garment, also was bothered by the impact of the unprecedented wave of protests on Nixon's foreign policy as everything started to become "unhinged." For some reason, he recalls people inside the White House turning to the poems of W. H. Auden for courage.[25]

Not everyone remembers things in such apocalyptic terms. Nixon himself was acutely aware of the need to show that he was unrattled, that the government was functioning. Although Garment himself was unnerved, he admires the president for having "maintained his poise" throughout those difficult days. Dwight

Chapin attributes this poise to Nixon's Quaker background, and how, in crises except for Watergate, the president practiced the Quaker concept of "peace at the center." James Keogh knows that Nixon was clearly "troubled and surprised," as was everyone in the White House, but there was no "siege mentality"—he and his colleagues went on about their business of running the government.[26]

Keogh may have exaggerated. Ray Price does not use the term "business as usual" to describe those days in May. They were all "caught by surprise and storm" by the "absolute public hysteria" that began even before Kent State. For this, the speechwriter blames the "frothing-at-the-mouth correspondents on the air." After May 4, they and the public went "completely bananas."[27]

Many of Nixon's activities during the second week in May revolved around the Kent State crisis. On May 6, he sent letters to the parents of the four dead students and met with a delegation from the university. The next day he discussed the situation with eight prominent university presidents, and on May 11, met with most of the nation's governors. In addition, an examination of his phone calls during the period reveal a dramatic increase in volume to old friends and supporters around the world. Despite the storm outside the White House and the acute anxiety within, the government did not *completely* stop, as some critics boasted.[28]

The administration contributed to that storm with an initial insensitive response to the Kent State killings. Ray Price, who wrote the first press release for Ron Ziegler, regrets dashing something off before he understood the full implications of the tragedy.[29]

Of all the members of the inner circle, Henry Kissinger may have been shaken the most by the reaction to the Cambodian invasion, if only because so much of the protesting took place on campuses. Especially after Kent State, the national security adviser began talking of himself as the major casualty of the affair.[30] He knew full well that as much as 70 percent of the population was supportive of the Cambodian invasion, but among the 30 percent that was not were most of the elite groups in society.[31] Despite Nixon's play to the Silent Majority, Kissinger still felt that his main audience was an eastern establishment that ultimately might prevail over a president who temporarily aroused the populist masses. Like the Wise Men before him in 1968, Kissinger worried about the almost universal opposition from the establishment to Nixon's foreign policy, especially after the campus response to Kent State. According to his boss, Kissinger was so rattled he wanted the United States to leave Cambodia as quickly as possible.[32]

It was true that the longer he associated with the Nixon people, the more unpopular he became with students, professors, intellectuals, and liberal journalist friends. Even before Cambodia, Kissinger had begun to cut his ties to them. He still liked the students, he wrote, in part because they could not help what they were doing, having been "brought up by skeptics, relativists, and psychiatrists." Characteristic was his impatience in April when he walked out of a meeting with graduate students at Johns Hopkins University when someone asked him if he thought he was a war criminal.[33]

On May 8, a group of Harvard professors met with their old colleague to brief him on the crisis on their campus and within the academic and intellectual communities at large. Among them were former Johnson advisers Edwin Reischauer, Adam Yarmolinsky, and Francis Bator. The meeting was acrimonious. The Harvard group hoped to influence Kissinger to alter American policy or even to resign in protest over the invasion. He felt that they implicitly threatened him with exile from Harvard if he persisted in backing Nixon. Over the years, members of this ad hoc group of academic experts from Cambridge had advised and lobbied both Republican and Democratic office holders. After storming out of the meeting with the national security adviser that day, they never again enjoyed the access and potential influence they had in the past.[34] The meeting helped to propel Kissinger more and more into the Nixon entourage, where his brand of unsentimental Realpolitik was appreciated.

The most dramatic meeting with protesters involved the president himself. On the morning of May 9, he left the White House at 5:00 A.M., along with his valet, Manolo Sanchez, Dr. Walter Tkach, and aide Egil Krogh, for a surprise visit with young people encamped at the Lincoln Memorial, awaiting the day's demonstration. This sensational nocturnal visitation revealed how much the protesters were bothering him. In 1969, he turned to football while the demonstrators gathered in Washington. Now, despite his bravado and the polls and Silent Majority strategy, he was distressed that so many young people around the nation were in such active opposition to his policies.[35]

Given all the staged events of the Nixon administration, one is tempted to consider the visit to the Lincoln Memorial as just another managed news opportunity, calculated to demonstrate that the president was concerned about young people. It was not staged and took Nixon's aides by surprise. Some were horrified by the dangers to which he exposed himself without advance security preparations. The only thing not surprising was the unexpected visit itself. Veterans of Nixon campaigns expected him to take off on his own every now and then, throwing their carefully laid plans into chaos.[36]

Explaining the motivations of such a complicated man like Nixon is difficult. Remembering that "hell of a rough weekend," Dwight Chapin thinks the president made his visit in part to show the world that he was not a captive in the White House and could move freely among his fellow citizens. The sensitive and caring Nixon, one of the many Nixons, was probably also concerned about the young people and their alienation.[37]

He did not expect to learn much about the protesters' arguments during the visit. From all accounts, it was a strange confrontation, with the president talking to sleepy, incredulous young people about their colleges' football teams, other sports, foreign travel, and general philosophical subjects. Although the discussions also touched on the war, he never did engage them in a serious Vietnam debate and obviously could not have hoped to win them over to his perspective. He wanted to show that he would listen to them, although he probably did not hear them. Despite Nixon's claims that the media did not portray his serious discussions accurately, his own account reveals almost no discussion of Vietnam, Cambodia, or Kent State. In his meetings with student demonstrators during the period, Ray Price found most of them arrogant and ignorant of the issues that brought them to Washington.[38]

The popular image of an unresponsive, unfeeling government

troubled some in the administration. Interior Secretary Walter J. Hickel, who was later fired for his lack of support for the Cambodian invasion, made public his concern that the president was not listening to the youth of the country. The response from Nixon and his advisers was that they were indeed listening. Aside from the president and his national security adviser, Rogers, Haldeman, and most of the other key players in the administration met with marchers and activists during early May.[39] Alexander Heard, the president of Vanderbilt University, was appointed White House special adviser on campus concerns and eight young White House staffers were dispatched to the campuses from May 21 to May 25 to listen to students and faculty.

All of this was window dressing and both sides were aware of it. The protesters knew that they were being listened to and noticed. They wanted the United States out of Vietnam at once, and the president did not agree with them. No amount of talking at the Lincoln Memorial or in H. R. Haldeman's office was going to change the basic incompatibility between the programs promoted by the movement and administration policy.

As in the Johnson administration, officials periodically went through the motions of listening to responsible antiwar critics. Commenting on an earlier Kissinger meeting with a Quaker group, Nixon asked, "Are they still worth the time?" and then answered ("I guess it would be worse if you didn't meet with them"). Such meetings were part of the administration's attempt to contain the damage from the demonstrators. The sensitive and caring strategy was devised by Jeb Stuart Magruder, who "feared more demonstrations" if the administration did not handle the Cambodian-Kent State protests generously. While he urged his colleagues to appear open and reasonable, he was one of the architects of a media campaign that enlisted the popular patriot Bob Hope to appear on the "Tonight Show" to wave the administration flag. Ultimately, Magruder felt that the White House rode out the storm employing strategies such as his.[40] If by riding out the storm he meant that the president was still president on June 1, the White House defenses were never breached, and the polls were with Nixon, then Magruder was correct.

Henry Kissinger worried about the long-term impact on young

people, the media, and Congress, all of whom could unite again to make another military escalation impossible. Even those in the Nixon inner circle were affected by the alienation of members of their own families after Cambodia.[41] Further, the Cambodian invasion led the Senate to revoke the Gulf of Tonkin Resolution and that body's passage of the Cooper-Church amendment to cut off funds for the invasion after June 30. Nixon withdrew the American soldiers before that date, and, in any event, the House did not pass Cooper-Church. It is impossible to determine whether Congress would have become so militant had it not been for the Cambodian invasion and, especially, the protests through the month of May.

It is also impossible to determine whether Nixon planned to keep the troops in Cambodia any longer than he did. He did not capture COSVN, if it ever existed in the form he described. Moreover, in terms of North Vietnamese body count and number of engagements, the invasion had to be considered a failure. Nevertheless, Nixon claimed success and that the capture of thousands of tons of equipment crippled communist offensive plans. He had bought time to allow the Vietnamization program to take hold. He also learned a painful lesson about the public's very strong opposition to any future Cambodias.

As the administration licked its wounds in the weeks after the invasion, weeks that also witnessed a dramatic decline in antiwar activity once the colleges closed, Nixon began planning a new and even more vigorous offensive against the movement. First he had to demonstrate that he could appear in public and be greeted with the support and respect his office demanded. On May 28, he appeared with evangelist Billy Graham at a large stadium rally in Knoxville, Tennessee, in part to show the many young people to whom it was directed that he was listening to them.[42] What they heard there and saw on television was a small coterie of uncivil, foul-mouthed demonstrators who rudely insulted Reverend Graham and the flag around which Nixon had carefully wrapped himself.

Nixon was cheered also by the rise of the hardhats. In an apparently spontaneous action, or at least one that could not be tied directly to White House operatives, a group of workers in New York City attacked a small antiwar group on May 20. Nixon endorsed the hardhats' bully-boy tactics when he greeted their representatives warmly at the White House on May 26.[43]

Despite these positive signs, Nixon and his aides still felt themselves "under siege" in the summer of 1970—under attack from the movement, the media, and the Congress.[44] The chief problem in the short run was the upcoming congressional election. Nixon planned to drive the doves from Congress through a renewed Silent Majority campaign. Charles Colson was the main operative here, as well as in the media campaign, working through the Tell It to Hanoi organization to defeat dovish Senate resolutions as well as dovish senators up for reelection themselves. In a related effort, the Committee to Support the President for Peace in Vietnam took an impressive full-page advertisement in the *New York Times* on August 31. The committee called for peace not surrender, a peace with honor that would be obtained through support for the president. Among the names that appeared on the steering and executive committees were New York Republican leader Whitney North Seymour, Donald Kendall of Pepsi Cola, and G. Keith Funston of the Stock Exchange.[45]

The Nixon administration's most serious anti-antiwar activity of the period was the secret intelligence war against the movement, radicals, and other enemies who were allegedly threatening national security. According to H. R. Haldeman, after Kent State Nixon felt that he could no longer count on the FBI and the CIA to protect the presidency. It was "the Vietnam war [that] had created almost unbearable pressures which caused him to order wiretaps and activate the plumbers in response to antiwar moves."[46]

On June 5, 1970, Nixon met with Hoover and Helms, as well as Admiral Noel Gayler, the head of the National Security Agency, Lieutenant General Donald Bennett of the Defense Intelligence Agency, Ehrlichman, and Robert Finch, the secretary of Health, Education and Welfare, to discuss ways to improve the intelligence-gathering apparatus of the government. He directed them to meet with White House aide Tom Huston to prepare new measures to deal with what Huston called a "serious crisis."[47]

After several meetings, the Huston Plan was devised, a plan to create a superintelligence agency, operating from the White House, coordinating the activities of the other intelligence agencies. Among other rationales presented for the development of this new agency was the danger to the nation posed by the thousands of foreign-inspired youths engaged in a conspiracy to destroy the country.[48]

Like their Democratic predecessors, Huston and Nixon did not see their intelligence activities as antithetical to democracy. Huston argued that if the radical Left was allowed to continue on its violent path, the Right would grow as a response and might create a repressive police state.[49] Police-state tactics would be used by the White House to head off the prospect of a police state. Nixon was confident that he had the authority to stretch and even violate the law to protect national security not only from the antiwar Left and other radicals, but from the dangerous Right.[50]

The FBI opposed the Huston Plan, which not only concentrated too much power in the White House, but also curtailed the agencies' independence. In a formal sense, the plan was operative for around five days in the summer of 1970, after which Nixon withdrew it.[51] As an implicit quid pro quo, the FBI accepted some of the new programs in the plan that it had initially resisted when they were first proposed. Among them was the lowering of the age of campus informants from twenty-one to eighteen.[52]

Although never adopted, the threat of the Huston Plan, as well as the White House's dogged insistence on expanding the scope of intelligence and harassment activities, caused all of the agencies to intensify the campaigns they already had in place.[53] The FBI, CIA, NSA, and even IRS combined to make it increasingly difficult for left-wing and liberal organizations to operate effectively in protest against the president's policies.

Perhaps the effort was not needed. The nationwide response to the Cambodian invasion and the Kent State killings was the last success for the antiwar movement during the Nixon administration, at least in terms of the quantity, quality, and impact of mass demonstrations. The paralysis of the nation's higher-education system during May ultimately redounded to Nixon's favor. Colleges closed, students' career plans were altered, buildings unrelated to the war were torched, and Nixon still commanded the support of the majority of the population, including many Democrats. Having dealt with the massive disruption and violence in their lives and on their campuses, students may have decided to draw back from the abyss after the paroxysm of May.

For whatever reasons, campus demonstrations and general antiwar activity declined after the spring of 1970, never to attain the heights of the 1967–70 period.[54] At least, the number and size of marches and protests declined as reported in the mass media. Sidney Lens, one prominent activist, suggests that one cannot evaluate the extent of political protests during the 1970–72 years from the media. For him, the nation was awash with marches, strikes, boycotts, and other forms of activism during the last two years of the first Nixon administration. Another antiwar leader, David Dellinger, considers 1972 to be the biggest year ever. Of course, as Dellinger noted, the media ignored most of the protests.[55] If that is the case, then it meant little whether the movement continued in its varied activities. If the media ignored them, then the impact on mass and elite opinion was minimal and the administration could ignore them as well.

Irrespective of Lens and Dellinger, some of the energy had clearly left the movement as the students prepared to return to the campuses in the late summer of 1970. On August 7, the *New York Times* commented on the apparent failure of an antiwar fund raiser when the New York City Rock Festival drew only twenty thousand people. At the end of the month, the movement suffered a severe blow: a young researcher at the University of Wisconsin was killed when the building in which he was working was fire bombed. On August 30, despite the previously announced threat that thousands of protesters would journey to Portland, Oregon, to disrupt the annual American Legion Convention, only one thousand of the faithful showed up. Three weeks earlier, Tom Huston had worried that the planned protest "could serve as a catalyst for widespread campus disorders" that fall. Finally, the traditional fall antiwar rally in New York was sparsely attended, as were the October 31 nationwide rallies planned to boost the doves in the upcoming congressional elections.[56] Two organizations formed after Kent State, the Movement for a New Congress and the

National Coalition for a Responsible Congress, had been focusing antiwar energies on those elections.

As seen in the Huston warning, the sudden decline in the size and fervor of the demonstrations may have caught the administration by surprise. Certainly Kissinger and Nixon expected a rough fall. As late as July, the president commented that the debate over the war was "sapping his domestic support."[57]

It was not just that the movement was doing poorly. Nixon himself was doing better. On September 16, he appeared to cheering crowds at Kansas State University. His speech of reconciliation mixed with patriotism drew the support of old adversary Hubert Humphrey. The Kansas State speech, although delivered in the conservative Midwest, suggested that he no longer had to relegate his campus appearances to General Beadle State or the Air Force Academy.[58]

The next month, with much fanfare, he announced a new initiative for peace. Despite the fact that it was merely a cosmetic repackaging of earlier initiatives, it served to maintain his support among those who wanted to see a little more progress in the peace talks. Further, Nixon was learning how to use the demonstrators against themselves. Although they did bother him at public events and, like others, threw off the rhythm of his speeches, playing to their intemperance became a political weapon. He came to sense more and more that the public had tired of the uncivil chanters and disrupters. A major theme in the 1970 congressional campaign was to concentrate attention on his enemies as representing noisy and violent radicals.[59]

On the eve of the election, at San Jose, California, Nixon encouraged heckling and stone throwing, all caught by the television cameras to show the nation how radicals treated his office. He set out to show "how little respect [he] had for their juvenile chanting."[60]

The strategy did not work as well as Nixon had hoped, especially when Lincolnesque Senator Edmund Muskie emerged in early November as a popular Democratic spokesperson. Muskie called for the softening of rhetoric on both sides and for reasoned debate in a democratic society. Further, although Americans sympathized with a president assailed by perceived violent revolutionaries, they were not prepared to accept another escalation in Vietnam. Nixon's Vietnamization policy was supported as far as that policy was understood as bringing the boys home. Kissinger still felt "constant pressure" to keep up the pace of withdrawals, and this pressure naturally affected his negotiating stance in Paris.[61]

In an unguarded moment in November 1970, Nixon may have revealed how he really felt about the movement, over which he had apparently triumphed. As he prepared to launch a raid to free prisoners of war at Sontay in North Vietnam, he supposedly remarked, contemplating a possible failure, "Christ, they surrounded the White House, remember? This time they will probably knock down the gates and I'll have a thousand incoherent hippies urinating on the Oval Office rug. That's just what they'd do."[62]

Nixon's fear of urinating hippies may have been exaggerated. His campaign against antiwar critics was working despite his relative failure at the polls in the fall elections. The abortive raid on the Sontay prison camp did not produce any outpouring of antiwar activity with the letter and telegram count running 1,112 to 87 in favor of the raid.[63] More important, the muted response to the Laos incursion had to be encouraging to the administration.

On February 8, the ARVN invaded Laos to destroy NVA sanctuaries comparable to those in Cambodia. This time, however, no American troops were involved. Nevertheless, Nixon was prepared for the worst. According to Henry Kissinger, the president withdrew into the same sort of protective shell into which he had withdrawn the previous May.[64]

Compared to demonstrations that followed earlier escalations, the demonstrations that were spawned by the Laos incursion were small and scattered. A generous estimate counts around fifty thousand people involved in nationwide protests on February 10. Not only were the protests relatively unimpressive; the media tended to stress more than ever the most violent activities of the protesters.[65]

The Laos incursion did produce a call from the National Peace Action Coalition, a group formed from the remnants of the old Mobilization Committee, for a mass Washington march on April 24, and a fast-growing new group, the Vietnam Veterans Against

TABLE 7.
MAJOR VIETNAM WAR–RELATED EVENTS OF 1971

Antiwar Activities	Percent Poll Respondents who Think War Was Mistake	Percent Poll Respondents for Withdraw
	Jan.: 59%	
		Jan.: 72%
April 23: Vietnam vets return medals		
	May: 61%	
April 24: Washington demonstration		
May 2–6: Mass arrest of protesters		
June 13: *Pentagon Papers* published		

dministration Activities	Troop Levels	*Battle Deaths (6-month totals)*
). 8: Laos invasion		
arch 29: Calley found guilty		
	June 30: 239,200	1,105
	Dec. 31: 156,800	276

the War (VVAW), planned their own event in the capital for the week beginning on April 19. They had made headlines in January with their "winter soldiers" investigation of Vietnam war crimes in Detroit. During this period, Kissinger reports feeling increasing antiwar pressure, especially from Congress and the media.[66] On the latter, influentials had to be impressed with the huge review by Neil Sheehan in the March 28, 1971, *New York Times Book Review* of thirty-three books on Vietnam. The provocative headline for this unprecedented review was: "Should We Have War Crimes Trials?"

On the other hand, the antiwar cause was not helped when a bomb exploded in the Capitol Building on March 1. This dramatic incident occurred less than two months after Father Philip Berrigan and five others had been indicted for planning to kidnap Kissinger and to bomb buildings in Washington.[67] Reports such as these helped isolate Nixon critics in a nation angered by violent radical activities. Given the relative satisfaction with Nixon's Vietnamization program and the phased withdrawal of American troops, antiwar critics could not afford to be tarred with the brush of violent radicalism. By the time that Lieutenant William Calley was found guilty of the My Lai murders on March 29, such news probably did not contribute to movement support. The White House surmised that doves opposed the verdict because they viewed Calley as taking the blame for the higher brass.[68]

Antiwar leaders on campuses were still capable of rallying some of their troops. On April 1, in the largest such action to date, over four hundred student presidents and editors issued an open letter opposing administration policies. Several of their leaders later had a perfunctory meeting with Nixon aides.[69] With this action, an indication of the continuing alienation of many college students, the stage was set for what would be the last major confrontation between the antiwar movement and a president, the series of rallies set to take place during the latter part of the month of April.

The first of the roughly one thousand VVAW began arriving on April 18 for a week of protests. Although they were dressed in khakis, many wore long hair, earrings, and other symbols of the counterculture. Some were disabled. Fearing adverse publicity, the administration tried to evict them from the Mall, where they were encamped. Although the Justice Department carried the day in the courts against the veterans (who were defended by former Attorney General Ramsey Clark), the administration did not follow through by attempting to remove them forcibly, although it never announced that it was not going to make any arrests. The policy was to keep the veterans guessing and off balance.[70]

The veterans' eventual protests were highlighted by a candlelight march on April 22 and the dramatic action of throwing their medals over a fence at the Capitol on the following day. Secretary of State Rogers played down the unusual event, noting that only twelve hundred veterans showed up, a small crowd to whom he would nevertheless listen. Several days later, Nixon too reported that he was listening to dissenters—"It is rather hard not to hear them, as matter of fact." He considered their arguments, he said, but they did not cause him to question his policies.[71]

On April 24, the ranks of the VVAW were swelled by an estimated 200 to 500,000 demonstrators who had answered the call from the National Peace Coalition to assemble in Washington.[72] With as many as 150,000 in San Francisco that day, the activities of April 24, 1971, resulted in one of the largest one-day antiwar demonstrations of the era. And it took place during a period when antiwar activism was allegedly approaching its nadir. Senators Gruening and Hartke were among those who addressed the Washington throng on the twenty-fourth.

The spring 1971 demonstrations are not remembered because of the impressive mass protest that day. A smaller army of demonstrators, some calling themselves the People's Coalition and the May Day Tribe, stayed on in Washington for more than a week, camping out along the Potomac in a political Woodstock. On May 2, after a week of random violence and disorganized protests, the District police began to rout the young people from their camps and ultimately arrested over ten thousand. This was the last stand for anti-Nixon demonstrators in Washington as the Justice Department and the police collaborated to rid the capital of the ragtag hippies, yippies, and radicals who had lingered on beyond May Day. White House speechwriter Ray Price refers to the action taken by the administration as a "military operation," a "military attack."[73]

In charge of defending the White House and the capital, Nixon counsel John Dean prepared an unsigned emergency declaration for Nixon to proclaim in case matters got out of hand. Further, he sent the president memos every few hours on May 4 and 5 that outlined the successes of the military activities.[74]

There was something reminiscent of Herbert Hoover's famous rout of the Bonus Marchers in 1932, a rout in effect repudiated the following year by the actions of his successor. Nixon and the Justice Department were in turn repudiated by the courts in 1975 when many of the mass arrests were judged to have been illegal and twelve hundred of those detained were awarded monetary damages.

The vindication for those arrested came too late to affect the antiwar movement. For many, including John Ehrlichman, the spring 1971 protests marked the end of mass public opposition to the war policies of the administration.[75] The very firm hand displayed by the Justice Department after May 1 suggested to many would-be demonstrators that future such activities would be counterproductive and even dangerous for the participants.

At first glance, the publication of *The Pentagon Papers* on June 13 should have rejuvenated the antiwar movement. Nixon fought a bitter losing battle against its publication and denounced the press for jeopardizing national security by revealing secrets of Vietnam diplomacy. On the other hand, *The Pentagon Papers* tempest may have helped Nixon obliquely by diverting attention from his policies to those of the Johnson and Kennedy administrations.[76] Moreover, most Americans accepted Nixon's national security arguments against publication and thus opposed almost reflexively the unpatriotic *New York Times*, which once again demonstrated that the eastern media were not operating in the best interests of the nation.[77]

As thoughtful readers analyzed the documents during the second half of June, some may have joined the majority of the population that by then thought getting into the war had been a mistake. Even so, why blame Nixon, when he was apparently working effectively to make the best of a bad situation by trying to escape from Southeast Asia with peace and honor?

The life had gone out of the movement. One prominent activist points to the tiny Evict Nixon rallies organized by the May Day Tribe in the fall as further proof of the end of demonstrations as an antiwar tool. This failure was duplicated in December when a well-publicized benefit for the People's Coalition (Women Strike for Peace, VVAW, War Resisters League, Communist party, Quakers, National Welfare Rights Organization, the National Peace Action Committee, and the Student Mobilization) in New York drew a surprisingly small crowd.[78]

In trying to explain the decline of the movement in the spring of 1971, even though the war continued for Americans until January 1973, antiwar leader Tom Hayden suggests that Nixon's confrontational tactics had worked. By 1971, many activists were simply "burned out" and could not muster their mental and physical energies for yet another protest, which would be opposed vigorously by the administration and, especially, the Silent Majority. Hayden and others also felt that traditional forms of peaceful protest had been exhausted—they had gone as far as they could go with marches and rallies in Washington, New York, and San Francisco. Some searched for new vehicles to rally the anti-Nixon forces; others, fearful of government oppression, went underground.

Hayden and some of his colleagues began to plan a massive protest for the Republican Convention in San Diego in the summer of 1972, but when the convention was switched to Miami, a city with much less of a youthful antiwar community in the surrounding region, Hayden decided to sit it out. He is emphatic, however, when he claims that the beginning of the draft lottery in December 1969, and the beginning of the end for the draft in general, had little to do with the decline in antiwar activity during the last eighteen months of American involvement in the war.[79]

On the other hand, Daniel Henkin, who was in charge of public relations for the Defense Department, sees the lottery as an important factor in the decline of protests. Beginning in 1970, with the lottery in place and the number of those drafted through the lottery declining, he recalls with pleasure a noticeable decrease in the amount of heckling that he received when he addressed youthful audiences.[80]

The winding down of the draft naturally related to the winding down of the war as far as American combat participation was concerned. During the last six months of 1971, American battle deaths dropped to 276, one-fourth of what they had been during the first six months of the year and only 3 percent of the bloody totals from Nixon's first six months in office. By the end of 1971, troop levels in Vietnam had plummeted to 157,000. The fewer the battle deaths, the less attention to the war in Vietnam, the more support for Nixon's policies.

In the more general sense, the tactics of the antiwar movement that stood it in good stead from 1965 to 1971 were stale and uninteresting to many potential demonstrators. A fatigue factor settled in, similar to the fatigue factor that contributed to the sudden decline in ghetto disturbances after 1968. Although the Nixon administration did little to address the problems that gave rise to Watts and Detroit and other cities wracked by riots, that form of black protest almost disappeared in 1969, after three of the most turbulent years in American urban history.

College students were not only tired of the demonstrations; their priorities had changed during the late sixties. The economy had taken a turn for the worse and good jobs were no longer taken for granted by young people in the emerging "Me" decade of the seventies.

Other aspects of Nixon's foreign policies contributed to the decrease in the intensity and frequency of antiwar activities. His promotion of détente with the Soviet Union and the opening to China in 1972 contributed to the slackening of ardor among his critics. In addition, the startling announcement in January 1972 that Henry Kissinger had been engaged in a promising series of secret negotiations with the North Vietnamese since August 1969 also made protest seem irrelevant and unnecessary for many.

A final ironic factor in the movement's decline has to do with its success. In the summer of 1971, 71 percent of those Americans polled agreed that it had been a mistake for the United States to become involved in the Vietnam War and 58 percent felt that involvement was immoral.[81] Critics in Congress, the media, and on the campuses, among other places, had helped to bring the public to that position. Most Americans wanted to get out of the mess as quickly as possible consistent with achieving a peace with honor and an opportunity for Vietnamization to take hold. Congress, responding in part to the many years of pressure from the movement, was keeping tight reins on the president, guarding against any attempt to involve Americans in escalatory moves. The success of the movement made it increasingly unnecessary in 1971.

On the other hand, considering the expansion of the air war and the increase in Asian casualties, many in the movement did not view their activities as successful. They had failed to compel Nixon to end American military activities in Southeast Asia. Could an antiwar movement truly be considered successful while the bombs continued to fall and Vietnamese, Cambodians, and Laotians continued to die?[82]

As the president planned his political and military strategies for 1972, he was confident that he had contained the movement and its mass protest activities. As the Left in the United States became more and more isolated, Nixon captured the Right and the growing center, a center that included some returning from the Left. In the important election year, he enjoyed the support of most Americans for his Vietnam initiatives, as long as he made progress toward bringing home the last American boys from combat.[83]

In March, the North Vietnamese launched another major offensive, a conventional invasion of the South, at a time when negotiations were stalemated over the political future of the Thieu regime. There had been little movement in the secret talks ever since the previous spring, when the United States dropped mutual withdrawal of foreign forces from the South as one of its key demands. With only ninety-five thousand American troops remaining in Vietnam, and only a handful of those combat troops, Hanoi hoped to make sufficient gains on the ground to compel the United States to cut South Vietnamese President Thieu loose.

An angered Nixon responded with sustained devastating bombing attacks, particularly in the Hanoi-Haiphong area, and then, in May, with the mining of Haiphong harbor. These actions produced ripples of protests that were drowned out by public expressions of approval for the president. Nixon's aides helped to create some of this support by orchestrating a telegram and letter-writing campaign from operatives in the Committee to Re-elect the President, whose congratulatory messages were announced as spontaneous reactions to the mining.

Even without the overkill from his committee, the public was willing to accept retaliatory escalation in the form of bombing as long as American ground troops were not involved and as long as the boys continued to come home. In addition, despite some strong language, the Russians did not withdraw their invitation for Nixon to visit their country after the mining. The North Vietnamese, as well as the Left in the United States, discovered that Nixon's détente and intricate China card diplomacy were more important to Moscow than its beleaguered socialist ally.

In some ways, the nomination of George McGovern by the Democrats in 1972 could be tied to the then declining antiwar movement. His nomination was secured in good measure because of Democratic party reforms brought about by the convulsions at the Chicago Convention in 1968. Moreover, McGovern's main attraction was a promise to end the war more quickly than Nixon.

Even with the polls running in his favor by wide margins, Nixon took no chances and pressed Kissinger to achieve a political agreement before the election. When, after a whirlwind series of negotiations, the popular national security adviser announced that he had an agreement—"peace is at hand"—in the week before the election, more of McGovern's already fleeting minority support evaporated.

After being reelected by an even larger margin in the Electoral College than Johnson in 1964, Nixon revealed that the peace agreement had fallen apart. Although he did not explain the full particulars to the public, in his haste to have peace in his hands before the election, Kissinger failed to secure the agreement of the South Vietnamese. It was they—not the North Vietnamese, whom Nixon blamed publicly—who squelched the deal.

Although some Americans had their suspicions, most accepted Nixon's explanations as he went to work trying to put together a new agreement.[84] To buy South Vietnamese compliance, he promised vast increases in economic and military aid, military support should the North Vietnamese break the agreement, and alterations in the original treaty language. When the North Vietnamese stubbornly stood by the agreement they had signed in October,

Nixon revealed the other facet of his twin-pronged approach to peace.

On December 18 and for eleven days thereafter, American B-52's pounded Hanoi and Haiphong with thirty-six thousand tons of bombs, more than had been dropped from 1969 through 1971. Domestic and international opinion was outraged, Nixon's approval rating dropped, and congressional leaders, who were on Christmas break, told the media they planned strong action against the president when they came back after New Year's.

The bombing stopped before Congress could take that action and before most Americans emerged from their holiday activities. Peace talks reopened on January 8. Despite the communists' claims to the contrary, Nixon proclaimed that his bombing, though a tough decision, had worked.[85] As on Inauguration Day in 1969, protesters turned up in Washington to denounce the president. A hundred thousand participated in counterinaugural activities; some were upset about the Christmas bombing, others about the social and domestic programs of the first administration. The media paid scant attention to their activities. A week later, on January 27, agreement was reached between all belligerents in the Vietnam War. The war, for Americans, was over.

Early in 1975, after the peace treaty that earned Henry Kissinger and Le Duc Tho Nobel Prizes had been violated thousands of times by all parties, Hanoi launched its final nationwide offensive. In a matter of months, Saigon fell, and all of Vietnam was unified under the communists.

The antiwar movement figured indirectly in this outcome. The Watergate affair that crippled the Nixon presidency and dominated his political life from the spring of 1973 to his resignation in August 1974, originated in part from the Plumbers, the Huston Plan, and other offensives against his foreign policy critics. During this period, he was far too weak to contest with Congress over a renewal of American military involvement in Vietnam. As the crisis in South Vietnam deepened in the middle of 1974, the new president, Gerald Ford, wanted to increase military aid to the faltering Saigon regime. A muscle-flexing Congress refused his requests to what it saw as pouring more money down a rathole.

There was no antiwar movement nor much of a foreign policy

debate in 1974 and 1975. The public, led by Congress and the media, all influenced by arguments presented earlier by the movement, simply would not countenance a renewed American combat role in Vietnam or even greater financial commitments to a discredited Saigon regime.[86] The struggle for the hearts and minds of Americans was over. There would be no more Vietnams—for a while.

Chapter Eight

Conclusion

"If we appear to be divided—if the Soviets suspect that domestic, political pressure will undercut our position—they will dig in their heels."
—*RONALD REAGAN**

As I was leaving Leonard Garment's office after an interview, he asked me whether I thought antiwar dissenters had affected the decision makers. I replied that I did not know yet, as my research was incomplete. "But surely," the lawyer responded, "you must have a theory of the case."

At that time, midway through my research, I was pursuing many theories. Among the most plausible were that the movement (1) exerted pressures directly on Johnson and Nixon that contributed to their deescalation policies; (2) exerted pressures indirectly by turning the public against the war; (3) encouraged the North Vietnamese to fight on long enough to the point that Americans demanded a withdrawal from Southeast Asia; (4) influenced American political and military strategies, since Johnson and Nixon were convinced that Hanoi counted on the movement; (5) retarded the growth of general antiwar sentiment because the public perceived the protesters as unpatriotic; and (6) combinations of these theories.

Although I still cannot answer Garment's question categorically, it is clear to me now that the antiwar movement and antiwar criticism in the media and Congress had a significant impact on the Vietnam policies of both Johnson and Nixon. At two key points at least—October 1967 and October 1969—mass demonstrations affected American foreign policy. The March on the Pentagon

*New York Times, August 1, 1983, p. 4.

shocked many in the Johnson administration and produced the public relations campaign that contributed to public shock after Tet. The Moratorium helped to convince Nixon that Americans would not accept the savage blows envisaged in Operation Duck Hook. On many other occasions, involving such issues as bombing pauses, diplomatic and military initiatives, and major speeches, antiwar activities and dissent were important factors for the decision makers. Even more dramatically, the movement played a role in Lyndon Johnson's decisions not to seek a second term and to wind down the war and played a major, if latent, role in restraining Richard Nixon from reescalating.[1] In addition, many of the Watergate crimes were related to Nixon's attempt to crush the movement. Thus, the movement played an indirect role in the first resignation of a president in American history.[2]

The extent of the impact of the movement on decision makers cannot be gauged through an empirical approach. The most ingenious attempt, which correlated policy and opinion changes with mass demonstrations, came up with inconclusive and unconvincing findings.[3] The historian must rely instead on traditional tools to flesh out the often impressionistic evidence that allows one to make educated guesses about policymaking.

It is never easy to determine the motivations behind any public policy. The motivations behind foreign policies are even more difficult to determine than the motivations behind domestic policies, if only because officials try to obscure the role of sordid domestic politics when they defend national security. Irrespective of the stated and attributed rationales for foreign policies, one can identify the factors that attracted the attention of the decision makers as they considered their options. Archival and published records reveal the external events that worried them enough to be taken into account as they decided what and when to bomb in Vietnam, how many soldiers to call up or send home, and what sorts of diplomatic initiatives to undertake. Further, one can assess the importance of the antiwar movement to Washington by the energies expended in monitoring and suppressing its activities.[4] If, as the key figures often said, the movement had no impact on their foreign policies, why was it that they spent so much of their time and attention on it?

Even those who downplay the importance of the movement

concede that public opinion was a crucial variable in the construction of Vietnam policies. It is in their links to public opinion that the movement and antiwar critics exercised their most profound influence on those policies. To be sure, throughout the terms of both presidents, public opinion polls revealed considerable support for whatever the military did in Vietnam. On the other hand, in both administrations, support for escalation tended to decrease as the war dragged on and as first Johnson and then Nixon proved incapable of terminating it with dispatch.

Antiwar activities helped convince more and more Americans to oppose the war, or at least begin to feel uncomfortable about the nation's involvement in Vietnam. At times, some of their activities, as framed by sensation-seeking media, may have produced a patriotic backlash. Overall, however, the movement eroded support for Johnson and Nixon, especially among college students at the best universities, their parents, and members of the attentive and informed public. Some groups of people in the United States count for more than others. The loss of Yale and the *New York Times* to Johnson and even Nixon meant more than the retention of support from state colleges in Texas and the Scripps-Howard chain of newspapers. Through their constant and often publicized attacks, experts in the movement, the media, and on the campuses helped to destroy the knee-jerk notion that "they in Washington know."[5] This was a very important development. For the first time since 1945, major reference figures in the bipartisan establishment began to speak out against an American cold war policy and led many citizens to question the judgment and wisdom of their presidents.

From the start, it was clear that the longer the war went on, the more likely Americans would tire of their increasingly costly involvement. If the United States could not win, in the absence of a strong initial and sustained commitment to wait out the patient and dedicated enemy in Vietnam, pressures for withdrawal had to increase over time.[6] Dean Rusk, who sees opposition rising at home because of Tet and other policy failures, irrespective of previous criticism from the antiwar movement, emphasizes this approach.[7]

Yet that previous criticism had to be important for several reasons. First, movement activities and elite opposition in the media helped to keep the war "on the front burner" from 1965 through 1971.[8] With the war an object of almost constant attention, presidents found it difficult to pursue military policies that the public would find objectionable. In addition, the critics presented arguments and information that provided a framework for those who did not know how to articulate their general opposition to what was becoming an endless war. The existence of any opposition helped to reinforce other opposition. Senator Morse's lonely stand against the war in 1964 encouraged some citizens in their opposition, as did Senator Fulbright's hearings in early 1966, which had been encouraged by the rising opposition on elite campuses during the previous year. That opposition was legitimized to some degree when congressmen read its letters and petitions into the *Congressional Record.*

The movement's impact on the public and on the administration was enhanced by the way the antiwar argument was presented. As one critic of the movement has argued, those who opposed the war stole the moral issue from the administration early on.[9] That issue, simplistic and naive from a Realpolitik perspective, was understood more easily than the incompetently presented limited war argument. The moral argument, with the bombing and destruction of peasant society as its cornerstone, was echoed in Western Europe as well as in neutral nations. As the war continued, the argument received "disproportionate media attention," according to Walt Rostow.[10]

The antiwar movement plus the course of events affected the intellectual and opinion-making community, which in turn encouraged the activists and weakened the administration. Much of the nation's intellectual elite was associated with the prestigious universities where mass protests began and were nurtured. Both Johnson and Nixon blamed pied-piper professors on those campuses, more than students, for their problems there.

Whether their animosity was properly targeted, Johnson and Nixon should have expected the criticism from those opinion leaders. Irving Kristol contends that "no modern nation ever constructed a foreign policy acceptable to its intellectuals."[11] Perhaps, but American intellectuals were not especially dovish in 1964 and 1965. By 1970, however, according to one survey, intellectuals were overwhelmingly antiwar, with more than two-thirds changing their views during the preceding years. Their favorite journals, the *New York Times*, the *New Yorker*, and the *New York Review of Books*, influenced them, and the journals, in turn, were influenced by many of the intellectuals themselves.[12]

The alienation of the American intellectual elite did not affect the policymakers directly, in part because there was little contact between that elite and the Oval Office.[13] That was to be expected. At the same time, the desertion of the intellectuals had an indirect impact on government officials. In a trickle-down effect, Democratic party leaders, as well as those members of the public who took their lead from favorite writers and professors, were influenced by the desertion from the cold war foreign policy consensus of many liberal intellectuals.[14] "Trickle down" is even too vague a term to describe the relationship between intellectual discontent and the rise of the Kennedy opposition faction within the party after 1965.

Kristol may have been correct about intellectuals generally disapproving of a nation's foreign policy, especially a policy that appears to be amoral or immoral, but it is the extent of that disapproval and the passion with which it was held that is important on the Vietnam issue. It is difficult for a democracy to operate effectively in the international sphere without the support of its intellectual leadership.

It is also clear that the disaffection of intellectuals and elite college students affected establishment types outside of government who feared for the future of their country.[15] Respected leaders such as Dean Acheson and Clark Clifford, who worried about the establishment in the next generation, ultimately urged the administration to cut its losses before the country fell apart.[16]

Antiwar protests, among others, in a period that witnessed unprecedented rowdy demonstrations, took a physical and emotional toll on the occupants of the White House. Neither Johnson nor Nixon could tolerate criticism, even when they expected it from the media or from liberals. Both were subjected to the most extensive and abusive criticism of any twentieth-century president. On occasion, they and their advisers went to great lengths to avoid the demonstrators, who nevertheless managed to appear almost every time the presidents stepped out of the White House. Johnson, in particular, was irritated by the incessant public manifestations of displeasure with his policies and that irritation may have been a background variable in his decision to leave Washington for the peace of his ranch.

Both Johnson and Nixon developed offensives against their critics, especially in the movement, which included the mobilization of the CIA and FBI to monitor and harass them. Both claimed that such activities were not a product of their own concern with demonstrations but their fear that Hanoi would misinterpret them. Further, both believed that some, if not most, of the antiwar movement was foreign inspired and financed; the government had to devote considerable energies to defend the country against subversion.

On the latter charge, they were mistaken. The intelligence agencies concluded in report after report that foreign influences in the antiwar movement were marginal. On the other hand, their major contention that the movement and all of its manifestations encouraged Hanoi is no doubt true. The key question, and an imponderable one at that, is whether that encouragement prolonged the war.

Without a strong antiwar movement that limited the administration's abilities to pursue a tougher military policy, goes the prolongation argument, the North Vietnamese would have accepted a half a loaf and the war would have ended much sooner. The antiwar movement here is linked to the general development of antiwar attitudes among the public.

The contest for the public's support between the government and its opponents was an important element in the making of Vietnam policy. For example, when Richard Nixon committed Washington to a Vietnamization program, domestic opinion was one "crucial variable." Vietnamization would convince the public that the war was not endless; the American commitment would decrease gradually. Domestic support would be maintained that would convince the North Vietnamese not to count on the American people to force Nixon's negotiating hand. There was a "logical flaw" in this position.[17] If Vietnamization cooled dovish fervor in the United States, it also revealed the light at the end of the tunnel for Hanoi. Why negotiate when the last American soldier would depart Vietnam in the foreseeable future?

Moreover, the prolongation-of-the-war argument deemphasizes the commitment of Hanoi to fight on virtually forever for its goal of an independent communist Vietnam. Further, one of the major reasons Johnson and Nixon did not use tougher tactics was their fear that the Russians and Chinese might be compelled to intervene to rescue their socialist ally.

The ability to employ tougher military tactics was not just crippled by an alert antiwar movement. It is likely that the population in general, with or without the leadership of antiwar critics, would not have countenanced the bombing of the dikes in the North or the use or threatened use of tactical nuclear weapons. Americans would not have needed the movement to express their strong displeasure over the employment of such drastic means in a limited war. Here, the administrations caused their own problems. By never explaining in a convincing fashion why the war was so important, Johnson and Nixon found it impossible to escalate in a manner that would only be justified in a full-scale war vital to America's very survival. Johnson kept a low rhetorical profile in the years from 1965 through 1967, in part to avoid encouraging the growth of the antiwar movement. We have come full circle. Although only strong presidential leadership and a declaration of national emergency would have given the presidents the backing to employ tougher tactics, one of the reasons they eschewed that approach was the fear of arousing the antiwar movement.

It is true that once Nixon talked and acted tougher in 1972, the communists accepted less than the whole loaf at the bargaining table. Whether that would have been the case before détente neutralized the Soviet Union, as well as before the destruction and the disbanding of the antiwar movement, is a difficult question.

Irrespective of the validity of the argument that the movement prolonged the war by encouraging Hanoi, Johnson and Nixon *believed* that the North Vietnamese counted on American opinion, influenced by the movement, as one of its main allies. Both administrations considered this alleged factor as they constructed their political and military strategies. Here, then, is irrefutable evidence of the impact of the movement on policymaking during the war, if only indirect impact.

Some critics ignore the movement and opinion and point to the media, where dissenters and dissenting commentators turned the nation around on the war. Unfair to both Johnson and Nixon, the media allegedly created the movement and undermined both administrations. George Christian thinks the press was lost by 1967. Hubert Humphrey saw the media in 1968, the crucial year of decision, as "viscerally and intellectually" anti-Johnson. In a similar vein, Edith Efron described television network news on Vietnam in the fall of 1969 as reflecting an antiadministration bias. Finally, the media were undoubtedly important in the popular understanding of Tet.[18]

Former antiwar leader and sociologist Todd Gitlin, who does not agree with such criticism, nevertheless points out that movement ideas and activities were publicized by the media.[19] One of his old colleagues, David Dellinger, has written that the movement had three explicit targets—the government, the public, and the activists themselves. Especially in the early days, when the public and government were not listening, media attention provided gratification for the foot soldiers who continued to turn out for the demonstrations. As the movement picked up steam, the media helped to legitimize dissent.[20]

For the most part, however, experts do not agree with the theory of an "oppositional" media. In a study comparable to but more sophisticated than Efron's, Daniel Hallin concluded that at least as far as the *New York Times* and television news were concerned, both administrations received more than a fair break from the media. Another expert, Herbert Gans, demonstrated how, early in the war, Lyndon Johnson dominated the airwaves. Even when critical reports came in from the field through 1967, editors in New York and elsewhere either did not print them or toned them down.[21]

Presidents' views dominate the media until major reference figures from the establishment begin to disagree with them and appear in such numbers that the media are forced to cover their criticism.[22] Both Johnson and Nixon began with overwhelming support in the media, which declined over time. Their slowly developing criticism was legitimate and generally without malice. The presidents' failing and controversial policies, as well as their own growing antagonism to the media, led to an entirely understandable decrease in media support.[23] Johnson, for example, blamed the media for creating the credibility gap, when in fact it was his invention.[24]

Even the Tet argument used by the media critics can be turned around to support the notion that the press and television were more than fair to Johnson. One reason for widespread public concern over Tet was the failure of the media to prepare the nation for such an event because it accepted so uncritically the light-at-the-end-of-the-tunnel pronouncements from Washington.[25]

The relationships between the media, the movement, public opinion, and foreign policy are complicated. They are far too complicated to blame the media for the decline of support over time for the Johnson and Nixon policies.[26]

The antiwar movement succeeded in capturing the attention of Johnson and Nixon and affecting their policies in Vietnam. One of the important lessons one can learn from studies such as this is that government officials do not always behave the way they should according to the neat academic models of opinion formation and policymaking. Johnson and Nixon simply did not behave rationally on many occasions when they confronted media criticism and antiwar demonstrations. Surprisingly thin-skinned for professional politicians, they overreacted to criticism in unpredictable and unstructured manners. One never knew when a few demonstrators in front of the White House, or a speech on a college campus, or an editorial in the *Washington Post* might set off one or the other, even at times when they enjoyed the support of the vast majority of their constituents.

It might well be that there is less to learn here than one might suspect. Johnson and Nixon were unusual residents of the Oval Office. Both were among the most volatile, unstable, and maybe even pathological of recent presidents. Comparing their behavior and personalities to those of Roosevelt, Truman, Eisenhower, Kennedy, Ford, Carter, and Reagan, one must be leery about generalizing from Johnson and Nixon to all presidents.

Yet, as I was told time and again by such experienced presidential counselors and observers as Bryce Harlow, George Reedy, and Jack Valenti, much of the time, *all* presidents are just like everyone else.

They react to criticism and challenges, even from a minority of their constituents, quite often from the gut and not from the brain. What this means is that those who exercise their rights as citizens to gather, protest, and petition in comparatively small numbers have more of an impact on their leaders than one would expect. Such a conclusion might help to sustain others who question present and future foreign policies.[27]

Notes

PREFACE

1. I describe some of my interviewing experiences in "Interviews as a Source for the History of American Involvement in the Vietnam War," *Society for Historians of American Foreign Relations Newsletter* 16 (March 1985):23–28.

CHAPTER 1: INTRODUCTION

1. Samuel Eliot Morison suggests that the 1812 dissent was more important. Morison et al., *Dissent in Three American Wars* (Cambridge, Mass.: Harvard University Press, 1970), 3. As for another famous antiwar dissent, Robert Beisner finds the Vietnam movement to be more complex and heterogeneous than its counterpart in 1898. Beisner, "1898 and 1968: The Anti-Imperialists and the Doves," *Political Science Quarterly* 85 (June 1970):187–216.

2. Paul Burstein and William Freudenberg, "Changing Public Policy: The Impact of Public Opinion, Antiwar Demonstrations, and War Costs on Senate Voting on Vietnam War Motions," *American Journal of Sociology* 84 (July 1978):99–122.

3. James N. Rosenau, *Public Opinion and Foreign Policy* (New York: Random House, 1961), 97–98. Much of the discussion that follows appeared in Melvin Small, "Public Opinion on Foreign Policy: The View from the Johnson and Nixon White Houses," *Politica* 16, no. 2 (1984):184–200; idem, "The Impact of the Antiwar Movement on Lyndon Johnson: A Preliminary Report," *Peace and Change* 10 (Spring 1984):1–22; and idem, "Influencing the Decision Makers: The Vietnam Experience," *Journal of Peace Research* 24, no. 2(1987):185–198.

4. Bill Moyers, "One Thing We Learned," *Foreign Affairs* 46 (July 1968):658; Charles Frankel, *High on Foggy Bottom: An Outsider's Inside View of Government* (New York: Harper & Row, 1968), 205. A comparable problem exists when one tries to explain how a movement begins from individual action. Paul Rogat Loeb, *Hope in Hard Times: America's Peace Movement in the Reagan Era* (Lexington, Mass. D. C. Heath, 1986), 64.

5. George Reedy, interview, Milwaukee, Wisconsin, January 25, 1984. See also Eric A. Goldman, *The Tragedy of Lyndon Johnson* (New York: Knopf, 1969), 490.

6. Valenti, interview, Washington, D.C., February 10, 1984.

7. Clark Clifford, interview, Washington, D.C., February 8, 1984. Supporting Clifford's views was George Christian, Johnson's press secre-

tary from 1967 through 1969. George Christian, interview, Austin, Texas, May 18, 1983.

8. Rostow, interview, Austin, Texas, May 20, 1983; McGeorge Bundy, interview, New York, March 9, 1984; Dean Rusk, interview, Athens, Georgia, February 23, 1984.

9. Quoted in Barry B. Hughes, *The Domestic Context of American Foreign Policy* (San Francisco: W. H. Freeman, 1978), 4.

10. Ibid., 90–96. The 1980 election is one obvious exception to the rule. One quantitative study that reports a correlation between war entries and punishment at the polls is Timothy Y. C. Cotton, "War and American Democracy: Electoral Costs of the Last Five Wars," *Journal of Conflict Resolution* 30 (December 1986):616–635.

11. Benjamin I. Page and Richard Brody, "Policy Voting and the Electoral Process: The Vietnam War Issue," *American Political Science Review* 66 (September 1972):994.

12. Winston Lord, interview, New York, March 8, 1984. For the famous meeting system, see David C. Humphrey, "Tuesday Lunch at the Johnson White House: A Preliminary Assessment," *Diplomatic History* 8 (Winter 1984):81–101; and Henry F. Graff, *The Tuesday Cabinet: Deliberation and Decision on Peace and War under Lyndon B. Johnson* (Englewood Cliffs, N.J.: Prentice-Hall, 1970). George Reedy, for one, thinks too much has been made of the Tuesday Lunch. He suggests that its members were meeting even before it became institutionalized and that the president, criticized for having a chaotic bureaucratic style, publicized the Lunch so that the media would think the White House was well organized. Reedy, interview. According to H. R. Haldeman, Johnson told Nixon that the Lunch was for the media. Haldeman, interview, Los Angeles, November 14, 1985.

13. Bryce Harlow, interview, Washington, D.C., February 7, 1984; Ray Price, interview, New York, March 9, 1984. One may appreciate Nixon's penchant for memo-writing by sampling the wide variety of memos available in the President's Personal Files (hereafter PPF), Memoranda From the President (hereafter MFRP), Nixon Presidential Materials Project (hereafter NP), National Archives, Alexandria, Virginia.

14. I. M. Destler, *Presidents, Bureaucracies and Foreign Policy* (Princeton, N.J.: Princeton University Press, 1974), 111; William P. Bundy, unpublished history of the Vietnam War, chap. 26, p. 24; Rusk, interview; Bromley E. Smith, oral history (hereafter oh), p. 26, Lyndon Baines Johnson Library (hereafter LBJL), Austin, Texas.

15. Dean Rusk pinpointed one of the problems in this area in recent years as the growth of the National Security Council bureaucracy. Rusk, interview. Nixon's memos reveal a constant concern about the "official sources" quoted in newspaper stories about his policies. At the highest levels, the Johnson administration, especially the secretaries of state and defense and the national security advisers, got along much better with less backbiting than their counterparts in the Nixon administration, as the many memoirs from the Nixon administration reveal.

16. Chester Cooper, *The Lost Crusade: America in Vietnam* (New York: Dodd, Mead, 1979), 414–415; Townsend Hoopes, *The Limits of Intervention* (New York: David McKay, 1969), 53; Humphrey, "Tuesday Lunch," 93–94; Smith, oh, pp. 24–25, LBJL. Cyrus Vance, who was not quite in the inner circle, disagrees with this portrayal. Vance, interview, New York, March 18, 1984.

17. For an account of the "Radford" affair, see Seymour M. Hersh, *The Price of Power: Kissinger in the Nixon White House* (New York: Summit, 1983), 465–474.

18. Reedy, interview.

19. Elihu Katz and Paul F. Lazarsfeld, *Personal Influence* (Glencoe, Ill.: Free Press, 1955), 102–103.

20. Harry S. Truman, *Memoirs* (Garden City, N.Y.: Doubleday, 1956), 2:219–220.

21. Christian, interview.

22. Rusk, interview. John P. Roche notes that the "boys in the firehouse in Boston" read the *Boston Herald*, not the *New York Times*. Roche, interview, Medford, Massachusetts, March 12, 1984.

23. Harlow; Valenti, interviews. With Johnson in particular, sources stressed his sensitivity to criticism. Christian; Reedy, interviews; telephone interview with Douglass Cater, February 8, 1984.

24. Rosenau suggests a similar approach in *Public Opinion and Foreign Policy*, 11.

25. See Michael Wheeler, *Lies, Damn Lies, and Statistics: The Manipulation of Public Opinion in America* (New York: Norton, 1976), chap. 7, for a general discussion in this area.

26. Leo Bogart, *Silent Politics: Polls and the Awareness of Public Opinion* (New York: Wiley, 1972), 4. See also Leonard A. Kusnitz, *Public Opinion and Foreign Policy: America's China Policy* (Westport, Conn.: Greenwood, 1984), 130, n. 153.

27. Louis Harris, *The Anguish of Change* (New York: Norton, 1974), 17. Bryce Harlow remembers H. R. Haldeman, especially, as an inveterate poll user. Harlow, interview.

28. Christian, interview.

29. Haldeman, interview.

30. Daniel Z. Henkin, interview, Washington, D.C., February 9, 1984; Rusk; Price, interviews. See also State Department opinion analyst H. Schuyler Foster's discussion in *Activism Replaces Isolationism: U.S. Public Attitudes, 1940–1975* (Washington, D.C.: Fox Hall, 1983), 9–11.

31. Hughes, *Domestic Context*, 108–110; William Caspary, "The Mood Theory: A Study of Public Opinion and Foreign Policy," in Dan Nimmo and Charles M. Bonjean, eds., *Political Attitudes and Public Opinion* (New York: David McKay, 1972), 439–454.

32. Don D. Smith, "Dark Areas of Ignorance Revisited: Current Knowledge about Asian Affairs," in Nimmo and Bonjean, *Political Attitudes*, 267–272.

33. Philip E. Converse and Howard Schuman, "Silent Majorities and

the Vietnam War," *Scientific American* 222 (June 1970):21; John E. Mueller, *War, Presidents, and Public Opinion* (New York: Wiley, 1973), 71–74.

34. Hughes, *Domestic Context,* 101–102. A fine survey on mail to Congress that has implications for the executive branch is Stephen E. Frantzich, *Write Your Congressman: Constituent Communications and Representation* (New York: Praeger, 1986). See also Abigail McCarthy, *Private Faces/Public Places* (Garden City, N.Y.: Doubleday, 1972), 288–291.

35. Bogart, *Silent Politics,* 53.

36. See, e.g., the weekly counts sent from the Defense Department to Lyndon Johnson by Joseph Califano in WH 5-1, White House Central Files (hereafter WHCF), LBJL; and Noble Mellencamp to Nixon, September 18, 1969, box 3, President's Handwriting (hereafter PH), President's Office Files (hereafter POF), NP, on the weekly flow of mail on Vietnam.

37. Cooper to McGeorge Bundy, April 6, 1965, box 16, National Security Country File, Vietnam (hereafter NSCVN), LBJL. Dean Rusk reports that he was impressed with well-written, literate letters that were not part of some organized campaign. Rusk, interview. Nixon similarly was on the alert for nonspontaneous letters as when he asked Kissinger to have his staff determine "how much is inspired" in the weekly mail on Vietnam. Note on Mellencamp to Nixon, September 18, 1969, box 3, PH, POF, NP. Presidential advisers Eric Goldman and John P. Roche also took mail seriously. Eric Goldman, interview, Princeton, New Jersey, March 5, 1984; Roche, interview.

38. Other examples are the fewer than one thousand telegrams and six hundred letters produced by Johnson's major October 31, 1968, bombing concession and the fewer than one hundred telegrams produced by Dean Rusk's television testimony in March 1968. See Rostow to Johnson, November 1, 2, 4, 1968, Presidential Document Series (hereafter PDS), *Vietnam, the Media, and Public Support for the War,* microfilm, reel 3 (Frederick, Md.: University Publications, 1986); and Lou Schwartz to Rostow, March 13, 1968, PDS, reel 4. It is more understandable that mail to a congressman's office, from a much smaller population, might serve as a useful reflector of district opinion. Hughes, *Domestic Context,* 101.

39. Bogart, *Silent Politics,* 53–54; Frantzich, *Write Your Congressman,* 81.

40. According to one poll, 2.5 percent of the respondents reported sending a letter to a publication, whereas 1 percent said they had taken part in a demonstration. Milton J. Rosenberg, Sidney Verba, and Philip E. Converse, *Vietnam and the Silent Majority: A Dove's Guide* (New York: Harper & Row, 1970), 33–34, 31.

41. For example, on one occasion Johnson requested a sample of a critical letter from a serviceman in order to get a feel for such sentiments. Juanita Roberts to Paul Popple, April 5, 1967, box 10, WH 5-1, WHCF,

LBJL. Ray Price often provided Nixon with a sampling of the mail for "weekend reading." Price to Nixon, May 21, 1971, box 3, PH, POF, NP. Nixon's marginal comments suggest that he read most of them.

42. George Reedy, *The Twilight of the Presidency* (New York: World, 1970), 86-87, 95-96; William P. Bundy, interview, New York, February 6, 1984; Reedy; Henkin; Harlow, interviews; Henry Kissinger, *White House Years* (Boston: Little, Brown, 1979), 300, 513; Kissinger, *Years of Upheaval* (Boston: Little, Brown, 1982), 93-94; Gerald R. Ford, *A Time to Heal* (New York: Harper & Row, 1979), 83; Curt Smith, *Long Time Gone: The Years of Turmoil Remembered* (South Bend, Ind.: Icarus, 1982), 217; McCarthy, *Private Faces*, 286-287. Gerald Ford remembers dinner table discussions but "never had the kind of estrangement that unfortunately existed in some families." Transcript of Representative David Bonior's interview with Ford, November 9, 1982.

43. Herbert Klein, *Making It Perfectly Clear* (Garden City, N.Y.: Doubleday, 1980), 338; Marvin and Bernard Kalb, *Kissinger* (London: Hutchison, 1974), 28.

44. Christian, interview.

45. Jeffrey Schevitz, *The Weaponsmakers: Personal and Professional Crisis During the Vietnam War* (Cambridge, Mass.: M.I.T. Press, 1979). See also Cohen, *The Public's Impact on Foreign Policy* (Boston: Little, Brown, 1973), 80-84.

46. Michael P. Rosenberg sees congressional doves affecting opinion, affecting politics, and influencing the executive. "Congress and the Vietnam War: A Study of the Critics of the War in 1967 and 1968" (Ph.D. diss., New School for Social Research, 1973), 10-16.

47. Eugene McCarthy, *The Year of the People* (Garden City, N.Y.: Doubleday, 1969), 254.

48. Harlow, interview. Dean Rusk also employed talks with legislators to gauge opinion. Rusk, interview. See also Goldman, *Tragedy of Lyndon Johnson*, 403.

49. Warren E. Miller and Donald E. Stokes, "Constituency Influence in Congress," in Nimmo and Bonjean, *Political Attitudes*, 543-561. The classic Miller and Stokes article may be outdated in terms of recent congressional behavior.

50. Bernard C. Cohen, *The Press and Foreign Policy* (Princeton, N.J.: Princeton University Press, 1963), 38-47. See also Smith, oh, p. 5, LBJL; and Reedy, *Twilight of the Presidency*, 99-118.

51. A study that examines most of those roles in detail is Kathleen Turner, *Lyndon Johnson's Dual War: Vietnam and the Press* (Chicago: University of Chicago Press, 1985).

52. David L. Altheide, *Creating Reality: How TV News Distorts Events* (Beverly Hills, Calif.: Sage, 1976), 173.

53. Valenti, interview; Chester Cooper, oh, pp. 10-11, LBJL.

54. James Aronson, *Deadline for the Media: Today's Challenges to*

Press, TV and Radio (Indianapolis: Bobbs-Merrill, 1972), 16; Todd Gitlin, *The Whole World Is Watching: Mass Media in the Making and Unmaking of the New Left* (Berkeley: University of California Press, 1980), 218.

55. Two notable exceptions were Morley Safer's 1965 report from Vietnam that featured the famous Zippo lighter incident and Walter Cronkite's editorial remarks in 1968 following the Tet Offensive.

56. The expert who ran the State Department's opinion bureau in many instances relied more heavily on a sample of newspaper editorials than on polls for a reflection of opinion trends. Foster, *Activism Replaces Isolationism*, 12.

57. Cohen, *The Press and Foreign Policy*, 134–136; Cater; Reedy; Valenti; Rusk, interviews. For an excoriation of the *New York Times* and its nefarious left-wing influence, see Russ Braley, *Bad News: The Foreign Policy of the New York Times* (Chicago: Regnery Gateway, 1984). Beyond Washington, Charles Kadushin reports that 98 percent of his sample of American intellectuals read the *Times*. Kadushin, *The American Intellectual Elite* (Boston: Little, Brown, 1974), 137.

58. For the "voracious" reader, Lyndon Johnson, they were required evening reading. He read the earliest editions before he went to bed each night. Tom Johnson, interview, Los Angeles, November 15, 1985.

59. BDM Corporation, "A Study of the Strategic Lessons Learned in Vietnam," vol. 4 (Washington, D.C.: U.S. Department of the Army, 1979), EX-5.

60. Note the instructions on how to flatter Lippmann in McGeorge Bundy to Johnson, March 15, 1965, box 3, vol. 9, National Security Council Aides File, LBJL.

61. Kissinger, *White House Years*, 298; and box 30 Annotated News Summaries, POF, NP, for Nixon's many marginal notes to Kissinger expressing concern about the media's failure to appreciate the progress he was making in Vietnam during the first six months of his administration. For Nixon's hatred for and fascination with the media, see Joseph Spear, *Presidents and the Press: The Nixon Legacy* (Cambridge, Mass.: M.I.T. Press, 1984).

62. Harlow; Reedy; Valenti, interviews. Naturally, the elite journalists can have an impact around the world. See W. Averell Harriman, February 24, 1966, box 1, Meeting Notes, LBJL, who reported that the *New York Times* and Walter Lippman had contributed to the questioning of America's will by her allies.

63. Reedy, interview.

64. Interview with J. William Fulbright, Washington, D.C., February 7, 1984. As Henry Adams wrote over seventy years ago, "The difference is slight, to the influence of an author, whether he is read by five hundred readers, or by five hundred thousand; if he can select the five hundred, he reaches the five hundred thousand." *The Education of Henry Adams* (Boston: Houghton Mifflin, 1918), 259. Lyndon Johnson told friendly *Washington Post* editor Russell Wiggins that his editorials were worth

fifty divisions. Ronald Steel, *Walter Lippmann and the American Century* (Boston: Little, Brown, 1980), 570.

65. Reedy, interview.

66. Interview with Harry Zubkoff, Washington, D.C., August 3, 1984; Richard Scheinin, "Harry Zubkoff and His Pentagon Papers, *Washington Journalism Review* (March 1985): 33–36, 38.

67. Haldeman, interview. The news summaries, available in POF in the Nixon Project, full of Nixon's marginalia, are not as impressive in breadth of coverage as Zubkoff's service.

68. Douglass Cater suggests that if an apparatus were set up to handle opinion and, especially, dissent in a sophisticated manner, it might look to outsiders like a counterpropaganda agency. Cater, interview. The Johnson administration did set up a Public Affairs Policy Committee for Vietnam in 1965 (later the Vietnam Information Group), but it dealt with all aspects of public and media relations.

69. Johnson, for example, convinced that the early mass demonstrations were organized, nonspontaneous actions of subversives, could easily ignore that type of manifestation of opinion. Christian, interview. Bernard C. Cohen finds intuition more important than science in evaluating public opinion in the State Department. Cohen, *The Public's Impact*, 65.

70. Other reflections of domestic opinion, although not public opinion as perceived by the president, would come from lobbies and interest groups and the official bureaucracies. Dean Rusk, for example, paid attention to resolutions that emanated from important national organizations that reflected accurately the sentiments of the organizations' memberships. Rusk, interview.

71. Despite presidential attempts to belittle the antiwar movement as not representing public opinion, it was carefully monitored, especially after 1966. Bogart, *Silent Politics*, 48.

72. Lars-Goran Stenelo, *The International Critic* (Lund, Sweden: Student-litteratur, 1984).

73. Valenti; Roche; Tom Johnson, interviews; Jeb Stuart Magruder to John R. Brown III, December 18, 1969, box 24, HU 3–1, WHCF; Kenneth Cole to Nixon, October 13, 1969, box 3, PH, POF; Alexander Butterfield to Nixon, January 9, 1970, box 4, ibid., NP. On Johnson and the press, see John Tebbel and Sara Miles Watts, *The Press and the Presidency: From George Washington to Ronald Reagan* (New York: Oxford University Press, 1985), 489–500.

74. Roche; Price, interviews. In fact, Johnson's attempts to browbeat publishers might have worked against him ultimately. Stewart Alsop, oh, pp. 7–9, LBJL.

75. Roche, interview.

76. Valenti, interview. Moreover, Johnson was an "extraordinarily sophisticated" man who understood the impact of one powerful columnist's criticism. Tom Johnson, interview.

77. Robert Weissberg, *Public Opinion and American Popular Govern-*

ment (Englewood Cliffs, N.J.: Prentice-Hall, 1976); Kusnitz, *Public Opinion and Foreign Policy.*

78. Benjamin I. Page and Robert Y. Shapiro, "Effects of Public Opinion on Policy," *American Political Science Review* 77 (March 1983):182–183.

79. Burstein and Freudenberg, "Changing Public Policy."

80. William Berkowitz, "The Impact of Anti-Vietnam Demonstrations upon National Public Opinion and Military Indicators," *Social Science Research* 2 (March 1973):1–14.

81. Leslie H. Gelb with Richard K. Betts, *The Irony of Vietnam: The System Worked* (Washington, D.C.: Brookings, 1979), 332. See also Hughes, *Domestic Context*, 113, 203.

82. When asked recently, Gelb could not remember his use of the term "essential domino" and certainly did not link opinion to dissent. Interview with Leslie Gelb, Washington, D.C., July 31, 1984.

83. Among those who deemphasize the impact of the antiwar movement are Gelb, "Dissenting on Consensus," in Anthony Lake, ed., *The Vietnam Legacy: The War, American Society, and the Future of American Foreign Policy* (New York: New York University Press, 1976), 112; John P. Roche, "The Impact of Dissent on Foreign Policy: Past and Future," in Lake, *Vietnam Legacy*, 132; E. M. Schreiber, "Anti-war Demonstrations and American Public Opinion on the War in Vietnam," *British Journal of Sociology* 27 (June 1976):229; William M. Lunch and Peter W. Sperlich, "American Public Opinion and the War in Vietnam," *Western Political Quarterly* 32 (March 1979):31; Walter LaFeber, "The Last War, the Next War, and the New Revisionists," *Democracy* 1 (January 1981):272–282.

84. Of course, it was possible to be both antiwar and antidemonstrator. Mueller, *War, Presidents and Public Opinion*, 164–165; Rosenberg, Verba, and Converse, *Vietnam and the Silent Majority*, 40–41; Harris, *Anguish of Change*, 66–67.

85. As many as 40 percent of those polled in 1966 and 1967 thought the demonstrators did not have a right to protest against the war. Jerome Skolnick, *The Politics of Protest* (New York: Simon & Schuster, 1969), 23. Many of those who actively demonstrated in favor of the administration were more antidove than prowar. John P. Robinson, "Balance Theory and Vietnam Related Attitudes," in Nimmo and Bonjean, *Political Attitudes*, 353.

86. Irwin Unger, *The Movement: A History of the American New Left: 1959–1972* (New York: Dodd, Mead, 1975), 207. Among those who credit the movement with success are Irving Louis Horowitz, *The Struggle Is the Message: The Organization and Ideology of the Anti-war Movement* (Berkeley, Calif.: Glendessary, 1970), 56–57; James O'Brien, "The Anti-War Movement and the War," *Radical America* 8 (May-June 1974):66; Jonathan Schell, *The Time of Illusion* (New York: Vintage, 1976), 18; William Westmoreland, *A Soldier Reports* (Garden City, N.Y.: Doubleday, 1976), 413–414; U. S. Grant Sharp, *Strategy for Defeat: Vietnam in Retrospect* (San Rafael, Calif.: Presidio, 1978), 205; and Peter L. Berger, "Indochina and the American Conscience," *Commentary* 69 (February

1980):29. Richard Nixon sees it as "a factor . . . but not the decisive factor." Richard Nixon, *No More Vietnams* (New York: Arbor House, 1985), 15.

87. This view would be comparable to Tom Wolfe's analysis during the same period of how black radicals achieved success by "mau-mauing the flak catchers." Wolfe, *Radical Chic and Mau-Mauing the Flak Catchers* (New York: Farrar, Straus & Giroux, 1970).

88. Interview with Bui Xuan Ninh, New York, June 15, 1983. Among others who stress the significance of the movement during the Nixon years are Nixon aide Price and Kissinger aide Lord. Price; Lord, interviews. See also John Mueller, "Reflections on the Vietnam Antiwar Movement and on the Curious Calm at the War's End," in Peter Braestrup, ed., *Vietnam as History: Ten Years after the Paris Peace Accords* (Washington, D.C.: University Press of America, 1984), 153.

89. For a useful definition of the "movement," see Charles DeBenedetti, "On the Significance of Citizen Peace Activism: America 1961–1975," *Peace and Change* 9 (Summer 1983):11–12. See also Paul Joseph, *Cracks in the Empire: State Politics in the Vietnam War* (Boston: South End, 1981), 154–156; and G. Louis Heath, ed., *Mutiny Does Not Happen Lightly: The Literature of the American Resistance to the Vietnam War* (Metuchen, N.J.: Scarecrow, 1976).

90. Although campuses were also aflame with civil rights and other protests, after 1965 the war colored all other issues. Skolnick, *Politics of Protest*, 45–46; Robert B. Smith, "Campus Protests and the Vietnam War," in James Short and Marvin Wolfgang, eds., *Collective Violence* (Chicago: Aldine, 1972), 250–277.

91. Theodore White, *The Making of the President, 1968* (New York: Atheneum, 1969), 69. The number of potential activists in this cohort is unusually large given the huge blocks of free time enjoyed by university people.

92. Milton Viorst, *Fire in the Streets: America in the 1960s* (New York: Simon & Schuster, 1980), 164.

93. The often violent opposition to administration policies from the elite colleges concerned administration officials such as Secretary of Defense Robert S. McNamara. Graff, *Tuesday Cabinet*, 122.

94. One scholar using the *New York Times* index counted 750 major antiwar demonstrations involving 2.25 million participants from 1964 through 1971. Berkowitz, "Impact of Anti-Vietnam Demonstrations," 1–14. See also Richard E. Peterson, *The Scope of Organized Student Protest, 1964–1965* (Princeton, N.J.: Educational Testing Service, 1966), 43–44.

95. For the history of the movement, most useful are Nancy Zaroulis and Gerald Sullivan, *Who Spoke Up? American Protest Against the War in Vietnam, 1963–1975* (Garden City, N.Y.: Doubleday, 1984); Gitlin, *Whole World Is Watching;* Fred Halstead, *Out Now: A Participant's Account of the American Movement Against the Vietnam War* (New York: Monad, 1978); Jack Newfield, *A Prophetic Minority* (New York:

New American Library, 1966); Thomas Powers, *The War at Home: Vietnam and the American People, 1964–1968* (New York: Grossman, 1973); and Kirkpatrick Sale, *SDS: Ten Years toward a Revolution* (New York: Random House, 1973). Charles DeBenedetti died in 1987, before he could bring his authoritative "The Antiwar Movement in America 1955–1975" to completion. His lengthy draft, edited by Charles Chatfield, will become the definitive work on the antiwar movement.

CHAPTER 2: THE AMERICANIZATION OF THE WAR AND THE RISE OF DISSENT

1. After the dust had settled from the election and Johnson began to bomb North Vietnam in February, wags commented, "They told me that if I voted for Goldwater we would start bombing North Vietnam. I voted for Goldwater and we started bombing North Vietnam."

2. Theodore Draper, *Abuse of Power* (New York: Viking, 1967), 67.

3. Michael G. Burton, "Elite Disunity and Collective Protest: The Vietnam Case," *Journal of Political and Military Sociology* 5 (Fall 1977):169–183. DeBenedetti sees all the parts in place for the launching of the movement by the end of 1964. DeBenedetti, "The Antiwar Movement."

4. An indispensable source for opinion data from State Department files is Foster, *Activism Replaces Isolationism.* Some early concern for opinion can be seen in Henry Cabot Lodge to W. Averell Harriman, March 3, 1964, box 1, National Security File, McGeorge Bundy Aides File, LBJL; and Bundy to Johnson, August 24, 1964, ibid.

5. See, e.g., McGeorge Bundy's long memo on "sustained reprisal" on February 7, 1965, to Lyndon Johnson, in *The Pentagon Papers* (hereafter *PP*), Senator Gravel ed. (Boston: Beacon, 1971), 3:687–691.

6. Bundy, interview; Bundy, unpublished history of Vietnam War, chap. 20, p. 15. Bundy does remember some explicit dovish advice concerning opinion given to the president by Senator Mike Mansfield on the eve of the bombing (chap. 22, p. 6).

7. Rusk; Vance, interviews.

8. Interview with George Ball, Trenton, New Jersey, March 5, 1984. William Bundy was also concerned about the Korean precedent during the period. Bundy, interview.

9. McGeorge Bundy, interview; December 1, 1964, box 1, Meeting Notes, LBJL. See also Chester Cooper, oh, tape 1, p. 12, LBJL.

10. Telephone interview with James C. Thomson, Jr., March 13, 1984. See also Hoopes, *Limits of Intervention,* 31; and Hubert Humphrey, *The Education of a Public Man: My Life and Politics* (Garden City, N.Y.: Doubleday, 1976), 319. For Humphrey's concern *after* the bombing began, as well as for his feeling of being an outsider in Johnson's White House, see Carl Solberg, *Hubert Humphrey: A Biography* (New York: Norton, 1984), 272, 274–275.

11. Moyers, "One Thing We Learned," 662.

12. For Goldwater and leftist intellectuals, see Sandy Vogelsgang, *The Long Dark Night of the Soul of the American Intellectual Left and the Vietnam War* (New York: Harper & Row, 1974), 56.

13. Roche, interview.

14. McNamara to Johnson, July 30, 1965, *PP*, 3:387.

15. Bundy, interview. For an interesting assessment of congressional and, to some degree, public opinion during the winter of 1965, see William Conrad Gibbons, *The U.S. in the Vietnam War: Executive and Legislative Roles and Relationships*, pt. 2 (Princeton, N.J.: Princeton University Press, 1986), 396–397.

16. Dean Rusk on "*Vietnam: A Television History*," PBS, program 4; Tom Johnson, interview.

17. Bundy to Johnson, February 7, 1965, *PP*, 3:688.

18. Barbara Tuchman, *The March of Folly: From Troy to Vietnam* (New York: Knopf, 1984), 326.

19. Harry G. Summers, Jr., *On Strategy: The Vietnam War in Context* (Carlisle Barracks, Pa.: US Army War College Strategic Studies Institute, 1981), 22. Johnson himself thought that a limited war required not telling the public any more than it needed to know, and most of his advisers approved of his policy of stealthy escalation. Philip Geyelin, "Vietnam and the Press: Limited War and an Open Society," in Lake, *Vietnam Legacy*, 180–181, 167.

20. Herbert Y. Schandler, *The Unmaking of a President: Lyndon Johnson and Vietnam* (Princeton, N.J.: Princeton University Press, 1977), 21–22; Stanley Karnow, *Vietnam: A History* (New York: Penguin, 1983), 416.

21. Eric Goldman believes that the phrase was first used by David Wise in the *New York Herald Tribune* on that date. Goldman, *Tragedy of Lyndon Johnson*, 409.

22. William P. Bundy, oh, tape 5, p. 9, LBJL.

23. For information on the so-called "nonspeech," see McGeorge Bundy, boxes 17–19, National Security Council Aides File, LBJL. His brother also writes about the speech that was never given in his unpublished history, chap. 22, p. 24. See also Turner, *Lyndon Johnson's Dual War*, 113–114, on the State Department's interest in improving public relations on the bombing issue.

24. Bundy, interview.

25. William Bundy, interview. Bundy called his chapter on the document "The White Paper Disaster," in his unpublished history, chap. 22, p. 35. His brother and George Ball also agree that the White Paper was a feeble effort. McGeorge Bundy; Ball, interviews. For reports on CIA fabrication of evidence, see George McT. Kahin, *Intervention: How America Became Involved in Vietnam* (New York: Knopf, 1986), 290.

26. Cooper, *Lost Crusade*, 265–266. For the refutation prepared by Richard Ewing for William Jorden of State, see box 16, NSCVN, LBJL. From time to time, department specialists prepared refutations of antiwar articles for their superiors. See, e.g., the critique of an article in the June

1965 issue of the *Bulletin of Atomic Scientists* written by doves George McT. Kahin and John Lewis (May 11, 1965, box 17, NSCVN, LBJL).

27. Paul M. Kattenburg, *The Vietnam Trauma in American Foreign Policy* (New Brunswick, N.J.: Transaction, 1980), 245.

28. Bundy to Johnson, February 9, 1965, box 13, NSCVN, LBJL.

29. Chase to Bundy, February 16, 1965, box 13, NSCVN, LBJL.

30. The SDS had originally called for a demonstration during a late December meeting. As early as the previous August, the organization began planning for an expected escalation. Interview with Tom Hayden, Los Angeles, November 15, 1985.

31. Frank Church, oh, pp. 20, 22–23, LBJL; Powers, *War at Home*, 48; Rowland Evans and Robert Novak, *Lyndon B. Johnson: The Exercise of Power* (New York: New American Library, 1966), 563.

32. Steel, *Walter Lippmann*, 559.

33. Powers, *War at Home*, 44–45.

34. For U Thant's activities, see Walter Johnson, "The U Thant-Stevenson Peace Initiatives in Vietnam, 1964–65," *Diplomatic History* 1 (Summer 1977):285–295. This incident became even more embarrassing for Johnson after the publication of an article by Eric Sevareid in *Look* magazine, "The Final Troubled Hours of Adlai Stevenson" (November 30, 1965):81–85. Another international response was Jean Paul Sartre's cancellation of an American speaking tour. *PP*, 3:365.

35. Spock to Johnson, March 23, 1965, Johnson to Spock, March 30, 1965, box 215, National Defense, 19, Country File 312 (hereafter, ND19CO312), WHCF, LBJL. McGeorge Bundy did urge Johnson to make the response brief so that it could not "be used as propaganda against us." See also Joseph, *Cracks in the Empire*, 155–156. One sees a similar line earlier when Benjamin Read of State advised Bundy not to respond to Bertrand Russell's telegram in order to deny him the publicity. Bundy to Johnson, McGeorge Bundy, vol. 9, box 3, NSC Aides File; Read to Bundy, January 21, 1965, box 214, ND19CO312, LBJL.

36. McNaughton to McNamara, March 24, 1965, *PP*, 3:698.

37. Interview with Helga Herz, Detroit, April 5, 1984; Shingo Shibata, *Phoenix: Letters and Documents of Alice Herz* (Amsterdam: B. R. Gruner, 1976). Two more widely publicized self-immolations occurred on November 2, when Norman Morrison burned himself to death at the Pentagon, and on November 9, when Roger LaPorte did the same at the UN.

38. Thomson to Bundy, February 19, 1965, tab 65, box 40, NSC Histories, Deployment (hereafter NSCDEP), LBJL.

39. Delaney to Bundy, March 3, 1965, box 14, NSCVN. See also Cooper to Bundy, March 4, 1965, box 14, NSCVN, on his meeting with leaders of SANE as well as a petition from faculty and citizens in the Rutgers University area.

40. Rusk, interview. It did take the media some time to begin to highlight the teach-ins as seen by the relatively subdued coverage in the *New York Times* on page 9 on March 25. See also comments on the lack of

media attention to a University of Wisconsin teach-in in James Gilbert, "The Teach-in: Protest or Co-optation," in Massimo Teodori, ed., *The New Left: A Documentary History* (Indianapolis: Bobbs-Merrill, 1969), 240–246.

41. Vogelsgang, *Long Dark Night*, 66.

42. Thomson, interview.

43. Reedy, interview.

44. Roche, interview.

45. George Ball, *The Past Has Another Pattern: A Memoir* (New York: Norton, 1982), 429. Eric Goldman, who worked in the White House in 1965 and 1966, thinks that Johnson wanted him to continue his "Open Mind" television program because of the prestige it lent to his administration among intellectuals. Goldman, interview.

46. Halberstam, *The Best and the Brightest* (New York: Fawcett, 1973), 762.

47. Valenti, interview. Another Harvard White House aide on whom he depended was Tom Johnson, who, like Valenti, was not from the East but from Georgia. On Johnson's admiration for Phi Beta Kappas, see Richard L. Schott and Dagmar Hamilton, *People, Positions and Power: The Political Appointments of Lyndon Johnson* (Chicago: University of Chicago Press, 1984), 19.

48. Reedy, interview. See also Walter Isaacson and Evan Thomas, *The Wise Men: Six Friends and the World They Made* (New York: Simon & Schuster, 1986), 643–646.

49. Roche; Christian, interviews.

50. Reedy, interview.

51. Ibid.

52. Interview with Harry McPherson, Washington, D.C., February 9, 1984. In his book on Henry Kissinger, correspondent Richard Valeriani noted that only Johnson rivaled Kissinger in his "determination to know every word said or printed about him." Valeriani, *Travels with Henry* (Boston: Houghton Mifflin, 1979), 331. Among other advisers, John Roche, not yet on board, worried about teach-ins, but Rostow says *he* did not. Roche; Rostow, interviews.

53. Johnson, interview. See also Kahin, *Intervention*, 322.

54. See notes on the March 26, 1965, National Security Council Meeting in box 1, Meeting Notes, LBJL, on Johnson's call for "new propaganda efforts" to support American policy in Vietnam. See also *PP*, 3:364–365; Goldman, *Tragedy of Lyndon Johnson*, 407.

55. Thomson, interview.

56. Ibid.; William Bundy, unpublished history, chap. 23, p. 29.

57. The haste with which the speech was prepared is reflected in Black's own lack of knowledge of the plan until almost the last minute. Evans and Novak, *Lyndon B. Johnson*, 568–570. An excellent treatment of the speech and its background is in Turner, *Lyndon Johnson's Dual War*, 111–134.

58. Evans and Novak, *Lyndon B. Johnson*, 544.

59. Reedy; Ball, interviews. See also Wayne Morse's comments in Mitchel Levitas, "Vietnam Comes to Oregon U.," in Louis Menashe and Ronald Radosh, eds., *Teach-Ins U.S.A.: Reports, Opinions, Documents* (New York: Praeger, 1967), 19.

60. Bundy, interview; William Bundy, unpublished history, chap. 23, pp. 25, 27, 31. Johnson was especially angry with Pearson.

61. McGeorge Bundy to Johnson, March 28, 1965, box 15, NSCVN, LBJL.

62. Roche, oh, p. 5, LBJL; Evans and Novak, *Lyndon B. Johnson*, 541–543; Halberstam, *Best and Brightest*, 694–695.

63. On others who saw the speech in advance, see Turner, *Lyndon Johnson's Dual War*, 124–126.

64. Halberstam, *Best and Brightest*, 36. William Bundy found him "aging but still influential." Bundy, unpublished history, chap. 20, p. 12. Eric Goldman thought his influence had declined, although Johnson and Jack Valenti did not think so. Goldman, interview.

65. Fulbright, interview. Lippmann was not considered an influential columnist in one important survey of intellectuals' reference figures. Kadushin, *America's Intellectual Elite*, 184.

66. Steel, *Walter Lippmann*, 555–556.

67. Rusk, interview.

68. Bundy to Johnson, March 15, 1965, vol. 9, box 3, McGeorge Bundy, Aides File, LBJL; Steel, *Walter Lippmann*, 562.

69. Steel, *Walter Lippmann*, 558–559, 572; Turner, *Lyndon Johnson's Dual War*, 132 and n. 75.

70. Bundy, interview. For criticism of Lippmann's column by the national security adviser, see Bundy to Lippmann, April 20, 1965, box 16, NSCVN, LBJL.

71. Cooper to Bundy, April 6, 1965, April 13, 1965, box 16, NSCVN, LBJL.

72. *New York Times*, April 9, 1965, p. 12; April 18, 1965, p. E7.

73. Bundy to Johnson, April 14, 1965, box 16, NSCVN, LBJL.

74. Newfield, *A Prophetic Minority*, 27. See also Charles DeBenedetti, *The Peace Reform in American History* (Bloomington: Indiana University Press, 1980), 173.

75. Interview with Abbie Hoffman, Detroit, October 17, 1985.

76. Gitlin, *Whole World Is Watching*, 58. Gitlin thinks that one motivation of the *Times* was its editors' concern about their own radical children (p. 37). See also on the same subject, ibid., 46–50; and Sale, *SDS*, 191. Newfield sees the media treating the marchers more favorably. Newfield, *Prophetic Minority*, 30.

77. Hayden, interview; Gitlin, *Whole World Is Watching*, 153. See also ibid., 127–128, and for the tension between peace liberals and peace radicals, Milton S. Katz, *Ban the Bomb: A History of SANE* (Westport, Conn.: Greenwood, 1986), 93–125.

78. Fulbright, interview. On media criticism of the invasion, see Turner, *Lyndon Johnson's Dual War*, 136–137. See also Kahin, *Intervention*, 321.

79. Ball to Johnson, April 21, 1965, box 17, NSCVN, LBJL. Ball is certain that his memos and comments at meetings were read and taken seriously by Johnson. Ball, interview; Ball, *Past Has Another Pattern*, 430.

80. He repeated the analogy at the Gerald R. Ford Presidential Library Conference in Ann Arbor on November 10, 1982, as well as in an interview, using almost the exact same words in each case. Rusk, interview.

81. Warren Cohen, *Dean Rusk* (Totowa, N.J.: Cooper Square, 1980), 252.

82. United States State Department, *Department of State Bulletin* (hereafter *DSB*) 52 (May 10, 1965):699. For a useful summary of all State Department activities in this area from February to July, see Inventory, August 13, 1965, PDS, reel 5.

83. Rusk, interview; Califano, *A Presidential Nation* (New York: Norton, 1975), 213. George Ball affirms Johnson and Rusk's position as outsiders. Ball, interview. See also Isaacson and Thomas, *Wise Men*, 704.

84. Valenti to Johnson, April 23, 1965, box 215, ND19CO312; Cooper to Valenti, April 24, 1965, box 17, NSCVN, LBJL.

85. Thomas F. Conlon, "The Truth Teams: A View from the Podium," in Menashe and Radosh, *Teach-Ins*, 129–130.

86. Gilbert, "The Teach-In," 240–246.

87. Valenti to Johnson, May 20, 1965, box 215, ND19CO312, LBJL. The administration was pleased with this program. See Thomson, Ropa, and Cooper to McGeorge Bundy, August 23, 1965, PDS, reel 5.

88. DeLoach to Valenti, June 9, 1965, and DeLoach memo, March 4, 1966, box 215, ND19CO312, LBJL. See also, in this area, the suggestion from Connecticut senator Thomas Dodd, one of Johnson's most faithful supporters, to obtain senatorial sponsors for an advertisement for a National Committee for the Defense of South Vietnam Against Communist Aggression. Dodd to McGeorge Bundy, May 11, 1965, box 17, NSCVN, LBJL.

89. Cooper to Valenti, April 24, 1965, box 17, NSCVN, LBJL.

90. Roche, interview. McGeorge Bundy also saw nothing wrong with the National Security Council assisting the so-called Dean Committee, organized later that year. Bundy, interview.

91. Bundy to Johnson, April 27, 1965, box 16, NSCVN, LBJL.

92. *New York Times*, June 2, 1965, p. 52.

93. Cabinet meeting minutes, June 18, 1965, reel 1, 0604, microfilm, Minutes and Documents of Cabinet Meetings of President Johnson (hereafter CAB) (Frederick, Md.: University Publications of America, 1982).

94. Fishel to Weinberg, April 30, 1965, American Friends of Vietnam, 1965 folder, box 2, AFV Collection, Michigan State University Archives

(hereafter MSU); Valenti to Johnson, April 23, 1965, box 215, ND19CO312; Cooper to Valenti, April 24, 1965 and May 5, 1965, box 19, NSCVN; Valenti to Johnson, May 20, 1965, box 215, ND19CO312, LBJL.

95. Valenti to Johnson, May 26, 1965, box 215, ND19CO312, LBJL.

96. Cooper to Valenti, June 7, 1965, box 18, NSCVN, LBJL.

97. AFV Policy Statement folder; Minutes of Board Meeting, April 1, 1965; Jonas to S. L. A. Marshall, August 19, 1965, Ryan Hearings folder, box 2, AFV Collection, MSU. Local hearings held by dovish legislators were another, often obscure, facet of the antiwar movement. They did, however, contribute to the debate over the war.

98. Jonas to Ropa, September 9, 1965, and Jonas to Jorden, September 10, 1965, General Publicity folder, box 2, AFV Collection, MSU.

99. Jonas to Young, March 12, 1965, AFV 1965 folder, box 2, AFV Collection, MSU. For similar links to the White House see Jonas to Fishel, January 11, 1966, AFV 1966 folder, ibid. Senator Dodd was another who lent support to the organization. See Addie Corradi (AFV secretary) to David Martin (Dodd's assistant), April 1, 1965, and Jonas to Frank Barnett (copy to Martin), September 10, 1965, AFV 1965 folder, ibid. See also Kahin, *Intervention*, 80.

100. See, e.g., the problems encountered in trying to raise a mere $700 for a *New York Times* advertisement. Jonas to Barnett, September 10, 1965, AFV 1965 folder, box 2, AFV Collection, MSU. See also Frank Trager to Fishel and Jonas, December 17, 1965, ibid.; Robert Shaplen to Jonas, April 23, 1966, AFV 1966 Policy Statement folder, ibid.

101. AFV 1966 folder, box 2, AFV Collection, MSU. The largest donors were the Ford Motor Company ($10,000), and John Loeb, Procter and Gamble, R. Lehman, and Arthur Krim ($5,000).

102. Memo, November 15, 1966, AFV 1966 folder, box 2, AFV Collection, MSU.

103. Memo, Gordon Chase, August 11, 1965, PDS, reel 5.

104. *PP*, 3:362. For a history of this pause and the diplomatic activities surrounding it, code-named Project Mayflower, see George C. Herring, ed., *The Secret Diplomacy of the Vietnam War: The Negotiating Volumes of the Pentagon Papers* (Austin: University of Texas Press, 1983), 49–73; and *PP*, 3:362–381.

105. *PP*, 3:362–363; Maxwell Taylor, *Swords and Plowshares* (New York: Norton, 1972), 352. Both Bundys do not think the pause was undertaken with much hope for success. McGeorge Bundy; William Bundy, interviews; William Bundy, unpublished history, chap. 24, p. 18. See also Goldman, *Tragedy of Lyndon Johnson*, 406.

106. Thomson, interview; Cooper, *Lost Crusade*, 278.

107. Bundy, unpublished history, chap. 25, p. 18.

108. Taylor, *Swords and Plowshares*, 351; Ball, interview; Bundy, unpublished history, chap. 13, p. 37.

109. May 16, 1965, box 1, Meeting Notes, LBJL.

110. Valenti, interview.

111. Bundy, interview. It is difficult to believe that Bundy would have made his plans without asking Johnson's permission.

112. William Small, *To Kill a Messenger: Television News and the Real World* (New York: Hastings House, 1970), 111.

113. McGeorge Bundy; William Bundy, interviews.

114. Bundy; Thomson, interviews.

115. *New York Times*, May 16, 1965, p. 1. For the teach-in at Yale, see ibid., May 17, 1965, p. 1.

116. Bundy, interview. For background on the arrangements for the teach-in, see Cooper to Bundy, June 4, 1965, PDS, reel 6, and reel 6, passim.

117. Halberstam, *Best and Brightest*, 753.

118. Thomson, interview. Thomson was personally disappointed with Bundy's concluding attack.

119. Bundy, interview.

120. Thomson, interview.

121. Small, *To Kill a Messenger*, 111.

122. Goldman, *Tragedy of Lyndon Johnson*, 421.

123. Bess Abell claimed it was her idea and not Goldman's. Abell, oh, tape 3, pp. 24–29, LBJL.

124. *New York Times*, June 3, 1965, p. 1; Goldman, *Tragedy of Lyndon Johnson*, 427–430, 445–447. Abell attacks Goldman for his mishandling of the affair. Abell, oh, tape 3, p. 26, LBJL. Bill Moyers asked Arthur Schlesinger, Jr., to try to get Lowell to change his mind. Arthur M. Schlesinger, Jr., oh, p. 24, LBJL.

125. Valenti, oh, tape 5, p. 33, LBJL.

126. Goldman, interview; Goldman, *Tragedy of Lyndon Johnson*, 461.

127. *New York Times*, June 15, 1965, pp. 1, 48.

128. Goldman, *Tragedy of Lyndon Johnson*, 458–459. Bess Abell also reports that Mark Van Doren altered his opening remarks a bit to make them less political. Abell, oh, tape 3, p. 29, LBJL.

129. Valenti, oh, tape 5, p. 34, LBJL. Valenti also commented on the left-wing critic's bad breath.

130. Goldman, *Tragedy of Lyndon Johnson*, 414, 501. The affair just would not go away. Lyndon Johnson tried to quote Robert Lowell on August 4 but ended up instead misquoting Matthew Arnold. *New York Times*, August 5, 1984, p. 13.

131. Goldman, *Tragedy of Lyndon Johnson*, 439–440, 434; Goldman, interview.

132. *New York Times*, September 16, 1965, p. 1. Leslie Gelb thinks it was very important. Gelb, "Dissenting on Consensus," in Lake, *Vietnam Legacy*, 216. See also Eugene Brown, *J. William Fulbright: Advice and Dissent* (Iowa City: University of Iowa Press, 1985).

133. Merle Miller, *Lyndon: An Oral Biography* (New York: Putnam, 1980), 460; Fulbright, interview.

134. Rosenberg, "Congress and the War," 86.

135. John J. Hamre does not think congressional dissenters were very important until 1967. Hamre, "Congressional Dissent and American Foreign Policy: Constitutional War-Making in the Vietnam Years" (Ph.D. diss. Johns Hopkins University, 1975), 102.

136. Social workers (June 20, 1965, p. E5), Women Strike for Peace (June 21, 1965, p. 23), and artists (June 27, 1965, sec. 2, p. 18) took ads against Johnson in the *New York Times*, whereas the Young Americans for Freedom–organized Student Ad Hoc Committee to Support the President's Policy in Vietnam offered him some good news (June 27, 1965, p. 9).

137. Sidney Lens, *Unrepentant Radical: An American Activist's Account of Five Turbulent Decades* (Boston: Beacon, 1980), 300. Throughout the Johnson years, the Pentagon was accessible to peaceful dissenters who wanted to talk to an official. McNamara prided himself on his open-door policy. Henkin, interview. Of course, as with the Lens visit, few protesters ever thought that they had changed any officials' minds.

138. Halberstam, *Best and Brightest*, 719. William Bundy saw the public as generally supportive at this juncture. Bundy, unpublished history, chap. 24, p. 29.

139. Thomson, interview. See also Isaacson and Thomas, *Wise Men*, 651–653.

140. Humphrey to Valenti, July 16, 1965, box 216, ND19CO312, WHCF, LBJL; Cabinet meeting minutes, June 18, 1965, reel 1, 0604, CAB.

141. Christian; Ball, interviews.

142. Bundy to Johnson, June 30, 1965, tab 354, box 53, NSCDEP, LBJL. Two weeks earlier, however, Bundy was not so bullish as he offered the president suggestions concerning another bombing pause. Bundy to Johnson, June 19, 1965, tab 320, box 42, NSCDEP, LBJL.

143. Chester Cooper's term for the hawks never caught on. Cooper, memo, November 30, 1965, PDS, reel 5.

144. Bundy, unpublished history, chap. 26, p. 21.

145. Ibid., chap. 26, p. 10; chap. 29, p. 1. Russell's standard response to constituents on the Vietnam issue was that he opposed the original commitment, but since we were there, we had better support the president and win it. See correspondence from this period with constituents in the Richard B. Russell Library, University of Georgia, Athens.

146. McNamara to Johnson, July 30, 1965, *PP*, 3:387. See also ibid., 4:29–30.

147. Bundy, unpublished history, chap. 30, p. 20.

148. Interview with Henry A. Graff, New York, March 6, 1984.

149. Ibid.

150. Henry A. Graff, "Decision in Vietnam," *New York Times Magazine*, July 4, 1965, pp. 4–7 and ff.

151. Bundy, interview.

152. Larry Berman, *Planning a Tragedy: The Americanization of the War in Vietnam* (New York: Norton, 1982); and Kahin, *Intervention,* 347–401. Wallace J. Thies in *When Governments Collide: Coercion and Diplomacy in the Vietnam Conflict, 1964–1968* (Berkeley: University of California Press, 1980) also has very little material on the opinion variable throughout his entire period.

153. Ball; McPherson; Valenti, interviews; Moyers, "Bill Moyers Talks about LBJ, Power, Poverty, War, and the Young," *Atlantic* 222 (July 1968):30. Douglass Cater felt that no one, not even Ball, offered the president a logical plan for how not to escalate. Cater, interview. See also Ball on *"Vietnam: A Television History,"* program 4.

154. Bundy to Johnson, July 1, 1965, *Declassified Documents* (hereafter *DD*), vol. 8, 001255 (Washington, D.C.: Carrollton Press, 1982); Bundy, interview. Labeling the late July meetings a "pseudo debate," John P. Burke is certain that the decision to escalate had already been taken when Johnson began to consult publicly his advisers. Burke, "Responsibilities of Presidents and Advisors: A Theory and Case Study of Decision-Making," *Journal of Politics* 46 (August 1984):838–839. Lending support to Burke is the account in Andrew P. Krepinevich, Jr., *The Army and Vietnam* (Baltimore, Md.: Johns Hopkins University Press, 1986), 131–163.

155. Reedy; Ball, interviews; Cooper, *Lost Crusade,* 284.

156. Ball, interview.

157. Valenti, interview; Ball, *Past Has Another Pattern,* 428.

158. James C. Thomson, Jr., "How Could Vietnam Happen?" *Atlantic* 221 (April 1968):47–53; Thomson, interview.

159. Valenti; Rusk, interviews.

160. Ball, interview; Ball, *Past Has Another Pattern,* 400; Berman, *Planning a Tragedy,* 109; Jack Valenti, *A Very Human President* (New York: Norton, 1975), 333. In using the Korean War case, Ball anticipated the main argument of Mueller, *War, Presidents and Public Opinion* (New York: Wiley, 1973).

161. Ball, *Past Has Another Pattern,* 402.

162. Berman, *Planning a Tragedy,* 117. Army secretary Stanley Resor supported Greene. Ibid., 119.

163. Valenti, *A Very Human President,* 300–301; Berman, *Planning a Tragedy,* 146.

164. Berman, *Planning a Tragedy,* 63n.

165. Goldman, *Tragedy of Lyndon Johnson,* 415; Bundy, unpublished history, chap. 29, pp. 1–2.

166. Bundy, unpublished history, chap. 27, p. 14.

167. Johnson may have remembered the political flap that attended Kennedy's Berlin buildup of 1961.

168. Robert Donovan, *Nemesis: Truman and Johnson in the Coils of War in Asia* (New York: Norton, 1984), 93.

169. Bundy, unpublished history, chap. 30, pp. 18–23, 26.

170. Among other things, Johnson felt that by making too much of the decision, he would elicit strong opposition. Turner, *Lyndon Johnson's Dual War*, 148–149.

171. July 21, 1965, box 1, Meeting Notes, LBJL.

172. McCloy to Bundy, July 29, 1965, box 216, ND19CO312, LBJL. Freedom House did sponsor a supportive advertisement on July 25 (*New York Times*, p. E5), which noted that "the Silent Center" must speak up. This may have been the first use of that phrase that was to become the Silent Majority under Nixon.

173. Busby to Johnson, July 21, 1965, box 3, Office Files of Horace Busby, Vietnam; Valenti, *Very Human President*, 65; McNamara to Johnson, July 28, 1965, box 40, NSCDEP, LBJL.

174. Memo, Bundy, June 17, 1965, tab 390, box 43, NSCDEP, LBJL; Bundy to Johnson, July 19, 1965, ibid. See also PDS, reel 5, passim.

175. Memo, Bundy, November 2, 1968 (concerning July 27 meeting), box 3, Meeting Notes, LBJL.

CHAPTER 3: THE OPPOSITION GATHERS

1. *New York Times*, July 16, 1965, p. 17; Rufus Youngblood to Marvin Watson, August 6, 1965, box 59, HU 4 Freedoms, WHCF, LBJL. Chester Cooper offered to talk with Muste, but the pacifist refused to see anyone but Johnson. Chester Cooper to Irwin Hogenauer, August 13, 1965, ibid.

2. See ND19CO312, LBJL, for the fall of 1965 and much of 1966 to see the wide use made of the pamphlet released to the public on August 20. The same title was given to a widely circulated film, narrated by Johnson, that was released several months later.

3. *New York Times*, July 21, 1965, p. 3; July 25, 1965, p. 5; 7; Bundy to Johnson, August 24, 1965, McGeorge Bundy, Office Files of the President, WHCF, LBJL; Johnson to Watson, August 24, 1965, ibid.

4. *New York Times*, August 5, 1965, p. 13.

5. Bundy to Johnson, September 9, 1965, vol. 14, box 4, McGeorge Bundy, National Security Council Aides File, LBJL; Bundy, interview. See also speeches prepared for possible use by Senators Stuart Symington, John Sparkman, and Gale McGhee in Rostow to Mike Manatos, July 14, 1966, PDS, reel 5.

6. Chester Cooper to Marvin Watson, September 20, 1965; Cliff Carter to Jack Valenti and Marvin Watson, September 24, 1965, box 16, ND19CO312, LBJL. For background, see memo, Fred Ricci, May 27, 1965, ibid.

7. *New York Times*, September 9, 1965, pp. 2, 30.

8. August 5, 1965, box 2, Meeting Notes, LBJL. On the antiwar bias of the Vietnam journalists, see Winant Sidle, "The Role of Journalists in Vietnam: An Army General's Perspective," in Harrison E. Salisbury, ed., *Vietnam Reconsidered* (New York: Harper & Row, 1984), 110–112; and

Robert Elegant, "How to Lose a War: Reflections of a Foreign Correspondent," *Encounter* 57 (August 1981):73–90.

9. Harry Castleman and Walter J. Podrazik, *Watching TV: Four Decades of American Television* (New York: McGraw-Hill, 1982), 187.

10. David Halberstam, *The Powers That Be* (New York: Knopf, 1979), 490.

11. Small, *To Kill a Messenger*, 113.

12. Castleman and Podrazik, *Watching TV*, 187–188.

13. McPherson to Johnson, September 22, 1965, box 28 (1752), McPherson Office Files, Vietnam 1965, LBJL.

14. Taylor, *Swords and Plowshares*, 358–359, 365; *New York Times*, August 25, p. 15. In addition, Hubert Humphrey's speech had been disrupted at the National Student Association Convention in Madison, Wisconsin, on August 23. *New York Times*, August 24, 1965, p. 12.

15. For preparations, see Roy Goodson, memo, September 14, 1965, box 216, ND19CO312; Joseph Califano to Johnson, October 14, 1965, box 59, HU 4 Freedoms, WHCF, LBJL; Memo, August 30, 1965, *DD*, 11, 002910.

16. Bundy to Johnson, September 29, 1965, box 2, Meeting Notes, LBJL.

17. Miller, *Lyndon*, 488–489; Lady Bird Johnson, *White House Diary*, 370.

18. Rufus Youngblood to Marvin Watson, July 13, 1965, box 59, HU 4 Freedoms, WHCF, LBJL.

19. Moyers to Johnson, September 25, 1965, Bill Moyers File, Office of the President, 1963, 1964, 1965; Goldman to Johnson, November 3, 1965, box 217, ND19CO312, LBJL. See also Goldman's advice to Johnson on how to deal with two radical Presidential Scholars. Goldman to Johnson, October 1, 1965, ibid.; Goldman, *Tragedy of Lyndon Johnson*, 501.

20. Califano, *Presidential Nation*, 237.

21. Doris Kearns, *Lyndon Johnson and the American Dream* (New York: Signet, 1977), 331–332; Goldman, *Tragedy of Lyndon Johnson*, 449–450.

22. Thomson; Reedy, interviews.

23. Reedy, interview.

24. Reedy, *Lyndon B. Johnson: A Memoir*, 86–87; 95–96.

25. Tom Johnson, interview.

26. Ibid.

27. *New York Times*, October 18, 1965, p. 7.

28. Sale, *SDS*, 230–231; Newfield, *A Prophetic Minority*, 143.

29. Ball, interview.

30. *New York Times*, October 21, 1965, p. 1; October 26, 1965, p. 2; October 29, 1965, p. 4; Humphrey to Johnson, November 9, 1965, box 217, ND19CO312, LBJL.

31. Cooper to Bundy, October 26, 1965, box 57, HU 4 Freedoms

(Confidential), WHCF, LBJL. For government preparation and intelligence, see Claude Sither to Marvin Watson, November 20, 1965, box 59, ibid. The concern was kept relatively low-key for fear of giving the demonstrators too much media attention. Don Ropa, memo, November 2, 1965, PDS, reel 5.

32. Cooper, *Lost Crusade*, 289. See also Katz, *Ban the Bomb*, 97–98.

33. *New York Times*, November 28, 1965, p. 1. See also Sale, *SDS*, 242.

34. Cooper, memo, November 29, 1965, NSC Name File, Chester Cooper; Humphrey to Johnson, December 2, 1965, NSC Name File, Hubert H. Humphrey; Humphrey to Rusk and Bundy, November 30, 1965, box 217, ND19CO312, LBJL.

35. *New York Times*, November 28, 1965, p. 1.

36. Sevareid, "Final Troubled Hours," 81–84; David Kraslow and Stuart H. Loory, *The Secret Search for Peace in Vietnam* (New York: Random House, 1968), 106.

37. *New York Times*, November 29, 1965, p. 1; December 10, 1965, p. 1.

38. Cooper to Bundy, Moyers, Valenti, Cater, December 14, 1965, box 71, ND19CO312 (Confidential), LBJL. Another call for a direct appeal came from George Reedy, who, after a visit to the University of Chicago, concluded that the dissenters were not "beatniks" or "radicals." Reedy to Johnson, January 27, 1966, box 219, ND19CO312, LBJL.

39. William Bundy, memo, December 1, 1965, *PP*, 4:34; William Bundy, oh, tape 2, p. 24, LBJL; Paul Warnke, "The Search for Peace—Vietnam Negotiations," in Lake, *Vietnam Legacy*, 314; Allen E. Goodman, *The Lost Peace: America's Search for a Negotiated Settlement of the Vietnam War* (Stanford, Calif.: Hoover Institution, 1978), 34.

40. January 10, 1966, box 2, Meeting Notes, LBJL; Rusk to Lodge, December 28, 1965, *PP*, 4:39.

41. McGeorge Bundy, interview; Hoopes, *Limits of Intervention*, 49; Cyrus Vance, oh, tape 3, p. 12, LBJL; Robert S. McNamara, deposition, *William Westmoreland vs. CBS et al.*, U.S. District Court, Southern District of New York, 281.

42. Hoopes, *Limits of Intervention*, 49.

43. *PP*, 4:33.

44. December 17, 1965, box 2, Meeting Notes, LBJL.

45. December 18, 1965, box 2, Meeting Notes, LBJL.

46. January 10, 1966, box 2, Meeting Notes, LBJL.

47. January 3, 1966, box 2, Meeting Notes, LBJL.

48. Arthur M. Schlesinger, Jr., *Robert F. Kennedy and His Times* (Boston: Houghton Mifflin, 1978), 734.

49. Roche, interview.

50. Valenti to Johnson, January 25, 1966, box 44, NSC Histories, Manila Conference, LBJL.

51. January 25, 1966, box 2, Meeting Notes, LBJL; Ball, interview.

52. Meeting Notes, January 27, 1966, *DD*, 8, 0012590.

53. Helms to Moyers, February 23, 1966, box 71, ND19CO312 (Confidential), LBJL.

54. Meeting Notes, January 27, 1966, *DD*, 8, 0012590; Sharp, *Strategy*, p. 26.

55. Meeting Notes, January 28, 1966, *DD*, 8, 0012590.

56. Meeting Notes, January 29, 1966, *DD*, 8, 0012590.

57. Cooper, *Lost Crusade*, 295; Bundy, interview. See also the army's contracted study by the BDM Corporation, *A Study of the Strategic Lessons Learned in Vietnam*, 4:1–29.

58. In one of the analyses of antiwar activity sent to the White House, Claude Sither reported that Norman Mailer was "a concealed communist." Sither to Watson, February 4, 1966, box 59, HU 4 Freedoms, WHCF, LBJL.

59. J. William Fulbright, *The Arrogance of Power* (New York: Random House, 1966), 66, 62–64.

60. Fulbright, interview.

61. Joseph C. Goulden, *Truth Is the First Casualty: The Gulf of Tonkin Affair—Illusion and Reality* (Chicago: Rand McNally, 1969), 172, 176–177.

62. Halberstam, *The Powers That Be*, 495–504.

63. Fred W. Friendly, *Due to Circumstances Beyond Our Control* (New York: Random House, 1967), 256. See also Small, *To Kill a Messenger*, 118–120.

64. Graff, *Tuesday Cabinet*, 99–101. Rusk was angry as well and called Kennan to tell him so. Isaacson and Thomas, *Wise Men*, 668.

65. Cater, interview.

66. Fulbright, interview.

67. Valenti; Bundy, interviews. See also, Cooper, *Lost Crusade*, 301; Church, oh, p. 27, LBJL.

68. Lady Bird Johnson, *White House Diary*, 360–361; Graff, interview.

69. U.S. Senate, Committee on Foreign Relations, *Supplemental Foreign Assistance Fiscal Year—1966—Vietnam*, (Washington, D.C.: GPO, 1966), 454, 499, 609, 530.

70. Cohen, *The Public's Impact*, 69.

71. *Supplemental Foreign Assistance*, 403, 504.

72. In early 1966, Johnson felt that 10 percent of the population was dove, 20 percent hawk, and the rest satisfied with the way the war was being conducted. Gelb, interview.

73. Valenti; Ball, interviews. William Bundy also downplays the significance of the hearings. Bundy, interview.

74. Kearns, *Lyndon Johnson*, 341–342; Taylor, *Swords and Plowshares*, 366.

75. Turner, *Lyndon Johnson's Dual War*, 157. Kintner had other duties as well. Schott and Hamilton, *People, Positions, and Power*, 28.

76. Tristram Coffin, *Senator Fulbright: Portrait of a Public Philosopher* (New York: Dutton, 1966), 308–309.

77. Zaroulis and Sullivan, *Who Spoke Up?* 75; Church, oh, 27, LBJL; DeBenedetti, *The Peace Reform*, 176; Halberstam, *Best and the Brightest*, 506; Bob Buzzanco, "The American Military's Rationale against the Vietnam War," *Political Science Quarterly* 101 (Winter 1986):559–576.

78. *Supplemental Foreign Assistance*, 387. See also Isaacson and Thomas, *Wise Men*, 717n.

79. Coffin, *Senator Fulbright*, 308.

80. Castleman and Podrazik, *Watching TV*, 188.

81. *New York Times*, February 13, 1966, sec. 4, pp. 7ff., sec. 1, p. 2.

82. Califano to Johnson, February 12, 1966, and Levinson to Califano, February 12, 1966, box 9, EX WH 5–1, WHCF, LBJL; Lady Bird Johnson, *White House Diary*, 360, 362.

83. February 24, 1966, box 2, Meeting Notes, LBJL.

84. Ropa to Moyers, March 25, 1966, box 59, HU 4 Freedoms, WHCF, LBJL.

85. An Amherst protest made the first page of the *New York Times* on June 4.

86. Valenti to Johnson, May 1, 1966, box 220, ND19CO312, LBJL.

87. *New York Times*, June 5, 1966, pp. E5, 6, 7.

88. On petition signing, see Everett C. Ladd, Jr., "Professors and Political Petitions," *Science* 163 (March 28, 1969):1425–1430; Laurel Walum, "Sociologists as Signers: Characteristics of Protestors of Vietnam War Policy," *American Sociologist* 5 (May 1970):161–164; and E. M. Schreiber, "American Public Opinion and the War in Vietnam, 1964–1968" (Ph.D. diss., Princeton University, 1970), 287.

89. Reedy; Christian; Cater; Ball, interviews.

90. Rostow; Bundy, interviews.

91. McPherson to Moyers, August 4, 1966, box 26, McPherson Office Files, Vietnam, 1966, LBJL.

92. Califano to Johnson, May 13, 1966, box 59, HU 4 Freedoms, WHCF, LBJL.

93. McPherson to Moyers, October 4, 1966, box 28, McPherson Office Files, Vietnam 1966, LBJL.

94. Moyers to Johnson, June 6, 1966, Office Files of the President, Moyers, 1966 and 1967 folder, LBJL.

95. July 26, 1966, CAB, reel 2, 0753. See also reel 2, 0607 and 0698, for other comments about the media at June 16 and July 15 cabinet meetings.

96. *DSB* 54 (April 4, 1966):542; *DSB* 55 (July 11, 1966):49; *DSB* 55 (July 25, 1966):118. See also Rusk's comments in *DSB* 55 (August 1, 1966):171, and *DSB* 55 (September 19, 1966):423.

97. Jewish professors were certainly disproportionately antiwar. David J. Armor et al., "Professors' Attitudes towards the Vietnam War," *Public Opinion Quarterly* 31 (Summer 1967):159–175.

98. *New York Times*, September 11, 1966, p. 4; September 9, 1966, p. 1.

99. *PP*, 4:81; Rusk to Johnson, June 7, 1966, *PP*, 4:104.

100. Rostow to Johnson, September 22, 1966, tab c8, box 45, NSC Histories, Manila Conference and President's Asian Trip, LBJL.

101. *DSB* 55 (November 7, 1966):710. See also comments in Townsville, Australia, on October 23 in *DSB* 55 (November 28, 1966):826.

102. Ball; Thomson, interviews.

103. Roche, interview.

104. Rostow, interview.

105. Rusk; Vance, interviews; Taylor, *Swords and Plowshares*, 371. See also McGeorge Bundy to Johnson, April, 1966, *PP*, 4:159, and McCaHoaxes, and Diplomatic One-Upmanship in Vietnam (South Bend, Ind.: Gateway, 1978), 219.

108. Bui Xuan Ninh, interview. For a Vietcong perspective with emphasis on the movement in the Nixon years, see Truong Nhu Tang, *A Vietcong Memoir: An Inside Account of the Vietnam War and Its Aftermath* (New York: Harcourt, Brace, 1985), 209–213. For an account of how one South Vietnamese dissident was impressed with the American college students who opposed the war, see Doan Van Toai with David Chanoff, *The Vietnamese Gulag* (New York: Simon & Schuster, 1986), 147–149.

109. Powers, *War at Home*, xv. Tom Hayden, who met with the North Vietnamese, concurs with Powers. Hayden, interview.

110. See box 59, HU 4 Freedoms, WHCF, LBJL.

111. Lady Bird Johnson, *White House Diary*, 430; Christian; Johnson, interviews.

112. Halberstam, *Best and the Brightest*, 779.

113. Goulding, *Confirm or Deny*, 175–176; Warnke, interview.

114. Graff, *Tuesday Cabinet*, 122.

115. Christian, oh, p. 21, LBJL.

116. William Bundy, interview. See Sale, *SDS*, 303–304, for coverage of the Harvard affair.

117. *New York Times*, November 11, 1966, p. 1.

118. Ibid., 32. Of course, since some pro-Johnson Democrats lost to Republicans, the election could be seen as a repudiation of his Vietnam policies. Richard Cummings, *The Pied Piper: Allard K. Lowenstein and the Liberal Dream* (New York: Grove, 1985), 323–324.

119. Rosenberg, "Congress," 132.

120. See the background story in *New York Times*, November 11, 1966,

p. 11. For Eisenhower's views on the war and advice to Johnson, advice generally calling for hitting them hard and getting out before Americans' patience flagged, see Henry William Brands, Jr., "Johnson and Eisenhower: The President, the Former President, and the War in Vietnam," *Presidential Studies Quarterly* 15 (Summer 1985):589–601.

CHAPTER 4: COMING APART

1. Harrison Salisbury, *Behind the Lines—Hanoi* (New York: Harper & Row, 1967), 11.

2. Warnke, interview. Harry Ashmore and William C. Baggs, *Mission to Hanoi—a Chronicle of Double-Dealing in High Places* (New York: Putnam, 1968).

3. Goulding, *Confirm or Deny*, 52, 92. Salisbury also felt that the administration should have been more forthcoming at once. Salisbury, oh, p. 32, LBJL. See also *PP*, 4:135. The State Department sent a telegram to all posts on December 30 pointing out the alleged errors of fact in Salisbury's account. *DD*, 12, 002782.

4. Bundy, interview; Kraslow and Loory, *Secret Search*, 82–83.

5. *PP*, 4:135; *DSB* 56 (January 23, 1967):130–131.

6. Salisbury, oh, p. 29, LBJL.

7. Gay Talese, *The Kingdom and the Power* (New York: World, 1969), 447–449. See also Karnow, *Vietnam*, 490–491.

8. *New York Times*, December 30, 1966, pp. 1, 4. Lowenstein also organized a Peace Corps protest several months later. Robert Kintner to Johnson, March 1, 1967, box 72, ND19CO312 (Confidential), LBJL.

9. McPherson to Johnson, December 30, 1966, box 227, ND19CO312, LBJL; *New York Times*, February 1, 1967, p. 7. For other White House concerns about the student leaders, see Dick Copaken to John Roche and Harry McPherson, January 3, 1967, and Tom Johnson to Johnson, February 2, 1967, box 224, ND19CO312, LBJL. For the follow-up to the affair, see entire box 227, ND19CO312, LBJL, especially Cater to Johnson, June 20, 1967. See also Cummings, *Pied Piper*, 331.

10. For a brief account of the meeting some editors found most unsatisfactory, see David Harris, *Dreams Die Hard* (New York: St. Martin's, 1982), 65–66.

11. *New York Times*, January 22, 1967, sec. 4, p. 5; January 16, 1967, p. 8; January 31, 1967, p. 3; January 27, 1967, p. 1. In addition, 600 Michigan professors and 151 University of Texas professors protested in the *New York Times* on February 23, 1967, p. 22, and March 5, 1967, p. 5, respectively.

12. William A. Williams et al., *America in Vietnam: A Documentary History* (Garden City, N.Y.: Anchor, 1985), 261–262.

13. Schlesinger, *Robert Kennedy*, 741–742; Roche, interview.

14. *Time* 89 (March 17, 1967):21; Schlesinger, *Robert Kennedy*, 769.

15. Eric Goldman attests to the political significance of the *Time* story. Goldman, interview.

16. *New York Times*, March 24, 1967, p. 1; April 6, 1967, p. 1; April 25, 1967, p. 16. For the background of King's decision to break with Johnson over Vietnam see David J. Garrow, *Bearing the Cross: Martin Luther King, Jr, and the Southern Christian Leadership Conference* (New York: Morrow, 1986), 543–546, 549–555. King was affected by a January 1967 article in *Ramparts* magazine on the use of napalm in Vietnam.

17. *New York Times*, April 16, 1967, pp. 1, 3; April 19, 1967, p. 3; Nigel Young, *An Infantile Disorder: The Crisis and Decline of the New Left* (Boulder, Colo.: Westview, 1977), 179.

18. Rusk; Clark, interviews; David J. Garrow, *The FBI and Martin Luther King: From Solo to Memphis* (New York: Norton, 1981), 180–182.

19. John T. Elliff, *Crime, Dissent, and the Attorney General: The Justice Department in the 1960's* (Beverly Hills, Calif.: Sage, 1981), 173; David Dellinger, *More Power than We Know* (Garden City, N.Y.: Doubleday, 1975), 115; Garrow, *Bearing The Cross*, 554–555; Alexander to Johnson, April 28, 1967, box 225, ND19CO312, LBJL.

20. Humphrey to Johnson, April 13, 1967, box 225, ND19CO312, LBJL; Bundy to Johnson, May 9, 1967, boxes 74–75, NSCVN, LBJL; Bundy, oh, tape 4, p. 31, LBJL. Among other favorable evaluations were, on the failure of Bertrand Russell's war crimes trial, Katzenbach to Johnson, February 17, 1967, box 91, NSCVN; and on the support even among young people in the polls, Panzer to Johnson, March 8, 1967, box 224, ND19CO312, LBJL. On the other hand, Under Secretary of Agriculture John A. Schnittker told McPherson that no one supported the war at Kansas State. Schnittker to McPherson, June 9, 1967, box 28 (1752), McPherson Office Files, Vietnam, 1967, LBJL.

21. McPherson to Johnson, April 20, 1967, McPherson Office Files, Vietnam, 1967, box 28 (1752), LBJL; Doug Nobles to Marvin Watson, May 4, 1967, ibid.; *New York Times*, May 14, 1967, p. 1; May 13, 1967, p. 15.

22. Roche, interview; Roche to Johnson, May 15, 1967, box 73, ND19CO312 (Confidential), LBJL; Roche to Douglas, July 31, 1967, ibid.

23. Roche to Johnson, October 16, 1967, box 73, ND19CO312, LBJL.

24. Roche, interview; Roche to Johnson, May 19, 1967, PDS, reel 7.

25. Roche, interview; Marks to Johnson, October 17, 1967, box 229, ND19CO312, LBJL; Rowe to Johnson, October 1, 1967, ibid.

26. Richard J. Whalen, *Catch the Falling Flag: A Republican's Challenge to His Party* (Boston: Houghton Mifflin, 1972), 32–33.

27. *DSB* 56 (May 8, 1967):725; ibid. (May 22, 1967):774; Rusk, interview. See also *DSB* 56 (April 17, 1967):744.

28. *DSB* 57 (October 2, 1967):432.

29. Christian, interview; Halstead, *Out Now*, passim.

30. Christian, interview.

31. Clark, interview.

32. Ball, interview. Roche feels that they reinforced each other's suspicions. Roche, interview.

33. Wayne S. Cole, *Roosevelt and the Isolationists, 1932–45* (Lincoln: University of Nebraska Press, 1982), 487–489.

34. U.S. Senate, Select Committee to Study Intelligence Activities and the Rights of Americans (hereafter Select Committee), *Final Report of the Select Committee to Study Governmental Operations with Respect to Intelligence Activities*, book 2 (Washington, D.C.: GPO, 1976), 251; Hoover to McGeorge Bundy, April 28, 1965, ibid. One FBI official reported pressure for information not only from Johnson but from then attorney general Robert F. Kennedy. Select Committee, *Hearings*, vol. 2 (Huston Plan), (Washington, D.C.: GPO, 1975), 103.

35. Athan Theoharis, *Spying on Americans: Political Surveillance from Hoover to the Huston Plan* (Philadelphia, Pa.: Temple University Press, 1978), 176–178; Frank J. Donner, *The Age of Surveillance: The Aims and Methods of America's Political Intelligence System* (New York: Knopf, 1980), 253; Select Committee, *Hearings*, vol. 6 (The FBI), 55, 61, 161, 720. Select Committee, *Final Report*, book 2, p. 228.

36. Hoover to Marvin Watson, June 4, 1965, Select Committee, *Hearings*, 6:638.

37. C. D. Brennan to W. Sullivan, May 9, 1968, Select Committee, *Hearings*, 6:638.

38. *Report to the President by the Commission on CIA Activities within the United States* (Washington, D.C.: GPO, 1975), 131.

39. Ibid., 152–154; Thomas Johns to Johnson, May 23, 1967, McPherson Office Files, Vietnam 1967, box 28 (1752), LBJL.

40. Select Committee, *Hearings*, 6:22, 785; Select Committee, *Final Report*, book 2, p. 247.

41. Select Committee, *Hearings*, vol. 3 (IRS) (Washington, D.C.: GPO, 1975), 28. See also p. 46.

42. Select Committee, *Hearings*, 6:24–48, 749; Clark, interview.

43. Kintner to Johnson, May 18, 1967, Kintner to Clark, May 19, 1967, box 57, HU 4, Freedoms (Confidential), LBJL; Panzer to Johnson, August 14, 1967, President's Appointment File, Diary Backup, LBJL.

44. Enthoven, memo, April 28, 1967, *PP*, 4:456–457; Enthoven to McNamara, May 1, 1967, *PP*, 4:463–464.

45. McNaughton, memo, May 19, 1967, *PP*, 4:477–485; Joint Chiefs staff memo, May 31, 1967, *PP*, 4:499–500. Despite their bravado, the Joint Chiefs worried about draft resistance. See ibid., 165, for Admiral Sharp's concern.

46. Roche to Johnson, March 27, 1967; Roche, *Sentenced to Life*, 113; Whalen, *Catch the Falling Flag*, 67–68; September 15, 1967, box 2, Meeting Notes, LBJL.

47. Paul H. Nitze in W. Scott Thompson and Donaldson D. Frizzell,

eds., *The Lessons of Vietnam* (New York: Crane, Russak, 1979), 199–200. Several months earlier, Walt Rostow told Johnson of McNamara's concern about the domestic political cost of continued bombing. Rostow to Johnson, May 19, 1967, *DD*, 10, 002233.

48. McNamara, Deposition, 360, 359.

49. Goulden, *Truth Is the First Casualty*, 181.

50. August 18, 1967, box 2, Meeting Notes, LBJL.

51. Ibid., September 5, 1967. On Johnson's anger with *Time-Life*, see Hedley Donovan, *Roosevelt to Reagan: A Reporter's Encounters with Nine Presidents* (New York: Harper & Row, 1985), 103. Of Donovan's defection, Johnson said the editor "betrayed me." Halberstam, *The Powers That Be*, 484.

52. A useful chronological summary of the dispute is found in Appendix A of the CBS Memorandum in Support of Defendant's Motion to Dismiss and for Summary Judgment: *William Westmoreland v. CBS Inc. et al.*, May 23, 1984. See also Don Kowet, *A Matter of Honor* (New York: Macmillan, 1984); and Renata Adler, *Reckless Disregard: Westmoreland v. CBS et al.; Sharon v. Time* (New York: Knopf, 1986).

53. Appendix B, CBS Memorandum, 374, 83, 586, 583; CBS Memorandum, 6. See also pp. 26–27 of Appendix B for Allen's testimony.

54. CBS Memorandum, 50; Appendix B, CBS Memorandum, 442, 509. See also Wheeler to Helms and Abrams to Wheeler, August 29, 1967, McNamara, Deposition, 239.

55. McNamara, Deposition, passim.

56. Smith, *Long Time Gone*, 34; Clark, interview. October also witnessed major demonstrations in Madison and Oakland. Dellinger, *More Power than We Know*, 53–54.

57. Norman Mailer, *The Armies of the Night: History as a Novel, the Novel as History* (New York: New American Library, 1968), 245–248.

58. For White House preparations, see Charles DeBenedetti, "A CIA Analysis of the Anti-Vietnam War Movement, October 1967," *Peace and Change* 9 (Spring 1983):31–42; and boxes 59–60, HU 4, Freedoms, WHCF, LBJL.

59. President's Appointment File, Diary Backup, September 20, 1967; September 20, 1967, box 2, Meeting Notes, LBJL.

60. *DBS* 57 (October 23, 1967):522; cabinet meeting of October 4, 1967, reel 3, 0871, CAB.

61. Memo, October 3, 1967 box 80, President's Appointment File, Diary Backup, LBJL; cabinet meeting of October 4, 1967, reel 3, 0871, CAB. Clark and his press secretary categorically deny leaking information about communists in the demonstration to the media. It is possible, explaining his comments charitably, that he was merely reporting what he knew the FBI had done. On another occasion, according to Martin Luther King, Jr., biographer David Garrow, he opposed such leaking. In addition, John Elliff gives him generally good marks during this period for protect-

ing civil liberties. Clark, interview; telephone interview with Cliff Sessions (Clark press aide), May 4, 1984; Garrow, *Bearing the Cross,* 570; Elliff, *Crime, Dissent,* 197.

62. *DSB* 57 (October 30, 1967):559; Johnson to Handlin, October 3, 1967, ND19CO312, LBJL.

63. Elliff, *Crime, Dissent,* 185–186, 181–182; comments on "Vietnam: A Television History," program 12. See also Hershey, oh, pp. 20–22, LBJL.

64. Califano to Johnson, October 16, 1967, box 59, HU 4, Freedoms, WHCF, LBJL. Elements of the 82nd Airborne had been dispatched to Washington as well as six thousand federal marshals.

65. Johnson to Clark, October 20, 1967, box 60, HU 4, Freedoms, WHCF, LBJL. See also October 18 cabinet meeting minutes, reel 3, 0915, CAB, and memo, October 20, 1967, Marvin Watson Files, box 32 (1375 C), Vietnam, LBJL. October 16 had witnessed nationwide draft-card-burning demonstrations sponsored by the Resistance.

66. This phenomenon is not just American. After a conservative protest march in Stockholm, Sweden, on October 4, 1983, the conservative Danish newspaper *Jyllands Posten* described a march of a hundred thousand (October 5, 1983, p. 17), whereas *Politiken,* a liberal paper, counted only fifty thousand demonstrators (October 5, 1983, p. 5). Ramsey Clark suggests the entire process generally produces underestimates by the government. Clark, interview.

67. *New York Times,* October 23, 1967, pp. 1, 44; *Time* (October 27, 1967):23, 24, 25; *Newsweek* (October 30, 1967):20–21; *Nation* (November 6, 1967):454–455. See also *Newsweek* (November 6, 1967):26–27, for more on the violence at the Pentagon.

68. Castleman and Podrazik, *Watching TV,* 204.

69. Hayden, interview.

70. One who did not was Abbie Hoffman, who was pleased with the "symbolic warfare" at the Pentagon and not surprised by the media attention to "sex and violence." Hoffman, interview.

71. Panzer to Johnson, October 26, 1967, box 60, HU 4, Freedoms, WHCF, LBJL.

72. Claude Sither to Watson, October 23, 1967; Califano to Johnson, October 24, 1967, box 60, HU 4, Freedoms, WHCF, LBJL.

73. October 22, 1967, Daily Diary of President Johnson, 1963–1969, microfilm, reel 10 (Frederick, Md.: University Publications of America, 1980). Johnson probably knew that the protest was a "profound" one that involved more than hippies. Tom Johnson, interview.

74. Marks to Johnson, October 23, 1967, box 229, ND19CO312, LBJL.

75. Each Johnson adviser tended to view demonstrations idiosyncratically, with personality, such as Rostow's "thicker skin," a factor. Christian, interview.

76. Fulbright, interview; McPherson, interview; Miller, *Lyndon,* 289.

Douglass Cater and William Bundy support McPherson's view of a kaleidoscope of events. Cater; Bundy, interviews.

77. Clifford; Rusk; Rostow (telephone), interviews.

78. Mailer, *Armies of the Night*, 95.

79. Warnke, interview.

80. Henkin, interview.

81. Paul Hendrickson, "McNamara: Specters of Vietnam," *Washington Post*, May 10, 1984, p. B1; Hoffman, interview.

82. Roche; Clark, interviews. McNamara himself was not impressed with their organization. Hendrickson, "McNamara," B9.

83. Christian, Tom Johnson, interviews. Agreeing with them on the impact is Sale, *SDS*, 406.

84. Roche, interview; November 1, 1967, box 2, Meeting Notes, LBJL.

85. Graff, interview.

86. Hendrickson, "McNamara," B10; Vance; Christian; Roche, interviews; Sharp, *Strategy*, 165. On other indications of McNamara's dovish leanings, see Goulding, *Confirm or Deny*, 179, 203, 213. Defense Secretary James Forrestal committed suicide in 1949. See also Isaacson and Thomas, *Wise Men*, 664.

87. Ernest Goldstein to Johnson, December 18, 1967, ND19CO312, LBJL.

88. Gelb, interview.

89. Hoopes, *Limits of Intervention*, 97–98.

90. "Changing Views on Vietnam," *Saturday Evening Post* (November 18, 1967):90; Moyers to Johnson, November 28, 1967, Moyers, Office Files of the President, 1966 and 1967, LBJL; see also his to Johnson of July 18, 1967, ibid., on the same theme.

91. For the next several months, McCarthy's challenge was not taken that seriously. John Roche told the president, after a McCarthy visit to Massachusetts, "Gene McCarthy spent a big day yesterday in Massachusetts. He was greeted enthusiastically by a mob ⅓ of whom were Californians and New Yorkers, ⅓ of whom were Japanese, Swedish, or Upper Voltan, and ⅓ of whom thought he was 'Joe.' " Roche to Johnson, January 26, 1968, PDS, reel 10.

92. Robert Ginsburgh to Rostow, December, 1967, box 98, NSCVN, LBJL; memo, December 11, 1967, Christian Office Files, Vietnam, box 2, LBJL.

93. Hoopes, *Limits of Intervention*, 111–112. One observer referred to them as "government-in-exile [folks] who flow in and out of different foundations and groups." William Connell to Humphrey, January 22, 1968, PDS, reel 4. An obscure Pentagon analyst named Daniel Ellsberg was also one of the Bermuda conferees.

94. The failure of Robert Lovett and John McCloy to attend the session may have indicated a crack in the ranks. Isaacson and Thomas, *Wise Men*, 678.

95. Clifford, oh, tape 3, p. 9, LBJL.

96. Ball, *Past Has Another Pattern*, 407; Taylor, *Swords and Plowshares*, 378. On the same theme, see an earlier letter from Humphrey to Johnson, September 13, 1967, Marvin Watson Office Files, box 32 (1375C), Vietnam, LBJL.

97. Bundy, interview.

98. Rostow to Johnson, November 2, 1967, box 2, Meeting Notes, LBJL; Jim Jones to Johnson, ibid.

99. Jones to Johnson, November 2, 1967, box 2, Meeting Notes, LBJL; Bundy to Johnson, November 10, 1967, President's Appointment File, Diary Backup, LBJL.

100. Jones to Johnson, November 4, 1967, box 2, Meeting Notes, LBJL.

101. On the offensive, see Turner, *Lyndon Johnson's Dual War*, 201–204; and PDS, reel 1, passim. Admiral Sharp worried at this time that the protests might lead to a bombing halt. Sharp, *Strategy*, 205.

102. *DSB* 57 (December 11, 1967):777, 779; ibid. (January 8, 1968):1489.

103. Ashmore and Baggs, *Mission to Hanoi*, 106.

104. McPherson to Johnson, October 10, 1967, Office Files of McPherson, Vietnam, 1967, pt. 2, LBJL; Bunker to Rostow, October 28, 1968, CBS Memorandum, 134. At the November 2 Wise Men's meeting, Henry Cabot Lodge, a former ambassador to South Vietnam, said, "Bunker should be well publicized when he returns." Jones to Johnson, November 3, 1968, box 2, Meeting Notes, LBJL. See also the attempt to enlist the aid of friendly academics in Roche to Watson, December 14, 1967, Office Files of McPherson, box 29 (1752); and Goldstein to Christian and Rostow, November 17, 1967, box 99, NSCVN, LBJL.

105. Westmoreland on "Vietnam: A Television History," program 7.

106. Warnke, interview. See also Bruce Palmer, *The 25-Year War: America's Military Role in Vietnam* (Lexington: University of Kentucky Press, 1984), 75, for comparable comments.

107. Rusk; Clifford, interviews.

108. Rostow; Roche; Henkin, interviews.

109. Warnke, interview.

110. For the campaign and its impact on opinion, see Peter Braestrup, *Big Story: How the American Press and Television Reported and Interpreted the Crises of Tet in Vietnam and Washington* (Boulder, Colo.: Westview, 1977), 52–85. For a brief comment on the theme, see Cooper, *Lost Crusade*, 389.

111. Most of those interviewed or who have written about the relationship between Tet and opinion have not drawn a causal link to the March on the Pentagon. Warnke, Christian, and William Bundy, however, tend to think the thesis is plausible. McGeorge Bundy agrees that the propaganda campaign was mishandled, but the possibility that it was triggered by the antiwar protestors is only "hypothetical." Warnke; Christian; William Bundy; McGeorge Bundy, interviews.

112. Dellinger, *More Power than We Know*, 126; October 31, 1967, box 2, Meeting Notes, LBJL.

113. Califano to Johnson, November 15, 1967, box 60, HU 4, Freedoms, LBJL; Clark to Johnson, December 16, 1967, ibid.

114. Rostow to Johnson, October 23, 1967, box 143, NSCVN, LBJL; Rostow to Johnson, December 13, 1967, box 230, ND19CO312, LBJL.

115. *DSB* 57 (November 27, 1967):705.

116. Helms to Johnson, November 15, 1967, box 3, National Security File, WHCF, LBJL. Abbie Hoffman flaunted his visits with North Vietnamese. Tom Hayden and other antiwar leaders met with North Vietnamese and Viet Cong representatives in Bratislava, Czechoslovakia, in September.

117. Miller, *Lyndon*, 408.

118. Helms to Johnson, February 29, 1968, April 9, 1968; box 3, National Security File, WHCF, LBJL.

119. Helms to Johnson, September, 1968, box 3, National Security File, WHCF, LBJL; McGhee to Johnson, January 17, 1969, ibid.

120. Skolnick, *Politics of Protest*, 79, 23.

121. *New York Times*, January 14, 1968, p. 5.

122. Graff, *Tuesday Cabinet*, 141; Lady Bird Johnson, *White House Diary*, 623; *New York Times*, January 20, 1968, pp. 5, 28. Johnson was so angered at the performer that he apparently succeeded in keeping her off network television for several years after the lunch. Interview with Eartha Kitt, "NPR Morning Edition," October 24, 1985.

123. Skolnick, *Politics of Protest*, 61.

CHAPTER 5: THE BEGINNING OF THE END

1. Tom Johnson, interview.

2. Thompson and Frizzell, *Lessons of Vietnam*, 100.

3. Godfrey Hodgson, *America in Our Time* (New York: Vintage, 1978), 356. See also Harry McPherson on "Vietnam: A Television History," program 7, for the impact of the assassination.

4. Tran Do and Rusk on "Vietnam: A Television History," program 7. One keen observer of North Vietnamese politics sees Hanoi as unprepared for the victory in the United States. Gabriel Kolko, *Anatomy of a War: Vietnam, the United States, and the Modern Historical Experience* (New York: Pantheon, 1985), 333.

5. Braestrup, *Big Story*, 671, 703, 338.

6. Charles Mohr, "Once Again—Did the Press Lose Vietnam?" *Columbia Journalism Review* 22 (November 12, 1983):51–56.

7. Tom Johnson, interview. Johnson thinks the announcement was not made because the president then feared that he would be too weak as a lame duck to forge a peace.

8. Hoopes, "LBJ's Account of March 1968," *New Republic* 162 (March 14, 1970):19.

9. Karnow, *Vietnam*, 546.

10. McPherson on "Vietnam: A Television History," program 7; Rostow, interview; Rostow on "Vietnam: A Television History," program 7; Clifford, oh, tape 5, pp. 13–14, LBJL.

11. Vaughan Bornet, *The Presidency of Lyndon Johnson* (Lawrence: University Press of Kansas, 1983), 289–305.

12. Wheeler, oh, p. 15, LBJL; McPherson; Clifford; Cater, interviews; Destler, *Presidents*, 111; Morris, *Uncertain Greatness*, 24. See also Karnow, *Vietnam*, 560.

13. Graff; Cater; Rusk, interviews; Clifford on "Vietnam: A Television History," program 7.

14. Karnow, *Vietnam*, 535; *PP*, 4:550.

15. Clark M. Clifford, "A Viet Nam Reappraisal: The Personal History of One Man's View and How It Evolved," *Foreign Affairs* 47 (July 1969):609.

16. Joseph, *Cracks in the Empire*, 235–238; Clifford, "Viet Nam Reappraisal," 610.

17. Humphrey, *Education*, 377–378.

18. Hayden, interview. Hayden's North Vietnamese sources made this point to him.

19. Cooper, *Lost Crusade*, 393; Schandler, *Unmaking of a President*, 345–346.

20. Goulden, *Truth Is the First Casualty*, 243; Schandler, *Unmaking of a President*, 211; Harry McPherson, *A Political Education* (Boston: Little, Brown, 1972), 436. See Joseph, *Cracks in the Empire*, 351, n. 44, for a list of Democratic defections in February and March. See also PDS, reel 4, passim.

21. United States Senate, Committee on Foreign Relations, *Foreign Assistance Act of 1968, Part I, Vietnam* (Washington, D.C.: GPO, 1968), 58. See also pp. 59, 172–174. Rusk did do well in the telegram count at the White House. Lou Schwartz to Rostow, March 13, 1968, PDS, reel 4.

22. Rostow, interview.

23. Stephen Lesher, *Media Unbound: The Impact of Television Journalism on the Public* (Boston: Houghton Mifflin, 1982), 4–6; Christian, oh (September 17, 1979), LBJL.

24. Tom Johnson, interview; George Christian on "Our World," ABC television, June 11, 1987.

25. Bert Spector, "A Clash of Cultures: The Smothers Brothers vs. CBS Television," in John E. O'Conner, ed., *American History/American Television* (New York: Ungar, 1983), 179–180. The owners of the CBS affiliate in Detroit chose not to run it. A year later, Richard Nixon advised his aides to monitor such entertainment shows as the "Smothers Brothers" for antiadministration propaganda. Nixon to Ehrlichman, March 11, 1969, box 1, MFRP, PPF, NP.

26. Wheeler, oh, tape 2, p. 8, LBJL; Taylor, *Swords and Plowshares*, 390.

27. Rusk, interview.

28. Christian on "Vietnam: A Television History," program 7; Rostow to Johnson, February 8, 1968, box 100, NSCVN, LBJL; Schandler, *Unmaking of a President*, 118, 178.

29. Rostow to Johnson, February 6, 1968, President's Appointment File, Diary Backup, LBJL. See also Lodge to Rusk, March 5, 1968, tab o, vol. 4, box 48, NSC File, March 31 Speech, LBJL.

30. President's Appointment File, Diary Backup, February 6, 1968; LBJL; *DSB* 57 (March 11, 1968):347.

31. Johnson, *Vantage Point*, 384; Westmoreland, *Soldier Reports*, 325, 365, 421–422; Wheeler, oh, tape 2, p. 2, LBJL; Taylor, *Swords and Plowshares*, 400; Marks to Maguire, February 8, 1968, box 231, ND19CO312, LBJL.

32. Johnson, *Vantage Point*, 415, 365; George Christian Office Files, February 12, 1968, Vietnam box, LBJL.

33. Rostow to Johnson, February 12, 1968, box 48, NSC Histories, March 31 Decision, LBJL.

34. Bill Crook to Johnson, February 8, 1968, box 231, NC19CO312 LBJL; John Macy to Johnson, March 30, 1968, box 32 (1375c), Vietnam, Marvin Watson Files, LBJL.

35. Cater to Johnson, March 8, 1968, March 23, 1968, box 231, ND19CO312, WHCF, LBJL.

36. Rostow, interview. James Thomson sees the establishment consensus beginning to come apart as early as 1965. Thomson, interview.

37. McPherson, *Political Education*, 433–434.

38. Rusk, interview.

39. Goulding, *Confirm or Deny*, 356; Hoopes, *Limits of Intervention*, 224; Rusk, interview.

40. Reedy, *Lyndon B. Johnson*, 151; Joseph, *Cracks in the Empire*, 266. George Christian also emphasizes Clifford's role. Christian, interview. One major actor who downplays Clifford's influence is Richard Helms. Helms, oh, tape 2, p. 28, LBJL.

41. Clifford, interview.

42. Johnson to Clifford and Rusk, February 28, 1968, box 49, vol. 7, tab K, NSC File, March 31 Speech, LBJL; Clifford; Christian, interviews. See also Clifford, "Viet Nam Reappraisal," 610.

43. February 27, 1968, box 2, Meeting Notes, LBJL; Johnson, *Vantage Point*, 390.

44. Bundy Background Paper, February–March 1968, box 2, Clark Clifford Papers, LBJL.

45. Study Paper, March 1, 1968, box 2, Clifford Papers, LBJL; Department of State Public Affairs, March 3, 1968, vol. 7, tab c, box 49, NSC File, March 31 Speech, LBJL.

46. *PP*, 4:559–561; Warnke, interview. Clifford and Vance do not remember the reserves being much of an issue at the time. Clifford; Vance, interviews.

47. John Mueller, "Reassessment of American Policy: 1965–1968," in Harrison E. Salisbury, ed., *Vietnam Reconsidered: Lessons from a War* (New York: Harper & Row, 1984), 48–52.

48. Karnow, *Vietnam*, 555.

49. Tom Johnson to Johnson, March 15, 1968, box 60, HU 4 Freedoms, WHCF, LBJL.

50. Memo, March 21, 1968, Office Files of the President, LBJL; Rusk, interview. See also March 14, 1968, box 2, Meeting Notes, LBJL.

51. Memo, March 16, 1968, Memos on Vietnam, February–August 1968, box 2, Clifford Papers, LBJL.

52. Clifford, interview. Clifford on "Vietnam: A Television History," program 7. Outside of the White House, Dean Acheson had already become "one of us" when he told Johnson through an aide on February 27 "that he can take Vietnam and stick it up his ass." Isaacson and Thomas, *Wise Men*, 687.

53. Bundy, interview. Vance and Ball also stress opinion in their observations of the meetings. Ball; Vance, interviews. See also Ball, *Past Has Another Pattern*, 409; and for Goldberg's March 15 memo to Johnson, Zaroulis and Sullivan, *Who Spoke Up?* 159.

54. March 26, 1968, box 2, Meeting Notes, LBJL; Taylor, *Swords and Plowshares*, 391.

55. Ernest R. May, *American Imperialism: A Speculative Essay* (New York: Atheneum, 1968). For another view of the relationship between elite consensus breakup and public disaffection, see Bruce Andrews, "Public Constraint and American Policy in Vietnam," Sage Professional Paper in International Studies, 02–042, IV (Beverly Hills, Calif.: Sage, 1976), 43.

56. Clifford, interview. Kissinger, *White House Years*, 29. Useful on the establishment are Godfrey Hodgson, "The Establishment," *Foreign Policy* 3 (Spring 1973):3–40; and Priscilla M. Roberts, "The American 'Eastern Establishment' and Foreign Affairs: A Challenge for Historians," *Society for Historians of American Foreign Relations Newsletter* 14 (December 1983):9–28.

57. Cater, interview.

58. Memo, Mike Mansfield, March 13, 1968, Meeting Notes of the Wise Men, LBJL; Warnke, interview.

59. Fred L. Block, *The Origins of International Economic Disorder: A Study of United States Monetary Policy from World War Two to the Present* (Berkeley: University of California Press, 1977), 193–194; Dean Acheson memoranda, March 14, 26, 1968, in David S. McLellan and David C. Acheson, eds., *Among Friends: Personal Letters of Dean Acheson* (New York: Dodd, Mead, 1980), 292–296. Gabriel Kolko stresses the international monetary crisis as fundamental to understanding the establishment's defection. Kolko, *Anatomy of a War*, passim.

60. Clifford, interview.

61. Goulding, *Confirm or Deny*, 347.

62. Clifford, interview. Christian is one of the few who thinks that

Johnson all along knew he was not going to escalate and that he recognized he had lost the public's support. Christian, interview.

63. Hoopes, *The Limits of Intervention*, 219.

64. McPherson on "Vietnam: A Television History," program 7; Tom Johnson, interview.

65. Tom Johnson, interview.

66. Schandler, *Unmaking of a President*, 328; Gelb, interview, and *Irony of Vietnam*, 332; Bundy, oh, tape 1, p. 39, LBJL. Gelb is emphatic, however, in pointing out that opinion became important only after Tet.

67. Graff; Clifford; Cater, interviews. White House aide Lloyd Hackler commented that Johnson had "suffered more than anybody about the war." Hackler, oh, tape 1, p. 24, LBJL.

68. Hackler, oh, tape 2, p. 7, LBJL; Hoopes, *The Limits of Intervention*, 164.

69. Clifford, Rostow, interviews. Tom Johnson, the aide closest to him in the retirement years, never heard him second-guess the decision. Johnson, interview.

70. Reedy, *Lyndon B. Johnson*, 142; William Bundy, oh, tape 4, p. 32, LBJL; Rusk interview.

71. Rostow, *Diffusion of Power*, 356.

72. Douglass Cater, George Reedy, and Tom Johnson agree with this interpretation. Cater; Reedy; Johnson, interviews.

73. Hackler, oh, tape 2, p. 8, LBJL.

74. Harlow, interview.

75. Taylor, *Swords and Plowshares*, 408; Christian, interview. See also Christian, oh, p. 20, LBJL; and George Christian, *The President Steps Down: A Personal Memoir of the Transfer of Power* (New York: Macmillan, 1970), 159.

76. Humphrey, *Education*, 428-429; Solberg, *Hubert Humphrey*, 372-385; Hoffman; Johnson, interviews.

77. Westmoreland, *Soldier Reports*, 225; Rostow, interview.

78. Cater, interview.

79. Clark, interview; Halberstam, *Best and Brightest*, 220; David Talbot, "And Now They Are Doves," *Mother Jones* (May 1984):33, 47; Hendrickson, "McNamara," p. B10.

80. Reedy, interview. See also Karnow, *Vietnam*, 506, on Gelb's wife.

81. Bundy, interview. He remembers also being "mad as hell" at old friend John Oakes of the *New York Times* for his editorial swipes at him and his colleagues. The war took a heavy physical toll on Bundy. Isaacson and Thomas, *Wise Men*, 657.

82. Talbot, "Now They Are Doves," 33; Tom Johnson, interview.

83. Reedy, *Lyndon B. Johnson*, 5; Reedy, interview.

84. Johnson, *Vantage Point*, 530, 418, 422.

85. "LBJ Reminisces," *Among Friends of LBJ* 27 (November 1, 1983):2-7.

86. Tom Johnson, interview.

87. Kearns, *Lyndon Johnson*, 328; Miller, *Lyndon*, 488; Ramsey Clark, oh, tape 5, pp. 23–25, LBJL. See also Graff, *Tuesday Cabinet*, 126.
88. Valenti, interview.
89. Reedy, interview. Johnson also decided against a proposed visit to Harvard for seminars in 1967. Zbigniew Brzezinski, oh, pp. 19–20, LBJL.
90. Rusk; Henkin, interviews.
91. Hershey, oh, pp. 43–45, LBJL.
92. McPherson, *Political Education*, 446.
93. Kearns, *Lyndon Johnson*, 325. For the comparable reaction of a Johnson aide to criticism, see Stenelo, *International Critic*, 135.
94. Graff, interview; Reedy, *Lyndon B. Johnson*, 148.
95. Humphrey, *Education*, 344.
96. Ball, *Past Has Another Pattern*, 43; Vance, interview; Reedy, *Lyndon B. Johnson*, 142; Humphrey, *Education*, 347; Kearns, *Lyndon Johnson*, 275; Irving L. Janis, *Victims of Groupthink: A Psychological Study of Foreign Policy Decisions and Fiascos* (Boston: Houghton Mifflin, 1972), 105.
97. Gelb, *Irony of Vietnam*, 150, 292. Of 224 surveyed Johnson appointees, only 2 said they left the administration because of the war. Schott and Hamilton, *People, Positions, and Power*, 201.
98. Christian, oh, p. 23; Clark; Reedy, interviews; Reedy, *Lyndon B. Johnson*, 148; Kearns, *Lyndon Johnson*, 334.
99. Rostow, interview; Humphrey, *Education*, 319. For comments from a recipient of the Johnson treatment toward critics, see Don Riegle, *O Congress* (Garden City, N.Y.: Doubleday, 1972), 197–199. See also how he dropped critical advisers in Kearns, *Lyndon Johnson*, 335.
100. Morris, *Uncertain Greatness: Henry Kissinger and American Foreign Policy* (New York: Harper & Row, 1971), 74; Thomson, "How Could Vietnam Happen?" 49. Thomson, oh, pp. 60–62, LBJL; Thomson, interview; Hackler, oh, tape 2, p. 27, LBJL. Rostow may have been less concerned than Thomson thought. See Rostow to Johnson, May 1, 1967, PDS, reel 6.
101. Christian, interview. Dean Rusk was especially upset about the loss of support for his Vietnam policy from old friends in the Western Alliance. Rusk, interview.
102. Rusk, interview; John P. Roche, *Sentenced to Life* (New York: Macmillan, 1974), 87, 93. See also Kearns, *Lyndon Johnson*, 327; and Schott and Hamilton, *People, Positions, and Power*, 42–43.
103. Graff, *Tuesday Cabinet*, 150; Christian, interview. Cyrus Vance, however, sees Johnson's intimate circle narrowing and becoming more insulated from critical opinion. Vance, interview.
104. Gelb, *Irony of Vietnam*, 286.
105. Goldman; Valenti; Rusk, interviews. See also Roche, *Sentenced to Life*, 152.
106. Reedy; Christian, interviews; McPherson, *Political Education*, 402.
107. Rostow; Cater, interviews; Roche, *Sentenced to Life*, 76.

108. Roche; Reedy, interviews; Califano, *Presidential Nation,* 75. Journalist Bernard Weinraub remembers this as an important influence on editors and publishers. Transcript of interview with Bernard Weinraub, David Bonior, 1982, 11.

109. Michael Ferber and Staughton Lynd, *The Resistance* (Boston: Beacon, 1971), 193; Steve Kelman, *Push Comes to Shove* (Boston: Houghton Mifflin, 1970), 118; Roche, "Impact of Dissent," in Lake, *Vietnam Legacy,* 129–130; Samuel Lubell, *The Future While it Happened* (New York: Norton, 1973), 193, 258–259.

110. Lawrence M. Baskir and William A. Straus, *Chance and Circumstance: The Draft, the War, and the Vietnam Generation* (New York: Knopf, 1978), 61, 69; James Fallows, "What Did You Do in the Class War, Daddy," in A. D. Horne, ed., *The Wounded Generation: America after Vietnam* (Englewood Cliffs, N.J.: Prentice-Hall, 1981), 20–21.

111. Westmoreland, *Soldier Reports,* 297; Adam Yarmolinsky, "The War and the Military," in Lake, *Vietnam Legacy,* 221.

112. David Cortright, *Soldiers in Revolt: The American Military Today* (Garden City, N.Y.: Doubleday, 1975), 12–13, 53; Westmoreland to Johnson, August 25, 1968, box 68, ND 7-2 (Confidential), WHCF, LBJL. The Pentagon did monitor opinion on the war in general. Jaya Krishna Baral, *The Pentagon and the Making of US Foreign Policy: A Case Study of Vietnam, 1960–68* (Atlantic Highlands, N.J.: Humanities Press, 1978), 298.

113. Warnke, interview; Palmer, *25-Year War,* 155.

114. Warnke; Cater, interviews.

115. Rusk, interview; March 22, 1968, box 2, Meeting Notes, LBJL. Rusk is fond of referring to his "country cousins" in Cherokee County, Georgia, as reflecting average American opinion. Some of them may have been affected by a country-and-western hit record of the period, "Ruby, Don't Take Your Love to Town." Recorded by Mel Tillis and Kenny Rogers and the First Edition, the song told the tragic story of a severely paralyzed veteran. The author is indebted to Dr. Gary Artinian of the Wayne State University Board of Governors for this information. Richard Nixon was disturbed when the song received three minutes on an NBC evening newscast ("What has been done to complain?") in October of 1969. Nixon note on Annotated News Summaries, October 7, 1969, box 31, POF, NP.

116. One journalist refers to the retirement speech as a "stunning victory" for the antiwar movement. Schell, *Time of Illusion,* 18.

117. *New York Times,* March 24, 1968, pp. 1, 72; Hoffman; Hayden, interviews; Zaroulis and Sullivan, *Who Spoke Up?* 179.

118. *New York Times,* April 28, 1968, pp. E7–10; May 3, 1968, pp. 31–34.

119. For the networks' own surprise on how their coverage was interpreted, see Hodgson, *America in Our Time,* 372–373; Small, *To Kill a Messenger,* 209–210.

120. Tom Hayden, on the other hand, was pleased with the ultimate result in Chicago because it produced dramatic reform in the Democratic party. Hayden, interview.

121. Panzer to Johnson, April 17, 1968, box 232, ND 19, WHCF, LBJL; Johnson to Rusk and Clifford, June 11, 1968, box 101, NSCVN, LBJL.

122. May 25, 1968, box 3, Meeting Notes, LBJL.

123. Vance, interview; May 4, 1968, box 3, Meeting Notes, LBJL; *DSB* 59 (September 16, 1968), 295; ibid. (November 4, 1968), 471.

CHAPTER 6: HANOI AND THE MOVEMENT CONFRONT A NEW PRESIDENT

1. Page and Brody, "Policy Voting," 994–995.

2. Riegle, *O Congress*, 20; Kalb and Kalb, *Kissinger*, 120. See also Hersh, *Price of Power*, 119. Later Kissinger changed his tune when he told Riegle that he should have asked the "sincere" doves to give him a three-year moratorium on demonstrations while he ended the war. Riegle, *O Congress*, 25.

3. Fulbright, interview.

4. Nixon, *RN: The Memoirs of Richard Nixon* (New York: Wagner, 1978), 755; Christian, interview. Dwight Chapin remembers Nixon saying that he was not going to fall into Johnson's trap. Telephone interview with Chapin, April 3, 1984.

5. Ehrlichman; Chapin, interviews.

6. Haldeman, interview. Haldeman is proud of how the Nixon administration tried to maintain this dialogue.

7. NSC Study Memo, February 13, 1969, *DD*, 8, 000646.

8. Chapin, interview.

9. Lord, interview. One can see the relative disinterest in public opinion displayed by the State and Defense departments, the Joint Chiefs, and the CIA in their hundreds of pages of responses to questions from the NSC about the situation in Vietnam in January of 1969. NSSM I, January 21, 1969, and responses, in Documents of the National Security Council, second supplement, microfilm, reel 3, 0321, 0328, 0558, 0753, 0920, 1035 (Frederick, Md.: University Publications of America, 1983). Only the State Department emphasized domestic opinion in its response to the first general question posed by the NSC.

10. Harlow, interview. Harlow may have exaggerated. A survey of Nixon's papers reveals his interests in such relatively trivial matters as the whereabouts of President Eisenhower's old football cleats, dinner seating and protocol, a picture of the family dog in a White House fountain, the relative merits of Bordeaux wine in the White House cellar, inviting Mexican comedian Cantinflas to the White House, and obtaining a wastebasket for the bathroom in his office in the Executive Office Building.

11. Price, interview.

12. Interview with James Keogh, New York, March 18, 1984.

13. Price, interview.

14. Haldeman, interview; Annotated News Summaries, POF, NP. Dwight Chapin and Ray Price extol Haldeman's fair and valuable opinion surveys. Chapin; Price, interviews.

15. Chapin, interview. Knowing that Secretary of State William Rogers and Secretary of Defense Melvin Laird were principal doves in his entourage, he tried to avoid seeing them when contemplating hawkish decisions. On such relative doves, see Spiro T. Agnew, *Go Quietly or Else* (New York: Morrow, 1980), 27, 32; and Elmo R. Zumwalt, *On Watch* (New York: Quadrangle, 1976), 380.

16. Ehrlichman, interview.

17. Haldeman, interview. See also Agnew, *Go Quietly*, 31.

18. Haldeman; Chapin, interviews.

19. Ehrlichman, interview.

20. Harlow, interview; Nixon to Haldeman, January 6, 1970, box 2; MFRP, PPF, NP. Nixon to Ehrlichman, June 16, 1969, box 1, ibid. See his advice to staffers in Tebbel and Watts, *Press and the Presidency*, 503, as well as their chapter on the media and Nixon (pp. 500–515). See also Whalen, *Catch the Falling Flag*, 13.

21. Price; Keogh, interviews.

22. Price, interview. The media may not have been entirely at fault in their coverage of Nixon. According to one of the joint chiefs, the administration was "not just like riding a roller coaster but like riding it blindfolded." Zumwalt, *On Watch*, 327.

23. Haldeman, interview; Nixon to Haldeman, June 15, 1971, box 3, MFRP, PPF, NP.

24. Interview with Leonard Garment, Washington, D.C., August 1, 1984. Garment thinks Nixon was the last liberal to be president. The four main newspaper enemies of Nixon were the *Times, Post, Boston Globe,* and *St. Louis Post-Dispatch.* Tebbel and Watts, *Press and the Presidency*, 503. Nixon once referred to *Times* reporter Charles Mohr as a "notorious Oakes liner." Nixon note on an undated memo (ca. January 12, 1971) concerning a television show on NET on which he felt four of the five journalists "want us to lose the war," box 4, PH, POF, NP.

25. Ehrlichman, interview. Ray Price also remembers good times with journalists who were often hostile professionally. Price, interview.

26. Haldeman, interview.

27. Nixon, *RN*, 757; interview with Peter Rodman, Washington, D.C., August 1, 1984; Kissinger, *Years of Upheaval*, 93–94.

28. Ehrlichman, interview. Old Washington hand Bryce Harlow also claims that his social life was unaffected by the town's hostility to Nixon. Harlow, interview.

29. Throughout his term in office, Kissinger maintained close ties to liberal Democrats. At a dinner of the International Association for Cultural Freedom in early December 1968, he told the audience that his door would always be open to intellectuals like them. During the same

period he confided to a journalist that "almost all my friends—were liberal democrats." Kalb and Kalb, *Kissinger,* 28.

30. Even before asked the question in an interview, Rostow walked to the window of his office at the University of Texas, and looked out proudly at the campus, where even his wife was dean of a prestigious school. Protesting too much perhaps, Rostow expressed pleasure in his move to the Southwest. Rostow, interview.

31. David Landau, *Kissinger: The Uses of Power* (Boston: Houghton, Mifflin, 1972), 98–101, 256, n.13. Kissinger himself comments on the Johnson aides' problems after leaving office. Kissinger, *White House Years,* 294–295.

32. Lord, interview. See also William Shawcross, *Sideshow: Kissinger, Nixon and the Destruction of Cambodia* (New York: Simon & Schuster, 1979), 96–97.

33. Haldeman, interview.

34. H. R. Haldeman, *The Ends of Power* (New York: Times Books, 1978), 69. Later, in 1973, he "said he wants to screw the universities, especially Harvard, by cutting back on research and development money." Zumwalt, *On Watch,* 419.

35. Moynihan remembers the Nixon years as "very hard and difficult" for him. Interview with Moynihan, en route between Washington and New York, August 4, 1985.

36. The scattered demonstrations were enough to convince Nixon that the district police should be tougher in the future. Nixon note on Egil Krogh, Jr., to Ehrlichman, January 24, 1969, box 1, PH, POF, NP. For coverage of the unsuccessful demonstrations against the inaugural, see *New York Times,* January 21, 1969, p. 24. See also Zaroulis and Sullivan, *Who Spoke Up?* 217, on the relative quiescence of the movement until the summer.

37. *Report of the President's Commission on Campus Unrest* (New York: Arno, 1970), 38–39. See also Zaroulis and Sullivan, *Who Spoke Up?* 301; Sale, *SDS,* 511–513.

38. See, e.g., how the "Days of Rage" played into his hands. Gitlin, *Whole World Is Watching,* 191.

39. See the Clergy and Laymen Concerned's large advertisement in the *New York Times* on March 30, 1969, sec. 4, p. 7. Nixon wrote to Herbert Klein on Women Strike for Peace, "Herb—Let's dig out the background on this outfit. As you probably know it's a front," on Alexander Butterfield to Klein, March 27, 1969, box 23, HU 3-1, WHCF, NP.

40. Harlow, interview; Tod Hullin to Jack Caulfield, October 9, 1969, box 51, Chronological File, John Ehrlichman Papers, NP; Haldeman, interview.

41. *New York Times,* April 30, 1969, p. 1.

42. Kalb and Kalb, *Kissinger,* 137; Hersh, *Price of Power,* 119.

43. *New York Times,* June 9, 1969, p. 49.

44. William B. Hixson, Jr., "Nixon, the War, and the Opposition: The

First Term," *Journal of American Culture* 4 (Summer 1981):67; Wilkinson to Kissinger, July 7, 1969, box 24, HU 3-1, WHCF, NP. See also Wilkinson to Ken Cole, August 22, 1969 and Tom Huston, Memo, August 18, 1969, ibid. After a tour of campuses during this period, George Ball expressed concern about the widespread alienation and radicalism among the students. Ball, *Past Has Another Pattern*, 412.

45. Halberstam, *The Powers That Be*, 484-485.

46. Av Westin, *Newswatch: How TV Decides the News* (New York: Simon & Schuster, 1982), 96-97.

47. For an intelligence report on Hanoi's strategy in the spring of 1969, see Thomas C. Thayer, *War without Fronts: The American Experience in Vietnam* (Boulder, Colo.: Westview, 1985), 52.

48. Burstein and Freudenberg, "Changing Public Policy," passim. Stretching his point, Magnus Jerneck in "Kritik som Utrikespolitiskt Medel: En Studie av de Amerikanska Reactionerna pa den Svenska Vietnamkritiken" (Ph.D. diss., Lund, Sweden, 1983) also includes the impact of foreign criticism, especially Sweden's, on Congress.

49. Rodman, interview; Nixon to Kissinger, October 27, 1969, box 1, MFRP, PPF, NP.

50. Rosenberg, "Congress and the Vietnam War," 178.

51. Haldeman, interview; Andrews, *Public Opinion*, 47. Leonard Garment also stresses Democratic senators' personal hostility to Nixon. Garment, interview.

52. Burstein and Freudenberg, "Ending the Vietnam War: Components of Change in Senate Voting on Vietnam War Bills," *American Journal of Sociology* 82 (March 1977):981-1006.

53. Haldeman, interview. Haldeman also felt that senators, unlike officials in the executive branch, often reacted irrationally to a handful of picketers sitting in their offices or to very small but well-organized pressure groups in their districts. Similarly, Ray Price felt senators were more receptive to transitory opinion and attitude shifts than the White House. Price, interview.

54. Harlow; Fulbright, interviews.

55. Alton Frye and Jack Sullivan, "Congress and Vietnam: The Fruits of Anguish," in Lake, *Vietnam Legacy*, 199.

56. Hamre, "Congressional Dissent," 88-89. In the years to come, the Senate's Cooper-Church resolution barring funds for direct military operations in Cambodia after July 1, 1970, and the Senate's repeal of the Tonkin Gulf Resolution in January 1971 were among the measures adding to Nixon's difficulties. Frye and Sullivan, "Congress and Vietnam," 200.

57. Haldeman, interview.

58. Karnow, *Vietnam*, 597.

59. Ibid., 594-595; Rodman, interview; Hersh, *Price of Power*, 125-130.

60. Two former NSC aides, Winston Lord and Peter Rodman, place the Sihanouk issue as clearly number one. Lord; Rodman, interviews.

61. Karnow, *Vietnam*, 592; Nixon, *RN*, 382; Kissinger, *White House Years*, 246, 252–253.

62. Landau, *Kissinger*, 204–205. According to Nixon, the "heart of the matter" in Vietnam policy in the spring of 1969 was to show the North Vietnamese that his tough talk was serious. Nixon to Kissinger, April 13, 1969, on Annotated News Summary, box 30, POF, NP.

63. Ibid., 217; Haldeman, *Ends of Power*, 98; Kissinger, *White House Years*, 254–255.

64. Defense Secretary Melvin Laird talks about pressures from Congress and the public in general in 1969 to end the war quickly. Laird on "Vietnam: A Television History," program 10. When *Times* reporter William Beecher wrote a bombing story in May of 1969, the public paid scant attention, however.

65. Morton H. Halperin, "The Lessons Nixon Learned," in Lake, *Vietnam Legacy*, 415. Opposing the secrecy, Melvin Laird felt that the public would accept the bombing if it was revealed. Henkin, interview.

66. Schell, *Time of Illusion*, 36–39.

67. *DSB* 60 (March 24, 1969):239, 243.

68. *DSB* 60 (June 2, 1969):461; ibid.,60 (October 13, 1969):316.

69. *DSB* 60 (June 2, 1969):465; ibid., 61 (July 21, 1969):43.

70. Raymond Price, *With Nixon* (New York: Viking, 1977), 157; Kissinger, *White House Years*, 290; Morris, *Uncertain Greatness*, 170. See also Agnew, *Go Quietly*, 27–28; Jeb Stuart Magruder, *An American Life: One Man's Road to Watergate* (New York: Atheneum, 1974), 74.

71. William Safire, *Before the Fall: An Insider's View of the Pre-Watergate White House* (Garden City, N.Y.: Doubleday, 1975), 140–141; Price, *With Nixon*, 165; Nixon, *RN*, 399. At a meeting on October 1, he again said he would not be affected by nor respond to the Moratorium. Ehrlichman memo, October 1, 1969, box 3, Notes of Meetings with the President, Ehrlichman Papers, NP. Press Secretary Ron Ziegler reiterated this position on October 15. Christopher H. Pyle, "Military Surveillance of Civilian Politics, 1969–1970" (Ph.D. diss., Columbia University, 1974), 248. See also John Mitchell's support for Nixon in Smith, *Long Time Gone*, 19–23.

72. Price, *With Nixon*, 158–160; *DSB* 61 (November 3, 1969):371–372; Nixon, *RN*, 403. The day before, appearing on "Meet the Press," Secretary Rogers warned Hanoi not to listen to the protesters in the upcoming Moratorium since they did not reflect majority opinion in the United States. *DSB* 61 (October 27, 1969):349.

73. Nixon to Harlow and Kissinger, September 23, 1969, box 1, MFRP, PPF; Ken Belieu to Harlow, September 29, 1969, box 79, MFP, POF; Jack Caulfield to Ehrlichman, October 10, 1969, box 3, PH, POF, NP.

74. Aronson, *Deadline*, 6.

75. Gitlin, *Whole World Is Watching*, 218, 221. Castleman and Podrazik, *Watching TV*, 219. One Nixon aide was less sanguine: James Keogh thought Agnew's media campaign was only partially successful. It

bought time, but the media were always a problem for Nixon. Keogh, interview.

76. *New York Times*, October 8, 1969, p. 1; October 11, 1969, p. 24; October 23, 1969, p. 7; October 12, 1969, pp. 1, 80. Abbie Hoffman played up the Kim Agnew story, supporting the rumor that she was one of his followers. Hoffman, interview.

77. *New York Times*, October 15, 1969, p. 1. The campaign was a product of the Citizens' Committee for Peace with Security.

78. Harriman considered his participation "a thrilling experience." Harriman, *America and Russia in a Changing World* (Garden City, N.Y.: Doubleday, 1971), 147. Harriman might have been neutralized had Nixon earlier asked him to help the new administration. Rita Hauser to Nixon, April 29, 1969, box 1, PH, POF, NP.

79. Memo, October 17, 1969, Demonstration 10/15/69 folder, box 81, John Dean Papers, NP. For extensive coverage of the Moratorium, see *New York Times*, October 16, 1969, pp. 1, 18–22. See also the page one advance story on October 15, as well as the page one follow-up on October 17.

80. Ehrlichman note, October 15, 1969, box 3, Notes of Meetings with the President, Ehrlichman Papers, NP; *New York Times*, October 20, 1969, p. 1; "Vietnam: A Television History," program 12. Read into the *Congressional Record*, the letter was signed "affectionately yours."

81. *DSB* 61 (November 3, 1969):370. See also Lodge's comments on Nixon's poll support in *DSB* 61 (November 24, 1969):444 and (December 15, 1969):547.

82. Rodman, Lord, and Garment, interviews. Letters for the week of October 16–22 ran 9,094 in favor and 7,974 against the Moratorium with telegrams tallied at 1,810 in favor, 957 opposed. Noble Mellancamp memo, October 22, 1969, box 3, PH, POF, NP.

83. Keogh, Ehrlichman, interviews; *DSB* 61 (November 10, 1969):395.

84. Price, Ehrlichman, interviews.

85. Haldeman, interview. Antiwar leader Tom Hayden refers to Haldeman's interpretation as "pathological." Hayden, interview. For support for Hayden's view, see Warnke, "Search for Peace," 318. On the other hand, James Keogh and Ray Price agree with Haldeman. Keogh; Price, interviews. See also Nixon, *RN*, 350–351.

86. Rodman, interview.

87. Haldeman, interview; Morris, *Uncertain Greatness*, 165.

88. Moynihan, interview; Hersh, *Price of Power*, 129–130.

89. George C. Herring, *America's Longest War: The United States and Vietnam, 1950–1975* (New York: Knopf, 1986), 228. The death of Ho in September might also have affected the situation.

90. Price, interview; Harlow, memo, October 24, 1969, box 79, MFP, POF, NP. See also Joseph, *Cracks in the Empire*, 438–439, for Moratorium organizer Sam Brown's evaluation.

91. Kalb and Kalb, *Kissinger*, 113–114; Price, *With Nixon*, 160; Nixon, *RN*, 409–410; Kissinger, *White House Years*, 307; Rodman, interview.

92. Important here was an October 16 memo from Dwight Chapin on the need to split the Moratorium from the Mobilization. Although Jeb Stuart Magruder calls attention to the value of the Chapin memo as laying out the game plan for weakening the Mobilization, Chapin does not recall it. Magruder, *American Life*, 81–83; Gitlin, *Whole World Is Watching*, 225; Chapin, interview. Haldeman and Kissinger were involved in the campaign as well. Ehrlichman, *Witness to Power* (New York: Simon & Schuster, 1972), 265; Hersh, *Price of Power*, 132.

93. "Intelligence Reports-Caulfield" file, box 20, Ehrlichman Papers, NP; memo in Demonstration 10/15/69 folder, Dean Papers, NP. For preparations for the Mobilization see box 82, ibid. The FBI and the army, among others, were keeping the White House informed about Mobilization logistics. U.S. Senate Select Committee, *Hearings*, 6:690; Donner, *Age of Surveillance*, 307.

94. William Safire appropriated the term. Zaroulis and Sullivan, *Who Spoke Up?* 279–280. Earlier Safire suggested "Middle Americans" while Nixon played with "Working Americans." Ehrlichman to Nixon, August 4, 1969, box 2, PH, POF, NP. In March of 1970, Nixon floated a new term, "New Majority." Nixon to Haldeman, March 2, 1970, box 2, MFRP, PPF, NP.

95. Safire, *Before the Fall*, 178; Kissinger, *White House Years*, 292–293, 298; James Keogh memo, November 5, 1969, box 79, MFP, POF, NP.

96. Smith, *Long Time Gone*, 213. As for Nixon's celebrated use of the term "bums," Haldeman suggests that description applied only to campus hangers-on, not to all protesting students. Haldeman, *Ends of Power*, 105.

97. Smith, *Long Time Gone*, 215, 216. Ray Price sees the students as "victims." Price, *With Nixon*, 152, 154–156.

98. Smith, *Long Time Gone*, 217. U.N. representative Rita Hauser was kinder in public when she expressed pride in the Moratorium on November 11: "Through reasoned dissent, man progresses." *DSB* 61 (December 1, 1969):472.

99. Haldeman, *Ends of Power*, 105; Morris, *Uncertain Greatness*, 168–169; Kissinger, *White House Years*, 299–302, 306.

100. Kissinger, *White House Years*, 288, 281.

101. Kalb and Kalb, *Kissinger*, 146; *Public Papers of the President, Richard Nixon, 1969* (Washington, D.C.: GPO, 1969), 901–909.

102. Nixon, *RN*, 412–413. He prepared a media defensive in advance with a memo calling for the careful monitoring of ABC, CBS, NBC, the *Post*, *Times*, *Newsweek*, and *Time* for critical coverage that would be met by congressional speeches and planted letters to the editors. Nixon to Haldeman, October 26, 1969, box 1, MFRP, PPF, NP. On the media's allegedly unfair treatment of the speech see James Keogh, *President Nixon and the Press* (New York: Funk and Wagnall, 1972), 137. See also Morris, *Uncertain Greatness*, 170.

103. Pyle, "Military Surveillance," 60. Other White House activities to

combat the movement included the release in November by the USIA of a fifteen-minute "Silent Majority" film and the appointment of astronaut Michael Collins as an assistant secretary of state who would be responsible for explaining American foreign policy to young people.

104. Agnew, *Go Quietly*, 29.

105. Castleman and Podrazik, *Watching TV*, 219. William Safire saw the real enemy not as the academics or liberals but as the press. Safire, *Before the Fall*, 341.

106. Gitlin, *Whole World Is Watching*, 227; Hodgson, *America*, 377; Chancellor on "Vietnam: A Television History," program 12; Aronson, *Deadline*, 16.

107. Lens, *Unrepentant Radical*, 359, 354–355. The CIA was pleased with the logistic support it rendered District police during the demonstration. Undated memo, *DD*, 9, 000091.

108. Pyle, "Military Surveillance," 300–301. On smearing antiwar critics see Nixon to Ehrlichman, November 24, 1969, box 1, MFRP, POF, NP.

109. Elliff, *Crime, Dissent*, 222–223. See the request for more information from the CIA on June 20, 1969, from Huston in Rockefeller Report, 135, and in the call for data on communist financial support for campus protests in Ehrlichman to Nixon, May 5, 1969, box 2, PH, POF, NP. John Ehrlichman saw supporting evidence for Nixon's beliefs. Ehrlichman, interview.

110. On other requests for the CIA to provide intelligence on the movement, see Theoharis, *Spying*, 16; U.S. Select Committee, *Hearings*, 2:401; and especially W. C. Sullivan to DeLoach, June 20, 1969, ibid., 112.

111. U.S. Senate Select Committee, *Final Report*, book 2, p. 107; *Hearings*, 6:785, 6:236.

112. One can see this, for example, in the mail flow to Senator Richard

SENATOR RICHARD B. RUSSELL'S ANSWERED MAIL ON VIETNAM
DURING SELECTED PERIODS, 1965–1970

Date	Hawk	Dove
Jan. 1, 1965– June 30, 1965	19	14
Jan. 1, 1967– Jan. 15, 1967	24	6
Oct. 18–31, 1967	9	8
Oct. 15–31, 1969	28	30
Nov. 10–26, 1969	34	8
May 16–28, 1970	26	13

Russell, the powerful head of the Senate Armed Services Committee (see table). Because he was perceived as antagonistic to doves and also because he came from Georgia, a conservative state, one might expect to find more hawkish than dovish mail on the Vietnam issue in his archives. The accompanying table evaluates the sentiments on Vietnam expressed in letters received by Russell during selected periods of the war. The March on the Pentagon produced only a handful of letters on the subject, with the usual hawk-dove margin a little closer than in previous periods. Then came the Moratorium, with dovish mail surpassing hawkish mail. Following the Silent Majority speech, and during the period of the Mobilization, the tide had apparently turned. Even after the Cambodian invasion in May 1970, hawks continued to outnumber doves in the senator's correspondence on Vietnam. Evaluated from the Vietnam folders in the Richard B. Russell Memorial Library, University of Georgia, Athens, Georgia. Russell and his staff apparently never made such a count. Moreover, given his state and his record, it is likely that domestic issues counted much more for him than issues relating to international affairs.

113. Price, interview.

114. The nation's press generally approved of the Moratorium, the Mobilization, *and* the Silent Majority speech. Foster, *Activism Replaces Isolationism*, 308.

115. Nixon's approval rating on Vietnam policy after the Mobilization was 64 percent. Ibid.

CHAPTER 7: THE WAR AND THE MOVEMENT WIND DOWN

1. Henry Kissinger said of the period, "We had withstood a military offensive by Hanoi, as well as the Moratorium." Kissinger, *White House Years*, 435.

2. Price, interview. Congress and the movement always posed a "latent" threat to Nixon, according to one Nixon aide. Rodman, interview.

3. In 1971, among a hundred randomly selected American soldiers, there were seventeen AWOL incidents, twenty individuals who used marijuana frequently, ten who used hard drugs frequently, and twelve who had written their congressmen to complain about the military. Baskir and Strauss, *Chance and Circumstance*, 110.

4. DSB 62 (January 5, 1970):3. See also ibid. (February 16, 1970):176, for a comparable warning, and Klein, *Making It Perfectly Clear*, 114.

5. *New York Times*, April 16, 1970, pp. 1, 44.

6. Nixon, *RN*, 448; Rodman, interview.

7. Herring, *America's Longest War*, 235.

8. Nixon, *RN*, 447; Hersh, *Price of Power*, 184. For his letters to the Smith College Board of Trustees, see Nixon to Herbert Klein, May 25, 1969, box 2, MFRP, PPF, NP.

9. Morris, *Uncertain Greatness*, 174.

10. In his preliminary, handwritten notes on the speech, Nixon listed division in the nation as one of the four negative aspects he feared. Notes of April 26; 1970, box 58, President's Speech File, PPF, NP; Charles W. Colson, *Born Again* (New York: Bantam, 1976), 34.

11. *DBS* 62 (May 11, 1970):604. See also William Rogers's comments in ibid. (March 2, 1970):217.

12. Keogh, *Nixon and the Press*, 101.

13. Morris, *Uncertain Greatness*, 69.

14. Ibid., 174. See also Kissinger, *White House Years*, 492. In another context, Kissinger talked about the establishment abdicating its responsibility to curb the radicals who ran the movement. Kissinger, *Years of Upheaval*, 86–87.

15. Ford, *Time to Heal*, 354–355.

16. Kissinger, *White House Years*, 499. Haldeman feels that Rogers and Laird were given ample opportunity to make known their dissent. Haldeman, interview.

17. Hersh, *Price of Power*, 191. Another cabinet member who was surprised by the Cambodian invasion was Interior Secretary Walter J. Hickel. Hickel, *Who Owns America?* (Englewood Cliffs, N.J.: Prentice-Hall, 1971), 223.

18. Yet according to one poll of eighteen hundred college presidents, only 4 percent of the campuses reported violent acts in May. Kenneth Keniston and Michael Lerner, "The Unholy Alliance," in Keniston, ed., *Youth and Dissent: The Rise of a New Opposition* (New York: Harcourt, Brace, 1971), 354.

19. Nixon, *RN*, 454; Ehrlichman, *Witness to Power*, 150; Safire, *Before the Fall*, 184. The perpetrators of the burning of the center, which was unrelated to Stanford and the Stanford Research Institute, have never been found. The author was in residence at the center that year, but his study escaped the apparently random torching. Nixon and his aides were helpful to Srinivas in raising money and providing experts to restore many of his burned documents. One study that suffered major damage was that of Harvard philosopher John Rawls. The only copy of his unpublished work "A Theory of Justice," which would become a classic, survived the blaze in a metal file cabinet.

20. Ehrlichman, interview. Although two students were killed at Jackson State, a black college, most attention focused on the Kent State killings.

21. Sale, *SDS*, 636.

22. Nixon, *RN*, 457, 458; Price, *With Nixon*, 162. Mostly negative petitions and letters are found in boxes 24, 36, and 37, HU 3–1, WHCF, NP.

23. Goodman, *Lost Peace*, 107; Rodman, interview. See also John Corelis, "Kent State Reconsidered as Nightmare," *Journal of Psychohistory* 8 (Fall 1980):137–147.

24. Kissinger, *White House Years*, 511; Ehrlichman; Haldeman, inter-

views; Colson, *Born Again*, 36-37; Moynihan, interview; Moynihan to Nixon, May 9, 1970, box 6, PH, POF, NP.

25. Klein, *Making It Perfectly Clear*, 341-342; Lord; Garment, interviews.

26. Garment; Chapin; Keogh, interviews. Some critics, on the other hand, report Nixon being close to a nervous breakdown. Shawcross, *Sideshow*, 154.

27. Price, interview. However, the television networks apparently offered balanced coverage of Cambodia, even to the point of using the administration's own word, *incursion*, instead of *invasion*. Castleman and Podrazik, *Watching TV*, 220.

28. May 6, 1970, Letters to Kent State, box 10, PPF; Edward L. Morgan memo, May 7, 1970, box 80, MFP, POF; Nils A. Boe memo, May 11, 1970, ibid.; President's Phone Calls for May 1970, box 105, POF, NP; Ehrlichman, interview.

29. Price, interview. See also Kissinger, *White House Years*, 511; and Kissinger on "Vietnam: A Television History," program 12.

30. Kalb and Kalb, *Kissinger*, 165.

31. Kissinger on "Vietnam: A Television History," program 12.

32. David Frost, *I Gave Them a Sword: Behind the Scenes of the Nixon Interviews* (New York: Morrow, 1978), 164.

33. Kissinger, *White House Years*, 510; Hersh, *Price of Power*, 196n.

34. Landau, *Kissinger*, 94-97. See also Kalb and Kalb, *Kissinger*, 165; Kissinger, *White House Years*, 514-515.

35. Keogh, interview. For Nixon's own account, see Nixon, *RN*, 460-466.

36. Haldeman, interview.

37. Chapin, interview; Safire, *Before the Fall*, 206.

38. Price, interview. Nixon referred to "our PR failure" in Nixon note on Ehrlichman to Nixon, July 8, 1970, box 6, PH, POF, NP. For his own private account see Nixon memo, May 13, 1970, MFRP, PPF, NP.

39. Price, *With Nixon*, 168; Haldeman, interview; *DSB 62* (June 1, 1970):674. The administration publicized these meetings to demonstrate its sensitivity. Larry Higby to Ron Ziegler, June 19, 1970, box 24, HU 3-1, WHCF, NP.

40. Nixon note on October 1969 news summaries, box 31, POF, NP; Magruder, *American Life*, 113-114, 118.

41. Kissinger, *White House Years*, 512-513. See also Karnow, *Vietnam*, 610, and Nixon supporter Edward Teller's pessimistic report from the campuses in Garment to Haldeman, June 7, 1970, box 24, HU 3-1, WHCF, NP.

42. Smith, *Long Time Gone*, 49.

43. Charles Colson memo, May 26, 1970, box 80, MFP, POF, NP; Aronson, *Deadline*, 11-12.

44. Klein, *Making It Perfectly Clear*, 285. See also Herring, *America's Longest War*, 239; Frost, *I Gave Them a Sword*, 109.

45. Klein, *Making It Perfectly Clear*, 285; Magruder, *American Life*, 66; *New York Times*, August 31, 1970, p. 18. For an example of the administration's work with such support groups, see the account of Nixon's meeting with H. Ross Perot and Frank Borman in Haldeman memo, December 4, 1969, box 79, MFP, POF, NP.

46. Haldeman, *Ends of Power*, 107, 121. Haldeman also calls attention to the need to plug up the leaks in Henry Kissinger's shop (p. 118).

47. U.S. Senate Select Committee, *Hearings*, 2:4, 17.

48. Ibid., 86, 316; Donner, *Age of Surveillance*, 265.

49. U.S. Senate Select Committee, *Report*, book 2, p. 146; *Hearings*, 2:32.

50. U.S. Senate Select Committee, *Report*, book 2, p. 160.

51. Ibid., 111.

52. U.S. Senate Select Committee, *Hearings*, 2:23, 102. See also 116, 123–124; and Hersh, *Price of Power*, 210, on the NSA.

53. The Nixon administration was not entirely pleased with the new efforts. See Huston to Haldeman, September 21, 1970, in U.S. Senate Select Committee, *Hearings*, 2:395, for complaints that the IRS was not doing enough in the area of the investigation of the financing of left-wing organizations.

54. Alan E. Bayer and Alexander W. Astin, "Campus Unrest 1970–1971: Was It Really All That Quiet?" *Educational Record* 52 (Fall 1971):301–313; Safire, *Before the Fall*, 298. Others see more campus- and not nationally related protests during the later period than before. Keniston and Lerner, "Unholy Alliance," 354.

55. Lens, *Unrepentant Radical*, 367–368; Dellinger, *More Power than We Know*, 60.

56. *New York Times*, August 7, 1970, p. 26; Huston to Haldeman, August 7, 1970, in U.S. Senate Select Committee, *Hearings*, 2:254; *New York Times*, November 1, 1970, p. 6.

57. Kissinger, *White House Years*, 968, 969.

58. Safire, *Before the Fall*, 288. For those who wanted a statement on the trouble on the campuses, Nixon sent out copies of a Sidney Hook column from the *Los Angeles Times* of August 30, 1970. See boxes 25–27, HU 3–1, WHCF, NP.

59. Safire, *Before the Fall*, 170–171; Harris, *Dreams Die Hard*, 219. In July, Nixon had proclaimed that he wanted "peace on the campus, but my major obligation is to adopt policies that I consider will bring peace to the world." *DSB* 63 (August 10, 1970):164.

60. Nixon, *RN*, 492. Sometimes Nixon tried to avoid such demonstrations. Chapin to Ron Walker, August 26, 1970, box 24, HU 3–1, WHCF, NP.

61. Kissinger, *White House Years*, 984, 976.

62. Schemmer, *The Raid*, 164.

63. Memo for Alexander Butterfield, November 28, 1970, box 8, PH, POF, NP.

64. Kissinger, *Years of Upheaval*, 101.

65. Zaroulis and Sullivan, *Who Spoke Up?* 347. Some in the movement had already decided that mass demonstrations had run their course. Katz, *Ban the Bomb*, 115–116. For the media treatment, see the *New York Times*, February 9, 1971, p. 16; February 11, 1971, p. 15; and February 12, 1971, p. 14.

66. Kissinger, *White House Years*, 1012. Of these days he wrote that the White House was "more absorbed in fending off the assaults of its critics at home than the assaults of the enemy in the field" and that, at home, almost a "civil war" was going on (pp. 1010, 1011).

67. Leslie Bacon, a prominent radical suspected of bombing activities, was arrested on April 27 as well.

68. Larry Higby to Haldeman, April 7, 1971, box 16, Alphabetic Subject file, Ehrlichman Papers, NP.

69. Meetings with protesters continued through the first two years of the Nixon administration. Kissinger himself counted nineteen meetings with students, twenty-nine with academics, and thirty with other assorted critics from April 1970 to April 1971. Kissinger, *White House Years*, 1015.

70. See Dean to Haldeman and Ehrlichman, April 24, 1971, box 83, Dean Papers, NP.

71. Schell, *Time of Illusion*, 148–149; *DSB* 64 (May 10, 1971):596, and (May 17, 1971):629.

72. Zaroulis and Sullivan report the 500,000 figure in *Who Spoke Up?* 358.

73. Price, interview. Bryce Harlow recalls vividly the violence of the week and how difficult and potentially dangerous he found it to try to drive to and from the White House. Harlow, interview.

74. See box 83 for the reports and box 87 for the declaration in the Dean Papers, NP. See also Dean's memo to John Nidecker on April 30, 1971, in box 83, Dean Papers, NP, on how to make the White House look like it was operating on a business-as-usual basis during the crisis.

75. Ehrlichman, interview. One author even dates the end of the movement to the previous year, with Cambodia "a brief swansong." Young, *An Infantile Disorder*, 360.

76. William Bundy, interview.

77. Many Americans did not know or care about *The Pentagon Papers*. Those that did split on the *Times'* action. Foster, *Activism Replaces Isolationism*, 319.

78. Dotson Rader, "The Day the Movement Died," *Esquire* 99 (June 1983):312. See also Sam Brown, "The Defeat of the Antiwar Movement," in Lake, *Vietnam Legacy*, 120–127; and Frederick D. Miller, "The End of SDS and the Emergence of Weathermen: Demise Through Success," in Jo Freeman, ed., *Social Movements of the Sixties and Seventies* (New York: Longman, 1983), 279–297.

79. Hayden, interview. Winston Lord agrees with Hayden's

deemphasis of the draft as a factor in the decline of the movement. Lord, interview. Abbie Hoffman stresses the success of Nixon's repressive tactics. Hoffman, interview.

80. Henkin, interview. Ray Price and George Ball concur. Price; Ball, interviews.

81. The same poll revealed only 31 percent support for Nixon's Vietnam policy at that point. Harris, *Anguish of Change,* 72–73. Nixon would soon recoup his losses on that question.

82. At the time, the author was not at all certain about the "success" of the movement. When Richard Nixon began to campaign on the platform that casualties in the war had been reduced 95 percent during his presidency, the author sent a letter to the *New York Times,* one of the papers carrying his advertisements, to point out that Nixon's campaign committee had left out the word *American* to modify "casualties" and thus had ignored the Asian death toll. The letter was not accepted for publication.

83. Gelb, *Irony of Vietnam,* 356–357; Lubell, *Future While It Happened,* 83, 88.

84. His approval rating on Vietnam policy in this period was close to 60 percent. "Report No. 90," *Gallup Opinion Index* (December, 1972):2.

85. The North Vietnamese claim their accurate antiaircraft fire, which brought down so many B-52's, compelled the United States to sue for peace on their terms. Bui Xuan Ninh, interview.

86. For a discussion of this theme, see Nguyen Tien Hung and Jarrold L. Schecter, *The Palace File* (New York: Harper & Row, 1986), 74–75.

CHAPTER 8: CONCLUSION

1. Dwight Chapin feels that the movement "brought down Johnson and tried to bring down Nixon." Chapin, interview.

2. Russ Braley titles his chapter on Watergate, "A Foreign Affair." Braley, *Bad News,* 434–451. Henry Kissinger also links the movement to Watergate. Kissinger, *Years of Upheaval,* 89.

3. Berkowitz, "Impact of Anti-Vietnam Demonstrations," 13.

4. Horowitz, *Struggle Is the Message,* 56–58.

5. Graff, interview. Dean Rusk centers on the role of only a few opinion leaders and chance. Things might have been different, he says, if John Oakes and Ben Bradlee had not been in charge of the editorial pages of the *Times* and the *Post.* Rusk, interview.

6. Palmer, *25-Year War,* 190.

7. Rusk, interview.

8. Harlow, interview.

9. Norman Podhoretz, *Why We Were in Vietnam* (New York: Simon & Schuster, 1982), 107–108, 124. On the significance of the moral argument with activists, see Ellen Frey-Wouters and Robert S. Laufer, *Legacy of a War: The American Soldier in Vietnam* (Armonk, N.Y.: M. E.

Sharpe, 1986), 105. Walt Rostow was offended by the simplicity of the argument. Rostow, interview, and *Diffusion of Power*, 492–495. John Roche, on the other hand, downplayed the moral issues and emphasized isolationism as the key to the relative success of the doves. Roche, "Impact of Dissent," 135.

10. Rostow, *Diffusion of Power*, 199.

11. Irving Kristol, "American Intellectuals and Foreign Policy," *Foreign Affairs* 45 (July 1967):596.

12. Kadushin, *American Intellectual Elite*, 127, 137, 178.

13. Ibid., 349–350.

14. Christian, interview; Goldman, *Tragedy of Lyndon Johnson*, 163.

15. That establishment is not revered by everyone. John Kenneth Galbraith noted that "the foreign policy elite was always the world's biggest collection of meatheads." Hodgson, "The Establishment," 4.

16. Christian, interview. Walt Rostow's brother, Eugene, told him toward the end of the Johnson administration that 90 percent of college students opposed the war. Although such news did not bother the national security adviser, he reports that it did bother others in the administration. Rostow, interview.

17. Lord, interview.

18. Christian, interview; Humphrey, *Education*, 363; Edith Efron, *The News Twisters* (Los Angeles: Nash, 1971); Braestrup, *Big Story*. See also Sidle, "Role of Journalists"; and Elegant, "How to Lose a War."

19. Gitlin, *Whole World Is Watching*, 242–243. Dean Rusk and Ramsey Clark also emphasize the importance of the media in publicizing the movement. Rusk; Clark, interviews.

20. Dellinger, *More Power than We Know*, 117; Small, *To Kill a Messenger*, 129–131; J. Fred MacDonald, *Television and the Red Menace: The Video Road to Vietnam* (New York: Praeger, 1985), 225–226.

21. Daniel C. Hallin, *The "Uncensored War": The Media and Vietnam* (New York: Oxford University Press, 1986); Herbert Gans, *Deciding What's News: A Study of the CBS Evening News, NBC Nightly News, Newsweek and Time* (New York: Random House, 1980), 279–280, 135–136. See also Aronson, *Press and the Cold War*, 232, on the decline of dovish views among the journalists in Vietnam *after* 1965; and Robert Entman and David L. Paletz, "The War in Southeast Asia: Tunnel Vision on Television," in William C. Adams, ed., *Television Coverage of International Affairs* (Norwood, N.J.: Ablex Pub. Co., 1982), 181–196; Phillip Knightley, *The First Casualty* (New York: Harcourt, Brace, 1975), 374–400; Michael Arlen, *The Living Room War* (New York: Viking, 1969), 8, 14–15, 239–240; and Ernest Gruening, *Many Battles: The Autobiography of Ernest Gruening* (New York: Liveright, 1973), 475–476. For the persistence of media opposition to dissent in our period, see Loeb, *Hope in Hard Times*, 214.

22. This is one general conclusion of Montague Kern, Patricia W. Levering, and Ralph B. Levering, *The Kennedy Crises: The Press, The*

Presidency and Foreign Policy (Chapel Hill: University of North Carolina Press, 1983).

23. Michael Baruch Grossman and Martha Joynt Kumar, *Portraying the President: The White House and the News Media* (Baltimore, Md.: Johns Hopkins University Press, 1981).

24. Kattenburg, *Vietnam Trauma*, 266.

25. Edward Jay Epstein, *Between Fact and Fiction: The Problem of Journalism* (New York: Vintage, 1975), 220–221.

26. For an interesting overview of the problem, see Michael Mandelbaum, "Vietnam: The Television War," *Daedalus* 3 (Fall 1982):157–169.

27. For an attempt to apply some of the lessons learned to protests in general, see Small, "Influencing the Decision Makers."

Selected Bibliography

The literature on the diplomatic, military, and political history of American involvement in the Vietnam War is a rich one. The best guide to that literature is Richard Dean Burns and Milton Leitenberg, eds., *The Wars in Vietnam, Cambodia and Laos, 1945–82* (Santa Barbara, Calif.: ABC Clio, 1983). For the period after 1982, the annotated listings in *Indochina Chronology*, a quarterly published by the University of California at Berkeley's Institute of East Asian Studies, are most valuable. The best single overview of the war, which also contains a perceptive bibliographic essay, is George C. Herring, *America's Longest War: The United States and Vietnam: 1950–1975* (New York: Knopf, 1986). Useful for the contemporary record of events, documents, and speeches were the *New York Times* and its index and the *Department of State Bulletin*.

What follows is a list of materials cited in the text. It represents only some of the many important sources available to the student of the Vietnam War.

I. UNPUBLISHED SOURCES

A. Interviews Conducted by the Author

George Ball, Trenton, New Jersey, March 5, 1984
Bui Xuan Ninh, New York, New York, June 15, 1983
McGeorge Bundy, New York, New York, March 9, 1984
William P. Bundy, New York, New York, March 6, 1984
Douglass Cater, telephone, February 4, 1984
Dwight Chapin, telephone, April 3, 1984
George Christian, Austin, Texas, May 18, 1983
Ramsey Clark, New York, New York, March 9, 1984
Clark Clifford, Washington, D.C., February 9, 1984
John Ehrlichman, telephone, May 1, 1984
Jana Hruska Fagan, Brockport, New York, February 8, 1987
J. W. Fulbright, Washington, D.C., February 7, 1984
Leonard Garment, Washington, D.C., August 1, 1984
Leslie H. Gelb, Washington, D.C., July 31, 1984
Eric F. Goldman, Princeton, New Jersey, March 5, 1984
Henry A. Graff, New York, New York, March 6, 1984
H. R. Haldeman, Los Angeles, California, November 14, 1985
Bryce Harlow, Washington, D.C., February 7, 1984

Tom Hayden, Los Angeles, California, November 15, 1985
Daniel Z. Henkin, Washington, D.C., February 9, 1984
Helga Herz, Detroit, Michigan, April 5, 1984
Abbie Hoffman, Detroit, Michigan, October 17, 1985
Tom Johnson, Los Angeles, California, November 15, 1985
James Keogh, New York, New York, March 18, 1984
Winston Lord, New York, New York, March 18, 1984
Harry McPherson, Washington, D.C., February 9, 1984
Daniel Patrick Moynihan, en route from Washington to New York,
    August 4, 1984
Ray Price, New York, New York, March 9, 1984
George Reedy, Milwaukee, Wisconsin, January 25, 1984
John P. Roche, Medford, Massachusetts, March 12, 1984
Peter Rodman, Washington, D.C., August 1, 1984
Walt W. Rostow, Austin, Texas, May 20, 1983; telephone,
    April 9, 1987
Dean Rusk, Athens, Georgia, February 23, 1984
Cliff Sessions, telephone, May 4, 1984
James C. Thomson, Jr., telephone, March 13, 1984
Jack Valenti, Washington, D.C., February 10, 1984
Cyrus Vance, New York, New York, March 8, 1984
Paul Warnke, Washington, D.C., July 31, 1984
Harry Zubkoff, Washington, D.C., August 3, 1984

B. Archival Sources

American Friends of Vietnam Papers, Michigan State University Archives,
    East Lansing, Michigan
Lyndon Johnson Papers and records of his presidency, Lyndon B. Johnson
    Presidential Library, Austin, Texas
Nixon Presidential Materials Project, National Archives, Alexandria,
    Virginia
Richard B. Russell Papers, Richard B. Russell Memorial Library, Athens,
    Georgia

C. Oral Histories from the Lyndon Johnson Library

Bess Abell	Lewis B. Hershey
Stewart J. Alsop	Benjamin H. Read
Zbigniew Brzezinski	John P. Roche
William P. Bundy	Harrison Salisbury
George E. Christian	Arthur M. Schlesinger, Jr.
Frank Church	Bromley K. Smith
Ramsey Clark	James C. Thomson, Jr.
Clark Clifford	Jack Valenti
Chester L. Cooper	Cyrus Vance
Lloyd Hackler	Earle G. Wheeler
Richard M. Helms	

D. Ph.D. Dissertations

Hamre, John J. "Congressional Dissent and American Foreign Policy: Constitutional War Making in the Vietnam Years." Johns Hopkins University, 1978.

Jerneck, Magnus. "Kritik som Utrikespolitiskt Medel: En Studie av de Amerikanska Reactionerna pa den Svenska Vietnamkritiken." Lund, 1983.

Pyle, Christopher H. "Military Surveillance of Civilian Politics, 1967–70." Columbia University, 1974.

Rosenberg, Michael P. "Congress and the Vietnam War: A Study of the Critics of the War in 1967 and 1968." New School for Social Research, 1973.

Schreiber, E. M. "American Public Opinion and the War in Vietnam: 1964–1968." Princeton University, 1970.

E. Other Unpublished Sources

Bundy, William. Unpublished and uncompleted manuscript on the history of the Vietnam War to 1965.

Christian, George. Comments on "Our World," ABC Television, June 11, 1987.

DeBenedetti, Charles. "The Antiwar Movement in America 1955–1975," unpublished manuscript.

Ford, Gerald. Transcript of interview conducted by Representative David Bonior, November 9, 1982.

Kitt, Eartha. Interview on National Public Radio's "Morning Edition," October 24, 1985.

"Vietnam: A Television History," Public Broadcasting System.

Weinraub, Bernard. Transcript of interview conducted by Representative David Bonior, 1982.

II. PUBLISHED PRIMARY MATERIALS

A. Documents

Appendices A and B to Memorandum in Support of CBS' Motion to Dismiss and for Summary Judgment, *William Westmoreland v. CBS et al.* U.S. District Court, Southern District of New York, 1984.

BDM Corporation. *A Study of the Strategic Lessons Learned in Vietnam.* Vol. 4. Washington, D.C.: United States Department of the Army, 1979.

Daily Diary of President Johnson, 1963–1969. Microfilm. Frederick, Md.: University Publications of America, 1980.

Declassified Documents. Washington, D.C.: Carrollton Press.

Documents of the National Security Council. Second Supplement. Microfilm. Frederick, Md.: University Publications of America, 1983.

McNamara, Robert S. Deposition. *William Westmoreland v. CBS et al.,* 1984.

Memorandum in Support of Defendant CBS' Motion to Dismiss and for Summary Judgment. *William Westmoreland v. CBS et al.*, 1984.

Minutes and Documents of the Cabinet Meetings of President Johnson, 1963–1969. Microfilm. Frederick, Md.: University Publications of America, 1982.

The Pentagon Papers. Senator Gravel edition. Vols. 3 and 4. Boston: Beacon, 1971.

Presidential Documents Series. *Vietnam, the Media, and Public Support for the War*. Selections from Holdings of the Lyndon Baines Johnson Library. Microfilm. Frederick, Md.: University Publications of America, 1986.

Public Papers of the President. Richard M. Nixon, 1969. Washington, D.C.: GPO, 1971.

Report of the President's Commission on Campus Unrest. New York: Arno, 1970.

Report to the President by the Commission on CIA Activity within the United States. Washington, D.C.: GPO, 1975.

United States House of Representatives. *Hearings Before the Select Committee on Intelligence*. 94th Congress, Part 3. Washington, D.C.: GPO, 1976.

United States Senate. Committee on Foreign Relations. *Foreign Assistance Act of 1968. Part I—Vietnam*. Washington, D.C.: GPO, 1968.

———. *Supplemental Foreign Assistance, Fiscal Year—1966—Vietnam*. Washington, D.C.: GPO, 1966.

———. *Select Committee to Study Intelligence Activities and the Rights of Americans. Final Report*. Book 2. Washington, D.C.: GPO, 1976.

———. *Hearings*. Vol. 2 (Huston Plan). Vol. 3 (IRS). Vol. 4 (NSA). Vol. 6 (FBI). Washington, D.C.: GPO, 1975.

B. Memoirs and Letters

Adams, Henry. *The Education of Henry Adams*. Boston: Houghton Mifflin, 1918.

Agnew, Spiro T. *Go Quietly . . . or Else*. New York: William Morrow, 1980.

Ashmore, Harry and William C. Baggs. *Mission to Hanoi—a Chronicle of Double-Dealing in High Places*. New York: Putnam, 1968.

Ball, George. *The Past Has Another Pattern: A Memoir*. New York: Norton, 1982.

Califano, Joseph. *A Presidential Nation*. New York: Norton, 1975.

Christian, George. *The President Steps Down: A Personal Memoir of the Transfer of Power*. New York: Macmillan, 1970.

Colson, Charles W. *Born Again*. New York: Bantam, 1976.

Dellinger, David. *More Power than We Know: The People's Movement toward Democracy*. Garden City, N.Y.: Doubleday, 1975.

Donovan, Hedley. *Roosevelt to Reagan: A Reporter's Encounters with Nine Presidents*. New York: Harper & Row, 1985.

Ehrlichman, John. *Witness to Power*. New York: Simon & Schuster, 1972.

Ford, Gerald. *A Time to Heal.* New York: Harper & Row, 1979.

Frankel, Charles. *High on Foggy Bottom: An Outsider's Inside View of Government.* New York: Harper & Row, 1968.

Friendly, Fred W. *Due to Circumstances Beyond Our Control.* New York: Random House, 1967.

Frost, David. *I Gave Them a Sword: Behind the Scenes of the Nixon Interviews.* New York: William Morrow, 1978.

Goulding, Phil G. *Confirm or Deny: Informing the People on National Security.* New York: Harper & Row, 1970.

Gruening, Ernest. *Many Battles: An Autobiography of Ernest Gruening.* New York: Liveright, 1973.

Haldeman, H. R. *The Ends of Power.* New York: Times Books, 1978.

Halstead, Fred. *Out Now: A Participant's Account of the American Movement Against the Vietnam War.* New York: Monad, 1978.

Harriman, W. Averell. *America and Russia in a Changing World: A Half Century of Personal Observations.* Garden City, N.Y.: Doubleday, 1971.

Hickel, Walter J. *Who Owns America?* Englewood Cliffs, N.J.: Prentice-Hall, 1971.

Humphrey, Hubert. *The Education of a Public Man: My Life and Politics.* Garden City, N.Y.: Doubleday, 1976.

Johnson, Lady Bird. *A White House Diary.* New York: Holt, Rinehart, 1970.

Johnson, Lyndon Baines. *The Vantage Point: Perspectives of the Presidency, 1963–1969.* New York: Holt, Rinehart, 1971.

Keogh, James. *President Nixon and the Press.* New York: Funk and Wagnall, 1972.

Kissinger, Henry. *White House Years.* Boston: Little, Brown, 1979.

———. *Years of Upheaval.* Boston: Little, Brown, 1982.

Klein, Herbert. *Making It Perfectly Clear.* Garden City, N.Y.: Doubleday, 1980.

Lens, Sidney. *Unrepentant Radical: An American Activist's Account of Five Turbulent Decades.* Boston: Beacon, 1980.

McCarthy, Abigail. *Private Faces/Public Places.* Garden City, N.Y.: Doubleday, 1972.

McCarthy, Eugene S. *The Year of the People.* Garden City, N.Y.: Doubleday, 1969.

McLellan, David S. and David C. Acheson, eds. *Among Friends: Personal Letters of Dean Acheson.* New York: Dodd, Mead, 1980.

McPherson, Harry. *A Political Education.* Boston: Little, Brown, 1972.

Magruder, Jeb Stuart. *An American Life: One Man's Road to Watergate.* New York: Atheneum, 1974.

Mailer, Norman. *The Armies of the Night: History as a Novel, the Novel as History.* New York: New American Library, 1968.

Nixon, Richard. *RN: The Memoirs of Richard Nixon.* New York: Warner, 1978.

Price, Raymond. *With Nixon.* New York: Viking, 1977.

Reedy, George. *Lyndon B. Johnson: A Memoir.* New York: Andrews and McMeel, 1982.

Riegle, Don. *O Congress.* Garden City, N.Y.: Doubleday, 1972.

Roche, John P. *Sentenced to Life.* New York: Macmillan, 1974.

Rostow, W. W. *The Diffusion of Power: An Essay in Recent History.* New York: Macmillan, 1972.

Safire, William. *Before the Fall: An Inside View of the Pre-Watergate White House.* Garden City, N.Y.: Doubleday, 1975.

Salisbury, Harrison E. *Behind the Lines—Hanoi.* New York: Harper & Row, 1967.

Sharp, U. S. Grant. *Strategy for Defeat: Vietnam in Retrospect.* San Rafael, Calif.: Presidio, 1978.

Tang, Truong Nhu. *A Vietcong Memoir: An Inside Account of the Vietnam War and Its Aftermath.* New York: Harcourt, Brace, 1985.

Taylor, Maxwell D. *Swords and Plowshares.* New York: Norton, 1972.

Toai, Doan Van and David Chanoff. *The Vietnamese Gulag.* New York: Simon & Schuster, 1986.

Truman, Harry S. *Memoirs.* Vol. 2. Garden City, N.Y.: Doubleday, 1956.

Valenti, Jack. *A Very Human President.* New York: Norton, 1975.

Valeriani, Richard. *Travels with Henry.* Boston: Houghton Mifflin, 1979.

Westmoreland, William C. *A Soldier Reports.* Garden City, N.Y.: Doubleday, 1976.

Zumwalt, Elmo R. *On Watch.* New York: Quadrangle, 1976.

III. PUBLISHED SECONDARY MATERIALS

A. Books

Adler, Renata. *Reckless Disregard: Westmoreland v. CBS et al.; Sharon v. Time.* New York: Knopf, 1986.

Altheide, David L. *Creating Reality: How TV News Distorts Events.* Beverly Hills, Calif.: Sage, 1976.

Arlen, Michael J. *The Living-Room War.* New York: Viking, 1969.

Aronson, James. *Deadline for the Media: Today's Challenges to Press, TV and Radio.* Indianapolis: Bobbs-Merrill, 1972.

———. *The Press and the Cold War.* Indianapolis: Bobbs-Merrill, 1970.

Baral, Jaya Krishna. *The Pentagon and the Making of U.S. Foreign Policy: A Case Study of Vietnam, 1960–1968.* Atlantic Highlands, N.J.: Humanities Press, 1978.

Baskir, Lawrence M. and William A. Strauss. *Chance and Circumstance: The Draft, the War and the Vietnam Generation.* New York: Knopf, 1978.

Berman, Larry. *Planning a Tragedy: The Americanization of the War in Vietnam.* New York: Norton, 1982.

Block, Fred L. *The Origins of International Economic Disorder: A Study of United States Monetary Policy from World War II to the Present.* Berkeley: University of California Press, 1977.

Bogart, Leo. *Silent Politics: Polls and the Awareness of Public Opinion.* New York: Wiley, 1972.

Bornet, Vaughan Davis. *The Presidency of Lyndon B. Johnson.* Lawrence: University Press of Kansas, 1983.

Braestrup, Peter. *Big Story: How the American Press and Television Reported and Interpreted the Crises of Tet in Vietnam and Washington.* Boulder, Colo.: Westview, 1977.

———, ed. *Vietnam as History: Ten Years After the Paris Peace Accords.* Washington, D.C.: University Press of America, 1984.

Braley, Russ. *Bad News: The Foreign Policy of the New York Times.* Chicago: Regnery Gateway, 1984.

Brown, Eugene. *J. William Fulbright: Advice and Dissent.* Iowa City: University of Iowa Press, 1985.

Castleman, Harry and Walter J. Podrazik. *Watching TV: Four Decades of American Television.* New York: McGraw-Hill, 1982.

Coffin, Tristram. *Senator Fulbright: Portrait of a Public Philosopher.* New York: Dutton, 1966.

Cohen, Bernard C. *The Press and Foreign Policy.* Princeton, N.J.: Princeton University Press, 1963.

———. *The Public's Impact on Foreign Policy.* Boston: Little, Brown, 1973.

Cohen, Warren. *Dean Rusk.* Totowa, N.J.: Cooper Square, 1980.

Cole, Wayne S. *Roosevelt and the Isolationists 1932–45.* Lincoln: University of Nebraska Press, 1983.

Cooper, Chester C. *The Lost Crusade: America in Vietnam.* New York: Dodd, Mead, 1970.

Cortright, David. *Soldiers in Revolt: The American Military Today.* Garden City, N.Y.: Doubleday, 1975.

Cummings, Richard. *The Pied Piper: Allard K. Lowenstein and the Liberal Dream.* New York: Grove, 1985.

DeBenedetti, Charles. *The Peace Reform in American History.* Bloomington: Indiana University Press, 1980.

Destler, I. M. *Presidents, Bureaucrats and Foreign Policy: The Politics of Organizational Reform.* Princeton, N.J.: Princeton University Press, 1974.

Donner, Frank J. *The Age of Surveillance: The Aims and Methods of America's Intelligence System.* New York: Knopf, 1980.

Donovan, Robert J. *Nemesis: Truman and Johnson in the Coils of War in Asia.* New York: St. Martin's, 1984.

Draper, Theodore. *Abuse of Power.* New York: Viking, 1967.

Efron, Edith. *The News Twisters.* Los Angeles: Nash, 1971.

Elliff, John T. *Crime, Dissent, and the Attorney General: The Justice Department in the 1960's.* Beverly Hills, Calif.: Sage, 1981.

Epstein, Edward Jay. *Between Fact and Fiction: The Problem of Journalism.* New York: Vintage, 1975.

Evans, Rowland and Robert Novak. *Lyndon B. Johnson: The Exercise of Power.* New York: New American Library, 1966.

Ferber, Michael and Staughton Lynd. *The Resistance.* Boston: Beacon, 1971.

Foster, H. Schuyler. *Activism Replaces Isolationism: U.S. Public Attitudes, 1940–1975.* Washington, D.C.: Foxhall, 1983.

Frantzich, Stephen E. *Write Your Congressman: Constituent Communications and Representation.* New York: Praeger, 1986.

Frey-Wouters, Ellen and Robert S. Laufer. *Legacy of a War: The American Soldier in Vietnam.* Armonk, N.Y.: M. E. Sharpe, 1986.

Fulbright, J. William. *The Arrogance of Power.* New York: Random House, 1966.

Gans, Herbert. *Deciding What's News: A Study of CBS Evening News, NBC Nightly News, Newsweek and Time.* New York: Random House, 1980.

Garrow, David J. *Bearing the Cross: Martin Luther King, Jr., and the Southern Christian Leadership Conference.* New York: Morrow, 1986.

———. *The FBI and Martin Luther King: From Solo to Memphis.* New York: Norton, 1981.

Gelb, Leslie H. with Richard K. Betts. *The Irony of Vietnam: The System Worked.* Washington, D.C.: Brookings, 1979.

Gibbons, William Conrad. *The U.S. Government and the Vietnam War: Executive and Legislative Roles and Relationships, Part II, 1961–1964.* Princeton, N.J.: Princeton University Press, 1986.

Gitlin, Todd. *The Whole World Is Watching: Mass Media in the Making and Unmaking of the New Left.* Berkeley: University of California Press, 1980.

Goldman, Eric F. *The Tragedy of Lyndon Johnson.* New York: Knopf, 1969.

Goodman, Allen E. *The Lost Peace: America's Search for a Negotiated Settlement of the Vietnam War.* Stanford: Hoover Institution, 1978.

Goulden, Joseph C. *Truth Is the First Casualty: The Gulf of Tonkin Affair—Illusion and Reality.* Chicago: Rand McNally, 1969.

Graff, Henry A. *The Tuesday Cabinet: Deliberation and Decision on Peace and War under Lyndon Johnson.* Englewood Cliffs, N.J.: Prentice-Hall, 1970.

Grossman, Michael Baruch and Martha Joynt Kumar. *Portraying the President: The White House and the News Media.* Baltimore, Md.: Johns Hopkins University Press, 1981.

Halberstam, David. *The Best and the Brightest.* New York: Fawcett, 1973.

———. *The Powers That Be.* New York: Knopf, 1979.

Hallin, Daniel C. *The "Uncensored War": The Media and Vietnam.* New York: Oxford University Press, 1986.

Harris, David. *Dreams Die Hard.* New York: St. Martin's, 1982.

Harris, Louis. *The Anguish of Change.* New York: Norton, 1974.

Heath, G. Louis, ed. *Mutiny Does Not Happen Lightly: The Literature of the American Resistance to the Vietnam War.* Metuchen, N.J.: Scarecrow, 1976.

Herring, George C. *America's Longest War: The United States and Vietnam, 1950–1975.* New York: Knopf, 1986.

——, ed. *The Secret Diplomacy of the Vietnam War: The Negotiating Volumes of the Pentagon Papers.* Austin: University of Texas Press, 1983.

Hersh, Seymour M. *The Price of Power: Kissinger in the Nixon White House.* New York: Summit, 1983.

Hodgson, Godfrey. *America in Our Time.* New York: Vintage, 1978.

Hoopes, Townsend. *The Limits of Intervention.* New York: David McKay, 1969.

Horowitz, Irving Louis. *The Struggle Is the Message: The Organization and Ideology of the Anti-war Movement.* Berkeley, Calif.: Glendessary, 1970.

Hughes, Barry B. *The Domestic Context of American Foreign Policy.* San Francisco: W. H. Freeman, 1978.

Hung, Nguyen Tien and Jarrold L. Schecter, *The Palace File.* New York: Harper & Row, 1986.

Isaacson, Walter and Evan Thomas. *The Wise Men: Six Friends and the World They Made.* New York: Simon & Schuster, 1986.

Janis, Irving L. *Victims of Groupthink: A Psychological Study of Foreign-Policy Decisions and Fiascos.* Boston: Houghton Mifflin, 1972.

Joseph, Paul. *Cracks in the Empire—State Politics in the Vietnam War.* Boston: South End, 1981.

Kadushin, Charles. *The American Intellectual Elite.* Boston: Little, Brown, 1974.

Kahin, George McT. *Intervention: How America Became Involved in Vietnam.* New York: Knopf, 1986.

Kalb, Bernard and Marvin Kalb. *Kissinger.* London: Hutchinson, 1974.

Karnow, Stanley. *Vietnam: A History.* New York: Viking, 1983.

Kattenburg, Paul M. *The Vietnam Trauma in American Foreign Policy: 1945–75.* New Brunswick, N.J.: Transaction, 1980.

Katz, Elihu and Paul F. Lazarsfeld. *Personal Influence: The Part Played by People in the Flow of Mass Communication.* Glencoe, Ill.: Free Press, 1955.

Kearns, Doris. *Lyndon Johnson and the American Dream.* New York: Signet, 1977.

Kelman, Steve. *Push Comes to Shove.* Boston: Houghton Mifflin, 1970.

Kern, Montague, Patricia W. Levering, and Ralph B. Levering. *The Kennedy Crises: The Press, the Presidency, and Foreign Policy.* Chapel Hill: University of North Carolina Press, 1983.

Knightley, Phillip. *The First Casualty.* New York: Harcourt, Brace, 1975.

Kolko, Gabriel. *Anatomy of a War: Vietnam, the United States and the Modern Historical Experience.* New York: Pantheon, 1985.

Kowet, Don. *A Matter of Honor.* New York: Macmillan, 1984.

Kraslow, David and Stuart H. Loory. *The Secret Search for Peace in Vietnam.* New York: Random House, 1968.

Krepinevich, Andrew F., Jr. *The Army and Vietnam.* Baltimore, Md.: Johns Hopkins University Press, 1986.

Kusnitz, Leonard A. *Public Opinion and Foreign Policy: America's China Policy, 1949–1979.* Westport, Conn.: Greenwood, 1984.

Landau, David. *Kissinger: The Uses of Power.* Boston: Houghton Mifflin, 1972.

Lesher, Stephen. *Media Unbound: The Impact of Television Journalism on the Public.* Boston: Houghton Mifflin, 1982.

Loeb, Paul Rogat. *Hope in Hard Times: America's Peace Movement in the Reagan Era.* Lexington, Mass.: D. C. Heath, 1986.

Lubell, Samuel. *The Future While It Happened.* New York: Norton, 1973.

MacDonald, J. Fred. *Television and the Red Menace: The Video Road to Vietnam.* New York: Praeger, 1985.

May, Ernest R. *American Imperialism: A Speculative Essay.* New York: Atheneum, 1968.

Miller, Merle. *Lyndon: An Oral Biography.* New York: Putnam, 1980.

Morison, Samuel Eliot, Frederick Merk, and Frank Freidel. *Dissent in Three American Wars.* Cambridge, Mass.: Harvard University Press, 1970.

Morris, Roger. *Uncertain Greatness: Henry Kissinger and American Foreign Policy.* New York: Harper & Row, 1977.

Mueller, John E. *War, Presidents, and Public Opinion.* New York: Wiley, 1973.

Newfield, Jack. *A Prophetic Minority.* New York: New American Library, 1966.

Nixon, Richard. *No More Vietnams.* New York: Arbor House, 1985.

Palmer, Bruce. *The 25-Year War: America's Military Role in Vietnam.* Lexington: University of Kentucky Press, 1984.

Peterson, Richard E. *The Scope of Organized Student Protest in 1964–1965.* Princeton, N.J.: Educational Testing Service, 1966.

Podhoretz, Norman. *Why We Were in Vietnam.* New York: Simon & Schuster, 1982.

Powers, Thomas. *The War at Home: Vietnam and the American People, 1964–1968.* New York: Grossman, 1973.

Radvanyi, Janos. *Delusion and Reality: Gambits, Hoaxes and Diplomatic One-Upmanship in Vietnam.* South Bend, Ind.: Gateway, 1978.

Reedy, George C. *The Twilight of the Presidency.* New York: World, 1970.

Rosenau, James N. *Public Opinion and Foreign Policy.* New York: Random House, 1961.

Rosenberg, Milton J., Sidney Verba, and Philip E. Converse. *Vietnam and the Silent Majority: A Dove's Guide.* New York: Harper & Row, 1970.

Sale, Kirkpatrick. *SDS: Ten Years toward a Revolution.* New York: Random House, 1973.

Schandler, Herbert Y. *The Unmaking of a President: Lyndon Johnson and Vietnam.* Princeton, N.J.: Princeton University Press, 1977.

Schell, Jonathan. *The Time of Illusion.* New York: Vintage, 1976.

Schemmer, Benjamin F. *The Raid.* London: MacDonald and Jane's, 1977.

Schevitz, Jeffrey M. *The Weaponsmakers: Personal and Professional Crisis During the Vietnam War.* Cambridge, Mass.: Schenkman, 1979.

Schlesinger, Arthur M., Jr. *Robert Kennedy and His Times.* Boston: Houghton Mifflin, 1978.

Schott, Richard L. and Dagmar Hamilton. *People, Positions, and Power: The Political Appointments of Lyndon Johnson.* Chicago: University of Chicago Press, 1984.

Shawcross, William. *Kissinger, Nixon and the Destruction of Cambodia.* New York: Simon & Schuster, 1979.

Shibata, Shingo. *Phoenix: Letters and Documents of Alice Herz.* Amsterdam: B. R. Gruner, 1976.

Skolnick, Jerome. *The Politics of Protest.* New York: Simon & Schuster, 1969.

Small, William. *To Kill a Messenger: Television News and the Real World.* New York: Hastings House, 1970.

Smith, Curt. *Long Time Gone: The Years of Turmoil Remembered.* South Bend, Ind.: Icarus, 1982.

Solberg, Carl. *Hubert Humphrey: A Biography.* New York: Norton, 1984.

Spear, Joseph. *Presidents and the Press: The Nixon Legacy.* Cambridge: M.I.T. Press, 1984.

Steel, Ronald. *Walter Lippmann and the American Century.* Boston: Little, Brown, 1980.

Stenelo, Lars-Goran. *The International Critic.* Lund, Sweden: Student Litteratur, 1984.

Summers, Harry G., Jr. *On Strategy: The Vietnam War in Context.* Carlisle Barracks, Pa.: U.S. Army War College, Strategic Studies Institute, 1981.

Talese, Gay. *The Kingdom and the Power.* New York: World, 1969.

Tebbel, John and Sarah Miles Watts. *The Press and the Presidency: From George Washington to Ronald Reagan.* New York: Oxford University Press, 1985.

Thayer, Thomas C. *War without Fronts: The American Experience in Vietnam.* Boulder, Colo.: Westview, 1985.

Theoharis, Athan. *Spying on Americans: Political Surveillance from Hoover to the Huston Plan.* Philadelphia: Temple University Press, 1978.

Thies, Wallace J. *When Governments Collide: Coercion and Diplomacy in the Vietnam Conflict, 1964–1968.* Berkeley: University of California Press, 1980.

Thompson, W. Scott and Donaldson D. Frizzell, eds. *The Lessons of Vietnam.* New York: Crane Russek, 1979.

Tuchman, Barbara. *The March of Folly: From Troy to Vietnam.* New York: Knopf, 1984.

Turner, Kathleen J. *Lyndon Johnson's Dual War: Vietnam and the Press.* Chicago: University of Chicago Press, 1985.

Unger, Irwin. *The Movement: A History of the American New Left, 1959–1972.* New York: Dodd, Mead, 1975.

Vargas Llosa, Mario. *The Real Life of Alejandro Mayta.* Translated by Alfred Mac Adam. New York: Farrar, Straus & Giroux, 1986.

Viorst, Milton. *Fire in the Streets: America in the 1960's.* New York: Simon & Schuster, 1980.

Vogelsgang, Sandy. *The Long Dark Night of the Soul: The American Intellectual Left and the Vietnam War.* New York: Harper & Row, 1974.

Warner, Denis. *Certain Victory: How Hanoi Won the War.* Kansas City: Sheed, Andrews and McMeel, 1978.

Weissberg, Robert. *Public Opinion and American Popular Government.* Englewood Cliffs, N.J.: Prentice-Hall, 1976.

Westin, Av. *Newswatch: How TV Decides the News.* New York: Simon & Schuster, 1982.

Whalen, Richard J. *Catch the Falling Flag: A Republican's Challenge to His Party.* Boston: Houghton Mifflin, 1972.

White, Theodore. *The Making of the President: 1968.* New York: Atheneum, 1969.

Williams, William A. et al. *America in Vietnam: A Documentary History.* Garden City, N.Y.: Anchor, 1985.

Wolfe, Thomas. *Radical Chic and Mau-Mauing the Flak Catchers.* New York: Farrar, Straus & Giroux, 1970.

Young, Nigel. *An Infantile Disorder: The Crisis and Decline of the New Left.* Boulder, Colo.: Westview, 1977.

Zaroulis, Nancy and Gerald Sullivan. *Who Spoke Up? American Protest Against the War in Vietnam, 1963–1975.* Garden City, N.Y.: Doubleday, 1984.

B. Articles

Andrews, Bruce. "Public Opinion and American Foreign Policy in Vietnam." *Sage Professional Paper in International Studies, 02-042. Vol. 4.* Beverly Hills, Calif.: Sage, 1976.

Armor, David J. et al. "Professors' Attitudes towards the Vietnam War." *Public Opinion Quarterly* 31 (Summer 1967):159–175.

Bayer, Alan E. and Alexander W. Astin. "Campus Unrest 1970–71: Was It Really All That Quiet?" *Educational Record* 52 (Fall 1971):301–313.

Beisner, Robert L. "1898 and 1968: The Anti-Imperialists and the Doves." *Political Science Quarterly* 85 (June 1970):187–216.

Berger, Peter L. "Indochina and the American Conscience." *Commentary* 69 (February 1980):29ff.

Berkowitz, William. "The Impact of Anti-Vietnam Demonstrations upon National Public Opinion and Military Indicators." *Social Science Research* 2 (March 1973):1–14.

Brands, Henry William, Jr. "Johnson and Eisenhower: The President, the Former President, and the War in Vietnam." *Presidential Studies Quarterly* 15 (Summer 1985):589–601.

Brown, Sam. "The Defeat of the Antiwar Movement." In Anthony Lake, ed., *The Vietnam Legacy: The War, American Society and the Future of American Foreign Policy* (New York: New York University Press, 1976), 120–127.

Burke, John P. "Responsibilities of Presidents and Advisers: A Theory and Case Study of Vietnam Decision Making." *Journal of Politics* 46 (August 1984):818–845.

Burstein, Paul and William Freudenberg. "Changing Public Policy: The Impact of Public Opinion, Antiwar Demonstrations, and War Costs on Senate Voting on Vietnam War Motions." *American Journal of Sociology* 84 (July 1978):99–122.

———. "Ending the Vietnam War: Components of Change in Senate Voting on Vietnam War Bills." *American Journal of Sociology* 82 (March 1977):991–1006.

Burton, Michael G. "Elite Disunity and Collective Protest: The Vietnam Case." *Journal of Military and Political Sociology* 5 (Fall 1977): 169–183.

Buzzanco, Bob. "The American Military's Rationale against the Vietnam War." *Political Science Quarterly* 101 (Winter 1986):559–576.

Caspary, William R. "The 'Mood Theory': A Study of Public Opinion and Foreign Policy." In Dan Nimmo and Charles M. Bonjean, eds., *Political Attitudes and Public Opinion* (New York: David McKay, 1972), 439–454.

Clifford, Clark M. "A Viet Nam Reappraisal: The Personal History of One Man's View and How It Evolved." *Foreign Affairs* 47 (July 1969):601–622.

Conlon, Thomas F. "The Truth Teams: A View from the Podium." In Louis Menashe and Ronald Radosh, eds., *Teach-Ins: U.S.A.: Reports, Opinions, Documents* (New York: Praeger, 1967), 128–131.

Converse, Philip E. and Howard Schuman. "Silent Majorities and the Vietnam War. *Scientific American* 222 (June 1970):17–25.

Corelis, John. "Kent State Reconsidered as Nightmare." *Journal of Psychohistory* 8 (Fall 1980):137–147.

Cotton, Timothy Y. C. "War and American Democracy: Electoral Costs of the Last Five Wars." *Journal of Conflict Resolution* 30 (December 1986):616–635.

DeBenedetti, Charles. "A CIA Analysis of the Anti-Vietnam War Movement, October, 1967." *Peace and Change* 9 (Spring 1983):31–42.

———. "On the Significance of Peace Activism: America, 1961–1975." *Peace and Change* 9 (Summer 1983):6–20.

Elegant, Robert. "How to Lose a War: Reflections of a Foreign Correspondent." *Encounter* 57 (August 1981):73–90.

Entman, Robert and David L. Paletz. "The War in Southeast Asia: Tunnel Vision on Television." In William C. Adams, ed. *Television Coverage of International Affairs* (Norwood, N.J.: Ablex, 1982), 181–202.

Fallows, James. "What Did You Do in the Class War, Daddy?" In A. D.

Horne, ed., *The Wounded Generation: America after Vietnam* (Englewood Cliffs, N.J.: Prentice-Hall, 1981), 15–29.

Frye, Alton and Jack Sullivan. "Congress and Vietnam: The Fruits of Anguish." In Lake, *Vietnam Legacy*, 194–215.

Gelb, Leslie H. "Dissenting on Consensus." In Lake, *Vietnam Legacy*, 102–119.

Geyelin, Philip. "Vietnam and the Press: Limited War and Open Society." In Lake, *Vietnam Legacy*, 166–193.

Gilbert, James. "The Teach-In: Protest or Co-optation." In Massimo Teodori, ed., *The New Left: A Documentary History* (Indianapolis: Bobbs-Merrill, 1969), 240–246.

Graff, Henry A. "Decision in Vietnam." *New York Times Magazine*, July 4, 1965, pp. 4–7ff.

Halperin, Morton H. "The Lessons Nixon Learned." In Lake, *Vietnam Legacy*, 411–428.

Hendrickson, Paul. "McNamara: Specters of Vietnam." *Washington Post*, May 10, 1984, pp. B1, 9–10.

Hixon, William B., Jr. "Nixon, the War and the Opposition: The First Year." *Journal of American Culture* 4 (Summer 1981):58–82.

Hodgson, Godfrey. "The Establishment." *Foreign Policy* 3 (Spring 1973):3–40.

Hoopes, Townsend. "LBJ's Account of March 1968." *New Republic* 162 (March 14, 1970):17–19.

Humphrey, David C. "Tuesday Lunch at the Johnson White House: A Preliminary Assessment." *Diplomatic History* 8 (Winter 1984): 81–101.

Johnson, Walter. "The U Thant–Stevenson Peace Initiatives in Vietnam, 1964–1965." *Diplomatic History* 1 (Summer 1977):185–195.

Keniston, Kenneth and Michael Lerner. "The Unholy Alliance." In Keniston, ed., *Youth and Dissent: The Rise of a New Opposition* (New York: Harcourt, Brace, 1971), 352–368.

Kristol, Irving. "American Intellectuals and Foreign Policy." *Foreign Affairs* 45 (July 1967):594–609.

Ladd, Everett C., Jr. "Professors and Political Petitions." *Science* 163 (March 28, 1969):1425–1430.

LaFeber, Walter. "The Last War, The Next War, and the New Revisionists." *Democracy* 1 (January 1981):272–282.

"LBJ Reminisces." *Among Friends of LBJ* 27 (January 1, 1983):2–7.

Levitas, Michael. "Vietnam Comes to Oregon U." In Menashe and Radosh, *Teach-Ins U.S.A.*, 16–23.

Lunch, William L. and Peter W. Sperlich. "American Public Opinion and the War in Vietnam." *Western Political Quarterly* 32 (March 1979):21–44.

Mandelbaum, Michael. "Vietnam: The Television War." *Daedalus* 3 (Fall 1982):157–169.

Miller, Frederick D. "The End of SDS and the Emergence of Weathermen:

Demise Through Success." In Jo Freeman, ed., *Social Movements of the Sixties and Seventies* (New York: Longman, 1983):279–297.

Miller, Warren E. and Donald E. Stokes. "Constituency Influence in Congress." In Nimmo and Bonjean, *Political Attitudes*, 543–561.

Mohr, Charles. "Once Again—Did the Press Lose Vietnam?" *Columbia Journalism Review* 22 (November 12, 1983):51–56.

Moyers, Bill. "Bill Moyers Talks about LBJ, Power, Poverty, War, and the Young." *Atlantic* 222 (July 1968):29–37.

———. "One Thing We Learned." *Foreign Affairs* 46 (July 1968):657–664.

Mueller, John E. "Reassessment of American Policy: 1965–68." In Harrison Salisbury, ed., *Vietnam Reconsidered: Lessons from a War* (New York: Harper & Row, 1984), 48–52.

———. "Reflections on the Vietnam Antiwar Movement and on the Curious Calm at the War's End." In Peter Braestrup, ed., *Vietnam as History: Ten Years after the Paris Peace Accords* (Washington, D.C.: University Press of America, 1984), 151–160.

O'Brien, James. "The Antiwar Movement and the War." *Radical America* 8 (May–June 1974):53–86.

Page, Benjamin and Richard Brody. "Policy Voting and the Electoral Process: The Vietnam War Issue." *American Political Science Review* 66 (November 1972):979–995.

Page, Benjamin and Robert Y. Shapiro. "Effects of Public Opinion on Policy." *American Political Science Review* 77 (March 1983): 175–195.

Rader, Dotson. "The Day the Movement Died." *Esquire* 99 (June 1983):304–320.

"Report No. 90." *Gallup Opinion Index* (December 1972).

Roberts, Priscilla M. "The American 'Eastern Establishment' and Foreign Affairs: A Challenge for Historians." *Society for Historians of American Foreign Relations Newsletter* 14 (December 1983):9–28.

Robinson, John P. "Balance Theory and Vietnam Related Attitudes." In Nimmo and Bonjean, *Political Attitudes*, 347–353.

Roche, John P. "The Impact of Dissent on Foreign Policy: Past and Future." In Lake, *Vietnam Legacy*, 128–138.

Scheinin, Richard. "Harry Zubkoff and His Pentagon Papers." *Washington Journalism Review* (March 1985):33–36, 38.

Schreiber, E. M. "Anti-War Demonstrations and American Public Opinion on the War in Vietnam." *British Journal of Sociology* 27 (June 1976):225–236.

Sevareid, Eric. "The Final Troubled Hours of Adlai Stevenson." *Look* 29 (November 30, 1965):81–84.

Sidle, Winant. "The Role of Journalists in Vietnam: An Army General's Perspective." In Salisbury, *Vietnam Reconsidered*, 111–112.

Small, Melvin. "The Impact of the Antiwar Movement on Lyndon Johnson: A Preliminary Report." *Peace and Change* 10 (Spring 1984):1–22.

————. "Influencing the Decision Makers: The Vietnam Experience," *Journal of Peace Research* 24, no. 2 (1987):185–198.

————. "Interviews as a Source for the History of American Involvement in Vietnam." *Society for Historians of American Foreign Relations Newsletter* 16 (March 1985):23–28.

————. "Public Opinion on Foreign Policy: The View from the Johnson and Nixon White Houses." *Politica* (Denmark) 16 (1984):184–200.

Smith, Don D. "Dark Areas of Ignorance Revisited: Current Knowledge about Asian Affairs." In Nimmo and Bonjean, *Political Attitudes,* 267–272.

Smith, Robert B. "Campus Protests and the Vietnam War." In James Short and Marvin Wolfgang, eds., *Collective Violence* (Chicago: Aldine, 1972), 250–277.

Spector, Bert. "A Clash of Cultures: The Smothers Brothers vs. CBS Television." In John E. O'Connor, ed., *American History/American Television* (New York: Ungar, 1983), 159–183.

Talbot, David. "And Now They Are Doves." *Mother Jones* (May 1984): 22–33, 47–50, 60.

Thompson, James C., Jr. "How Could Vietnam Happen?" *Atlantic* 221 (April 1968):47–53.

Walum, Laurel. "Sociologists as Signers: Some Characteristics of Protestors of Vietnam War Policy." *American Sociologist* 5 (May 1970):161–164.

Warnke, Paul. "The Search for Peace—Vietnam Negotiations." In Lake, *Vietnam Legacy,* 312–330.

Yarmolinsky, Adam. "The War and the Military." In Lake, *Vietnam Legacy,* 216–235.

INDEX